Syntactic Development

William O'Grady

Syntactic
Development

The University of Chicago

Chicago and London

William O'Grady is professor of linguistics at the University of Hawai'i at Mānoa. He is the author of *Principles of Grammar and Learning,* also published by the University of Chicago Press, and coauthor of *Contemporary Linguistics: An Introduction.*

The University of Chicago Press, Chicago 60637
The University of Chicago Press, Ltd., London

© 1997 by The University of Chicago
All rights reserved. Published 1997

Printed in the United States of America

06 05 04 03 02 01 00 99 98 97   5 4 3 2 1

ISBN (cloth): 0-226-62075-1
ISBN (paper): 0-226-62077-8

Library of Congress Cataloging-in-Publication Data

O'Grady, William D. (William Delaney), 1952–
    Syntactic development / William O'Grady.
        p.   cm.
    Includes bibliographical references.
    ISBN 0-226-62075-1. — ISBN 0-226-62077-8 (pbk.)
    1. Language acquisition.   2. Grammar, Comparative and general—
Syntax.   3. English language—Acquistition.   I. Title.
    P118.027   1997
    401'.93—dc21   96–46257
                                                                            CIP

∞ The paper used in this publication meets the minimum requirements of the American National Standard for Information Sciences—Permanence of Paper for Printed Library Materials, ANSI Z39.48-1984.

For C. M.,
who learned two languages while I was trying
to finish this book

Contents

Acknowledgments

During the preparation of this book, I benefited enormously from interaction and discussion with a number of people, including Derek Bickerton, Robert Bley-Vroman, Gigi Glover, Hui-hua Hwang, Kazue Kanno, Seongchan Kim, Michael Long, Michael O'Grady, Ann Peters, Mark Sawyer, Akihiko Shimura, Kate Wolfe-Quintero, Yoshie Yamashita, and Naoko Yoshinaga. Additional valuable feedback came from an anonymous reviewer and from students who have read parts of the manuscript in classes that I have taught in recent years. Thanks are also due to Geoff Huck of the University of Chicago Press for his valuable advice during the review process, Peter T. Daniels for his superb copyediting work, and Naoko Yoshinaga for her assistance in preparing many of the graphics used in this book.

I owe a very special debt of gratitude to three people. First, Yutaka Sato went through the entire manuscript, double-checking the data and sources; his careful work uncovered a number of discrepancies and saved me a great deal of time. Second, Paul Bloom, serving as a referee for the University of Chicago Press, provided a very detailed commentary on an earlier version of the book, making important suggestions and offering much constructive criticism. Finally, I must express special thanks to Kevin Gregg, who read two versions of the manuscript in its entirety, each time providing me with incisive comments about matters great and small. I invariably found these comments helpful, and in many cases I have incorporated his insights directly into my discussion.

I

The Study of Language Acquisition

Children master the intricacies of their native language before they are able to tie a knot, jump rope, or draw a decent-looking circle. This achievement is so routine and so expected that most people rarely give it a second thought. But its significance has not been lost on linguists, who are only too aware of the complexity of language and of the mysteries that surround its acquisition.

A central tenet of virtually all research on language acquisition is that the ability to use language stems from the fact that, as children, all normal human beings acquire a grammar—a cognitive system that determines the relationship between form and meaning in all possible sentences of their language. As it is currently understood, a grammar includes two major components (see table 1.1). The first is a lexicon or 'dictionary', which serves as a repository for information about the properties of individual words (e.g., their form and meaning, the types of elements with which they can or must occur, and so forth). The second component of a grammar consists of various systems of principles that regulate the language's sound pattern (phonology), the structure of its words (morphology), and the form and interpretation of its sentences (syntax and semantics). Working together, the different components of the grammar determine that in a sentence such as *Sue's mother purchased several pictures of herself,* the word *mother* will be more heavily stressed than *Sue* (setting aside the possibility of contrastive intonation); that the verb *purchase* takes both a 'subject' (corresponding to the purchaser) and a 'direct object' (corresponding to the thing bought), that the subject precedes the verb; that the verb precedes its object and that together they form a structural unit; that the pictures depict Sue's mother (not Sue); and so forth. Much of this information can be represented in the form of a tree structure, as depicted in (1). (Various details, such as the internal structure of the NPs, are ignored here; indexing represents coreference.)

(1)

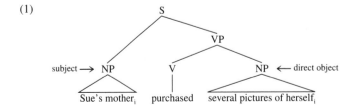

Table 1.1 The Grammar

Lexicon	Principles
Information about words	Phonology
	Morphology
	Syntax
	Semantics

There is good reason to think that "grammar" rather than "language" should be the focal point of research on linguistic development. As suggested several decades ago by Bloomfield (1926:155), a language is "the totality of utterances that can be made in a speech community." Since no one could ever learn such an infinitely large set of utterances, it follows that a language per se cannot be acquired. What can be acquired, however, is the finite grammar that allows members of a speech community to understand and use their language. Although I will continue to use the term 'language acquisition' for the sake of convenience and tradition, this book is concerned with the emergence of a particular cognitive system (i.e., the grammar), not a set of utterances. More specifically, it focuses on what is known about 'syntactic development', the (subconscious) process whereby children become able to form sentences from words and other smaller structural units. Because of this focus, it will often appear that I am using the terms 'grammar' and 'syntax' interchangeably; in fact, of course, the syntactic system makes up only one part of the grammar that is the product of the language acquisition process.

1. The Acquisition Process

Traditionally, the study of grammar and the study of language acquisition have been conducted more or less independently of each other. This contrasts with the view adopted here, which is that the two types of research can and should be pursued as part of a single joint enterprise. No grammatical theory can be considered satisfactory if there is no plausible account of how the grammars that it posits for particular languages emerge in response to experience. (N. Chomsky 1965:25 introduces the term 'explanatory adequacy' to describe this criterion.) By the same standard, no theory of language acquisition can be considered adequate if it cannot account for the emergence of the type of grammar believed to underlie adult linguistic competence.

The recognition that the end product of 'language acquisition' is a grammar does more than simply establish a point of principle. It also shapes and informs the study of language acquisition by shedding light on the nature of the system that is acquired and the sort of data to which learners do—and do not—have access. Let us briefly consider each point in turn.

THE FINAL SYSTEM

It is generally acknowledged that the mature grammar for any human language is a complex and abstract system. There is ongoing controversy about how to describe many parts of this system, and various phenomena continue to resist insightful analysis altogether. This is not to say that the existence of a grammar is in doubt, or even that its properties cannot be deduced with reasonable certainty. Quite to the contrary, there is a near-consensus that (the syntactic component of) the grammar for any human language must include both a set of categories such as 'noun' and 'verb' and a set of operations that can combine these categories to create an unlimited number of sentences with a particular linear and hierarchical organization. In addition, a grammar must contain principles that regulate phenomena such as pronoun interpretation (*him* can refer to John in *John's friends praised him,* but not in *John praised him*) and the relationship between a 'gap' and the 'displaced' element (e.g., a *wh* word) with which it is associated (compare *Who did you see a picture of __?* with **Who did a picture of __ frighten you?*).

From the point of view of language acquisition, then, it follows that we must find a way to explain how language learners discover categories such as 'noun' and 'verb', how they determine the precise architecture of the phrases formed by combining these categories, and how they come to have particular constraints on pronoun interpretation and gap placement. In each case, the more we know about the particular component of the mature grammatical system, the more precisely we can formulate hypotheses about the mental structures and types of experience that are necessary for its development.

THE DATA

One of the more puzzling revelations of the grammar-oriented study of language acquisition has to do with the type of linguistic 'data' available to children. When linguists set out to discover the grammatical system of a language that they do not speak, they invariably rely on so-called 'grammaticality judgments'— assessments by native speakers of the acceptability and interpretation of various real and hypothetical sentences. Imagine, for example, that a group of Chinese linguists studying English observed that some question structures contain two *wh* words. In order to determine whether all combinations of *wh* words are possible, they would prepare a list of hypothetical sentences such as those in (2)–(6) and solicit judgments from native speakers of English.

(2)   Who saw what?
(3)   Who gave a gift to whom?
(4)   Who went where?
(5)   ?*Who went when?
(6)   *Who went why?

In order to test subsequent hypotheses, they would make up further sentences and check their status, continuing in this manner until they had arrived at a successful analysis.

Children learning a first language cannot proceed in this way, however. As we will see in more detail in part II of this book, young language learners neither request nor receive judgments about the grammaticality of actual or hypothetical sentences in their language. Their sole source of information about the grammar that they must acquire is the normal, day-to-day use of language by those around them. Although no linguist could construct a grammar on the basis of such restricted data, children somehow succeed in doing just this.

2. The Acquisition Device

As we have just seen, language acquisition involves the emergence of a cognitive system containing categories and principles of a particular type. Much of this system exists subconsciously and is acquired without deliberate effort at an early age. More surprisingly, this system develops even though children do not have access to the type of evidence that bears most directly on its properties (i.e., grammaticality judgments). Taken together, these facts suggest that the human brain must contain a mechanism that is somehow especially suited for grammar-building and that is available from very early in life. For the sake of convenience, let us refer to this mechanism as the **acquisition device.**

The acquisition device can be thought of as a 'function' from experience to a grammar. That is, as depicted in figure 1.1, it takes as its input the type of experience that comes from being exposed to the language in one's environment and gives as its output a grammar that permits productive use of that language. (For early statements of this idea, see N. Chomsky 1966:20 and McNeill 1966:39; for some discussion, see McCawley 1976:171.)

In general, the study of the acquisition device is oriented around two major research themes, one involving **learnability** and the other **development.** The learnability issue, also called the 'logical problem of language acquisition', is concerned with the type of acquisition device needed to construct a grammar in response to the experience that is available during the first years of life. The study of development, on the other hand, focuses on the step-by-step emergence of grammatical patterns and the types of errors that may occur prior to the attainment of mature linguistic competence (e.g., *Daddy goed* and *Me want that*).

FIGURE 1.1 The Acquisition Process

These two research themes have often been pursued independently (for some commentary on this state of affairs, see Bowerman 1985:1259–60, 1987:443; and L. Bloom and Harner 1989:207–8). However, both lines of inquiry are in fact closely related, since each seeks to understand the acquisition device, although from somewhat different perspectives. Study of the learnability problem provides clues about the internal structure of the acquisition device, the type of grammar that it yields, and the type of experience that it requires. In contrast, investigation of developmental phenomena yields information about the real-time operation of the acquisition device in response to children's day-to-day experience with language. Put another way, learnability research focuses on *how* the acquisition device does what it does, while developmental research focuses on *when* it does it (and why).

Given their different goals and orientations, it is not surprising that the two approaches to language acquisition draw on very different types of data. The study of the learnability problem tends to make very limited use of data from child language, relying instead on argumentation involving the relationship between the types of experience available to the acquisition device and the principles of adult grammar that it must eventually produce (see chaps. 12–14). In contrast, research into development draws very heavily on child language data both from naturalistic studies and from experimental research (table 1.2).

Naturalistic studies of child language involve the examination of recordings and transcripts of children's spontaneous speech that have been collected over a period of months or even years. In contrast, experimental research attempts to assess children's knowledge of particular structure types by having them carry out a particular task (usually involving comprehension, production, or imitation). Experimental work is generally cross-sectional, involving the comparative study of different groups of children (say, 2-year-olds and 4-year-olds) at a particular moment in their development. On the other hand, naturalistic studies tend to be longitudinal in that they track the development of a particular child (or group of children) over a period of time.[1]

Each type of study has its advantages and disadvantages. Naturalistic studies are able to investigate speech in an uncontrived setting and are ideal for examining the step-by-step progression of the acquisition process—as manifested, for instance, in the emergence of tense inflection or pronominal case, changes in the rate of subject deletion, or the increase over time in the average length of children's sentences (so-called 'mean length of utterance' or **MLU**). However, this type of study is limited by the fact that certain structures (e.g., passives or relative clauses) occur infrequently in spontaneous speech and are thus difficult to investigate using data of this sort. Moreover, because of their longitudinal character, naturalistic studies are sometimes impractical due to the time required to collect

Table 1.2 Principal Methods of Data Collection

Method	Comments
Naturalistic (usually longitudinal)	
Recording & transcribing	Requires a substantial long-term commitment of time and effort on the part of the researcher; because only a small amount of the child's speech is recorded, infrequently used words or structures may not show up in the sample; speech may be difficult to interpret when it is being transcribed, and (unless videotaping is used) the precise context in which sentences are uttered may be difficult or impossible to reconstruct.
Diary study	Has the advantage of being carried out by the caregiver, who is best able to interpret what is being said and who hears more of the child's utterances than anyone else; best suited for the study of vocabulary and simple structures that can be identified by people with no professional training; there is some reason for concern about the reliability of diary reports (e.g., Pine 1992).
Experimental (usually cross-sectional)	
Comprehension	The most commonly used procedure (having the child act out the meaning of the sentence) requires considerable processing and planning beyond the simple interpretation of the sentence; these complications may be reduced by techniques that test comprehension by having the child match the sentence with a depiction of its meaning (see Cocking and McHale 1981; Hirsh-Pasek and Golinkoff 1991). At best, comprehension tests provide information about a sentence's interpretation; they usually cannot shed light on whether children think a particular pattern is well-formed (grammatical).
Imitation	Care must be taken to ensure that children are using their grammatical knowledge rather than just short-term memory to perform the task (see Slobin and Welsh 1973; Lust, Chien, and Flynn 1987; and Masterson 1993 for some guidelines); imitation can provide insights into how children perceive and analyze sentence structure, but it offers little information about meaning (O'Grady, Cho, and Sato 1994).
Production	Many structures are natural only in specific contexts which may be difficult to reproduce in experimental situations; children's performance on production tasks often lags behind their ability to comprehend and imitate particular structures.

and transcribe tape-recorded data. (This problem is alleviated somewhat in the case of English and a few other languages by the availability of previously collected and transcribed data from various sources, including CHILDES—the Child Language Data Exchange System; see, for instance, MacWhinney 1991.)

Experimental studies allow investigators to focus on particular phenomena, including structures that may occur rarely in spontaneous speech, and to work with relatively large numbers of subjects at once. However, this flexibility comes at some cost. Because of its cross-sectional design, experimental research cannot document the progression of individual children through developmental stages, although tentative proposals about the existence and nature of such stages are sometimes based on this type of work.

A limitation common to all methods for the study of syntactic development is that they are likely to underestimate subjects' actual competence: the fact that children fail to produce or comprehend a particular structure or a particular sentence type in an experiment does not allow one to conclude with certainty that they lack the relevant grammatical knowledge. A variety of extraneous factors—including inattention, nervousness, processing limitations, and a failure to understand what is expected—can interfere with children's ability to use language to the full extent of their grammatical capabilities. It is therefore perhaps not surprising that the evolution of ever more refined techniques of data collection in recent years has resulted in consistent downward revisions in estimates of the age at which various milestones in syntactic development are achieved.

In subsequent chapters, we will have occasion to consider concrete instances of the problems and shortcomings of the various types of data collection in more detail. For now it suffices to note that despite these limitations, work on each of the two major research themes in the study of language acquisition (i.e., learnability and development) has yielded important results in recent years. It is the goal of this book to examine these results in as comprehensive a manner as possible, with an eye to shedding light on the structure and operation of the acquisition device. Where possible, findings from different studies are brought together to give a synthesis; where this is not possible, note is made of the contradictory results and unsolved problems that must await future resolution.

Part I of this book is devoted largely to a survey of the developmental facts, focusing on the steps or 'stages' that language learners pass through on the way to acquiring the grammar of their language. These chapters discuss phenomena that are by all accounts central to the syntax of human language—category assignment, word order, passivization, question formation, relativization, and pronoun interpretation, to name a few. The emergence of these phenomena is considered in approximate chronological order, beginning with children's first primitive utterances and ending with complex syntactic patterns of various sorts. To the extent possible, these chapters present a historical overview of the relevant research literature and characterize the known facts in a relatively theory-neutral way. Although explanatory proposals are considered from time to time, no general theory of development is put forward, and only quite conservative assumptions are made about the grammar whose emergence is reflected in the developmental data.

In contrast, part II of this book is intentionally theoretical in orientation. The learnability problem is considered for the first time, and development is reconsidered from a theoretical perspective. The focus of these chapters is on the internal structure of the acquisition device, the type of experience that it requires to operate successfully, and the type of grammar that it ultimately yields. Different theories of learnability and development are considered and evaluated in light of the data described in earlier chapters.

Despite the technical nature of much of the work on syntactic development, every effort has been made to ensure that this book will be accessible to readers who have no advanced training in either linguistics or psychology. In general, the discussion assumes only an introductory course in linguistics, and concepts that may not be familiar to the average reader are explained as they are introduced. (In addition, a glossary provides brief definitions for key terms and abbreviations.) The chapters are intended to be read in sequence, since later parts of the book often presuppose familiarity with material covered in earlier sections.

3. Some Limitations

The literature on language acquisition is enormous, thanks in large part to the intense research activity of the past two decades. It goes almost without saying that no book can purport to provide a comprehensive treatment of the field. In order to limit the scope of the present study, several difficult choices had to be made.

First, it was necessary to choose between a detailed study of the acquisition of a single language and a much more general overview of acquisition phenomena in several different languages. (The ideal, of course, would be a detailed study of many different languages, but this is simply not a practical option—in part because of gaps in the research literature and in part because of limitations on time and space.) As readers will quickly discover, this book draws predominantly on research studies involving the acquisition of English—this being the language for which the currently available data provide the most complete picture of syntactic development. Occasional reference is made to the acquisition of languages other than English when relevant information is available, but no attempt is made to survey this part of the acquisition literature in a systematic way.

Second, it was necessary to limit the investigation to a set of syntactic phenomena whose acquisition can be described in a coherent and relatively self-contained way. It was therefore decided to exclude from the domain of this book most issues pertaining to lexical properties of words (meaning and subcategorization), morphology, and discourse even though these phenomena clearly play a role in sentence formation. The resulting picture of the language acquisition process will therefore of necessity be incomplete, but hopefully not distorted.

Third, because of the large number of studies on syntactic development, it was necessary to be somewhat selective in reviewing the relevant research literature. In part for practical reasons, it was decided to focus on studies that have appeared in the published literature. (In addition to their accessibility, these studies have the advantage of having been filtered through the peer review process.) However, where warranted, occasional reference is made to research that has appeared only in dissertations and conference presentations.

Still another difficult decision had to do with the choice of theoretical framework. A good deal of work on development is formulated within the grammatical framework known as 'Government and Binding (GB) theory' (also called 'Principles and Parameters theory'). However, since the findings of these studies do not in general entail the correctness of GB theory (or any other framework), I thought it advisable to restate them in more 'theory-neutral' terms. I have followed this policy as closely as possible throughout my survey of the developmental facts, keeping formalism to a minimum and employing syntactic representations that are compatible with (or at least easily translated into) a variety of contemporary theories.

The theoretical discussion that dominates the second part of this book requires a different approach, since many of the proposals considered there are inextricably linked to GB theory. In order to accommodate this fact, I have devoted an entire chapter to a review of work on the learnability problem within this framework. However, a subsequent chapter outlines various alternatives to the GB approach to learnability, although these alternatives are considerably less developed and less encompassing in their scope.

Within the limitations just outlined, the discussion of syntactic development contained in this book seeks to be as comprehensive and objective as possible. Facts and proposals from a wide variety of sources are brought together and integrated in an attempt to provide a coherent outline of how the acquisition device is structured and how it operates. Of course, important gaps remain, and many of the proposals I make may prove controversial, but perhaps it is not too much to hope that this exercise will contribute to further advances in the field of language acquisition research.

PART I

The Developmental Facts

2

One-Word Utterances

Between the ages of 12 and 18 months, the first utterances based on adult words make their appearance in child language. This chapter explores a series of topics pertaining to the emergence of these early utterances, including the strategies that allow children to identify their first words, the syntactic status of these words, and the role of the one-word stage in the overall process of syntactic development. Consistent with the general focus of this book, the discussion concentrates on structural matters, for the most part setting aside issues pertaining to phonology and semantics. (For discussion of the latter issue, see Barrett 1985.)

1. The First Words

On average, children have acquired ten words by age 15 months (Nelson 1973: 35) and fifty words by age 18 or 19 months (ibid. 36; Garman 1979:183). At about this time or a little later, most (and perhaps all) children evidence a sudden spurt in vocabulary growth, with between 30 and 50 new items learned in a single month (Nelson 1981:151; Goldfield and Reznick 1990; Mervis and Bertrand 1995). At later ages, lexical development may be even more rapid, with as many as 20 new words learned per day (see Nelson 1981 and the references cited there).

Peters (1994) observes that children's early one-unit utterances rarely coincide exactly with words in the adult language. Rather, they often consist either of a word fragment (e.g., /fənt/ for 'elephant') or a whole phrase (e.g. /əsæt/ for 'What's that'). This raises the question of how the acquisition device goes about identifying words and morphemes in the continuous stream of speech sounds to which it is exposed. Peters (1983, 1985) offers an interesting preliminary proposal that focuses on two processes: extraction and segmentation.

Extraction involves the identification of chunks of speech that can be treated as grammatical units. Peters (1983) suggests that the acquisition device often extracts whole utterances from the speech stream and remembers them together with salient features of the situational context. Some of these utterances are words (e.g., names such as *Daddy, Mommy,* and so on), but many are phrases or even sentences. For example, many children initially treat *what's that?, look at that, come here,* and similar expressions as single units that are linked holistically to a particular situational context. Utterances that are 'suprasegmentally delimited' (e.g., marked by special intonation or otherwise highlighted) are especially good candidates for extraction, as the examples in (1) help illustrate.

(1)   *Examples of extraction* (cited by Peters 1985 : 1035):
      a. MOTHER: Jane, here's a bottle. Where's the bottle? Here's a bottle.
         JANE: wah-wah
         MOTHER: Bottle
         JANE: bah-bah.

      b. ADULT: That's an elephant, *isn't it?* What is it?
         ADAM: intit.

Extraction works in tandem with **segmentation,** a process that seeks to analyze previously identified units into smaller constituent parts. Segmentation is notably sensitive to auditory salience, which has led Slobin (1985 : 1166) to propose that the acquisition device makes use of the strategies listed in (2).

(2)   a. Segment off a stressed syllable of an extracted unit and store it separately.
      b. Segment off the last syllable of an extracted unit and store it separately.
      c. Segment off the first syllable of an extracted unit and store it separately.

Especially salient are initial or final syllables that are also stressed. Peters (1985 : 1039) cites the examples in table 2.1A (from Velten 1943) of early words that seem to have been formed by focusing on an initial stressed syllable. I have added examples of words formed by focusing on a final stressed syllable. Sensitivity to stress has potential advantages when it comes to segmentation. As Peters notes, stress is a reliable indicator of word boundaries in many languages. Of the 444 languages surveyed by Hyman (1977), for instance, 406 have stress that predictably signals the beginning or end of a word.

Sometimes, the sensitivity of the acquisition device to stressed syllables can initially lead to incorrect segmentation. Many striking examples of this can be found in Pye's (1983) study of the acquisition of Quiché, a Mayan language spo-

Table 2.1 Some Early Words

Adult Word	Child's Word
A. Early Words Derived from Initial Stressed Syllables	
coffee	daf
faucet	fas
towel	daw
high chair	hats
B. Early Words Derived from Final Stressed Syllables	
giraffe	faff (Gleitman and Wanner 1982 : 18)
moustache	tass (Wilson and Peters 1988 : 262)
goodnight	na (French 1989 : 81)
away	way (Ingram 1976 : 31)

ken in Guatemala (see also Mithun's 1989 study of Mohawk). Consider in this respect the verb form in (3) meaning 'to be sleeping'.

(3) ka-war-ik
     ASP-sleep-INTR
     'He's sleeping.'

This form consists of three parts: the prefix *ka-* marking the incompletive aspect, the root *war* meaning 'sleep', and the suffix *-ik* indicating that the verb is intransitive. When this form is pronounced in the adult language, the /r/ of the root becomes part of the last syllable, which is also stressed, as in (4).

(4) ka.wa. rik

At age 2;2 (i.e., 2 years and 2 months), one of the children Pye was studying expressed the meaning 'He is sleeping' by saying *lik*. Setting aside the substitution of /l/ for /r/ (a common phenomenon), the child's pronunciation reflects the strategy of focusing on a stressed final syllable—resulting here in the production of a form consisting of the last consonant of the root and the intransitive suffix. Although there is no such word in the adult language, this became the child's first way of expressing the meaning 'He's sleeping'.

Another important segmentation strategy, outlined in (5), is based on distributional factors (Peters 1985:1041; Slobin 1985:1169).

(5) *The Matching Strategy:*
     When two extracted units share a phonologically similar portion, the shared portion can be segmented and stored as a unit, and so can the residue.

Thus, if the acquisition device has extracted the units *big car* and *big dog,* both of which start with *big,* it can treat *big* (the shared portion) as well as *car* and *dog* (the residue) as separate units.

Evidence for the operation of this strategy comes not only from children's successful segmentations (many of their utterances correspond to words in the adult language), but also from their errors. One such error is manifested in the frequently cited example *I was [heyv],* used to mean 'I was good'. Here, the acquisition device apparently misapplies the Matching Strategy to sentences such as *Please be good* and *Please behave,* incorrectly concluding that both contain the words *please* and *be.* This leaves the residue *good* in the first case and *-have* ([heyv]) in the second, both of which should be words according to the Matching Strategy. A similar error is cited by Peters (1985:1059), who reports that a child who had just heard a story about the Wizard of Oz and the Land of Oz declared that she was going to *Voz.* This suggests the mis-segmentation depicted in (6), in which *voz* is taken to be the unit shared by both utterances.

(6)   wizard ə voz (in response to wizardəvoz)
       land ə voz (in response to landəvoz)

Still another segmentation error can be seen in the examples in (7) from the speech
of Adam between 28 and 36 months (Brown 1973:392–93).

(7)   It's fell.
       It's has wheels.
       There it's goes.

Here it is likely that frequent exposure to utterances such as *It's Daddy, It's hot,*
and *It's time to eat* drew attention to the recurring form *it's,* leading to its analysis
and storage as a simple unit. Subsequent exposure to utterances that dissociated
it and *'s* (e.g., *It looks good, That's fine*) presumably allows the acquisition device
to carry out the necessary further segmentation.

TWO ACQUISITION STYLES

Not all children approach the problem of identifying the grammatical units of
their language in the same way. One approach, called **analytic** by Peters (1977),
focuses on relatively small chunks of speech and is characterized by clear, one-
word-at-a-time utterances. In contrast, the **gestalt** approach focuses on whole
phrases or sentences rather than single words. Children using this approach tend
to produce larger chunks of speech, such as *what happened?* and *stop that,* often
with inconsistent and relatively poor articulation. Peters and Menn (1993:745)
propose that the analytic style pays more attention to the " 'vertical' segmental
information contained in single (usually stressed) syllables, focusing on the details
of their consonants and vowels," while the gestalt approach concentrates more on
" 'horizontal' [prosodic] information, such as number of syllables, stress, and intonation patterns."

The analytic and gestalt styles need not be mutually exclusive. Rather, as observed by Peters (1977), the two approaches seem to make up a continuum. While
some children adopt one or the other style almost exclusively, many others use
both styles to varying degrees (see also Bretherton et al. 1983:312; Bates and
MacWhinney 1987).

The analytic/gestalt contrast often parallels a contrast in styles of vocabulary
development first identified by Nelson (1973). Of the eighteen children that she
studied, ten initially used language primarily to name things. These children,
whom Nelson called **referential,** had early vocabularies that consisted mostly of
noun-like words (75% of their first 50 words, on average). The other eight children
in Nelson's study used language less for naming (only 53% of their first 50 words
were nominals) and more for expressing feelings, needs, and social interactions.
These children, whom Nelson called **expressive,** quickly acquired (unsegmented)

phrases and expressions useful for making requests and carrying on rudimentary conversations: *go-away, stop-it, don't-do-it, thank-you, there-you-go, I-want-it.*[1]

As noted by Bretherton et al. (1983:312), the expressive speech style is the result of learning whole phrases and therefore represents a gestalt approach to language learning. In contrast, the referential style requires segmentation of individual words and is hence more representative of the analytic approach. For further discussion and data, see Lieven, Pine, and Barnes (1992).

The differences between the referential and expressive styles last until age 2 and perhaps much longer (Horgan 1981). Indeed, Goldfield and Snow (1985) suggest that some differences of this sort survive into the adult years, where they are manifested in distinct second language learning styles.

What underlies the different approaches to language learning that are reflected in the referential and expressive styles? One possibility, put forward by Nelson, is that the two approaches reflect attention to different functions of language—one focusing on its naming function (the referential approach) and the other on its social function (the expressive approach).

There are also apparent differences in language use by mothers that can be correlated with the child's speech style, but the relationship is not completely clear.[2] The most important such difference, reported by Furrow and Nelson (1984), is that mothers of referential children use nouns to refer to objects more often than do mothers of expressive children. In contrast, the latter group of mothers use nouns more often to refer to persons than do the former group. It remains to be determined whether and why this difference contributes to the adoption of one or the other speech style. Moreover, as observed by Paul Bloom (pers. comm.), it is possible that any correlation in the speech styles of mother and child reflects the mother's response to the child's manner of speaking rather than vice versa.

At any rate, notwithstanding differences in children's early speech and in maternal speech styles, it is important not to lose sight of the fact that the acquisition device ultimately yields essentially the same final grammar for all speakers of a language. Accounting for this fact is a central challenge for acquisition research.

2. The Syntactic Status of Early Words

A central tenet of both traditional and contemporary grammatical theory is that words belong to syntactic categories that help determine their combinatorial properties (e.g., a noun can combine with a determiner, but a verb cannot). This raises the question of whether children's early words belong to syntactic categories and, if so, which categories emerge first.

It is difficult to determine with any certainty at what point the acquisition device first discovers syntactic categories in English. We cannot simply assume that words used by children to refer to things are nouns and words used to denote actions are verbs, since it is widely agreed that syntactic categories in human language cannot be equated with such semantic notions. On the other hand, the most obvious independent signs of category membership (e.g., occurrence with a determiner or with the possessive suffix -'s in the case of nouns, occurrence with tense marking in the case of verbs) are largely absent from early child speech.

Given the lack of direct evidence for or against syntactic categories in the one-word stage, how can this issue be resolved? Researchers on both sides of the question are forced to resort to methodological arguments to support their positions. For example, opponents of the view that early child language includes syntactic categories typically appeal to the need for conservatism in linguistic description. One should not, they argue, attribute to children abstract categories or rules for which there is no direct evidence (e.g., Bowerman 1973; Braine 1976; Maratsos 1983; Ninio 1988:107).

On the other hand, Pinker (1984) outlines a methodological argument in favor of the view that syntactic categories are available from the beginning of the acquisition process. As noted earlier, linguistic development reflects the emergence of a grammar—a system of categories and principles that allows the formation and interpretation of sentences. Given that the acquisition device must ultimately construct a grammar, the argument goes, it makes sense to believe that it starts doing this from the outset rather than initially trying to build a linguistic system without syntactic categories and later switching to a system that has them.

An important assumption underlying Pinker's argument is that the full inventory of notions needed for grammar construction, including syntactic categories, is available to the acquisition device from the earliest developmental stages. Often referred to as the **Continuity Hypothesis,** this assumption constitutes a sort of 'null hypothesis' (e.g., Macnamara 1982:233; Pinker 1984:7), since it takes the cognitive mechanisms of children and adults to be the same in the absence of evidence to the contrary. (We consider this idea in more detail in chaps. 13 and 15.)

The Continuity Hypothesis is far from universally accepted, however. Some linguists (e.g., Felix 1987; Radford 1990; Bickerton 1991), believe that the acquisition device is the product of maturation and may not even be involved in children's first attempts at language. Of course, if this is so, there is no reason to suppose that children's early speech will include adult linguistic categories. We will return to a more careful examination of this issue in chapter 15 after we have had the opportunity to examine a broader range of developmental phenomena. For now, I will tentatively assume that at least some syntactic category distinctions (in particular, those involving nouns, verbs, and adjectives) emerge at an early point in language development.

THE EARLY PRIMACY OF NOUNS

What, then, is the first syntactic category to emerge in child language? Based on a study of early speech in English and several other languages, Gentner (1982) concludes that nouns have primacy in that words belonging to this category are acquired first (p. 305) and are predominant in children's early vocabulary (p. 307). (E. Clark 1983:800–1 arrives at a similar conclusion.) Table 2.2 gives a history of the words produced by Tad, whose linguistic development was studied by his mother and Gentner. Nouns are clearly the predominant early category here. Not

Table 2.2 Tad's Early Words (from Gentner 1982:306)

Age (months)	Nominal	Predicate	Expressive	Indeterminate
11	dog			
12	duck			
13	Daddy Mama teh (teddy bear) car	yuk		
14	dipe (diaper) owl toot toot (horn)			
15	keys cheese			
16	eye			
18	cow cup truck	hot		bath
19	kitty juice bottle spoon bowl towel apple teeth cheek knee elbow map ball block bus jeep	happy down up	oops boo hi bye uh oh	pee pee TV

only are all but one of the first dozen words to emerge nouns; this category remains numerically dominant throughout the first several months of linguistic development.

The second most common word class in Tad's speech—what Gentner calls the 'predicate' category—consists of words that name a property. This category later divides into verbs and adjectives, corresponding roughly to the distinction between action-type properties like 'running' and 'reading' and state-like properties such as 'tall' and 'good'.

Findings similar to those in table 2.2 have been reported in many other studies, including the naming study conducted by Goldin-Meadow, Seligman, and Gelman (1976); see box 2.1 and table 2.3. Consistent with Gentner's claim, nouns far outnumber verbs in the production data from all three subjects and are the first words used in the children's own speech. The difference between nouns and verbs is less dramatic in the comprehension task but still favors the noun category by a factor of about 2.[3]

Box 2.1

THE STUDY: Goldin-Meadow, Seligman, and Gelman 1976
SUBJECTS: 3 children aged 8–26 mos.
THE TASK: production (naming objects and actions) and comprehension (pointing to objects and acting out actions in response to the experimenter)

Table 2.3 Results of Goldin-Meadow, Seligman, and Gelman 1976

	No. of Different Words Produced		No. of Different Words Comprehended	
Age (mo. wk.)	Nouns	Verbs	Nouns	Verbs
Lexie				
22.0	7	0	35	22
24.2	17	0	54	26
25.0	28	3	58	27
25.1	40	7	61	27
Melissa				
19.1	5	0	22	14
22.1	9	0	40	16
Jenny				
14.0	10	0	27	9
16.0	19	0	33	14
17.0	29	4	38	18
17.1	34	6	45	18

Further support for the early predominance of nouns can be found in more recent studies as well. For example, based on their longitudinal study of 30 children, Bates, Bretherton, and Snyder (1988:153) report that at age 20 months, nouns were dominant (46.8% of total vocabulary) compared to verbs (8.3%) and adjectives (7.5%). Drawing on diary data collected from 1803 subjects aged 8 months to 2;6, Bates et al. (1994:95) report that 'common' nouns make up almost 40% of the first 50 words in children's early vocabulary; the next largest word class (so-called 'predicates') accounts for less than 10% of early vocabulary items. (Bates and her colleagues did not include proper names (e.g., *Johnnie, mommy*) or places in their calculations; had they done so, the proportion of nouns in early speech would have been even larger.)

Nelson, Hampson, and Shaw (1993) provide information about the subclasses of nouns found in children's early vocabulary; see box 2.2 and table 2.4. They were especially interested in the contrast between basic level object categories (BLOCs), which denoted a category of 'discrete whole individual objects'—e.g., *puppy, cheerios, toy, animal.* All other count nouns, including those denoting locations (*beach, kitchen*), single actions (*kiss, help*), events (*lunch, party*), person

Box 2.2

THE STUDY: Nelson, Hampson, and Shaw 1993
SUBJECTS: 45 children, aged 13–20 mos.
THE DATA: Mothers completed a vocabulary inventory for their children at age 18 mos.

Table 2.4 Mean Proportion of Word Types in Productive Vocabularies at 20 mos. (based on Nelson, Hampson, and Shaw 1993:70)

Word Type	Mean Proportion (%)		
Nouns			65
count nouns		54	
BLOCs	36		
XBLOCs	18		
proper nouns		4	
mass nouns		7	
Dual category[a]			6
Verbs			10
Other			19

a. Dual category items are words that can belong to more than one category (e.g., *drink,* which can function as either a noun or a verb).

roles (*doctor, brother*), natural phenomena (*sky, snow*), temporal entities (*morning, day*), parts of objects (*button*), quantities (*drop*), and material (*wood*), were grouped together and dubbed XBLOCS. Excluding words that can belong to more than one category, the mean proportion of nouns in the vocabulary of the children in Nelson et al.'s study stood at 65%, including a sizeable component (one third of all count nouns) that did not refer to basic level objects.

At first glance, the general predominance of nouns in early child language seems inconsistent with Nelson's (1973) contrast between the expressive and referential styles of language acquisition (see section 1). In fact, however, there is no inconsistency: although expressive children use fewer nouns in early speech than do referential children, no other syntactic category is dominant. Instead, as noted earlier, expressive children use more unanalyzed phrases (e.g., *what's-that*) and social formulas (e.g., *hi, please*)—items that do not belong to a conventional syntactic category. This can be seen by considering the data in table 2.5 (adapted from Gentner 1982), which records the first 8 to 10 words of eight children in Nelson's study. The first four children were classified by Nelson as referential and the last four as expressive. The dominant category for all eight children consists of proper and common nouns, which make up at least 50% of each child's early vocabulary. A similar finding is reported by Lieven, Pine, and Barnes (1992) in their study of the referential–expressive contrast in 12 British children.

Do nouns remain dominant beyond the earliest stages of lexical development? Based on a longitudinal study of 18 children learning English, Goldfield and Reznick (1990: 175 ff.) report that nouns make up more than 50% of all words in lexicons of 75 to 99 items in size.[4] Since the remaining portion of the lexicon

Table 2.5 The First Words of Eight Children

Child	Proper Nouns	Common Nouns	Predicates	Expressive	Other
1	Daddy, Mommy, Daniel	girl, ball, school, cracker, cookie		bye	that
2	Daddy, Momma, Papa	boat, truck, map	sit		this, um
3	Daddy	duck, ball, apple, doggie, kitty, donkey, bottle	bow wow	thank you	
4	Daddy, Mommy, Nana	doggie, dolly, milk	go-go	hi, hi-there	
5	Daddy, Mommy, Daisy	puppy, ball	see	hi, yes	where
6	Mommy, Daddy	woof-woof, ball		hi	there, hot, dirty
7	Ma	dog, milk, car, water		bye bye, no	here
8	Daddy, Mommy	dog, cat, tiger, milk		hi, no	
Totals:	18	30	4	11	8 = 71

includes several other word classes (verbs, adjectives, prepositions, 'social' words, and so on), nouns are clearly still the dominant category at this point in lexical development.

Gentner notes that the early primacy of nouns has also been reported for other languages, including German, Kaluli (Papua-New Guinea), Mandarin Chinese, Turkish, and Japanese (recently confirmed by Yamashita 1995). However, some recent work appears to call into question the generality of Gentner's findings; see box 2.3.

Box 2.3

THE STUDY: Choi and Gopnik 1993
SUBJECTS: 9 Korean-speaking and 9 English-speaking children
THE DATA: Speech samples were taken every 3–4 weeks, beginning around age 14 mos. and ending around age 22 mos. Supplementary information was obtained from a language questionnaire filled out by the parents.

Choi and Gopnik report that six of the nine Korean children showed a 'verb spurt' (defined as a session in which ten or more new verbs were used) before the corresponding 'noun spurt'. Interestingly, this happened in none of the English-speaking children in their study. The authors attribute this difference to the fact that Korean-speaking mothers produce significantly fewer nouns and more verbs than their English-speaking counterparts. In addition, it was noted that Korean mothers typically use language more often to direct the child's activities than to label objects (45% vs. 9% of all utterances). By contrast, the proportion of these two uses of language is almost identical among the English-speaking mothers in Choi and Gopnik's study (25% and 24%, respectively).

Choi and Gopnik's results point to important cross-linguistic differences in lexical development, but they do not actually refute Gentner's claim that nouns are the first category to emerge in the course of language acquisition. As the data cited in tables 2.2 to 2.4 show, Genter's conclusion is based primarily on the status of the first 10 to 20 words acquired by children and not on the timing of a verb spurt relative to a noun spurt. To the extent that Choi and Gopnik's findings focus on the nature of the vocabulary spurt, which normally does not take place until after children have acquired 30 words (Goldfield and Reznick 1990:180), they leave the core of Gentner's claim intact. Moreover, a subsequent study by Au, Dapretto, and Song (1994) of 4 Korean-speaking children aged 15 to 25 months found a much higher incidence of nouns than verbs in their early vocabularies. A similar finding is reported by Seongchan Kim (pers. comm.): diary records and speech samples from his son show that the child's first 10 words (and 18 of his first 25) were nouns.

WHY NOUNS?

This brings us to the question of why the acquisition device should favor nouns in early stages of syntactic development. The fact that Gentner is able to find evidence of noun primacy in languages other than English helps narrow down the possibilities. For example, the early preference for nouns over verbs cannot be attributed to inflectional factors (e.g., the fact that in English more verbs than nouns have irregular inflections and therefore do not present the child with a single, fixed root). This is because there is also an early preference for nouns in Mandarin Chinese, in which neither verbs nor nouns are inflected, as well as in Turkish, which exhibits heavy but regular inflection on both nouns and verbs.

It is likewise unlikely that word order is the crucial factor. While nouns can appear sentence-finally in English (this being a highly salient position in the sentence for the child—see section 1), they normally do not in Japanese, which is uniformly verb-final. (TOP = topic marker; AC = accusative case, used to mark a direct object)

(8)   Gakusei-wa hon-o   yonda.
       student-TOP book-AC read
       'The student read the book.'

However, the force of this argument has been somewhat diminished by the more recent finding that Japanese mothers apparently use nouns in isolation more often than do American mothers (Fernald and Morikawa 1993) and that Turkish mothers sometimes abandon the usual subject-object-verb order of their language and place nouns in the final position of sentences directed toward children (Golinkoff, Mervis, and Hirsh-Pasek 1994:137). Nonetheless, Au, Dapretto, and Song (1994:573) found that verbs are almost five times more common than nouns in final position in the utterances produced by the three Korean mothers whose speech they investigated, whereas nouns are far more likely in this position in English. Yet, in both languages, nouns are the dominant category in early child speech.

Gentner also claimed that the early emergence of nouns could not be attributed to frequency effects. Relying on data from adult-to-adult speech, she noted that nouns are less frequent than either verbs or prepositions and that of the 100 most frequent words in English, 20 are verbs and only 6 are nouns (1982:316–17). Crucially, however, recent work suggests that this may not be so in adult-to-child speech, which is presumably the more important input for the acquisition device. For example, Goldfield (1993) examined the frequency of nouns and verbs in 17-minute speech samples involving 12 one-year-old children and their mothers in situations involving play with toys and play with each other (tickling, peekaboo, and so forth). She reported that while there is indeed an overall frequency advantage for verbs (9.67 tokens per minute during play with toys vs. 7.01 tokens per minute for nouns; see also Au, Dapretto, and Song 1994:572), this advantage is diminished and may even disappear if copulas are excluded from consideration (pp. 90–91). Moreover, nouns consistently occur more often than verbs in shorter maternal utterances (one or two words), which may well be easier for children to attend to, and appear more often than verbs in the salient final position of these utterances (p. 94). On the other hand, Au, Dapretto, and Song (1994:572) report that verbs are overall twice as frequent as nouns in the speech of Korean mothers and are far more frequent than nouns utterance-finally (see above); yet nouns are still the dominant early category in the speech of Korean children.

Gentner's own explanation for the early primacy of nouns is based on semantic considerations, particularly the idea that the referents of nouns tend to have perceptual correlates that are comparatively easy to identify and are therefore more 'accessible' to children than those of verbs. According to this theory, even infants see objects as coherent and stable parts of their perceptual world. Because the denotation of most nouns is relatively easy to identify, Gentner explains (p. 303), "half the problem" of matching form with meaning is solved in advance in the case of nouns. (See Golinkoff, Mervis, and Hirsh-Pasek 1994; P. Bloom to appear; and the references cited there for further discussion of the principles that enter into the acquisition of noun-type meanings.)

In contrast, verbs and other predicates are claimed to have a less transparent relationship to the perceptual world. To illustrate this point, Gentner takes the example of a bottle floating down a stream into a cave. Although all languages pick out the bottle as a salient component of the situation and use a single word or phrase to refer to it, there are differences in how the movement is encoded. Whereas English encodes it with the help of a verb and a preposition (e.g., *floated into the cave*), Spanish uses two verbs and a preposition (e.g., *entró en la cueva, flotando*). (For detailed discussion of this phenomenon, see Talmy 1985.) Gentner takes this as evidence that the types of meanings encoded by verbs are not so obviously 'packaged' as those of nouns, which makes them correspondingly more difficult to acquire.

Still another possible explanation for the early primacy of nouns, put forward by O'Grady (1987:40), involves a category's role in determining thematic relations such as agent, theme and location.[5] A fundamental difference between verbs and the types of nouns used by children in the early stages of linguistic development is that the former categories imply one or more thematic roles while the latter do not (table 2.6). Thus the verb *fall* implies a theme role, *eat* an agent and theme, and so on. In contrast, nouns such as *Daddy, cat,* and *tree* do not have the types of meanings that imply thematic roles. To the extent that a word's association with one or more thematic roles complicates its acquisition, this could contribute to the

Table 2.6 Thematic Properties of Some Early Words

Verbs	Implied Thematic Roles	Nouns	Implied Thematic Roles
run	agent	*daddy*	Ø
fall	theme	*cat*	Ø
eat	agent, theme	*tree*	Ø
give	agent, theme, recipient		

relatively early development of the noun category compared to verbs and other predicates.

(Interestingly, some nouns do have the types of meanings that imply thematic roles, but they are not among the first words acquired by children. The most obvious examples of this involve nominalizations of various sorts, including *bath, work,* and *kiss.* Nelson, Hampson, and Shaw [1993] report that a small number of these words are used by children aged 1;1 to 1;8, but they seem not to be among the first 10 vocabulary items to be acquired. If this is so, their emergence presumably overlaps with that of the small number of verbs that also appear at roughly this time.)

In sum, there are a number of considerations which may be responsible (individually or together) for why the acquisition device favors nouns in the earliest stages of English lexical development. Further research must establish whether the early primacy of nouns is indeed universal and whether potential causal factors (such as semantic transparency and frequency in shorter utterances) hold for all languages.

3. Further Properties of the One-word Stage

A striking feature of children's one-word utterances is that they often express sentence-type meanings. Such utterances are called **holophrases** (literally 'whole sentences'). McNeill (1970:24) gives the example of a child who used the word *hot* (pronounced [ha]) between the ages of 12 and 15 months not only when something hot was before her, but also when she saw an empty coffee cup and a turned-off stove. He suggests that these uses show that *hot* "was not merely the label of a hot object but was also something said of objects that could be hot. It asserted a property." At age 15 months, this same child used *door* to mean 'close the door', *water* to mean 'water is in my eye', and *baby* to mean 'the baby fell down'.

Another example of the holophrastic use of one-word utterances comes from L. Bloom (1973:98), whose daughter said *Mama* when she looked at, touched, or pointed to her mother's lunch, gloves, and dress. Since the child could not have confused her mother with these things, it is likely that she was trying to make a comment about the identity of their owner. In so doing, she was using her one-word utterances to express a proposition, not simply to refer to a person or thing.

The examples in table 2.7 from Matthew, whose early speech patterns were studied by Greenfield and Smith (1976), help illustrate the different uses to which one-word utterances can be put. (Although it is often difficult to determine the intended meaning of holophrastic utterances by themselves, the physical and linguistic context generally makes it possible for researchers to interpret them with a reasonable degree of confidence. The practice of treating simple utterances as the expression of relatively complex meanings is known as 'rich interpretation' — see Ingram 1989:241 ff. for some discussion.)

The use of single-word utterances to communicate relatively complex messages seems to require considerable ingenuity on the part of the child. Drawing on data from children's spontaneous speech and from imitation studies, Greenfield et al. (1985) conclude that children use their one-word utterances to express new, changing, and/or uncertain information. (Greenfield et al. call this the 'informativeness principle'.) Previously known or background information is rarely encoded, although it may be indicated with the help of a gesture. Thus, to take one of their examples, a child trying to get down from a box was observed to say *down*, taking the agent (himself) for granted and encoding the action, which represented

Table 2.7 Types of One-Word Utterances
(adapted from Greenfield and Smith 1976:70)

Utterance and Context	Semantic Interpretation	Age (mos., days)
hi, while waving	performative	7,22
dada, looking at father	performative object	8,12
nana, responding to *no*	volition	11,24
dada, offering bottle to father	recipient	11,28
ball, having just thrown ball	theme/patient	13,0
daddy, hearing father approach	agent	13,3
up, reaching up and in answer to *Do you want to get up?*	action or state of agent	13,16
down, having just thrown something down	action or state of theme	14,6
caca, ('cookie'), pointing to door of room where cookies are kept	object associated with another object	14,29
box, putting crayon in box	location	15,20
fishy, pointing to empty fish tank	animate being associated with object or location	15,29
again, when he wants someone to do something again	modification of event	18,1

the change in the situation. Bates and MacWhinney (1979) suggest that this type of strategy may reflect a natural tendency on the part of the human attention system in both children and adults to focus on novel, changing, and/or uncertain elements in both linguistic and nonlinguistic settings.

However, a somewhat different view is put forward by Ninio (1992), based on a study of Hebrew-speaking infants and their mothers; see box 2.4. Focusing on the speech samples from 24 of the children at age 1;6 and comparing them with the utterances collected from all 48 of the mothers over the duration of the study, Ninio found that 97% of the children's one-word utterances resembled maternal models. This raises the possibility that children's use of one-word utterances to express sentence-type meanings is based in part at least on a similar practice by their mothers or other caregivers.

Box 2.4

THE STUDY: Ninio 1992
SUBJECTS: 48 Hebrew-speaking mother–child dyads (the children's age at the time of
     the study varied from 0;10 to 2;8)
THE DATA: a 30-minute cross-sectional speech sample from 24 of the dyads and six
     30-minute bimonthly speech samples from the other 24 dyads

KNOWLEDGE OF SENTENCE STRUCTURE

Turning now to a different matter, it has generally been believed that children's knowledge of *sentence structure* is not well developed during this initial period of language development. Surveying the literature on this subject, Barrett (1982) found that while children use one-word utterances for a variety of communicative functions, including questioning (as indicated by intonation) and predication (often with the help of pointing), there is no evidence that they are expressing actual structural relations during this period (see also Atkinson 1985). A similar conclusion is advanced by Radford (1990:22 ff.), who notes that children in the one-word stage produce speech without inflection or combinatorial patterns and frequently respond in a grammatically inappropriate way to even simple questions, as in (9).

(9)   *Some inappropriate responses in one-word speech* (Radford 1990:32):
       What's that? *There.* (16 mos.)
       What should I do? *Baby.* (16 mos.)
       Who says bow wow? *Home.* (19 mos.)
       Who rides the car? *Gone.* (16 mos.)

Experimental evidence in support of the same conclusion comes from an earlier study by de Villiers and de Villiers (1973), who found that children with an average utterance length of between 1 and 1.5 morphemes (i.e., essentially children in the one-word stage) correctly act out the meaning of sentences such as *The truck pushes the car* less than one third of the time. (This study is considered in more detail in chap. 4.)

However, recent work by Hirsh-Pasek and Golinkoff (1991) has yielded a much more optimistic assessment of young children's syntactic capabilities, especially as they pertain to word order; see box 2.5. In Hirsh-Pasek and Golinkoff's experiment, the child sits facing two TV monitors. Once his or her attention has been drawn to a light directly between the two monitors, an auditory stimulus such as *Hey, Cookie Monster is tickling Big Bird. Find Cookie Monster tickling Big Bird* is presented. Two videotapes are played simultaneously on the monitors, one depicting Cookie Monster tickling Big Bird and the other depicting Big Bird tickling Cookie Monster. The amount of time it takes for the child to look at one of the monitors (latency) and the amount of time he or she watches it (fixation time) are then measured. (Of course, the test itself is preceded by a familiarization exercise to allow the child to realize that the presentation of an auditory stimulus is accompanied by activity on the TV screens; moreover, the linguistic stimuli are counterbalanced so that half the subjects hear a stimulus that matches one of the video sequences and half hear a stimulus that matches the other sequence.)

Box 2.5

THE STUDY: Hirsh-Pasek and Golinkoff 1991
SUBJECTS: 48 children, aged 16–18 mos.
TEST SENTENCES: (4 tokens, each with a different verb) Cookie Monster tickles
    Big Bird
TASK: preferential looking (described in text)

Unlike comprehension tests involving an act-out procedure (as in de Villiers and de Villiers 1973), participants in a preferential looking task can focus almost entirely on the linguistic stimulus since there is no need to plan and carry out actions involving toys or other props. Preferential looking is thus a 'purer' test of linguistic knowledge than conventional comprehension experiments.

Although the children's performance on Hirsh-Pasek and Golinkoff's experiment was not perfect, they did demonstrate a significant preference for the screen that matched the auditory stimulus. This preference was manifested both in how quickly they looked at that screen (latency) and how long they looked at it (fixation). This seems to show that even children in the one-word stage have some knowledge of the word order contrasts that are used to distinguish subject/agents from direct object/themes in English active transitive sentences, even though they are not able to produce such sentences themselves.

4. Beyond the One-word Stage

Why is there a one-word stage in syntactic development? Why don't children simply produce utterances containing two or more appropriately segmented words from the beginning of the language acquisition process? The answer to this question apparently does not lie in the size of children's vocabulary. In a study of four children making the transition to multi-word speech, L. Bloom (1973:43–44) notes that the child with the largest vocabulary produced the smallest proportion of utterances longer than one word.

Another possibility is that the one-word stage results from limitations on the articulatory skills needed to produce full sentences. However, there are at least three problems with this idea. First, a full sentence can consist of as few as two or three syllables (e.g., *Sue left*). Second, many children (especially 'slow' developers) produce utterances consisting of a word and a seemingly meaningless 'filler syllable' (L. Bloom 1970, 1973; Dore et al. 1976; see Peters and Menn 1993 for a discussion of how at least some of these elements develop into full-fledged morphemes). For instance, utterances like those in (10) are common near the end of the one-word stage, where they may make up as much as 40% of the child's speech (Ramer 1976:55).

(10)   [ə] more. (Dore et al. 1976)
        Mama [widə]. (L. Bloom 1973:35)
        uh oh down. (L. Bloom 1973:42)

Finally, as noted earlier, children who use the 'gestalt' approach to language analysis produce unsegmented multisyllabic utterances during the one-word stage (e.g., *what's-that, come-here*). These considerations suggest that children have the articulatory skills required to produce at least short sentences, forcing us to look elsewhere for an explanation of the one-word stage.

A plausible motivation for the existence of the one-word stage lies in the nature of the grammar that the acquisition device is constructing. As explained earlier, phrases are formed by combining categories of a particular type. Thus, a determiner can combine with a noun to form an NP (e.g., *the boy*), but it cannot combine with an adverb (**the quickly*). Similarly, a verb can combine with a noun to form a VP (e.g., *see John*), but it cannot combine with a determiner (**see the*). What this means is that before children can form phrases, they must have access to at least some of the category distinctions underlying word combination. The two crucial categories in this regard are N and a predicate category that combines with it to give a larger phrase.

Interestingly, these are the two dominant categories that emerge during the one-word stage (setting aside formulas such as *uh-oh, please,* and *hi* and unanalyzed phrases such as *What's-that,* which arguably have no syntactic category).

As the studies reviewed earlier in this chapter show, children's first words are predominantly nouns. The second most common class of words consists of predicates that will later be combined with nouns to form phrases and sentences—e.g., operators such as *more* and *allgone,* location-naming words such as *up* and *there,* and action-naming words such as *stop* and *sit.* Since nouns and predicates constitute the two category types that are required for even the most rudimentary structure-building, it makes sense to think of the one-word stage as the period during which the acquisition device—having already begun the task of building a grammar—identifies an initial set of categorial distinctions.

Near the end of the one-word period, children typically begin to produce strings of single words, each of which refers to some aspect of a particular situation. The examples in (11) are from L. Bloom 1973:40–41.

(11)   Gia (19 mos.) looking at a picture of a boy in a toy car: *car/ride*
Eric (19 mos.) looking out the window at the street below: *car/see*
Allison (18 mos.) giving a peach and a spoon to her father so that he can get her another piece: *Daddy/peach/cut*

Such **chained one-word utterances** can be quite frequent in children's speech. Of the 320 utterances collected from David between the ages of 1;7 and 1;10, Branigan (1976) found that 90 consisted of sequences of one-word utterances (compared to 167 single word utterances and 63 two-word utterances). Figure 2.1 depicts the relative proportions of these different utterance types during the period of the study.

L. Bloom (1973:61) notes that the strings of single words produced near the end of the one-word stage differ from genuine multi-word utterances in three respects: they exhibit free word order, there is a slight pause between the words, and

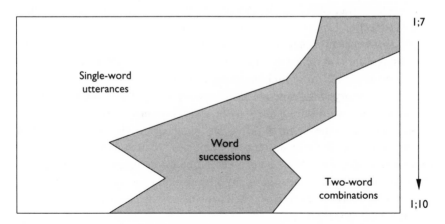

FIGURE 2.1   Relative Frequency of Three Utterance Types (from Garman 1979:187)

$$\overset{\frown}{\text{kick}} \quad \overset{\frown}{\text{that}}$$

$$\overset{\frown}{\text{kick}} \overset{\frown}{\text{that}}$$

FIGURE 2.2 Intonation Contours (de Villiers and de Villiers 1978:50)

each word has it own intonational contour. In bona fide sentences, in contrast, there are strict word order constraints, there is no pause between words, and there is a single intonational contour.

Branigan (1976) refined Bloom's observations somewhat, noting that sequences of single words exhibit properties intermediate between those of true one-word utterances and genuine two-word utterances, thereby constituting a transition between the two. He reported that while the intonation does fall after each word in a sequence of single words (the upper line in figure 2.2), it does not fall as sharply as it does at the end of an utterance (the lower line). Similarly, while there is a slight pause after each word, it is not as great as the pause between true one-word utterances.

These facts suggest that even as children are producing the first word in a sequence of single words, they are anticipating the production of a subsequent word. This prior planning for an additional constituent is doubtless a prerequisite for the formation of the true multi-word utterances that lie just ahead in the language acquisition process.

5. Conclusion

Even at this early point in our survey of syntactic development, it is possible to draw some tentative conclusions about the acquisition device. For example, by studying the form of children's first words and their attempts to repeat adult utterances (see section 1), we can infer that the acquisition device favors louder stimuli, stimuli that occur in isolation, and stimuli that are heard most recently. At the same time, there is evidence that the acquisition device permits considerable latitude in terms of early word-finding strategies: some children initially extract and commit to memory multi-word chunks of speech (the gestalt style), while others focus on smaller word-sized units from the outset (the analytic style).

Another clue to the nature of the acquisition device comes from the fact that despite differences in the character of children's early vocabulary (e.g., the referential–expressive distinction), nouns seem to be the dominant category in early child language—reflecting a sensitivity to semantic considerations such as the 'accessibility' of a word's referent (Gentner's theory) and perhaps to its thematic role-assigning properties.

The motivation for the one-word stage is somewhat harder to discern. One possibility, suggested in section 4, is that this period marks the emergence of the two category types that are minimally required for sentence formation (a nominal and a 'predicate' category that can combine with it). If this is so, then the existence of the one-word stage may be attributable not so much to the acquisition device itself as to the nature of the combinatorial system (the grammar) that it must ultimately construct.

3

Early Multiword Utterances

The phenomenon of word combination begins modestly and is dominated by two-word utterances. According to Nelson's (1973:37) study of 18 children, the mean age by which language learners have produced ten phrases is 19.8 months (with a range from 16 to 28 months). Children's first two-word utterances exhibit relatively little variation. In Braine's (1963) study of Gregory, for instance, the number of two-word combinations grows as in (1) in successive months.

(1)   14   24   54   89   350   1400   2500+

While it is possible that the first phrases produced by children are memorized units, the rapid increase in the number of multiword utterances suggests that productive rules must enter into play at some relatively early point.

A major issue in the study of two- and three-word utterances has to do with how they should be described. The principal point of contention involves a dispute over whether the acquisition device employs the same notions at all stages of development (the Continuity Hypothesis, see chap. 2, p.18). If it does, the rules for sentence formation in the two-word stage should be formulated in terms of syntactic categories such as N, V, NP, and VP, since these are the notions used in the mature grammar. In contrast, if the Continuity Hypothesis is wrong and the acquisition device does not employ the same notions from beginning to end, we need not assume that children use categorial concepts in the first stages of sentence formation simply because more mature speakers of the language do. In what follows, we will consider three approaches to early sentence formation that assume a discontinuous view of language acquisition and one approach that takes it to be continuous.

1. The Thematic Analysis

One widely used approach to early multiword speech makes use of semantic notions such as 'agent', 'action', 'patient' (= 'theme'), 'location', and 'modifier' to classify children's utterances. This sort of approach, which we can call the **thematic analysis** because of its extensive use of thematic role labels,[1] has been adopted by a large number of researchers, including Bowerman (1973), Brown (1973), Schlesinger (1974, 1982), Braine & Hardy (1982), Gleitman & Wanner (1982), Matthei (1987), and Budwig (1990b).

In and of itself, the use of thematic labels to describe child language does not entail a rejection of the Continuity Hypothesis, since it is widely agreed that thematic contrasts are relevant to the functioning of certain phenomena in adult speech (see, e.g., Wilkins 1988 for extensive discussion). However, proponents of the thematic analysis typically assume that these notions are used *instead of* (and not in conjunction with) more formal syntactic notions in the early stages of linguistic development.[2] Moreover, it is assumed, children use thematic notions to characterize phenomena (such as word order) that are constrained in the adult grammar by generalizations referring to structural notions (subject, verb, and so forth). Such a practice does imply rejection of the Continuity Hypothesis.

Using the descriptive tools of thematic analysis, it is possible to identify a variety of semantic relations and operations in the two-word stage. (The examples and classification in table 3.1 are based on Maratsos 1983:712. There is no universal agreement on how these relations should be characterized; for alternative views, see Dale 1972:44–45 and Braine 1976:56–57.) Brown (1973:178–79) reports that about 70% of children's utterances can be classified in terms of these and other less common thematic patterns.

As table 3.2, from Brown 1973:174, helps show, the relative frequency of the different thematic role patterns varies from child to child (see also Garman 1979: 195–97; Maratsos 1983:716) and possibly from language to language as well (Adam, Eve and Sarah were learning English, Kendall Finnish, and Sipili Samoan). Although all five children represented in table 3.2 have a mean length of utterance (MLU) between 1.48 and 2.06 morphemes, they differ in terms of the pattern they use most frequently: Adam prefers the action–theme structure, Kendall the agent–action pattern, and Sipili the possessor–head construction; the other two children exhibit no single dominant pattern. As is the case in the one-word stage, the acquisition device is evidently flexible enough to accommodate differences in children's communicative needs and preferences. In addition, extra-

Table 3.1 Patterns in the Two-Word Stage

Pattern	Examples
Semantic Relations	
agent + action	Eve read, Adam put
action + theme	hit ball, put book
agent + theme	Daddy cookie (= 'Daddy eat cookie')
possessor + head	Daddy shoe, Adam checker
modifier + head	big train, red train
entity + location	book table, sweater chair
action + location	come here, walk street
Referential Operations	
nomination (naming)	that book, it cat
recurrence	more cookie
nonexistence	no milk

Table 3.2 Relative Frequency of Selected Two-Word Patterns
(percentage of total multi-morpheme utterances)

Pattern	Adam	Eve	Sarah	Kendall	Sipili
agent – action	7	10	6	20	3
action – theme	16	10	4	10	8
action – location	5	1	1	3	1
possessor – head	11	10	7	9	14
agent – theme	0	9	0	3	0
entity – location	2	5	1	9	1

neous factors can sometimes enter into play. For example, relatively few of the utterances produced by Sarah and Sipili can be classified in terms of the thematic role patterns in table 3.2 for the simple reason that they produced so many one-word utterances in response to '*What's that?* questions' from their mothers during the taping sessions.

2. The Pivot Analysis

A second analysis of two-word utterances was put forward by Braine (1963), who proposed that children distinguish between two basic word classes, neither of which involves notions used in the adult grammar. (A larger number of word classes is permitted in the otherwise similar system proposed by Miller and Ervin 1964.)

1. The **pivot** (**P**) class consists of high-frequency words that occur in fixed position (only the beginning or only the end of an utterance). Although the set of pivot words varies somewhat from child to child, frequent members include the equivalent of prepositions (e.g., *up, off*), pronouns (*my, it, that*), certain verbs and adjectives (e.g., *see, do, pretty*), as well as 'relational' expressions such as *other, more, allgone,* and *bye-bye.* The pivot class is divided into two sub-classes, P_1, whose members occur utterance-initially, and P_2, whose members occur utterance-finally.

2. The **open** (**O**) class (called the 'X class' by Braine) consists of words that occur in different positions from structure to structure and can occur alone in one-word utterances. All non-pivot words in the child's vocabulary belong to the open class.

Thus, the four possibilities in table 3.3 are permitted. Table 3.4 (from Braine 1963:4–5) contains additional examples of the first three of these patterns, of which the P_1 + O combination is the most frequent.

One of the most serious problems with the pivot analysis is that some children simply do not produce speech with the 'pivot look' in the two-word stage (L. Bloom 1970; Bowerman 1973:30ff.). The words used by these children do

Table 3.3
Four Types of Utterances in
Pivot Grammar

Type	Examples
P_1 + O	it ball, it checker
O + P_2	bunny do, Daddy do
O + O	find bear, Candy say
O	Daddy

Table 3.4 Some Two-Word Combinations

P_1 + O	O + P_2	O + O
	Gregory	
see boy	push it	Mommy sleep
see sock	move it	milk cup
see hot	close it	oh-my see
pretty boat	do it	
pretty fan		
my Mommy		
my milk		
my Daddy		
allgone shoe		
allgone egg		
allgone watch		
allgone vitamins		
more taxi		
more melon		
	Andrew	
all broke	boot off	Papa away
all fix	water off	pants change
I see	airplane by	dry pants
I sit	siren by	
no bed	mail come	
no fix	Mama come	
more juice	hot in-there	
more fish	milk in-there	
other bib		
other milk		
Hi Calico		
Hi Mama		

not exhibit properties typical of either the pivot or the open class, and the variety of multi-word utterances is inconsistent with the limited set of possibilities permitted by a pivot grammar.

In fact, as noted by Braine himself (see also Bowerman 1973:30ff.; Brown 1973:100), even children whose speech does have the 'pivot look' produce a sig-

Table 3.5 Semantic Relations in O + O Patterns

Child's Utterance	Apparent Interpretation
baby highchair	Baby is in the highchair.
Mommy eggnog	Mommy had her eggnog.
Eve lunch	Eve is having lunch.
Mommy sandwich	Mommy will have a sandwich.
sat wall	He sat on the wall.
throw Daddy	Throw it to Daddy.
pick glove	Pick up the glove.

nificant number of utterances that do not fit into any of the four patterns in table 3.3. Some pivot words occur alone (e.g., *more, allgone, broken*), some occur with another pivot (e.g., *that off, want do, want more*), and still others can occur at either the beginning or the end of an utterance (e.g., *that book, see that*).

Finally, pivot grammar fails to account for important facts about the internal organization of children's two-word utterances. As noted by Brown (1973:105), for example, O + O utterances can exhibit a wide variety of semantic relations between their component parts (table 3.5). In treating all these utterances as instances of the same O + O structure, the pivot analysis ignores the fact that several different patterns of thematic relations are represented here: entity–location in the case of *baby highchair,* agent–theme in *Eve lunch,* action–location in *sat wall,* action–theme in *pick glove,* and so on. This problem was first observed by L. Bloom (1970:5), whose subject Kathryn used the utterance *Mommy sock* at age 21 months in two quite different ways—once to mean 'Mommy's sock' and another time to mean 'Mommy is putting the sock on me'. Since the pivot analysis treats both utterances as instances of the O + O pattern, it cannot account for the difference between them as things now stand. (In retrospect and at the risk of violating the spirit of the original proposal, a case might be made that such differences should be accounted for in the sentence's semantic representation rather than its syntactic structure.)

For these and related reasons, the pivot analysis is no longer considered viable by language acquisition researchers. It is still of historical interest, however, both because it constitutes a radical rejection of the Continuity Hypothesis and because its influence can be seen in the more contemporary characterization of early child language described in the next section.

3. The Limited Scope Analysis

A third type of analysis, advocated by Braine (1976) and Maratsos (1983), is based on the claim that the utterances produced by children in the first stages of multiword speech do not always manifest categories as general as those used in the adult grammar. Instead, productive patterns are described in terms of **limited**

scope formulas that specify the relative ordering of narrowly circumscribed semantic classes. Although a small number of these formulas make use of traditional thematic notions (most notably the formulas 'agent + action' and 'possessor + head'), most consist of a **constant** such as *big* or *see* and an **open position** that can be filled by a large set of words. To see how this analysis works, let us consider the set of multiword utterances in table 3.6 that Braine (1976:43) observed during several two-hour recording sessions with the child David at the age of 21 months. As Braine (p. 45) notes, there are two dominant patterns here. The first, which can be captured by the formula *here + X,* is used to indicate objects in the child's surroundings, while the second, corresponding to the formula *want + X,* is used for making requests. (A less common request formula involves the constant *can-I* or *can-I-have.*) Nowhere in this corpus is there direct evidence that David is making use of more general grammatical notions such as thematic roles (e.g., agent and theme) or syntactic categories (e.g., noun and verb).

Although the particular limited scope formulas used in the early stages of word combination differ considerably from child to child, Braine claims that the utterances produced in the two-word stage are always narrowly restricted. This point can be illustrated by considering the dominant patterns (table 3.7, based on Braine 1976:32) in the speech of Braine's son Jonathon at the age of 23 months

Table 3.6 David's Word Combinations at 21 Months

Indicating or Identifying Forms			
here wowwow	here pink	here this	here, Daddy, soap
here flower	here jump	here milk	
here bread	here break-it[a]	here apple	

Requesting Expression + What Is Requested			
want fix it	want light	want daddy fix it	can-I-truck
want car	want jump	want open door	can-I-have-this
want cookie	want milk	want this	can-I-have soap
want balloon	want babywant	this one here	
want book	want read	want this . . . egg	gimme . . . this . . . toy
want egg	want Brad	want this . . . soap	please get down
want pocket	want soap	want more	[u] get down
want ball	want it	want more milk	[u] get out

Other Combinations			
more balloon	sit down	help it	gimme
more open door	go away	fix it	no mike
more book	come here	break it	no wanna
David play	open door	drink milk	I can't
			where apple
			where wowwow
			this one

a. break-it = broken object.

Table 3.7 Dominant Patterns in Jonathon's Speech at 23 Months

Name + X	*big* + X	*little* + X	*more* + X
mommy bread	big plane	little stick	more juice
mommy shoe	big book	little rock	more bee
daddy shoe	big car	little ball	more stick
daddy car	big sock	little plane	more book
daddy book	big stick	little lamb	more catch
daddy pipe	big rock	little blue	more plane
daddy banana	big ball	little key	more dice
	big chicken	little duck	more ball
	big lamb	little bread	more duck
	big dog		more blue

(see also the profile of Andrew in Garman 1979:196). The pattern in the leftmost column parallels the 'possessor + head' pattern posited by thematic analysis. However, the other three patterns all involve a constant term and an open position: *big* + X, *little* + X (perhaps reduceable to a slightly more general *SIZE* + X), and *more* + X. Although these formulas are different from those posited for David (see table 3.6), they are comparable in their narrow scope.

The relative lack of diversity in children's early two-word utterances may not be as significant as proponents of the limited scope analysis believe. In fact, it may reflect nothing more than the size of children's vocabularies at this point in syntactic development. According to Bates, Bretherton, and Snyder (1988:98–99), for example, children at age 20 months (the common onset time for multiword structures) have vocabularies of fewer than 150 words, less than 10% of which are verbs. This places obvious limitations on the variety of utterances that they can initially produce, making it difficult to infer anything definitive about the types of categories that are present.

4. The Syntactic Analysis

All three of the approaches to early multiword utterances considered thus far have in common one important characteristic: they assume that the child's first attempts at constructing grammatical rules bypass the syntactic notions (e.g., N, V, etc.) that are used in the adult grammar. This raises an obvious problem since it is difficult to believe that the acquisition device is 'designed' to initially formulate entirely erroneous hypotheses about the grammar, so that it later has to backtrack and reconstruct the sentence-building system in very fundamental ways.

The obvious way to avoid this problem is to assume that the acquisition device makes use of syntactic notions from the outset, consistent with the Continuity Hypothesis. This assumption has been adopted by many researchers over the past thirty-five years, including Brown and Fraser (1963), Klima and Bellugi (1966),

McNeill (1970), L. Bloom (1970), and Pinker (1984); for further discussion of this work, see chapter 15. On this view, utterances in the two-word stage have the sorts of syntactic representations show in (2). (Proponents of the syntactic analysis differ in the details of the structural representations they use.)

(2)   a. action–location   b. agent–theme

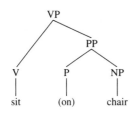   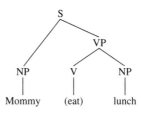

The most obvious feature of these representations is that they include positions for unexpressed categories (written here in parentheses)—such as the preposition *on* in (2a) and the verb *eat* in (2b).

Although abstract, this analysis is not unconstrained. Unexpressed P and V categories are posited in syntactic representations such as (2) only because overt prepositions and verbs appear in other utterances produced at this stage. In contrast, empty determiner categories are typically not used in these representations, since *the* and *a* are simply not found in children's early multiword utterances.[3]

In the long run, the postulation of unexpressed categories may actually contribute to a simpler account of children's syntactic system than would otherwise be possible. Were the unexpressed categories posited in (2) not present, we would have to assume that intransitive verbs such as *sit* can take a complement NP in child language and that subjects can combine directly with direct objects to form a sentence.

(3)   *Tree structures without empty positions:*
       a. action–location   b. agent≠theme

Since such patterns are not possible in adult English and hence do not occur in the speech to which children are exposed, questions arise as to why the acquisition device would permit them in child language. On the other hand, if we make use of unexpressed categories, the resulting syntactic patterns are commonplace: an intransitive verb with a PP complement as in (2a) and a subject–verb–object construction as in (2b).

This brings us to the question of why children have unexpressed categories in their syntactic representations in cases where the adult language does not permit this option. One possibility is simply that children have not yet learned the corresponding English word. This seems especially likely in the case of structures with an understood copula verb (e.g., *Daddy tired*), since this element is normally absent from two-word speech in general (Brown 1973:271 ff.; Ramer 1976:59). However, this cannot be the whole story, since at least some of the missing elements in early speech are vocabulary items known to the child (Ninio 1988: 112 n.). For example, L. Bloom (1970:166) reports that during the two-word stage Kathryn produced the verbless phrase *Baby cheek* with the meaning 'Baby hurt cheek' even though she had the word *hurt* in her active vocabulary.

A more general explanation, put forward in greatest detail by Pinker (1984: 160 ff.), is that a type of 'processing bottleneck' occurs between the representation of meaning and the syntactic structure that is supposed to encode it. The key idea is that the mechanisms responsible for realizing units of meaning as words in a particular syntactic configuration can handle only a very limited number of units per utterance (perhaps as few as two). As depicted in figure 3.1, a representation containing three semantic units (SIT, ON, and CHAIR) must pass through a filter that generally allows the expression of only two elements. As a result, one element (here the preposition) is left unexpressed—giving a two-word utterance. (Greenfield et al. 1985 suggest that the notions most likely to be encoded under such circumstances are those highest in informativeness.) As children mature, this constraint is gradually relaxed, leading to the production of the complete sentence structures that their grammars required from the outset.

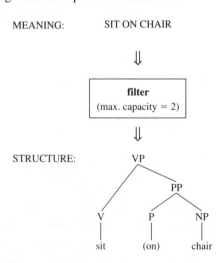

FIGURE 3.1 The Processing Bottleneck

Children seem to differ from each other in terms of how frequently they employ structures with unencoded categories. While the agent–theme pattern is marginal in the speech of many children (Brown 1973:194) and not used at all by some (Macrae 1979:164), L. Bloom (1970:224) reports that it was used productively by two of the three children she studied.[4] Similarly, whereas Valian (1986:573) found few examples of structures with a missing preposition in the speech of six 2-year-olds that she studied, Brown (1973:194) reports many such patterns (e.g., from the speech of Adam: *sit water, put truck window, write paper, sit Adam chair*) as does Braine (1976:34) (e.g., from the speech of Jonathon: *sand eye, ball house, sand toe, raisin cup*). Tomasello (1987) describes the development of prepositions in his daughter from age 1;0 to 2;0, noting that spatial prepositions such as *up, on, in,* and *over* were acquired earlier and omitted less frequently than nonspatial prepositions such as *by, to,* and *for.*

ARGUMENTS FOR THE SYNTACTIC ANALYSIS

The fact that the syntactic analysis alone is consistent with the Continuity Hypothesis does not in itself establish its correctness, since we cannot be sure at this point that the acquisition device really does employ the same notions throughout development. Indeed, even some linguists who are strongly committed to the view that the adult grammar includes abstract formal categories believe that these categories are not present in children's earliest speech (e.g., Felix 1987, 1988; Radford 1990); see chapter 15 for further discussion. To show that the syntactic analysis is right, it is therefore necessary to find independent evidence that children's early grammars do in fact employ syntactic notions rather than some other type of concept.

One such piece of evidence involves the emergence of syntactic categories such as noun and verb. Data from later stages in syntactic development suggest that children make strikingly few errors in syntactic categorization. For example, Maratsos (1982:252) reports that during his study of 74 hours of speech from 21 children between the ages of 2 and 4 years, he found only nine errors involving the assignment of a word to the wrong syntactic category. This is consistent with Cazden's (1968) report that she found only four such errors in her study of 150 hours of speech by Adam, Eve, and Sarah. Table 3.8 (from Maratsos 1982:253; Clark 1982) exemplifies the occasional categorial errors found in the speech of children aged 2 to 4 years. For some other examples, see Pinker (1984:114). The low error rate for syntactic categorization suggests an early sensitivity to categorial phenomena. There is simply no indication in the developmental data that children must make a transition from a semantically based system of classification to the more formal system of syntactic categorization found in adult grammars.

A different type of argument in support of the syntactic analysis has been put

Table 3.8 Some Syntactic Category Errors (ages 2–4 yrs.)

Error Type	Example
Noun used as verb	You have to *scale* (= weigh) it first.
	Mummy *trousers* me.
	I'm *crackering* my soup.
	It's *snowflaking*.
Adjective used as noun	I will be many *talls*.
	Where's the *dirties* at?
	That one's got a *happy*.
Verb used as adjective	They call me a *grumble* boy.
	See the *go* cars.
Adjective used as adverb	And they went *loud*.

forward by Pinker (1984:118 ff.). The key observation is that the syntactic analysis assigns identical category labels to elements found in different positions within the sentence.

(4)   a. [$_{NP}$ my mommy] read
        b. read [$_{NP}$ my book]

This allows the syntactic analysis to make an important prediction: since the elements occurring in preverbal and postverbal position are supposed to be instances of the same category (i.e., NP), they should exhibit a common range of semantic and structural diversity.

Consider first the question of semantic diversity. The traditional view is that preverbal and postverbal elements in child language differ in that the former designate animate entities while the latter have inanimate referents (e.g., Bloom 1970, Brown 1973, and Bowerman 1973, all cited by Pinker 1984:128); see table 3.9. Crucially, however, Pinker (p. 129) shows that this is only a statistical tendency, not an absolute contrast. As the utterances in table 3.10 demonstrate, early child speech does include examples of both inanimate subjects and animate complements. In sum, the elements occurring in preverbal and postverbal positions do not constitute distinct, semantically homogeneous classes in early child language. Rather, they exhibit the internal semantic diversity that one expects of syntactic categories, whose boundaries do not coincide with those of semantic notions such as animacy.

Turning now to structural properties, it has been claimed that the elements occurring in preverbal and postverbal positions can be distinguished in terms of their respective length and complexity. In particular, it has been noted that the preverbal position tends to be filled by simple nouns or pronouns while the post-verbal position is more likely to contain a noun together with a modifier such as a

Table 3.9 Some Examples of Animate
             Subjects and Inanimate
             Objects

Animate Subjects	Inanimate Objects
Mummy do it.	Hayley draw *boat.*
Mummy cry.	Laura eat *that.*
Pig go in.	Read *book.*
Hayley talk.	Baby drive *truck.*

Table 3.10 Inanimate Subjects and
              Animate Complements in
              Adam's Speech

Inanimate Subjects	Animate Complements
towtruck come here	me get *John*
shadow stay night	get *you*
horn playing	find *Kitty*
paper go?	give *Cromer*
shoe go?	throw *Daddy*
screwdriver hurt	see *Mommy*
truck broken	hit *mosquito*
windmill turn on	move *doggie*
tummy hurt	call *Daddy*

possessive (e.g., *John's book*), an adjective (e.g., *good dog*), or a determiner (e.g., *that book*) (e.g., Menyuk 1969:34; Limber 1976; Pinker 1984:131).

Crucially, though, this does not mean that there is a *grammatical* distinction between the two positions. Perhaps, as Pinker (1984:133) suggests, subjects are shorter because they express old or given information and therefore do not require as much lexical content as postverbal constituents that express new information (on this, see also chap. 5 and P. Bloom 1990a). To establish the existence of a grammatical contrast between the preverbal and postverbal positions, it would be necessary to show that certain types of phrases are systematically excluded from one or the other position. However, this does not seem to happen, as illustrated by the summary in table 3.11 of subject and object types in the speech of Adam, Eve, and Sarah. As Pinker (p. 133) notes, both positions exhibit a comparable range of structural diversity: although not particularly frequent, possessor–noun sequences do occur in subject position (e.g., **Dale panda** *march*) as do modifier–noun patterns (e.g., **little boy** *sleeping*) and determiner–noun sequences (e.g., **a bunny** *[is] there*).

Very similar findings (table 3.12) are reported by Limber (1976:315) in his study of the spontaneous speech of 8 children aged 2 to 4 years. Once again, all

Table 3.11 Types of Subject and Objects (frequency of
occurrence) (from unpublished work by
Roger Brown, cited by Pinker 1984:134)

Type of NP	Subject	Object	Total
Bare noun	36	163	199
Modifier[a]–noun	8	42	50
Total	44	205	249

a. Possessors, determiners, adjectives.

Table 3.12 Types of Subject and Object
(percentage of total)

Type of NP	Subject (846 tokens)	Object (654 tokens)
Impersonal pronouns	17	29
Personal pronouns	65	5
Inanimate nouns	5	54
Animate nouns	11	9

structural types occur in both subject (preverbal) and object (postverbal) position.
This is consistent with the claim that these positions are occupied by identical
syntactic categories (NPs) whose internal composition and semantic type must
therefore exhibit similar ranges of variation.

This conclusion is strengthened by the results of Valian's (1986:570) study of
the spontaneous speech of six 2-year-old children. As table 3.13 shows, Valian
found NPs of different sorts in three separate positions—subject (preverbal), direct object (postverbal), and object of a preposition. (Similar results are reported
by Ihns and Leonard 1988 for their study of Adam.)

English word order rules provide still another opportunity to determine
whether the acquisition device is formulating generalizations in terms of syntactic categories in the two-word stage. The grammar of English places the subject
NP in preverbal position regardless of its thematic role. If this is the type of
grammatical system being built by the acquisition device, then we would expect
children to place both agentive and nonagentive subjects in preverbal position.
Table 3.14, from Pinker 1984:142, describing data collected from Adam when
his MLU was between 1.5 and 2.75, suggests that this is what happens. (However,
matters may not be so straightforward for all children; see chap. 4 for discussion.)
Notice that agentive and nonagentive subjects are correctly positioned with approximately equal success, suggesting that both types of element belong to the
same category (presumably 'subject'), consistent with the syntactic analysis.

Table 3.13 The Distribution of NP Types in Three
Positions (percentages)

NP Type	Subject	Direct Object	Object of a Preposition
Det Adj N	0.4	2.5	0.4
Det N	5.4	18.9	7.8
N	2.1	6.8	1.8
Pronoun	31.4	11.8	2.6
Name	3.9	3.7	0.8
Total	43.2	43.7	13.4 (= 100%)

Table 3.14 Positioning of Subjects in Adam's Early Speech

	SUBJECT PLACEMENT		
	Correct	Incorrect	Total
Agentive subject	83	7	90
Nonagentive subject	33	3	36
Total	116	10	126

Yet another consideration favoring the syntactic analysis is outlined by P. Bloom (1990b), who reports on word order data from spontaneous speech that points toward a subtle distinction between subtypes of nominal elements. Bloom notes that whereas children in the two-word stage place modifiers in front of common nouns (*big dog*) and indefinite pronouns (*big one*), they never produce this pattern with definite pronouns (**big he*) even though the reverse order is found (*he [is] big*). The ability to make this distinction, which corresponds to a parallel contrast in adult speech, suggests a refined sensitivity to categorial information at an early age.

Nothing in the preceding discussion precludes the possibility that the acquisition device makes use of nonsyntactic notions *in addition to* syntactic concepts in the construction of early grammars. In fact, there is good evidence to suggest that thematic roles may interact with syntactic notions to yield 'best exemplars' of various category types in both adult and child grammars. In adult grammar, for instance, it has been claimed that the prototypical transitive clause has an agent subject and a theme direct object (e.g., Givón 1984:96). Consistent with this view, Slobin (1985:1176) reports that children learning Kaluli initially use the ergative case only for the subjects of transitive verbs that are highly agentive ('hit', 'cut', 'eat', etc.) rather than for the subjects of transitive verbs in general. Similarly, Gvozdev (1961:173, cited by Braine 1976:67 and Slobin 1985:1176) reports that his Russian-learning child initially employed the accusative case only for direct objects whose referents undergo a change in position (prototypical themes). Thus he used the accusative for the direct object of verbs such as 'give', 'carry', 'put', and 'throw', but not 'draw', 'read', and 'make'. (Angiolillo and Goldin-Meadow 1982 and Matthei 1987 provide additional examples of the interaction between syntactic and semantic notions.)

It is important to emphasize here that the preceding examples point to the possible joint use of syntactic and thematic notions by the acquisition device, not to the use of the thematic notions alone. For instance, the accusative case rule described by Gvozdez applies only to *direct objects* that are also prototypical themes; subjects bearing the theme role (as in the Russian equivalent of *The man fell*) do not appear with the accusative case. There is therefore nothing in this phenomenon to contradict the view that structural notions are available to the acquisition device from a very early point in the developmental process.

5. Evidence for Hierarchial Structure

A key claim of contemporary syntactic analysis is that the words that make up a sentence are not simply strung together like beads on a string but rather are organized into (for the most part) binary-branching hierarchical structures such as those in (5).

(5)   a.   b.

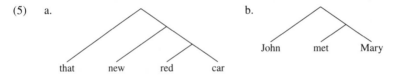

How can we know whether the grammars used by young children impose a hierarchical structure on the utterances they produce? A first set of considerations is theory-internal. According to one popular view (e.g., Marantz 1984), the syntactic configuration reflects the manner in which the meanings of words combine to give the meaning of a sentence (the so-called 'compositional semantics'). If this is right, then we can predict the relatively early emergence of hierarchical structure. In particular, representations of this sort should appear at the point that children start combining word-level meanings to express sentence-level meanings.

An experiment (box 3.1) by Hirsh-Pasek and Golinkoff (1991) suggests that even children in the one-word stage realize that sentences are formed by combining the meanings of their component words. As the children heard a test sentence such as *She's kissing the keys,* they were presented with different scenes on the TV monitors in front of them (figure 3.2). One scene depicted a woman kissing keys, with a ball held in the foreground; the other depicted a woman kissing a ball, with keys held in the foreground.

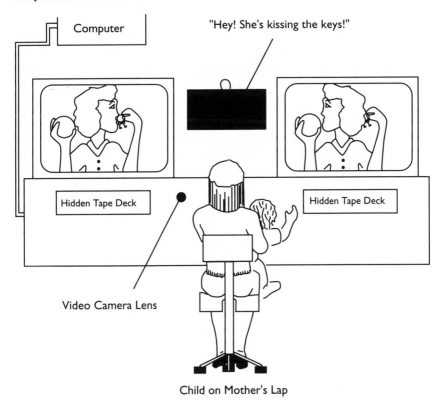

FIGURE 3.2 The Preferential Looking Task (from Hirsh-Pasek and Golinkoff 1991 : 303)

Box 3.1

THE STUDY: Hirsh-Pasek and Golinkoff 1991
SUBJECTS: 16 infants (8 boys, 8 girls), aged 13–15 mos.
SENTENCE TYPES:
    SVO sentences, such as 'She's kissing the keys.'
TASK: preferential looking (as described in chap. 2)

If infants understand that the meanings of the words *kiss* and *keys* are supposed to combine to create a more complex meaning, they can be expected to prefer the screen depicting the woman kissing the keys to the screen that shows the woman kissing the ball. (Recall from chap. 2 that infants prefer to look at scenes that 'match' their understanding of the auditory stimulus; preference is measured in terms of latency and/or fixation time.) If, on other hand, the infants are processing word meanings as unconnected, they should distribute their attention equally between the two screens, since each depicts a kissing action as well as a set of keys. Interestingly, Hirsh-Pasek and Golinkoff report (p. 308) that the infants exhibited a statistically significant preference for the screen that depicted the woman kissing the keys.

Hirsh-Pasek and Golinkoff's result seems to indicate that even children who are in the earliest stages of linguistic development understand that the meanings of the words making up a sentence combine with each other. This is arguably the crucial prerequisite for the emergence of syntactic structure (see above), but it would obviously be desirable to find some independent evidence that young language learners make this connection. Unfortunately, such evidence is very difficult to come by.

The tests most often used to verify claims about hierarchical structure in adult language (table 3.15) are typically inapplicable in the early stages of syntactic development, either because the utterances in child speech are too short or because they do not include the right types of elements.

Although there is no direct evidence for hierarchical structure in the earliest stages of multiword speech, children's use of the indefinite pronoun *one* at a somewhat later period offers a potentially promising avenue of inquiry. In adult English, *one* can be substituted for a unit consisting of a noun and its modifier, as in (6).

(6)   John chose this *white ball* and Harry chose that *one*.
      (*one* = *white ball*)

Table 3.15 Some Tests for Hierarchical Structure in Adult Language (showing that *hit the ball* is a structural unit)

Test Sentence	Problem
a. Movement John said that he would hit the ball, and [*hit the ball*] he did ___ .	VP fronting is relatively unusual even in adult speech; it occurs only in special contexts and requires stranding of an auxiliary verb—a type of category that does not occur in early child language (see ch. 15).
b. Substitution John hit the ball, and Sam *did* too. (*did* = *hit the ball*)	The element that is substituted for the VP is an auxiliary verb, which is nonexistent in early child speech.
c. Deletion John will hit the ball and Sam will Ø too. (Ø = *hit the ball*)	Deletion leaves behind an auxiliary verb, a type of category that is missing from early child speech.
d. Coordination John will [hit the ball] and [run to first base].	Coordination does not emerge until age 2;6 or later (see chap. 6).

This supports the contention that the noun and its modifier make up a syntactic unit that excludes the determiner *this,* consistent with the view that syntactic structure in the adult language consists of binary hierarchical relations, as in (7).

(7)   [this [white ball]]

Interestingly, Radford (1990:65) notes that young children also produce utterances in which *one* apparently refers back to modifier + noun sequences, as in (8).

(8)   a. nice [yellow pen], nice *one.* (23 mos.)
          (*one = yellow pen*)
       b. That's a [brown eye]. Another [brown eye]. No, that *one.* (26 mos.)
          (*one = brown eye*)
       c. ADULT: Ah! Nice little chicken!
          CHILD: Stroke that *one.* (23 mos.)
          (*one = nice little chicken*)

Although (as Radford admits) the precise reference of *one* is not always clear (e.g., does *one* in (8a) replace *yellow pen* or just *pen?*), independent experiments by Hamburger and Crain (reported below) provide strong support for the view that *one* refers to adjective + noun sequences in the speech of young children.

Not all research on child language has converged on the view that hierarchical structure is present from the early stages of syntactic development. In fact, this thesis has been directly challenged by Matthei (1982), based on the results of an intriguing experiment (box 3.2). The key part of the experiment involves children's responses to the biased array, in which the second ball overall is green (but does not qualify as the 'second green ball');[5] in the neutral array, in contrast, the second ball overall is red.

Box 3.2

THE STUDY: Matthei 1982
SUBJECTS: 35 children aged 3;9 to 6;3 (19 girls, 16 boys)
PHRASE TYPES: *the second green ball* (4 tokens for each of the two arrays described below)
TASK: The children were shown arrays of balls arranged as follows, and asked to select 'the second green ball'.
          biased array: RED   GREEN   RED   GREEN   GREEN   RED
          neutral array: GREEN   RED   GREEN   RED   RED   GREEN
          Pre-testing established that children knew the meanings of the words making up the phrases, and pre-training ensured that the children could count the members of a set and that they counted from left to right.

When asked to do this task, adults take *the second green ball* to refer to the second ball from among the set of green balls. Thus, they choose ball number 4 in the first array and ball number 3 in the second array. This is consistent with the view that phrases have binary hierarchical structure in adult speech, as in (9).

(9)
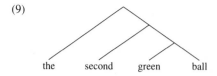

Here there is a syntactic unit corresponding to the set of green balls, to which the modifer *second* then applies to pick out the second object of this sort.

Interestingly, many of the children in Matthei's study responded quite differently, selecting ball number 2 in the biased array over half the time—on average, 2.08 times out of 4 (compared to 0.86 for the neutral array).[6] (There was no significant correlation between age and number of correct responses.) Matthei suggests that the children tended to treat the modifiers *second* and *green* as if they applied independently to the noun *ball,* thereby deriving an interpretation involving a ball that is both second among the balls and green, not second among the green balls. This interpretation seems to presuppose the non-hierarchical syntactic structure depicted in (10), in which *second* is a sister of *ball* rather than *green ball.*

(10)
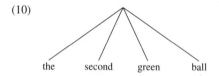

From this Matthei concludes that 'children initially make the hypothesis that the syntactic structure of [a] construction is not hierarchically organized' (p. 328).

This conclusion can be disputed for various reasons. First, if in fact the children in Matthei's study were systematically assigning the wrong syntactic structure to the stimulus phrases, one would expect their responses to be uniformly incorrect, so that they would always choose the wrong ball from the biased stimulus array. In fact, though, the children gave correct responses 45.5% of the time. This suggests confusion rather than a systematic error in the assignment of syntactic structure.

This conclusion receives support from the results of a second experiment that Matthei did with the same group of children, this time asking them simply to choose 'the second ball' from arrays as in (11).

(11)   BOX   BALL   BOX   BALL   BALL   BOX

The children should have had no trouble interpreting these patterns, since (as depicted in (12)) no adjective complicates the relationship between the numeral and the noun, in contrast with the situation in phrases like *the second green ball.*

(12)

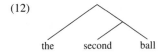

the   second   ball

Yet, the children still responded incorrectly 36% of the time (by choosing the second item in the sample array). This suggests that the real problem lies in children's inability to match ordinal numbers (*second, third,* etc.) with a subset of items in an array. In the case of stimuli such as *the second ball,* for example, the target item must be selected from the set of balls which is itself a subset of a larger set of items (the array of balls and boxes). Similarly, in the case of phrases such as *the second green ball,* the target item must be chosen from a subset of the set of items to which the children are exposed. (They are shown a picture of several balls, but they must only pay attention to the green balls in picking the second item.) Hamburger and Crain (1984) provide a detailed formalization of the planning required to respond appropriately to this task.

Additional experimental work by Hamburger and Crain sheds further light on what made Matthei's original experiment so difficult for his subjects. In one series of tasks in Hamburger and Crain's study, the experimenter asked children to hand him felt cutouts (saying, for example, 'hand me four of those' and 'hand me five of those'). The experimenter next used the cutouts to construct test arrays on a feltboard out of the children's sight. The children were then presented with the stimulus sentence in its entirety before being shown the array from which the selection was to be made. (In Matthei's experiment, the children had the array in sight as they heard the stimulus sentence—opening the possibility that they might begin to point as soon as they hear the word *second* without waiting for the additional information that was needed to make the right selection.) With these relatively minor modifications, error rates fell to as low as 14% on the sentences that had caused the most trouble to children of a comparable age in Matthei's experiment.

A further experiment by Hamburger and Crain (box 3.3) provides independent evidence that young children have hierarchically organized syntactic representations.

Box 3.3

THE STUDY: Hamburger & Crain 1984
SUBJECTS: 25 children with an average age of 4;10 (no age range is given)
TASK: The children were given an array such as the following and were asked: 'Point to the first green ball; point to the second one'.

GREEN	RED	GREEN	RED	GREEN	RED
SQUARE	SQUARE	BALL	BALL	BALL	BALL

Children who interpret *one* in the second part of the experimenter's request as 'ball' will select item 4 while those who interpret it as 'green ball' will select item 5. Both interpretations are possible, of course, but the latter is especially interesting since it treats *green ball* as a syntactic unit, consistent with the view that phrase structure is hierarchically organized. Hamburger and Crain report that 42 of 50 responses took *one* to mean 'green ball', consistent with the view that children make use of hierarchically structured syntactic representations. (This also confirms Radford's contention (see above) that language learners use *one* to refer to adjective + noun sequences, although Hamburger and Crain's subjects were evidently somewhat older than the children studied by Radford.)

In sum, there is good reason to think that the problems encountered by Matthei's subjects lie not in the hierarchical properties of syntactic structure, but rather in the conceptual difficulty associated with finding and counting the relevant sub-array of elements. This leaves intact the conclusion that hierarchical syntactic representations are present from the early stages of syntactic development.

6. Conclusion

A variety of considerations suggest that the acquisition device discovers both syntactic categories and hierarchical structure at an early point in linguistic development. First, there is evidence from children's own speech (reviewed in section 4) which demonstrates that elements occurring at different places in the sentence exhibit the internal structure and the semantic diversity that one would expect of true syntactic categories. Second, children's use of the indefinite pronoun *one* both in naturalistic speech and in experimental studies points toward the existence of binary branching within NPs from the earliest point at which evidence of this sort can be gathered. Finally, methodological considerations militate against the view that the acquisition device would initially use notions irrelevant or inappropriate to the adult grammar, only to replace these notions with a new set of concepts at some intermediate point in the acquisition process.

We are left, then, with an important conclusion about the acquisition device: it is designed to 'discover' syntactic categories and hierarchical structure in the speech to which it is exposed from a very early point (maybe even the beginning) of the language acquisition process. The question of precisely *how* this happens would take us well beyond the developmental data that are our current primary concern. However, we will return to this issue in part II of this book. First, though, a number of other important developmental phenomena must be considered.

4

Word Order and Case

For language to fulfill its communicative function, it must have a way to mark the grammatical roles of the various phrases that can occur in a clause. In a sentence such as *The girl helped the boy,* for example, there must be a way to indicate that the first NP functions as subject and the second as direct object. Two of the most common ways to convey this sort of information in human language are through linear position ('word order') and affixation ('case').

As a 'fixed word order' language, English requires most syntactic relationships to be encoded by a consistent word order pattern even when there is no danger of ambiguity or misunderstanding.[1] Thus, adjectives uniformly precede the nouns that they modify (*old house,* not **house old*), prepositions systematically precede their complements (*on the bench* vs **the bench on*), and so on. The primary means of distinguishing between subjects and direct objects in English is also through word order: as in the example sentence considered in the preceding paragraph, the subject characteristically occurs before the verb and the direct object after it.

Case too has a role to play in distinguishing between subjects and direct objects, but only when these elements are pronouns. A subject pronoun has the **nominative** form, while a pronoun that functions as direct object has the **accusative** form. Thus, we say *She helped him* (not **Her helped he*), with both case and word order identifying the first pronoun as the subject and the second one as the direct object.

The purpose of this chapter is to consider the developmental path followed by the acquisition device as it uncovers the function of word order and case in English.

1. The Development of Word Order

The sentence-building component of a grammar must specify not only which constituents can combine to form a larger phrase (e.g., a transitive verb combines with a direct object NP), but also their relative order. While the categorial inventory is more or less the same across languages (e.g., all languages have transitive verbs and NPs), word order conventions vary quite dramatically. The three most commonly found word orders within 'basic' transitive clauses are illustrated in (1).

(1) a. *English* (SVO):
       The man fixed the car.

b. *Tagalog* (VSO):
   Binili ng-nanay   ang-bigas.
   bought ERG-mother ABS-rice
   'The mother bought the rice.'

c. *Korean* (SOV):
   Haksayng-i chayk-ul ilkessta.
   student-NOM book-AC read
   'The student read the book.'

A particularly intriguing system of word order contrasts is found in German (2), where a verb in the sole or topmost clause occurs in second position if it is finite but must be placed in sentence-final position if it is nonfinite.

(2)   a. *Finite verb: occurs in second position:*
          Karl *kauft* das Buch.
          Karl buys the book

       b. *Nonfinite verb: occurs in sentence-final position:*
          Karl hat das Buch *gekauft.*
          Karl has the book bought
          'Karl has bought the book.'

Clahsen (1986:108) reports that just prior to mastery of the finite–nonfinite distinction, the three German children he was studying were confused about verb placement, using the 'verb-second' order in only about 40% of the sentences where it is required by the adult grammar. Immediately following mastery of this contrast, however, the incidence of the verb-second order in required contexts rose to 90%. This suggests that the acquisition device is able to treat a category's combinatorial properties independently of its positioning: well before the children in Clahsen's study had mastered the peculiarities of German word order, they were using verbs with direct objects and modifiers of various sorts. The acquisition device had thus correctly identified the combinatorial properties of the verb category before it determined the precise details of its relative positioning. Atkinson (1992:261) reviews several studies of other languages in which a comparable developmental phenomenon seems to occur.

Compared to German, the conventions governing the relative order of a verb and its arguments in English are straightforward. As a result, the acquisition device seems generally to master the verb's combinatorial and positional properties more or less simultaneously, so that English-speaking children employ the appropriate word order in the vast majority of their utterances from the earliest stages of multiword speech. In fact, Brown (1973:156) estimates that of the many thousands of utterances recorded in studies of more than a dozen English-speaking children, only about 100 contain word order errors. Three such errors, from the speech of Adam at age 2;3, are reproduced below. (For a sampling of other errors of this type from various sources, see Brown 1973:125 and Maratsos 1983:724.)

(3)   Dirty my hands
      Paper find
      Must go Catherine

Comparable findings are reported by Pinker (1984:123), who calculates that 95% of the utterances produced by the twelve children studied by Braine (1976) exhibit the correct word order. In a similar vein, Valian (1986) reports complete mastery of NP-internal word order (e.g., *the black dog,* not **black the dog*) in the speech of six 2-year old children that she studied. Other commentators have drawn similar conclusions both for English (e.g., Radford 1990:79) and for other languages with relatively fixed word order (e.g., Maratsos 1983:726; Pinker 1984:122–23). All of this suggests both that the acquisition device is extremely sensitive to word order phenomena (as first proposed by Slobin 1973) and that it proceeds very conservatively, perhaps even 'record[ing] one by one the word orders found in parental speech' (Pinker 1984:120).

THE NATURE OF WORD ORDER ERRORS

Notwithstanding the findings just cited, the literature on syntactic development does include reports of systematic word order errors in both comprehension and production. Errors of the former type are commonly observed in experimental studies investigating children's interpretation of transitive clauses such as *The truck pushes the car.* Clauses of this sort are called **reversible,** since their component NPs can be reversed without yielding an ungrammatical or nonsensical result. They therefore cannot be comprehended without at least a rudimentary knowledge of word order, since the relative positioning of the two NPs provides crucial information about which entity does the pushing and which is pushed. An early study of such patterns (box 4.1) was carried out by de Villiers and de Villiers (1973). They found that even children whose MLU approaches 3 have some difficulty interpreting active sentences (table 4.1). Note that even the most mature group of speakers made reversal errors (interpreting the first NP as the theme

Box 4.1

THE STUDY: de Villiers and de Villiers 1973
SUBJECTS: 33 children aged 19–37.5 mos.
SENTENCE TYPES: Reversible active and passive sentences embedded in the context
       'Make . . .'; 6 tokens of each type
TASK: Children were asked to act out the meaning of the test sentences with the help
       of toys.

Table 4.1 Interpretation of Reversible Active Sentences (percentage correct)

MLU	Correct	Reversed	Child as Agent	Refusals
1–1.5	31	21.4	33.3	14.3
1.5–2	75.5	5.6	12.2	6.7
2–2.5	70	11	16.2	2.8
2.5–3	81	14.2	2.4	2.4

Table 4.2
Interpretation of Reversible Active Sentences

Age Group (months)	Percentage Correct
24–28	58
32–36	75
40–44	88
48–52	92

and the second one as the agent) almost 15% of the time (col. 2). Roughly comparable results are reported by Slobin and Bever (1982:241) for a similar task. There were 12 children in each of the age groups for which results are reported in table 4.2.

At first glance, these results seem puzzling. We know from the study of children's own speech that the acquisition device identifies basic word order relations at an early stage in syntactic development and that these tend to be correctly encoded in sentence production. Why do even relatively advanced children perform poorly on the comprehension of reversible sentences? One possibility is that they are simply not accustomed to using word order as a clue to sentence interpretation. As Slobin and Bever (1982:234) note, most of the SVO utterances children hear are non-reversible (e.g., *The boy threw the ball*) and can therefore be interpreted on the basis of pragmatics without reference to word order. Moreover, encounters with reversible sentences (e.g., *The dog is chasing the cat*) are likely to occur in situations where the intended meaning can be inferred by simply observing what is happening in the immediate environment.

Another possibility is that the act-out experiments used in the studies cited above provide an inaccurate assessment of children's real grammatical knowledge, perhaps because of the processing demands created by the need to select and manipulate toys in response to the test sentences. Consistent with this idea, we have already noted (chap. 2) that experimental work involving the much less demanding 'preferential looking' task suggests that even children in the one-word stage are able to use word order to distinguish between the subject and direct object in reversible sentences (Hirsch-Pasek and Golinkoff 1991).

Turning now to children's speech production, occasional errors of various sorts have been reported. For instance, Braine (1976) claims that some children use variable word order for short periods during the early stages of acquisition. He observed that at age 25 months, Kendall (one of Melissa Bowerman's subjects) placed the verb after its theme argument in 7 of 15 phrases containing these two constituents, as in (4).

(4)   Kimmy kick. (for 'kick Kimmy')
      Doggy sew. (for 'sew doggy')
      Kendall pick up. (for 'pick up Kendall')
      Doggy look-it. (for 'look at the doggy')

Another seven utterances had the appropriate verb–theme order and one had the theme both before and after the verb (*Kimmy look at Kimmy*) (Braine 1976:20).

Although Braine treats such utterances as nonproductive 'groping patterns' that reflect short-lived uncertainty about the appropriate word order conventions for English, Radford (1990:231 ff.) proposes an alternative analysis. The key to his proposal is the observation that the theme–verb pattern in Kendall's speech occurs only when the agent is not expressed. When an agent is mentioned, Kendall invariably uses the verb–theme order, as in (5).

(5)   Kimmy ride bike. (not *Kimmy bike ride)
      Kendall turn page.
      Kimmy eat hand.
      Mommy pick-up . . . Kendall.

Radford suggests that the theme NP is actually the subject, not a preverbal direct object, in the utterances that Braine treats as word order errors. In other words, the sentences in (4) are parallel in the relevant respects to patterns such as those in (6) in adult English, in which the agent has been suppressed and the theme becomes the subject.

(6)   a. *Anticausatives:*
         The water boiled. (cf. He boiled the water.)
      b. *Middles:*
         This blackboard cleans easily. (cf. The student cleaned the blackboard.)
      c. *Passives:*
         The car has been washed. (cf. Someone has washed the car.)

A somewhat similar analysis is offered by L. Bloom (1970:167), who observed a small number of theme–verb patterns such as *book read* and *balloon throw* in the speech of Gia at the age of 19 and 20 months. She suggests (p. 88) that these structures may actually be instances of the 'topic–comment' pattern illustrated in (7), except that the subject is suppressed.

(7)   That book, I read.

The proposals put forward by Radford and Bloom imply that the patterns in (4) do not involve an actual word order error. Rather, they reflect the inappropriate use of either agent deletion (Radford) and/or topicalization (Bloom). Additional work is required to determine whether such operations are independently attested in child language at this stage of syntactic development (on the emergence of passives, see chap. 10).

A different type of word order error is highlighted by MacWhinney (1985: 1120), who reports that data from English and other languages (French, Italian, German, Japanese, and Hungarian) reveal a short period at the onset of multiword speech during which children use a 'predicate-first' order. He suggests that this reflects a tendency on the part of language learners to place the newest or most informative element first, and that this pattern is employed to describe a novel activity or property involving a familiar person or object. Adam's utterance *dirty my hands,* cited in (3), is a possible example of this phenomenon in English.

Déprez and Pierce (1993:43) note an important restriction on verb-initial patterns in early English. In 90% of such cases, they observe, the subject bears a theme role (i.e., it denotes the entity undergoing an action or movement). The examples in (8) help illustrate this tendency.

(8)   a. Going it. (Naomi, 1;10)
        b. Going (re)corder. (Naomi, 1;10)
        c. Come car. (Eve, 1;6)
        d. Came a man (Eve, 1;8)
        e. Fall pants. (Nina, 1;11)
        f. Fall down lady. (Nina, 1;11)
        g. Come Lois. (Peter, 2;1)
        h. Broken the light. (Peter 2;2)

Although such errors are infrequent, the fact that they occur primarily with a particular type of subject suggests that they are not unsystematic. A possible source for this mistake lies in transitive clauses such as *Lois drove the car* in (9), in which the verb regularly precedes the NP bearing the theme role. (TR = thematic role; GR = grammatical relation)

(9)   *Pattern produced by the child:* Come car
                                        TR: theme
                                        GR: subject

Possible source of confusion: Lois drove the car
TR: theme
GR: direct object

According to this view, the patterns in (8) arise because children sometimes focus on an NP's thematic role to the exclusion of its grammatical relation, grouping together the theme argument in an intransitive clause with its counterpart in a transitive clause (a direct object) rather than with other subjects.

Consistent with the suggestion made in the preceding chapter (section 4), this proposal implies that the acquisition device attends not only to grammatical relations such as subject and direct object (a type of syntactic notion) but also to thematic roles such as agent and theme. Word order phenomena in languages other than English confirm this: in adult Chinese, for example, subjects bearing the theme role are allowed to occur post-verbally (Mulder and Sybesma 1992:441)— resulting in structures parallel to (8). In learning Chinese, then, the acquisition device must be able to formulate a word order convention that refers both to the theme role and to subjecthood. Examples of even subtler interactions between semantic and syntactic notions will be considered later in this chapter.

Ben's Optative

The production errors considered above all involve relatively minor departures from the word order conventions of standard English. Typically, they occur among very young children and are comparatively infrequent (recall that Kendall's theme– verb order was observed only seven times). An error pattern of a very different sort is described by Sadock (1982), who observed an unusual optative construction in the speech of his son, Ben, between the ages of 19 and 30 months. (An optative expresses a wish.) Although Ben used the regular SVO order of English in indicative clauses, the subject occurred post-verbally in optative patterns.

(10)   Fall down *Daddy*. (= 'Daddy should fall down.')
        Eat *Benny* now. (= 'Let Benny eat now.')

Of special interest are optative constructions containing a transitive verb.

(11)   Pick up Benny for Daddy. (= 'Daddy should pick Ben up.')
        Read a story for Mommy. (= 'Mommy should read a story.')
        Erase it for Daddy. (= 'Daddy should erase it.')
        Play the recorder for Daddy. (= 'Daddy should play the recorder.')

Here the verb is immediately followed by the direct object. The subject occurs at the end of the sentence and is marked by the preposition *for,* resulting in the pattern in table 4.3. As Sadock notes, this system for encoding grammatical relations is essentially the one found in **ergative** languages: the subject of an intransitive

Table 4.3 Ben's Representation of Subjects and Objects in the Optative

	Intransitive Verb	Transitive Verb
Subject	immediately postverbal	sentence-final; marked by *for*
Direct object	——	immediately postverbal

ADULT PATTERN   CHILD'S PATTERN

Get up, Daddy $\Rightarrow$ perceptual $\Rightarrow$ Get up Daddy

verb   vocative   misanalysis   *verb   subject*

FIGURE 4.1 The Source of Ben's Error

verb and the direct object of a transitive verb are treated alike (both occur directly after the verb in Ben's speech) and are distinguished from the subject of a transitive verb (which Ben marks with the preposition *for*).

How could the acquisition device have arrived at such a system for English? Sadock speculates that Ben's optative constructions originated in the misanalysis of intransitive imperatives such as *Get up, Daddy,* in which the post-verbal NP is misinterpreted as the subject rather than a vocative (fig. 4.1). Sadock's explanation for Ben's use of *for* to mark the subject of a transitive verb is somewhat less straightforward. The key observation is that ergative languages often mark the subject of transitive verbs in the same way as they do a possessor. (In Inuktitut, for example, both nominals are marked by the suffix *-up.*) Interestingly, Ben also used *for* to mark possession, so that *That's a nose for Maggie* meant 'That's Maggie's nose'. Sadock speculates that Ben's use of *for* with subjects of transitive verbs was motivated by whatever property underlies the link between subjects of transitive verbs and possessors in ergative languages in general.

If this suggestion is right, then the emergence of Ben's optative structures does not reflect a failure of the acquisition device with respect to word order per se. Rather, the error originates in the misinterpretation of a vocative as subject, perhaps because of inattention to the intonation break that often signals a vocative. Once this error is made, the normal sensitivity of the acquisition device to linear order guarantees that it will note the post-verbal position of what has been (incorrectly) identified as the subject, giving the pattern observed in Ben's speech.

Pre-subject Negation

Children's earliest use of negation in English and other languages seems to make reference to a preceding utterance (Wode 1977). The most straightforward examples of this so-called 'anaphoric negation' involve the use of *no* to respond to questions such as *Are you hungry?* and *Are you ready for bed?* Of more interest to us are patterns in which the *no* or *not* is used to negate the sentence in which it occurs. One of the most interesting but also most controversial word order phenomena in child language involves the possible existence of patterns of this type in which the negative precedes the subject.

(12) *Examples from Eve* (age 1;6–2;0); cited by Bellugi (1967):
No the sun shining.
No I see truck.
Not Fraser read it.
No Mommy giving baby Sarah milk.

(13) *Examples from Nina* (age 1;11–2;3); cited by Déprez and Pierce (1993:34):
No Mommy doing. David turn.
No lamb have it. No lamb have it.
No lamb have a chair either.
No dog stay in the room. Don't dog stay in the room.
Don't Nina get up.
Never Mommy touch it.
No Leila have a turn.
Not man up here on him head.

Pre-subject negation was first noted by Bellugi (1967) in the speech of Adam, Eve, and Sarah. However, its status was subsequently called into question by L. Bloom (1970:160–62), based on her work with a different set of children. Contrary to Bellugi's assumption that the pre-subject negative in these constructions negated the verb, Bloom claimed that it was almost always 'anaphoric' in the data she examined and that it actually negated the *preceding* proposition. Thus, *No car going there* meant 'No, the car is going there' rather than 'The car is not going there'.

Déprez and Pierce (1993:35) argue against this interpretation of pre-subject negation patterns in general, claiming that non-anaphoric negation outnumbers anaphoric negation by a factor of 2 to 1 in Nina's speech. They give the examples in (14) to illustrate non-anaphoric negation.

(14) MOTHER: Can you put it on the floor?
NINA: *No have it, Mommy.*
MOTHER: You don't want me to have it?
NINA: *No. No. No lamb have it. No lamb have it.*
MOTHER: You don't want the lamb to have it either.
NINA: *No lamb have a chair either.*

(15) MOTHER: Let me try it. [as mother takes the whistle]
NINA: Yeah.
MOTHER: What's mommy doing?
NINA: *No mommy doing. David turn.* [as Nina brings whistle to David]

However, there is a possible problem here. Although the italicized utterances are clearly not examples of anaphoric negation, they seem not to involve verb negation, either—contrary to what Déprez and Pierce assume. Rather, the pre-subject negative in these patterns seems to carry a meaning that might be para-phrased as 'I don't want'. Thus, *No lamb have it* in (14) does not mean 'The lamb doesn't have it' (verbal negation); rather, it means something like 'I don't want the lamb to have it.' Similarly, *No mommy doing* in (15) seems to mean 'I don't want Mommy to do it', not 'Mommy isn't doing it'. (L. Bloom 1991:144 notes the existence of similar sentences in data collected by Peter and Jill de Villiers from their son when he was 23–29 months old.)

Drozd (1995) develops this idea in considerable detail, examining instances of pre-subject negation in speech samples from more than 100 children aged 0;11 to 3;4. He claims that pre-subject *no* and *never* are used as instances of 'metalinguistic exclamatory negation' (the equivalent of 'no way' or 'don't say'). This can be illustrated with the help of examples (16) and (17) from Peter at age 2;2 and Nathaniel at age 2;7. (The paraphrases in parentheses are provided by Drozd.)

(16)   MOTHER: Do you want me to cut it? (Let me cut it.)
       PETER: *No Mommy cut it.* (No way Mommy cut it!)

(17)   MOTHER: It's not ice cream time.
       NAT: What's this?
       MOTHER: That's your glass. 'Bai' knocked your glass off. Ooh, King Nathaniel.
       NAT: *No King Nathaniel.* (Don't say 'King Nathaniel' to me!)
       MOTHER: Is Nathaniel a king?
       NAT: *No Nathaniel a king.* (Don't say Nathaniel's a king!)
       MOTHER: What is Nathaniel?
       NAT: *No King Nathaniel.* (Don't say 'King Nathaniel' to me!)

Drozd suggests that in (16), the child is objecting to the idea that his mother should cut the balogna that he himself wants to cut; and that in (17), the child is objecting to his mother's mocking reference to him as 'King Nathaniel'. Neither of these uses of *no* involves the simple denial of a proposition's truth, as would be expected if they were examples of verbal negation.

Independent support for Drozd's idea that pre-subject *no* and *never* patterns are not instances of verbal negation comes from the fact that the majority are 'echoic' (they repeat most of the preceding utterance to which they object)—a characteristic of exclamatory negation in the adult language as well.

Interestingly, however, Drozd found that pre-subject negation involving *not* is frequently non-echoic, as example (18) from Eve at 1;9 helps illustrate.

(18)   COLIN: Will I read it or will you read it?
       EVE: Eve read it.
       COLIN: Oh, Eve's going to read it.
       EVE: *Not Fraser read it.*

In such cases, Drozd suggests (p. 602) that *not* is being used contrastively, perhaps applying just to the constituent *Fraser* in the sentence above (giving the interpretation 'Not Fraser but Eve').

If the proposal put forward by Drozd can be maintained, it would call into question the very existence of pre-subject *verbal* negation in child language. At the very least, it seems clear that the relatively high frequency of pre-subject verbal negation calculated by Déprez and Pierce (over 90% for early periods of development) will have to be revised downward.[2]

Assuming, though, that there are at least some instances of pre-subject negation in children's speech, the question that then arises is why the acquisition device permits this pattern of negation, given the apparent lack of a model in adult English. (In adult English, of course, the negative element occurs sentence-internally, as in *The sun isn't shining* or *The dog didn't stay*.) Déprez and Pierce suggest that the appearance of these patterns in child language supports a proposal in contemporary government and binding theory known as the VP-Internal Subject Hypothesis (19), according to which the subject occurs inside VP in deep structure and subsequently 'raises' to the NP position immediately under S.

(19)   *The VP-Internal Subject Hypothesis:*

   Deep structure: $[_S$ — $[_{VP}$ John read the book]]
   Surface structure: $[_S$ John $[_{VP}$ — read the book]]

On the assumption that the negative occurs outside VP (or at least at the left boundary of VP), children's erroneous negative patterns would have the structure depicted in (20), in which the subject NP has failed to raise from its VP-internal position.

(20)   *Structure for pre-subject negation proposed by Déprez and Pierce:*
   $[_S$ — no(t) $[_{VP}$ the sun is shining]]

Déprez and Pierce suggest that, whereas subject raising is obligatory in the adult grammar of English, children initially treat it as optional, thereby producing patterns of pre-subject verbal negation. (In Déprez and Pierce's theory, 'case' assignment determines whether movement takes place, but this need not concern us here.)

There is perhaps another possibility, however. Contrary to Déprez and Pierce's assertion that there is nothing in children's linguistic experience that could lead the acquisition device to license pre-subject negation, at least one potential trigger arguably exists. Consider, for example, sentences such as (21).

(21)   a. No, it isn't. (In response to: Is the sun shining?)
       b. NO, don't eat that.

Here the negated sentences contain two negatives—a stressed sentence-initial *no* and a contracted and unstressed *n't*. Suppose that, for reasons of salience (see chap. 2), the acquisition device takes note only of the first negative, incorrectly treating it as applying to the verb. Then, sentences such as those in (21) might in fact provide the model needed to trigger the patterns of pre-subject negation observed in child language. This in turn would explain why children generally use *no* rather than *not* in cases of pre-subject negation (Drozd 1995:583).

One way to test this idea would be to examine languages such as French, in which the sentence-internal negative (*pas*) is a full syllable. The expectation would be that in such languages, sentences equivalent to (21) would not constitute such a liability for the acquisition device. Interestingly, as Déprez and Pierce note (pp. 40–41), *non* 'no' is never used in place of *pas* 'not' in the speech of French children, and pre-subject negation is extremely infrequent (a fact for which they offer a very different type of explanation, proposing that in French the verb 'raises' out of the VP to a position higher than the negative).

2. Case

Now let us consider the emergence of case, the second major mechanism (along with word order) that is used to encode structural relations in human language.

The genitive suffix *-'s* is the only case inflection found on nouns in Modern English. However, because of the role of word order in distinguishing between possessors and head nouns (as in *the teacher's child* vs. *the child's teacher*), this suffix has a comparatively light functional load. This, together with the morpheme's relative lack of phonetic salience, probably explains why it is generally ignored during the first several months of syntactic development, as in (22).

(22) *Possessives produced by Jonathon at 24 mos.* (Braine 1976:35):
      Daddy coffee
      Daddy hat
      Elliot juice
      Elliot diaper
      Andrew book
      Mommy tea
      Mommy book

In Brown's (1973) ground-breaking study of morphological development in the children Adam, Eve, and Sarah, the genitive suffix came to be used with 90% accuracy around age 3. It was the sixth of fourteen morphemes studied by Brown to be acquired at this level of proficiency, emerging after *-ing, in, on,* and the plural but before determiners, auxiliaries, and copulas.

English pronouns make use of case to a much greater degree than nouns. As

Table 4.4 The Case System for English Pronouns

	SINGULAR			PLURAL		
PERSON	Nom	Acc	Gen	Nom	Acc	Gen
1st	I	me	my	we	us	our
2nd	you	you	your	you	you	your
3rd	he	him	his	they	them	their
	she	her	her			
	it	it	its			

the paradigm in table 4.4 illustrates, three distinct case categories have to be recognized within the English pronoun system. Of special interest here is the fact that, unlike the -'s suffix of nouns, case inflection for pronouns cannot be dropped in children's speech. Because the form of a pronoun simultaneously represents its person,[3] number, and case (e.g., *we* is 1st person, plural, nominative), a pronoun cannot be pronounced without indicating its case.

This fact creates special problems for the acquisition device. Since pronominal case cannot be dropped (it is an inherent part of the pronoun's form) and apparently cannot be acquired instantaneously, errors are inevitable. Up to at least age 2, a common strategy seems to involve overgeneralization of accusative case forms. As in the adult language, the accusative is used for direct objects (23).

(23) *Accusative pronouns used as direct objects* (Radford 1990:175):
  Paula put *them*. (18 mos.)
  Pinch *him*. (21 mos.)
  Cuddle *me*. (Jem 21 mos.)
  Want *them*. (24 mos.)
  Help *me* out. (20 mos.)

However, in contrast to what is found in adult English, the accusative is also used for subjects as in (24) and even genitives as in (25).

(24) *Accusative pronouns used as subjects* (Radford 1990:175, 190):
  Me got bean. (17 mos.)
  Her do that. (20 mos.)
  Him gone. (20 mos.)
  Me want one. (21 mos.)
  Me sit there. (21 mos.)
  Me have biscuit. (22 mos.)
  Him naughty. (24 mos.)

(25) *Accusative pronouns used as genitives* (Radford 1990:190 [first 4 examples]; Déprez and Pierce 1993:34):
  Me eye (20 mos.)
  Me dad (24 mos.)

Me hand (24 mos.)
Me bot[tle] (18 mos.)
. . . on *him* head (26 mos.)

There is some disagreement on how common the use of accusative case for subject pronouns is. Valian (1991:52) reports that the 21 children (ages 1;10–2;8) whose speech she studied 'overwhelmingly used the nominative case' for pronominal subjects, with no more than 2% of the subjects bearing the incorrect case (p. 44). On the other hand, in a study of the speech of one girl between the ages of 2;5 and 3;0, Ingham (1992:142) observed only 18 instances of third person singular nominative pronouns (i.e., *she* or *he*) in subject position, compared to 179 instances of the accusative in that position. Moreover, Radford (1992:243) reports that 30 of the 60 two-year-olds that he studied made at least some use of accusative case for subject pronouns. Radford (1990:175) notes even more widespread overgeneralization of the accusative in children under age 2 (as exemplified in (24) above), noting that that the nominative occurs only sporadically in the speech of these children, mostly in fixed expressions such as *Off we go* (p. 177). For at least some children, then, the use of accusative pronouns in subject position seems to be a common occurrence during syntactic development. In contrast, the reverse error—nominative case on direct object pronouns, as in **Jane saw he*— is usually reported to be rare or even nonexistent (Aldridge 1989:193–94; Valian 1991:52; but see the discussion of Rispoli 1994 below).[4]

The Emergence of Nominative Case

In some children at least, the transition from accusative to nominative subjects includes a 'mixed stage' in which nominative and accusative pronouns alternate with each other in subject position. Aldridge (1989:193ff.) provides numerous examples (table 4.5) of this alternation from the speech of six children (aged 22–32 mos.). Indeed, Radford (1994:154) notes that children can even alternate between two case forms within the same sentence (e.g., *Me can't, I can't* in the speech of Penny at age 31 mos.)

Table 4.5 The Nominative–Accusative Alternation in Michelle (29 mos.)

Nominative Subjects	Accusative Subjects
I play with bricks.	What *me* have after?
I had a book.	*Me* can get this off.
I can't open this.	*Me* having a house.
I know	What *me* play with.
Can *I* put it on.	Wonder where *him* gone.

In the final step in the emergence of case, accusative forms are eliminated from the subject position, resulting in the adult system. Drawing on data from 8 children (aged 23–32 mos.), Aldridge (1989:180) suggests that the acquisition device often identifies the correlation between finite verbs and nominative subjects around age 24 months; see (26). (However, Huxley 1970:148–59 reports on a child for whom this distinction was not mastered until well after age 3.)

(26) *Nominative subjects with tensed Vs in the speech of Angela* (25 mos.) (Aldridge 1989:181):
I'm hot.
I got it.
I keep it on.
She won't.
He's got.
I will get it.
I put it on.

A key component of Aldridge's claim is that the acquisition device associates nominative pronouns with the subject position of *finite* (essentially 'tensed') verbs and not just with subject positions in general, so that verbal inflection for person and tense emerges contemporaneously with the nominative case. (A similar claim is put forward by Vainikka 1993/94.) A potential problem for this idea is that Aldridge's data include examples of nominative subjects that occur either with a nonfinite verb or with no verb at all (the last three examples in (27)); for additional examples of this sort, see Pierce (1994:328).

(27) *Some examples of nominative subjects without finite verbs* (Aldridge 1989:181– 82, 186):
I swinging. (Christie, 23 mos.)
I singing. (Angela, 25 mos.)
He hiding. (Katy, 28 mos.)
I playing flute. (Angela, 25 mos.)
He go there (Ester, 29 mos.)
He been hitting the sad one. (Ester, 29 mos.)
He on there. (Andrew 32 mos.)
He happy clown. (Ester 29 mos.)
He naughty boy. (Laura, 32 mos.)

At first glance, it might seem that these children are employing the nominative case without regard for whether there is a finite verb. However, Aldridge argues against this view, noting (p. 190) that the problematic nominative subjects almost all appear in contexts where a contracted copula or auxiliary would occur in adult speech. Thus, *I swinging* would be *I'm swinging* in adult speech, *He on there* would be *He's on there,* and so on. From this she infers that the sentences in question reflect the presence of an unexpressed tensed verb (*am, is, are,* etc.) rather than the operation of a nominative case rule that is insensitive to finiteness (see Radford 1994 for an alternative suggestion).

A crucial part of Aldridge's argument (p. 192) is the occurrence of (28), in which the italicized 'tag' structure seems to 'refer back' to an understood copula. (In adult speech, tag questions require a finite verb in the sentence to which they are attached.)

(28)   I on this one, *aren't I?* (Sarah, 26 mos.)

Assuming that tag patterns in this child's speech follow the adult rule, this example supports Aldridge's claim that the use of a nominative subject implies the presence of a finite verb.

Aldridge bases a second argument for her analysis on the *absence* of a particular pattern from child language. She observes (p. 187) that if children allowed nominative case to occur without a finite verb, nominative pronouns should be able to occur as subjects of *untensed* infinitival verbs in sentences such as (29).

(29)   *Mummy wants [*I* to eat it]. (cf. Mummy wants [*me* to eat it].)
       *I want [*he* to do it]. (cf. I want [*him* do it].)
       *Let [*I* do it]. (cf. Let [*me* do it].)
       *Let [*he* go there]. (cf. Let [*him* go there].)

Since no such errors occurred in the speech examined by Aldridge, she concludes that children must know that the nominative is used only for subjects of tensed verbs and that the sentences in (27) therefore contain an unexpressed finite copula.

A first problem for this conclusion comes from the developmental data itself. Although errors of the sort exemplified in (29) are apparently rare, they are not unattested—see (30).

(30)   *Case alternations in the speech of Sally at age 2;4* (Chiat 1981:89):
       Let *he* go in bed.
       Let *she* go on your swing.
       No, let *him* put his hat on.

As these examples show, this child seems to alternate between the nominative and accusative forms of pronoun in '*let* constructions', contrary to Aldridge's prediction.

A second problem with Aldridge's argument is its assumption that the italicized pronouns in (29) occupy a subject position. In fact, the analysis of these sentences is very much in dispute, with many linguists claiming that the position in question is associated with direct objects rather than subjects. (Authier 1991 and Bowers 1993 argue for such an analysis within government and binding theory, the model of grammar adopted by Aldridge.)[5] If this is right, then the occurrence of accusative case forms in sentences like (29) tells us nothing about how children encode *subject* pronouns.

In sum, the developmental evidence reviewed to this point reveals tendencies that are consistent with up to three developmental stages for the emergence of nominative pronouns in English.

(31)   *Possible stages in the emergence of nominative case:*
    i. Overgeneralization of the accusative form to all positions.
    ii. Alternation between the nominative and accusative in subject position; use of the accusative for other argument positions.
    iii. Use of the nominative for subjects of (finite) verbs; use of the accusative for other argument positions.

It is possible that not all children pass through the first two steps of this developmental sequence. At least some children seem to attain the system described in step (iii) immediately (recall Valian's observation that many children use the nominative correctly from the outset); still others may skip the first step. In addition, further refinements may be needed to take into account possible 'substages' in the emergence of the nominative case: Huxley (1970:159) reports that Douglas (a child whose speech she studied between 2;3 and 4;0) used the nominative case form *I* correctly from age 3;3—10 weeks before *he, she,* and *they* were mastered and 24 weeks before *we* was acquired.

Other Possible Stages

At least three other stages in the development of pronominal case have been proposed in the acquisition literature. First, Bellugi (1971:112) observes that case is apparently mastered later for pronouns that occur in coordinate structures than for those that occur alone as subjects or direct objects. She supports her observation with the examples in (32) of case errors in the speech of Adam at ages 4 and 5.

(32)   *Me* and Paul have string, huh?
    Can *me* and *him* play with this?
    Me and Robin are friends.

Assuming that these are not simply examples of a nonstandard dialect (Bellugi notes that Adam's mother did not use such patterns), it may be necessary to add a fourth step to the developmental sequence in (31) to accommodate the emergence of case inflection on pronouns in coordinate structures.

Second, as noted by Aldridge (1989:198), Bellugi (1967) proposes a stage in which the form *I* is used only for *sentence-initial* subjects. This yields contrasts such as those in table 4.6, which Bellugi uncovered in the speech of Adam be-

Table 4.6 Case Contrasts in the Speech
of Adam

Sentence-Initial Subject	Non–Sentence-Initial Subject
I laughing.	When *me* want it?
I making coffee.	Where *me* sleep?
I here.	Why *me* spilled it?

Table 4.7 The Children in Budwig's
Study (Budwig 1990a : 124)

Child	Initial Age (months)	Mean MLU
Megan	20	2.07
Grice	22	1.72
Jeffrey	30	2.82
Eric	28	3.48
Keith	31	3.22
Thomas	32	3.91

tween the ages of 28 and 35 months. Here, the nominative form *I* is used for sentence-initial subjects, while *me* marks subjects that do not occur in this position. Aldridge (1989 : 199) notes that such a stage seems not to have been observed in other children and that its existence in the speech of Adam is supported by only a handful of examples. However, Vainikka (1993/94) reports that such a stage occurred in the four children she studied, noting the pronominal subjects do not occur in the nominative case in early *wh* questions although the nominative case is used at this time in other patterns.

A third possible stage in the development of pronominal case is outlined by Budwig (1989b, 1990a), who describes an unusual and surprising contrast involving the first person pronouns *I, me,* and *my* in subject position. Budwig's finding is based on data from six children (table 4.7), each of whom was videotaped twice a month for a four-month period. The children ranged in age from 20 to 32 months at the beginning of the study. The three most advanced children (in terms of MLU) relied primarily on the form *I* for first person singular subjects (Budwig 1990a : 133). However, the other three children (Megan, Grice, and Jeffrey) also used *me* and *my,* as illustrated in (33) from Budwig 1989b : 272.

(33)   *I* like Anna.
       I cried.
       My want the little ones.
       My taked it off.
       Me jump.

Table 4.8 Self-Reference Options (Budwig 1990a: 126)

CHILD	Own Name	*I*	*My*	*Me*	Other
			OPTIONS (percentage)		
Megan	32	33	23	10	3
Grice	10	30	32	28	1
Jeffrey	3	38	46	6	7

Table 4.8 presents data on the relative proportion of these and other options for first person subjects in the speech of the three children. The use of *my* for subjects had been previously noted by L. Bloom (1970:159), Huxley (1970:148), Hamburger (1980), and Vainikka (cited by Lebeaux 1987:36; see also Vainikka 1993/94). However, Budwig goes beyond these earlier observations in proposing a principled semantic basis for the *I–me–my* alternation.

According to Budwig's analysis, *I* tends to be associated with low agentivity, as in the expression of internal states and intentions. In contrast, *my* generally appears with action verbs, especially when the child acts as a prototypical agent bringing about a change of state. This contrast is illustrated in (34)–(35), from Budwig 1989b:273.

(34)   *Use of* I *for the expression of states and intentions:*
       I like peas.
       I no want those.

(35)   *Use of* my *for the expression of agent-controlled actions:*
       My blew the candles out.
       My cracked the eggs.

Budwig also found a tendency for *my* to appear in "control acts—in directives, requests, challenges, protests and disputes over the control of objects and enactment of activities" (1989b:276). Conversations (36)–(37) help illustrate this point.

(36)   *Conversation illustrating use of* I:
       JEFFREY: No no my turn. [taking microphone from mother]
       RESEARCHER: You want me to put it on you for a minute?
       JEFFREY: Yeah.
       MOTHER: You wanna wear it.
       RESEARCHER: Okay [begins to clip mike on Jeffrey]
       JEFFREY: *I* wear it [smiling and looking at mike]

(37)   *Conversation illustrating use of* my:
       JEFFREY: What's that? [holding mike that was hidden on couch]
       RESEARCHER: Oh it's just some equipment.
       FRIEND: That's Eric [pointing at photo of himself]

RESEARCHER: Um-hmm.
JEFFREY: *My* wear it [gives mic. to researcher]
RESEARCHER: You wanna wear it.
JEFFREY: Yeah.
RESEARCHER: Okay I'll pin it right here.

The form *I* is used in (33) to describe a situation in which the child is already wearing the microphone. In (34), in contrast, the child is requesting the microphone—a control act that motivates the choice of *my* as subject.

Budwig's comments on the use of *me* as subject are much less detailed. She suggests (1989b:279) that this form tends to occur with predicates expressing actions that affect the child. The only examples offered in support of this claim are *Me jump, Me to do,* and *Me in there,* all of which supposedly involve the child "acting as instigator of actions that are directed back onto the Self." In contrast, *my* rarely occurs with intransitive verbs (p. 273) and is used primarily for actions in which the child brings about a change in some other entity (p. 279).

The use of first person genitive subjects is apparently not universally attested among children learning English. Although Vainikka (1993/94) observed the phenomenon to some degree among three of the four children she studied, Valian (1991:52) reports that *my* or *me* in subject position occurred in less than 1% of all utterances produced by the 21 children she studied. Based on data from 100 children aged 24–42 months, Radford (1992:243) concludes: "A couple of 2-year-olds made very sporadic use of what seemed to be genitive *my* as a subject, producing a handful of examples like 'My want a wee' but otherwise used only nominative subjects." Drawing on a 4-hour speech sample from each of twelve children (ages 1–3), Rispoli (1994:168) observed 191 instances of *my* in subject position, compared to 798 instances of *me* and 11,791 of *I*. He notes that *his* was never used in subject position, although Ingham (1992:142) reports that *our* was systematically used in this way by a 2-year-old that he studied. At best, then, it seems that the alternation considered by Budwig is not found in all children and that (even more curiously) it occurs only with first person pronouns.

One of the most important issues raised by Budwig's work has to do with why the acquisition device should attempt to use pronoun case to express contrasts involving agency and control in the first place (assuming that this is what is actually happening; see Vainikka 1993/94 for an alternative syntactic account). Interestingly, there are languages in which case does have this function: according to Mithun (1991), for example, agency and control are relevant to case marking in the Amerindian languages Lakhota, Central Pomo, Caddo, and Mohawk, among others. Moreover, as Budwig notes (1989b:265), Slobin (1985:1176) reports that agency seems to play a role in children's early hypotheses about case in Russian and Kaluli (although this phenomenon is apparently not limited to first person subjects in these languages).

Although these considerations suggest that the acquisition device must be able to take note of contrasts involving agency and control, this cannot be the whole story. Given the apparent rarity of the *I–me–my* alternation in the acquisition of English, we must still ask whether there is something special in the experience of certain children that directs their acquisition device to focus on this contrast. Budwig and Wiley (1991) uncover a potentially important clue, noting that 59% of the *I* forms used by Megan, Grice, and Jeffrey's caregivers occurred with state verbs. Since this is also the dominant use for *I* in the children's system, these two facts may well be connected in some way. What remains to be explained, however, is why the acquisition device ignores other uses of *I* in adult speech and ends up using *my* and *me* in ways which are never observed in adult English.

REASONS FOR OVERGENERALIZATION OF THE ACCUSATIVE

The single most frequent error in the development of English case undoubtedly involves the overuse of the accusative form illustrated in (24), repeated as (38).

(38) *Me* got bean. (17 mos.)
       Her do that. (20 mos.)
       Him gone. (20 mos.)
       Me want one. (21 mos.)
       Me sit there. (21 mos.)
       Me have biscuit. (22 mos.)
       Him naughty. (24 mos.)

As noted in the previous section, Budwig offers a semantic explanation for at least some case errors of this type. However, most researchers have sought to explain this phenomenon in structural terms.

One possibility, put forward by Gruber (1967), Guilfoyle (1984), and Lebeaux (1987), is that the accusative pronouns in (38) are not really subjects. Rather, it is suggested, they are topic NPs analogous to the italicized pronouns in (39).

(39) *Her*, I really like.
       Him, you should be careful with.

According to this analysis, the sentences in (21) have the structure depicted in (36), with the pronoun adjoined to S as a topic phrase and a null pronoun in subject position (Lebeaux 1987:37).

(40)

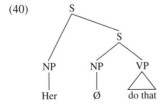

Of course, if the sentence-initial pronoun in this structure is a topic rather than a subject, it can be expected to occur in the accusative form—just what we find in examples like (38).

Although initially attractive, this proposal encounters various problems. For one thing, children's utterances with accusative subjects lack the intonation break after the purported topic that is typical of topic structures in adult speech (note the comma in the examples in (39)). A second problem arises because of the patterns illustrated in (41), from Aldridge 1989:202.

(41)   What *me* play with? (Michelle, 29 mos.)
        Can *me* put lots and lots? (Hannah, 28 mos.)
        Can *me* have biscuit? (Angharad, 22 mos.)
        Wonder where *him* gone? (Michelle, 29 mos.)
        There *her* is. (Angharad, 22 mos.)
        He doesn't know where *them* are. (Elizabeth, 26 mos.)

Here, as Aldridge notes, the accusative-marked subjects occur sentence-internally—in positions that are not open to topics, which are almost always sentence-initial.

A further problem stems from the existence of the utterances in (25), repeated as (42), which illustrate the use of the accusative case form to encode the genitive in English.

(42)   *Me* eye (20 mos.)
        Me dad (24 mos.)
        Me hand (24 mos.)
        Me bot[tle] (18 mos.)
        . . . on *him* head (26 mos.)

Unlike subjects, genitives do not normally indicate 'what the sentence is about'. This creates yet another problem for the topic analysis, suggesting that we must look elsewhere to explain why the accusative form of pronouns is overgeneralized in the early stages of syntactic development.

One possibility worth considering is put forward by Tanz (1974), who observes that the accusative case form has a much wider range of uses (see (43)) than the nominative. Whereas the latter form is employed only for subjects (of tensed verbs), the former is used for direct objects, complements of prepositions, and topics, in addition to pronouns used in isolation.

(43)   *Some uses for the accusative pronoun:*
        a. Direct object:
            John helped *her/*she*.
        b. Complement of a preposition:
            John sat near *her/*she*.

c. Topic:
    Her/*She, John likes.

d. Pronoun in isolation:
    Who just came in? *Her/*She.*

Tanz suggests that the comparatively wide range of uses associated with the accusative makes it more salient to the acquisition device, guaranteeing that it will be the first form acquired and used by children.

    Independent evidence in support of this conclusion comes from the acquisition of Dutch. As described by Kaper (1976), the Dutch nominative and accusative forms each have several uses and neither can be considered dominant in the way that the English accusative is. The acquisition device therefore has no grounds for selecting either form as more basic. Interestingly, Kaper reports that between the ages of 2 and 7, children learning Dutch often substitute the nominative for the accusative as well as vice versa, as in (44).

(44) a. *Nominative substituted for accusative:*
       Pappa met *ik.* (48 mos.)
       'Daddy with I'

     b. *Accusative substituted for nominative:*
       Mij moet ət hebbə. (31 mos.)
       'Me must have it.'

Still a different error pattern has been observed in the speech of children learning Japanese, a language in which nouns are marked for case (pronouns are usually null) and the nominative has a broader range of uses than the accusative. As Tanz's hypothesis would predict, Japanese children systematically overgeneralize the nominative to NPs that should be accusative (Clancy 1985:388–93).

    An additional factor favoring accusative case forms in English, also noted by Tanz, is that they can occur sentence-finally (as in *I saw him, She talked to me,* etc.)—the position of maximal perceptual salience. In contrast, nominative pronouns typically occur in the less salient initial position (for more on this, see Gerken 1991 and the next chapter). There is one exception to this, however: the nominative occurs sentence-finally in 'tag questions' (e.g., *Those guys are good, aren't they?*). Significantly, Tanz observes that nominatives appeared first in tag questions in the speech of Douglas, a child studied by Huxley (1970). In the following examples from Huxley's paper, Douglas uses the nominative in the tag question but the accusative in the subject position of the main clause. (For additional examples, from the speech other children, see Radford 1994:154.)

(45)   *Him* did get strong, didn't *he?*
       Them are only little, aren't *they?*
       Her is jolly strong, isn't *she?*

Table 4.9 Case Overextension Errors in Rispoli's Data

Type of Pronoun	No. of Errors	No. of Correct Uses
1st person singular (*I/me/my*)	1037	16742
3rd person feminine (*she/her*)	195	574
3rd person masculine (*he/his/him*)	72	1183
3rd person plural (*they/their/them*)	43	1062

Table 4.10 Proportion of Overextensions in Rispoli's Data

TYPE OF PRONOUN	NOMINATIVES		OBLIQUES	
	Example	% Occurrence	Example	% Occurrence
1st person singular	*I* for *me/my*	0	*me/my* for *I*	10
3rd person feminine	*she* for *her*	0	*her* for *she*	47
3rd person masculine	*he* for *him/his*	9	*his/him* for *he*	5
3rd person plural	*they* for *them/their*	4	*them/their* for *they*	6

Recently, yet another hypothesis about case substitution errors has been put forward. Rispoli (1994) examined speech samples from 12 American children who had been audiotaped at one-month intervals between the ages of 1 and 3. Focusing on 2 hours of speech from the first year and 2 hours from the second year for each of the children, Rispoli (pp. 164–65) examined a total of 20,908 uses of first person singular and third person pronouns, of which 1347 involved case errors (table 4.9). An intriguing feature of Rispoli's data (pp. 165–67) involves the percentage of nominative vs. oblique (i.e. accusative and genitive) overextensions (table 4.10). There are two crucial findings here. The first is that for the third person masculine pronouns (*him/him/his*) and for plural pronouns (*they/them/their*), overextensions run in both directions with roughly the same frequency: not only can an oblique replace a nominative (the familiar type of error discussed previously), but a nominative can replace an oblique, as illustrated in (46) and (47).

(46)   *Overextension of* he:
       I got *he* out. (child 8, age 2;4)
       He got back in *he* house (child 10, age 2;11)

(47)   *Overextension of* they:
       I'll put *they* in. (child 3, age 2;11)
       They stay with *they* mothers. (child 8, age 2;10)

The second major finding is that for first person pronouns (*I/me/my*) and third person feminine pronouns (*she/her*), substitution errors are essentially unidirectional: an oblique can replace a nominative, but not vice versa.

Table 4.11 A Partial Paradigm for English Pronouns

Case	1st sg.	3rd fem. sg.	3rd masc. sg.	3rd plural
Nominative	I	she	*he*	*the*y
Accusative	*me*	*he*r	*hi*m	*the*m
Genitive	*my*	*he*r	*hi*s	*their*
'Phonetic core'	*m-*	*h-*	*h-*	*th-*

Why should this be so? Rispoli suggests that the answer lies in the form of English pronouns. Consider in this regard the partial paradigm in table 4.11. The key observation here is that nominative forms for the third masculine singular and the third plural share the 'phonetic core' (*h-* and *th-*, respectively) also found in the other members of their paradigms. In contrast, the nominative forms for the first singular and third feminine (*I* and *she,* respectively) are suppletive: they bear no phonetic resemblance to other members of the paradigm.

Rispoli suggests that when direct access to the appropriate pronominal form fails, language users try to access the form through its phonetic core. In the case of the third masculine and third plural pronouns, this can lead to substitutions in either direction, since the nominative, accusative, and genitive forms all share a phonetic core.

In the case of first singular and third feminine pronouns, on the other hand, the nominative does not have the phonetic core of other members of the paradigm. In cases where direct access to an objective or genitive form fails, the nominative is therefore not accessible (given its lack of a phonetic core), and overgeneralization of the nominative is blocked. In contrast, where direct access to nominative *I* or *she* fails, the accusative and genitive forms are accessible since they each include the phonetic core of their respective paradigm (*m-* and *h-*). Thus, overgeneralization of the accusative and genitive is possible, giving the pattern of errors observed in Rispoli's data.

Rispoli's proposal is a fascinating one, and a number of points obviously deserve further study. For one thing, it would be useful to uncover independent evidence (perhaps from adult speakers) for the psychological reality of the phonetic cores on which Rispoli's theory is built. (Note that these elements are not morphemes in the conventional sense.) In addition, an attempt should be made to determine whether the overextension asymmetries reported by Rispoli are typical of English-speaking children in general. (One potential problem in this regard is that some previous work reports nominative overextensions of the type Rispoli reports in (46) and (47) to be essentially nonexistent—e.g., Aldridge 1989:193–94, Valian 1991:52, as noted earlier.) Furthermore, it will be necessary to see whether Rispoli's theory makes correct predictions for languages other than English. As Rispoli himself notes (p. 171), the overextension of the nominative first person pronoun *ik* 'I' in Dutch (see (44) above) is an apparent problem for his theory, although a more thorough and extensive analysis of the Dutch data remains to be done.

3. Conclusion

With the exceptions noted in section 1, the acquisition device makes remarkably few errors in determining a language's word order, which it seems to analyze using a combination of structural and thematic notions. Indeed, the overall success of the acquisition device in dealing with word order has led to the suggestion that it is somehow especially sensitive to the linear arrangement of constituents. For example, Slobin (1973) proposes that the acquisition device includes an innate 'operating principle' that predisposes language learners to 'pay attention to the order of words'. We consider this type of proposal in more detail in part II of this book.

As for case, the evidence reviewed in this chapter suggests that the acquisition device commonly makes at least two different types of errors. First, it is generally agreed that accusative pronouns are commonly overextended at the expense of their nominative and genitive counterparts, perhaps because the accusative exhibits a broader range of uses than either of the other two forms or because it is phonetically more salient. A second type of error underlies the apparently less frequent *I-me-my* alternation discussed by Budwig. Here, it appears that, for reasons not yet understood, the acquisition device underextends the form *I* in subject position, leaving room for the innovative use of *my*.

5

Subject Drop

As many of the examples in previous chapters show, children learning English and other languages produce sentences that have no overt subject. The following examples of subjectless sentences, collected by L. Bloom (1970:41 ff.), were produced by Kathryn at age 21 months.

(1)   No turn.
      Ate meat.
(2)   Touch milk.
      Helping Mommy.

Because the traditional analysis of subjectless sentences attributes their formation to an operation that deletes a subject pronoun, these patterns are often referred to as 'pro drop sentences'. However, for expository purposes, I will use the more neutral term 'subject drop'.

Linguists have taken a deep interest in why the acquisition device should initially conclude that overt subjects are optional in English despite evidence to the contrary in the adult speech to which it is exposed. We begin our discussion of this issue by considering a representative sampling of the many different proposals that have been put forward to account for this apparent anomaly.

1. Theories of the Subject Drop Stage

Theories of subject drop in child language can be divided into three types: those that attribute the phenomenon to processing considerations, those that link it to confusion over a language's typological status, and those that explain it in terms of a temporary morphological deficit. Let us consider each type of proposal in turn.

Processing Theories

P. Bloom (1990a) suggests that very young children drop subjects because of processing limitations that prevent them from consistently planning and producing complete sentences of more than two or three words (see chap. 3, section 4). (An earlier version of this idea can be found in L. Bloom 1970.) On this view, then, even two-year-olds understand that English does not permit subject drop. Their grammars are like those of adults in this respect, but a 'processing bottleneck' sometimes prevents the production of subjects where they are required.

Paul Bloom suggests that the processing theory makes an interesting and straightforward prediction: overt subjects are more likely to be dropped when the

VP is relatively long (thereby increasing the processing load). Testing his hypothesis on 20 hours of speech from the appropriate developmental period for each of the three 'Harvard children' (Adam, Eve, and Sarah), he found a statistically significant correlation between VP length and the likelihood of subject drop (p. 497).

Subsequently, Valian (1991:71) found that at least some of children that she studied (3 of the 5 children under age 2;3) showed the predicted correlation. Furthermore, she found a significant correlation between use of overt subjects and both MLU and age (i.e., the older the children were and the greater their MLU, the more overt subjects they produced). This seems to provide further support for the view that 'performance factors' of some sort underlie (or at least contribute to) the subject drop phenomenon.

Hyams and Wexler (1993:436) challenge the processing theory, arguing that there is no independent evidence that the beginning of a sentence is harder to process. However, Gerken (1991:436) offers a possible phonological basis for just such a processing difficulty. The key observation is that children show a tendency to delete the first syllable in iambic metrical feet (i.e., feet with a weak-strong stress pattern). Hence, they are more likely to pronounce *giráffe* as *raffe* (deleting a weak syllable from initial position) than to pronounce *mónkey* as *mon* (deleting a weak syllable in final position). Gerken goes on to note that pronoun subjects (but not pronoun objects) typically constitute the unstressed syllable in a (weak-strong) iambic pattern (e.g., *He léft*), which should facilitate their omission. Designing an experiment to test her hypothesis (box 5.1), Gerken found that children deleted subjects more often than objects (19% vs. 0.3%), and that pronouns were omitted in subject position significantly more often than either proper or common nouns (32% vs. 11% and 13%, respectively).

Box 5.1

THE STUDY: Gerken 1991
SUBJECTS: 18 children aged 23–30 mos. (mean MLU = 2.54)
SENTENCE TYPES: (2 tokens of each type)
    1. he KISSED her
    2. he KISSED JANE
    3. he KISSED the LAMB
    4. PETE KISSED her
    5. PETE KISSED JANE
    6. PETE KISSED the LAMB
    7. The BEAR KISSED her
    8. The BEAR KISSED JANE
    9. The BEAR KISSED the LAMB
TASK: imitation

It is unclear whether prosodic considerations constitute the principal (let alone the only) factor in children's production of subjectless sentences. Since subject drop seems to be a universal feature of syntactic development (see discussion below), further work will be required to ascertain whether it can invariably be associated with prosodic properties that are independently known to favor deletion, as is the case in English. (As noted by Lillo-Martin 1994:308, Gerken's theory seems to predict that subject drop should not occur in the speech of children learning a non–subject drop language in which the subject does not occur sentence-initially—e.g., a verb–subject–object or verb–object–subject language.) However, it does seem safe to conclude for now that prosody is at the very least capable of facilitating subject drop.

Evidence of a different sort for the role of processing in subject drop has been put forward by Valian (1989, 1991), who conducted a comparative study of English-speaking and Italian-speaking children. Table 5.1 summarizes the composition and characteristics of the English-speaking children in Valian's study. The children were taped talking with their mothers for a total of about 1.5 hours, typically spread over two sessions no more than two weeks apart. Table 5.2 depicts the proportion of their non-imperative utterances that contained verbs with an overt subject. The significance of these findings lies in their relationship to data on subject drop gathered from Italian-speaking children.

Valian's Italian data were gathered from five children in a series of 15- to 30-minute monthly sessions over a one-year period. For purposes of analysis, the data were divided into Time I, when the children ranged in age from 1;6 to 1;10, and Time II, when they were between 2;0 and 2;5. Interestingly, the Italian-speaking

Table 5.1 English-Speaking Children in Valian's Study (based on Valian 1991:38)

Group	No. of Children	Age range	MLU
I	5	1;10–2;2	1.53–1.99
II	5	2;3–2;8	2.24–2.76
III	8	2;3–2;6	3.07–3.72
IV	3	2;6–2;8	4.12–4.38

Table 5.2 Proportion of Utterances Containing a Subject (based on Valian 1991:44–45)

Group	Mean	Range
I	69%	55–82%
II	89	84–94
III	93	87–99
IV	95	92–97

children differed dramatically from their English-speaking counterparts in terms of their use of overt subjects. Whereas the youngest English children employ overt subjects in almost 70% of their utterances, this figure is under 30% for both developmental periods in the case of the Italian children.

Valian concludes that even the youngest English-speaking and Italian-speaking children have determined whether their respective languages permit subject drop (Italian does; English does not). This, she suggests, is why the English-speaking children produce overt subject phrases so much more frequently than their Italian counterparts. If this is right, then sentences without overt subjects in the early speech of English-speaking children are presumably the product of processing limitations, not the erroneous belief that English is a subject drop language.

Valian's proposal encounters at least two problems. First, the relative proportion of overt subjects in the speech of her youngest group of children is considerably higher than what has been reported for other children. For example, Hyams and Wexler (1993:426) claim that Adam produced overt subjects only 45% of the time in the early phases of multiword speech; P. Bloom (1990a:500) offers a similar calculation for Eve. While this does not rule out a processing explanation for early subject drop in English, it does raise questions about the generality and sharpness of the contrast between English-speaking and Italian-speaking children found in Valian's data.

It is also important to note that children learning different subject drop languages apparently vary in the rate at which they suppress subjects. Whereas Italian children use overt subjects only about 30% of the time (see above), the figure is around 50% for Korean children by age 2;6 or so (Y. Kim 1992b:133) and has been observed to be as high as 80% in some contexts (D. Kim 1990). Wang et al. (1992) report that Chinese children aged 2;0 to 4;4 employ null subjects in about 53% of their sentences on average, while Ingham (1992:146) found a subject drop rate of 77% in a speech sample from a three-year old Japanese girl. Such contrasts show that the acquisition device may be sensitive to relatively subtle differences in the *rate* of subject drop. As Valian (1991:49) herself notes, this opens the possibility that the differences between the English and Italian children simply reflect perceived differences in the rate of subject drop in adult varieties of the two languages. The English children in Valian's Group I might have produced overt subjects more often than the Italian children simply because the acquisition device had concluded that subject drop was relatively infrequent in English, not that it was prohibited. (On this point, see also Hyams 1994:293.)

GRAMMAR-BASED THEORIES

In sharp contrast to processing theories of subject drop, other approaches to this phenomenon draw heavily on grammatical theory. The best known approach of this type is based on the striking resemblance between 'subjectless' patterns in child language and certain sentences used by adult speakers of languages such as Italian, which permits a null pronoun (represented as *pro*) in subject position, as in (3).

(3)   *pro* ha visto Piero.
        '(S/he) has seen Peter.'

The fact that subject drop occurs both in the structures used by children learning English and in those produced by mature speakers of Italian led Hyams (1986) to propose that the acquisition device initially 'assumes' that it is learning an Italian-type language. Although this accounts for the appearance of subject drop sentences in child language, there are several problems. First, the early speech of children acquiring English is almost completely devoid of verbal inflection, and even the adult language has extremely limited person and number agreement (the only affix of this type being the -*s* of the third person singular of regular verbs in the present tense). In contrast, it is generally accepted that the admissibility of subject drop in Italian stems from the fact that verbs in this language are inflected to indicate the person and number of the subject. (For example, the form *ha* in (3) is third person singular.) This makes it hard to believe that the acquisition device could err to the point of assuming that English is an Italian-type language.

A second problem for Hyams's theory stems from her prediction that early English should resemble Italian in ways other than just subject drop. For example, she predicted that, like adult speakers of Italian, children in the 'subject drop stage' should not have modal auxiliaries such as *will* or *can;* [1] rather, she suggests, these elements should appear only after the subject drop stage ends. However, this prediction seems to be incorrect. O'Grady, Peters, and Masterson (1989) report that modals do in fact occur during the subject drop stage (see (4)), some in subjectless sentences.

(4)   *Some modals in Seth's speech during the subject drop stage* (to age 2;6):
        So *can* roll it?
        Would i' fall off?
        C'n you close za door?
        I *can* fwow again?
        Now *can* go!
        Se *ca'* dry ya hair dryer
        We *could* make a . . .
        I *will* put the meem away.

Valian (1991:59) reports that the use of modals "neither suddenly begins . . . nor dramatically increases when subject use becomes more consistent."

A further prediction of Hyams's theory is somewhat harder to test. Because languages with null pronominal subjects lack expletives such as *there* and *it* (compare English *it is raining* with Italian *piove* 'rains'), Hyams predicted that expletives should not be present during the subject drop stage, when the acquisition device is treating English as if it had null pronouns. Further, she suggests that exposure to expletives might even force the acquisition device to revise its initial hypothesis that English is a null pronoun language (1986:92).

Consistent with Hyams's prediction, expletives are absent from children's early speech, see (5).

(5)   *Sentences from child speech that lack an expletive* (Hyams 1986:93):
      Outside cold.
      Is toys in there.
      No more cookies.
      No morning.

However, it is much harder to establish a correlation between the emergence of expletives and the end of the subject drop phenomenon. Hyams claims that the two developments coincide (p. 93), but Valian (1990:115, 1991:52–53) found that expletive patterns in her 21-child speech sample occurred too infrequently to allow any conclusion on this point. Ingham (1992) reports that expletives emerge several months *after* the end of the subject drop stage in the speech of a child he studied (see below for a description of his study).

In an attempt to overcome these and related deficiencies, Hyams (1992) offers a new explanation for the subject drop stage. The key idea is that null subjects are licensed by **morphological uniformity,** a property of verb paradigms.[2]

(6)   *Morphological uniformity:*
      An inflectional paradigm is uniform if all its forms are morphologically complex or none of them are. (Hyams 1992:254)

According to this definition, both Italian and Chinese are morphologically uniform—Italian because all of its finite verb forms are inflected for person and number and Chinese because none of its verb forms are. This is illustrated in table 5.3 for verbs in the present tense. In contrast, English is morphologically **mixed** since its paradigm (table 5.4) includes inflection for only the 3rd person singular of the present tense.

Table 5.3 Verbal Paradigms for Italian and Chinese (present tense)

	ITALIAN (*parlare* 'speak')		CHINESE (*shuo* 'speak')	
	Singular	Plural	Singular	Plural
1st	parl-o	parl-iamo	shuo	shuo
2nd	parl-i	parl-ate	shuo	shuo
3rd	parl-a	parl-ono	shuo	shuo

Table 5.4 Verbal Paradigm for
English (present tense)

	Sing.	Plural
1st	speak	speak
2nd	speak	speak
3rd	speak-s	speak

Jaeggli and Safir (1989:29) propose the correlation in (7) between morphological uniformity and subject drop in human language.

(7) *The Null Subject Parameter:*
Null subjects are permitted in all and only languages with morphologically uniform inflectional paradigms.

This correctly predicts that, like Italian (see (3)), Chinese should permit subject drop. (Given the lack of person and number agreement, the understood subject in Chinese is identified with the help of the sentential topic. However, this element need not be overt; it too may be dropped if it can be linked to a discourse topic. See Hyams 1992:260 and Rizzi 1994.)

(8) bang le   Lisi.
help PAST Lisi
'(S/he) helped Lisi.'

The proposed null subject parameter also correctly predicts that English should *not* allow subject drop, since it is a morphologically mixed language.

Drawing on this analysis, Hyams suggests that the subject drop stage in early child language arises because the acquisition device initially treats English as a morphologically uniform language of the Chinese type (i.e., without verbal inflection). This neatly accounts for the fact that children in the subject drop stage do not inflect verbs for person, number, or tense, circumventing a major criticism of her earlier theory.

However, new problems arise. For one thing, it is unclear whether the proposed connection between morphological uniformity and subject drop can be maintained. Jaeggli and Safir themselves admit that they have no idea why such a correlation should exist in the first place (1989:41). Moreover, some morphologically mixed languages do permit subject drop, contrary to what Jaeggli and Safir's theory predicts. Two such languages are Persian and Wichita, from which sample paradigms are presented in table 5.5. (With Hyams 1992:259, I assume that zero inflection is a sign of a morphologically mixed system.) If the correlation between morphological uniformity and subject drop cannot be maintained typologically, Hyams's attempt to correlate the two in the early stages of linguistic development is seriously weakened.

Table 5.5 Verbal Paradigms for Persian and Wichita: Subject Agreement

	PERSIAN (past) (Lambton 1967:16)		WICHITA[a] (Rood 1976:227)		
	Singular	Plural	Singular	Dual	Plural
1st	-am	-im	Ø	hi-	ra.k/hi-
2nd	-i	-id	Ø	hi-	ra.k/hi-
3rd	Ø	-and	Ø	hi-	hi-

a. From the set used for transitive verbs with a 3rd singular direct object.

A second problem for Hyams's new theory involves the developmental data themselves. In a study of the early speech of three French-speaking children, Weissenborn (1992) found that subject drop continued even after the system of verbal morphology had been mastered, as in (9).

(9)   *Some subjectless sentences with inflected verbs in French* (Weissenborn 1992: 280–81):

    a. Peux le faire. 'can do it' (24 mos.)

    b. Ai mangé des quettes [crêpes]. 'have eaten pancakes' (26 mos.)

    c. Est sale. 'is dirty' (22 mos.)

    d. A fait. 'had made' (25 mos.)

    e. Est tombé. 'has fallen' (25 mos.)

    f. Veux manger. 'want to eat' (22 mos.)

Since French has the type of morphologically mixed verbal paradigm that does not license subject drop, this finding contradicts the major prediction of Hyams's new theory: even after French children learn that their language is morphologically mixed, they continue to drop subjects in violation of the constraint embodied in the version of the Null Subject Parameter outlined in (7).

Still another problem is noted by Wang et al. (1992). If children's English is indeed like adult Chinese, as Hyams's theory suggests, we would expect it to have not only null subjects but also null objects (Chinese allows both types of element).[3] However, Wang et al. show that while 2- and 3-year-old Chinese-speaking children drop objects around 20% of the time, English-speaking children do so only 3–8% of the time. (This point is discussed in more detail in section 3 below.) This further weakens the claim that the syntactic development of English includes a stage in which children use a Chinese-type grammar.

Finally, if English-speaking children do in fact initially believe that they are learning a null pronoun language, we would expect their production of overt pronouns such as *I, you,* and *he* to be quite limited. (A defining feature of null pronoun languages is that overt pronouns are used primarily for contrast and emphasis, and are thus relatively infrequent.) However, Valian (1989, 1991) found that even the youngest group of American children in her study used pronouns for over 70% of their overt subjects—more than twice the rate found in the speech of comparable Italian children. This further undermines the view that young language learners take English to be a null pronoun language.

TENSE-BASED THEORIES

Yet another explanation for the subject drop stage is proposed by O'Grady, Peters, and Masterson (1989), who try to link this developmental phenomenon to the emergence of tense. As they note, tense (or 'finiteness') plays a key role in determining which verbs require an overt subject in adult speech.

(10) *The overt subject requirement:*
      Tensed verbs require overt subjects.

The effects of the overt subject requirement are illustrated in table 5.6. (Tense in English can be associated with either verbal inflection or a modal auxiliary.) In contrast with tensed verbs, nonfinite verbal forms, such as infinitives and participles (table 5.7), do not require or take overt subjects.[4] There is a prima facie connection between tense and overt subjects in child language: Guilfoyle (1984) observes that children in the subject drop stage do not inflect verbs for tense, and Hyams (1992:255) acknowledges that the end of the subject drop stage coincides with the emergence of tense inflection.

O'Grady et al. build on this observation, proposing that the subject drop stage arises because the absence of tense contrasts makes it impossible for the acquisition device to distinguish between the inflectional subclasses of verbs that take an overt subject and the ones that do not. It therefore concludes from sentences such as those in (11) that overt subjects are optional. (A dot marks a missing subject in these examples.)

(11) We plan . to leave soon.
      Before . leaving, she checked the stove.

Table 5.6 Some Tensed Verbs in English

Tense Expressed by	With an Overt Subject	Without an Overt Subject
Inflected V	John [left yesterday].	* Left yesterday
Modal	John [will go tomorrow].	* Will go tomorrow
Inflected Aux	John [has gone]	* Has gone
Inflected copula	John [is here]	* Is here

Table 5.7 Some Untensed Verbs in English

Type	With an Overt Subject	Without an Overt Subject
Participle	* Harry [to work now]	To work now (is hard).
Infinitive	* Harry [leaving today]	Leaving today (would be nice).

O'Grady et al. note that a further confounding factor is the existence in the input of genuine subjectless sentences as in (12), of which all except the final two involve untensed verbs (see Schmerling 1973; Valian 1989).

(12)   Gotta go.
       Look OK?
       Been there yet?
       Wanna play?
       Already saw it.
       Seems like a nice day.

In the absence of a distinction between tensed and untensed verbs, this type of input could further facilitate the conclusion that overt subjects are optional.

O'Grady et al.'s analysis makes the following two predictions about how the subject drop stage should be manifested in children's actual speech patterns:

(i) *The initial absence of modals and inflection.* The subject drop phenomenon in child language stems from the absence of the tense-based contrasts needed to distinguish between subject-taking and non–subject-taking verbs. Thus, the initial part of the subject drop stage should be characterized by a paucity of modals and inflected verbs.

(ii) *Gradualness and variation.* The subject drop stage comes to an end as the acquisition device associates the overt subject requirement with the appropriate morphologically defined subclasses of verbs (modals, tensed auxiliaries, tensed main verbs, and tensed copulas). Two types of variation are expected. First, because there are differences in the frequency and morphology of the various subtypes of tensed verbs found in English, they will likely come to be used consistently with overt subjects at different times. Second, because no two children are exposed to the same input, there should also be variation from child to child in terms of which morphologically defined subclass of verbs is first recognized as subject-taking.

In order to test these predictions, O'Grady et al. examined transcripts of the speech of three children in the subject drop stage: Adam and Eve from Brown's (1973) longitudinal study, and Seth, a visually impaired child whose linguistic development was being studied by Peters. The children's ages and MLUs during the period studied are summarized in table 5.8. The transcripts were searched for instances of modals (*can, will,* etc.), semi-auxiliaries (*gonna, hafta*), regular auxiliaries (*have, be*), copulas, and main verbs inflected for tense—these being the type of elements that require an overt subject in English.

Table 5.9 profiles the emergence of subjects with various subtypes of verbs in the speech of Adam, whose development is representative of the other two children as well. O'Grady et al. assumed that a verb type could be considered 'subject-taking' once it appeared with an overt subject 90% of the time. The horizontal

Table 5.8 Ages and MLUs for Adam, Eve,
and Seth

Child	Age Range	MLU Range
Adam	33–36.5	2.35–3.55
Eve	21–25.5	2.55–3.4
Seth	24.5–30	2.10–4.44

Table 5.9 Proportion of Verbs with Overt Subjects in Adam's Speech

Age	Modal	Semi-Aux	Aux	Inflected Main Verb	Copula
33	0% [0]	0% [4]	0% [2]	60% [10]	100% [6]
33.5	100 [1]	25 [4]	60 [10]	42 [12]	89 [28]
34	100 [6]	0 [3]	77 [26]	63 [19]	94 [18]
34.5	0 [0]	10 [11]	20 [15]	100 [7]	96 [23]
35	100 [2]	68 [31]	65 [40]	100 [12]	100 [16]
35.5	80 [5]	81 [16]	94 [18]	75 [16]	100 [19]
36	100 [5]	99 [74]	98 [44]	100 [23]	100 [17]
36.5	67 [3]	100 [21]	100 [25]	93 [14]	100 [23]

lines in the table indicate the point at which this happened for the various subtypes of verbs. (The figures in square brackets indicate the number of tokens.) Adam's modals develop very late, consisting almost entirely of *can* and *can't* through 36.5 months. His auxiliaries have optional subjects until 35.5 months and his semi-auxiliaries until 36 months. Finally, his tensed main verbs come to have obligatory subjects 90% of the time at 34.5 months.

As predicted, the subject drop stage is initially characterized by the virtual absence of tense inflection. Inflected main verbs were extremely rare in the first months of the transcripts (occurring fewer than a dozen times in any child), compared to hundreds of uninflected verb forms. In the speech of Adam, for example, only 10 tokens of inflected verbs were observed at age 33 months. This is consistent with the view that the inability to distinguish between tensed and untensed verbs lies at the heart of the subject drop stage.

Moreover, also as predicted, the subject drop stage does not end abruptly. Rather, it disappears gradually, with each child identifying the various subtypes of verbs that obey the overt subject requirement in different orders, as summarized in table 5.10.

In sum, then, the developmental data garnered from the speech of Adam, Eve, and Seth offer two pieces of evidence that the subject drop stage originates in the

Table 5.10 Rank Order for Development of the Subject-Taking Property

Child	Rank Order	Time Span
Adam	cop > infl. main V > aux > semi-aux > modal	> 3 mos.
Eve	modal > {semi-aux, aux, cop} > infl. main V	1 mo.
Seth	cop > aux > {modal, semi-aux} > infl. main V	5 mos.

inability to distinguish between tensed and untensed verbs. First, the morphological signs of tense (verbal inflection and modals) are absent during the early portion of the subject drop stage, consistent with the claim that the tensed–untensed contrast has not yet been identified. Second, the appearance of tense inflection coincides with the gradual reduction and eventual elimination of illicit subject drop, as the various subtypes of tensed verbs are assigned to the subject-taking class. (Paul Bloom [pers. comm.] observes that the case for the tense-based theory could be strengthened by establishing a correlation between subject omission and the absence of tense, independent of age. To date, the statistical analysis needed to uncover such a correlation has not been attempted.)

There is at least one report of developmental data that is inconsistent with O'Grady et al.'s predictions. Ingham (1992) conducted a detailed case study of the speech of a single child (Sophie), examining speech samples taken every few days between ages 2;5 and 2;8. (The samples contained a total of 5580 utterances.) He reports (p. 144) that while Sophie's use of overt subjects reached the 90% level at age 2;5, tense inflections were not used productively until age 2;8—apparently contradicting the prediction that the contrast between tensed and untensed verbs must precede mastery of the overt subject requirement.

A possible explanation for this finding is that in addition to ignoring irregular inflection (e.g., *saw, ran,* etc.), Ingham counted instances of *-ed* that were used to indicate the immediate past as aspect rather than tense (p. 139), relying on Sophie's mother to determine the relevant time reference points. This in turn suppressed the rate of tense inflection during the period in which subject drop was diminishing. Further work is required to determine whether Ingham's criterion for calculating tense is appropriate and whether the findings he reports for Sophie are representative of language learners in general.

By itself, the tense-based theory cannot provide a full account of the subject drop phenomenon. Although it correctly predicts that overt subjects will be underused in certain contexts in child language, it seems to incorrectly predict that they will be *overused* in other places. For example, given that children cannot distinguish between tensed and untensed verbs, what is to rule out use of an overt subject in patterns such as (13), where the adult language does not permit such elements because of the untensed verb?

(13) *gonna [*me* go]. (cf. me gonna . go)

   *Mommy try [*me* (to) go]. (cf. Mommy try . to go)

Since such patterns are apparently not attested in child language, the tense-based theory must account for their absence with the help of some additional mechanism.[5]

2. Subject Drop and Embedded Clauses

As noted above, even adult English includes some sentences in which there is no overt subject, as in (12), repeated as (14).

(14) Gotta go.

   Look OK?

   Been there yet?

   Wanna play?

   Already saw it.

   Seems like a nice day.

Additional examples of this are provided by Valian (1989, 1990), as in (15).

(15) Wash the dishes. [imperative]

   Seems like she always has something.

   Want lunch now?

   Having a good time?

It seems reasonable to suppose that exposure to a sufficient number of sentences of this type could mislead the acquisition device into believing that English is a subject drop language. Continued exposure to such sentences would further complicate matters by preventing the acquisition device from correcting its initial error.

   Roeper and Weissenborn (1990) propose an interesting way out of this dilemma. The key observation is that the apparent subject drop found in (14) and (15) never occurs in embedded clauses in English, as shown in (16).

(16) *I know that [. gotta go].

   *Do you think that [. look OK]?

   *He wonders whether [. been there yet].

   *She asked if [. seems like a nice day].

In true subject drop languages, on the other hand, null subjects are permitted in embedded clauses.

(17) *Italian:*

   Il signore ha detto che [. è arrivato ieri].

   the gentleman said   that is arrived yesterday

   'The gentleman said that he arrrived yesterday.'

(18)   *Chinese:*
       Zhangsan shuo [. bu renshi Lisi].
       Zhangsan said   not know Lisi
       'Zhangsan said that he did not know Lisi.'

Roeper and Weissenborn focus on this fact, suggesting that the acquisition device determines a language's subject drop status by examining embedded clauses. It will thus unerringly conclude that English does not allow subject drop, but that Italian and Chinese do. (Interestingly, there is independent reason to believe that the acquisition device is sensitive to embedded clauses: a common early word order for single-clause sentences in German is the verb-final pattern found in embedded clauses rather than the verb-second order that occurs in the root clause— e.g., Clahsen 1992:63.)

Although embedded clauses do not appear in large numbers in children's own speech until *after* the subject drop stage has ended (Valian 1991:67), Roeper and Weissenborn's proposal enjoys significant support. First and foremost is the simple fact that children acquiring non–subject drop languages avoid using null subjects in those tensed embedded clauses that they do produce. Valian (1991:65) reports that none of the 21 English-speaking children in her study ever produced a null subject in a tensed embedded clause that was introduced by a complementizer (*that, if,* etc.). Similarly, Weissenborn (1992:285) observes that French-speaking children do not produce null subjects in tensed embedded clauses, although subject drop in tensed matrix clauses does take place (see the examples in (9) above). An experimental study (box 5.2) by Núñez del Prado et al. (1994) provides independent confirmation that children learning English do not drop subjects in embedded clauses. They report major contrasts in the frequency with which the proper name or pronoun in the second clause is deleted in the children's imitations. (In English, such deletion is permitted in the coordinate pattern, but

Box 5.2

THE STUDY: Núñez del Prado et al. 1994
SUBJECTS: 42 English-speaking and 63 Spanish-speaking children aged 2;2–4;5
RELEVANT SENTENCE TYPES: (in English and Spanish; 2 tokens of each type)
    Coordination pattern:
      Mickey sneezes and Mickey/he whistles.
    Complement pattern:
      Bunny says that Bunny/he dances.
    Adjunct pattern:
      Oscar whistles when Oscar/he jumps up.
TASK: elicited imitation of the appropriate sentences in the child's native language

---

not in the complement or adjunct patterns; in Spanish—a subject drop language—
it is permitted in all three structures.) Even among the youngest English children,
deletion took place far more often in coordinate structures than in the complement
or adjunct patterns; in contrast, deletion occurred with roughly the same frequency in all three patterns in the responses from the Spanish-speaking children.
This suggests a very early sensitivity on the part of language learners to the fact
that Spanish permits subjects in embedded complement and adjuncts clauses to be
dropped whereas English does not.

Even if the acquisition device is especially sensitive to embedded clauses, this
cannot be the whole story. As the pairs of sentences in (19)–(20) show, overt
subjects are found in embedded clauses only when the verb is tensed; untensed
verbs characteristically occur without an overt subject.

(19) *Tensed embedded clause:*
    a. With subject
        John decided [that *Bob* had won the prize]
    b. Without subject
        *John decided [that . had won the prize]

(20) *Untensed embedded clause:*
    a. With subject
        *John decided [*Bob* to win the prize]
    b. Without subject
        John decided [. to win the prize]

Thus, even if it relies on data from embedded clauses, the acquisition device must
still be sensitive to the distinction between tensed and untensed verbs.

Still another possibility is that the acquisition device is able to determine a
language's subject drop status by examining *wh* questions. Only true subject drop
languages permit null subjects in such structures, as the contrast in (21) between
Spanish and English illustrates.

(21) *Subject drop in wh questions:*
    a. Spanish
        Porqué . com-erán?
        why   eat-3.PL.FUT
        'Why will they eat?'
    b. English
        *Why will . eat?

Interestingly, Weissenborn (1992:285 ff.) notes that children acquiring French
(a non–subject-drop language) generally do not omit subjects in *wh* questions.
Valian (1991:39) makes a similar observation for English, noting that only 9 of

the 552 *wh* questions in her speech sample lacked an overt subject, and Rizzi (1994:251) reports that the rate of subject drop in the speech of Adam and Eve is far smaller than in declarative sentences.[6]

The picture that emerges from these observations, then, is that children learning English use overt subjects more or less invariably in two contexts: in *wh* questions and in embedded clauses introduced by a complementizer.

(22)   *Contexts that strongly favor an overt subject:*
        a. *Wh* questions
               What will *he* eat?
        b. Embedded clauses introduced by a complementizer
               I think [that *he* is here].

To see what these two contexts have in common, it is necessary to reassess a widely accepted assumption about the structure of clauses with null subjects.

The standard assumption of virtually all theoretical work on subject drop in child language is that verbs without overt subjects occur in syntactic structures such as those in (23), in which there is a null subject.

(23)

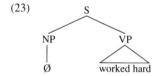

But there is perhaps another possibility, namely that young children treat utterances without overt subjects as simple VPs—that is, as incomplete sentences rather than as sentences with a null subject. Incomplete sentences consisting of other phrases are extremely common, of course, (e.g., NPs such as *this one,* PPs such as *on the table,* and AdvPs such as *over here*), and there is no a priori reason to rule out the production of sentence fragments that consist of just a VP.

Interestingly, there are two contexts where a plain VP is not permitted in adult English. First, it cannot occur with a complementizer such as *that,* which selects a full sentential complement, not just a VP. Second, it cannot occur in a *wh* question: as we will see in chapter 8, it is generally agreed that fronted *wh* words occur in syntactic structure as 'sisters' of an S category, not of a VP. Crucially, these are the very contexts in which Weissenborn, Valian, and Rizzi have independently noted that overt subjects consistently occur in the speech of children acquiring non–subject drop languages. It is possible, then, that the acquisition device is not positing a null subject at all in the type of 'subjectless' utterances considered in this chapter. Rather, the patterns in question may be simple VPs, as in (24b).

(24) a. *Traditional view:* utterance = S   b. *Alternative view:* utterance = VP

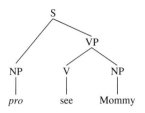

As if anticipating this proposal, Hyams (1986:70) notes two considerations that support the postulation of a null pronoun in sentences without an overt subject (see also Radford 1990:205 ff.; Hyams and Wexler 1993:441). As in languages with null pronoun subjects, the 'understood' subject in these sentences has the same definite reference as overt pronouns such as *he* and *she*. Moreover, it can alternate with an overt subject, as shown by the fact that (a) verbs that occur in subjectless sentences are also used in sentences with overt subjects by the same children, and (b) a subjectless sentence is sometimes immediately followed by an expanded variant that contains an overt subject, as in *Fall . . . Stick fall* or *Go nursery . . . Lucy go nursery* (both from Stevie at 25–26 months, as reported by Braine 1973).

However, neither of these arguments is convincing. There may be pragmatic reasons why a simple VP in child language must be predicated of a definite entity in the discourse context (e.g., to facilitate its identification by the addressee). And there is certainly no reason why a verb that appears in a simple VP in one utterance could not appear in a full sentence in another utterance (even a neighboring one).

It is thus possible that most of the utterances that seem to have null pronoun subjects in early phases of English are actually simple VPs. They bear a superficial resemblance to the null subject sentences found in a genuine subject drop language, but their true character is revealed by their failure to appear in embedded clauses and *wh* questions.[7]

What changes if subjectless utterances in early child language are actually simple VPs? On this view, the acquisition device actually has two tasks to perform with respect to subjects around age 2. First, it must determine whether the language to which it is exposed allows null subjects with tensed verbs (i.e., whether it is a pro drop language). As noted above, the data bearing most directly on this decision come from *wh* questions and embedded clauses. The fact that English-speaking children seem almost never to produce subjectless tensed verbs in such patterns suggests that the inadmissibility of subject drop in English is determined quite straightforwardly.

Second, the acquisition device must determine under what conditions an utterance can consist simply of a VP. It is possible that processing factors initially encourage the production of VP-size utterances (consistent with Paul Bloom's hypothesis), but eventually the acquisition device must discover the conditions under which such subsentential phrases are appropriate. The conditioning factors cannot be stated simply in terms of verb morphology (although tense is probably still a factor); rather, subtle (and still unidentified) lexical and contextual factors must apparently be brought into play. (Roeper 1991:181 notes a contrast between *seemed pretty as a picture* and ?**appeared pretty as a picture*.)

3. Missing Direct Objects

From the early theoretical work on subject drop, it has been assumed that there is an asymmetry in the rate of occurrence of overt subjects and direct objects. For instance, Hyams claims that while "missing subjects are pervasive, sentences with missing objects are strikingly rare" (1987:10) and that "we do not find regular production of objectless sentences" (1986:97). However, not all studies have reported this result. Early work by L. Bloom (1970) on argument dropping in child language suggested that object suppression is common, as manifested in 'subject–verb' patterns such as *Mommy pull*. (A similar claim is put forward by Slobin 1973:195.) Aldridge (1989:64) and Radford (1990:214–18) draw the same conclusion, citing numerous examples such as those in (25) from several dozen children.[8]

(25)   put __ in there. (18 mos.)
        touch __. (18 mos.)
        Lady do __. (21 mos.)
        Lady draw __. (21 mos.)
        push __ in there. (23 mos.)
        Jem have __. (24 mos.)
        not reach __. (24 mos.)
        put __ on. (23 mos.)
        Mummy get __. Man taking __. (23 mos.)

Based on these examples, Radford concludes: "There would seem to be no empirical evidence of any subject/object asymmetry in the [subject drop stage]" (p. 218).

Examples such as these demonstrate that object drop occurs in child language and even that it is not uncommon. By themselves, though, these examples do not establish its relative frequency with respect to subject drop, and the authors in question do not provide any estimates of the overall rate at which objects are suppressed compared to subjects. Interestingly, the data on this phenomenon point toward an asymmetry between subjects and objects. A good example of this comes from Valian's (1991) study of subject drop in the speech of 21 English-speaking children. The crucial figures in table 5.11 are those for obligatorily transitive verbs. On average, even the youngest children (Group I, age 1;10–2;2) used overt direct objects more than 90% of the time in these patterns. This compares

Table 5.11 Frequency of Direct Objects in Valian's Data (percentages) (based on Valian 1991:72–73)

	OBLIGATORILY TRANSITIVE		OPTIONALLY TRANSITIVE		INTRANSITIVE	
GROUP[a]	Mean	Range	Mean	Range	Mean	Range
I	93	86–100	49	33–67	4	0–9
II	93	80–100	66	14–93	5	0–10
III	98	96–100	66	16–86	3	0–10
IV	97	93–100	59	52–67	4	0–13

a. See table 5.1 for characteristics.

Table 5.12 Percentage of Missing Subjects and Objects from Obligatory Contexts

	Adam	Eve	Sarah
Subjects	57	61	43
Objects	8	7	15

with a figure of slightly less than 70% for overt subjects (see table 5.2 above). In the study described in section 1 of this chapter, P. Bloom (1990a:500) reports an even sharper contrast in the speech of Adam, Eve, and Sarah (table 5.12). (His calculation of object drop is for obligatorily transitive verbs; roughly comparable figures for Adam and Eve are reported by Hyams and Wexler 1993:426, whose speech samples and techniques of calculation were somewhat different.) Note that missing subjects are about seven times more common than missing objects in the speech of Adam and Eve. A similar asymmetry is reported for three 2-year-olds by Wang et al. (1992); see also L. Bloom, Miller, and Hood (1985). Overall, then, it seems impossible to avoid the conclusion that while object drop does occur, it is significantly less common than subject drop.

Why should overt subjects be suppressed more frequently than objects? Various possibilities are worth considering. For example, pragmatic factors pertaining to the distribution of new and old information within the sentence must be taken into account. Since the subject tends to express old, known, or recurring information (e.g., Givón 1984:138), this element is arguably more 'dispensable' than a constituent that carries new or unknown information (Greenfield and Smith 1976; P. Bloom 1990a:501, 1993:726). (For a critique of this type of proposal, see Hyams and Wexler 1993:428 ff. and Bloom's 1993 rebuttal.)

Prosodic factors may also be relevant. If the subject is to be encoded as an unstressed pronoun, the likelihood of omission may be increased by its occurrence in the weak initial position of an iambic foot, as argued by Gerken (1991)—see section 1 above.

Still another possibility comes to mind if we assume that 'null argument' patterns involve a missing constituent rather than a null constituent (consistent with the suggestion that 'subject drop sentences' are really simple VPs). Under these circumstances, structural considerations arguably play a role in determining why subjects are far more likely to be dropped than objects. As the tree structure in (26) helps illustrate, the type of grammar widely assumed in contemporary syntactic theory builds syntactic representations in which there is a structural unit consisting of the verb and its direct object (or other complements) and a structural unit consisting of the entire VP and its subject.

(26)

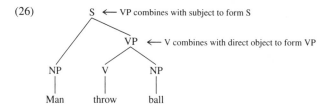

Crucially, however, there is no structural unit consisting of the subject and just the verb. Assuming that children's grammars favor the production of complete constituents (vs. either non-constituents or incomplete phrases), it follows that verb–complement patterns (with subject drop) will be preferred to subject–verb structures (with object drop).

4. Conclusion

There are still many mysteries and open questions in the study of subject drop in child language. Nonetheless, it seems safe to conclude at this time that there is an asymmetry in the suppression of overt subjects and objects, with the former elements being more susceptible to omission. While the ultimate motivation for subject drop is not yet known, it is possible that language learners are struggling with two quite different problems during this period of syntactic development.

On the one hand, the acquisition device must determine whether the language being acquired permits true null subject pronouns. As we have seen, the most reliable data in this regard come from *wh* questions and embedded clauses (assuming a prior contrast between tensed/untensed verbs). On the other hand, the acquisition device must also determine which subsentential constituents can occur as freestanding utterances in normal discourse. This issue is somewhat harder to resolve, since various subtle contextual factors seem to be involved. It is possible that many of the 'subjectless' utterances produced in child language reflect confusion over the latter issue: that is, they may actually be simple VPs rather than full sentences with null pronominal subjects of the sort found in either Italian or Chinese.

6

Embedded Clauses

English contains many different sentence structures built around two or more verbs. Among the most frequent structures of this sort are those in which a verb takes a clause rather than an NP or a PP as its complement. Table 6.1 illustrates the major subtypes of complement clauses in English. (A dot (.) marks a missing or 'understood' subject; for a discussion of patterns in which an untensed verb apparently takes an overt subject, see note 4 to chap. 5.) As examples (1)–(2) show, embedded clauses can also serve as adverbial modifiers and as conjuncts in coordinate structures.

(1) *Embedded clauses serving as adverbial modifiers:*
    a. John ate supper [after he got home].
    b. [Because Sue worked hard], she passed the exam.
    c. The pilot circled the airport [before . landing the aircraft].
(2) *Embedded clauses serving as conjuncts in coordinate structure:*
    [He's light] and [he's big].

This chapter focuses on the development of embedded clauses of various sorts. It begins by examining what is known about the emergence of the complement clause patterns exemplified in table 6.1. Section 2 concentrates on the interpretive strategies that are employed in embedded infinitival clauses, an area that has been the subject of quite intense investigation during the past two decades. Finally, section 3 offers a brief survey of adverbial clauses and coordinate structures. A later chapter is devoted to the emergence of relative clauses, yet another type of embedded structure.

Table 6.1 English Complement Clauses

Complement Type	Without Overt Subject	With Overt Subject
Unmarked infinitive	He helped [. fix it].	He watched [John play].
Marked infinitive	He tried [. to work].	He wanted [John to work].
Participle	He likes [. playing ball].	He watched [John working].
Tensed clause	——	He said [(that) John works].

1. The Development of Complement Clauses

Pioneering work on the development of complement clauses in child language was done by Limber (1973), who studied the spontaneous speech of 12 children

Table 6.2 Complement-Taking
Verbs Observed in Limber's Study
(from Limber 1973:176)

Age 1;11–2;5	Age 2;5–3;0
want	think
need	tell
like	guess
watch	know
see	hope
lookit	show
let	remember
ask	finish
say	wonder
make	wish
gonna	help
hafta	say
supposta	pretend
	decide
	forget

between the ages of 1;11 and 3;0 (table 6.2). Limber found thirty-some verbs used with complement clauses in his data.

The first complement clauses to appear in children's speech are subjectless infinitival phrases (e.g., *I wanna [do it]*). Shortly thereafter, infinitival complements with overt subjects make their appearance. (The examples in (3) of these structures in the speech of 2-year-olds are from Limber 1973:177.)

(3) a. I don't want [you read that book].
     b. Watch [me draw circles].
     c. I see [you sit down].
     d. Lookit [a boy play baseball].

As (3a) and the examples in (4) from Radford 1990:140 illustrate, the infinitival marker *to* is absent both where the complement clause contains an overt subject and where it is subjectless.

(4) a. want *with a complement containing an overt subject:*
        want [teddy drink]. (Daniel, 19 mos.)
        want [mummy come]. (Jem, 21 mos.)
        want [mummy do]. (Anna, 24 mos.)
        want [lady open it]. (Daniel, 22 mos.)

     b. want *with a subjectless complement:*
        want [. do it]. (Daniel, 19 mos.)
        ə want [. see]. (Angharad, 22 mos.)

> want [. open it]. (Daniel, 22 mos.)
> want [. drive car]. (Stephen, 19–24 mos.)

The morpheme *to* begins to occur with infinitives around age two, at about the same time as modal auxiliaries also make their appearance (Aldridge 1989:104). It typically shows up first with subjectless infinitives and then with infinitives that take overt subjects (L. Bloom, Tackeff, and Lahey 1984:400), as in (5).

(5)   *Early examples of infinitival to* (Aldridge 1990:132):
       Me want *to* get down. (Michael, 24 mos.)
       Jem want *to* draw. (Jem, 24 mos.)
       Going *to* sleep. (Lucy, 24 mos.)
       You go *to* sleep. (Angela, 25 mos.)
       Trying *to* push them away. (Elizabeth, 26 mos.)

Aldridge observes that infinitival *to* is not overgeneralized in early child language, so that sentences of the sort in (6) are not attested.

(6)   *I can to go there.
       *Let me to do it.

A possible developmental relationship between infinitival *to* and its prepositional counterpart (as in *to school*) remains in dispute. Aldridge (p. 133) states that infinitival *to* clearly precedes prepositional *to* in the speech of the five children she investigated. However, Bloom et al. (p. 403) found that infinitival *to* appeared "at essentially the same time" as the spatial preposition *to* in the speech of the four children aged 19–36 months that they studied. They further note that children's early use of *to* takes place with matrix verbs expressing a wish or intention *toward* an action (e.g., verbs such as *want* and *go*), suggesting that language learners may perceive a semantic similarity between the two types of *to*. Pinker (1984:226) goes one step further, interpreting Bloom et al.'s data as evidence for the prior acquisition of prepositional *to* and proposing that this may make it easier to locate and identify the homophonous infinitival marker.

Around age 2;4 or 2;6, two new structures typically make their appearance: complements beginning with a *wh* word (e.g., (7)) and tensed non-*wh* complements such as (8).

(7)   Do it [*how* I do it].
       I show you [*who* to do it].
       I don't know [*who* it is].
(8)   I think/guess [she is sick].

Figure 6.1, from L. Bloom et al. (1989:108), records the mean frequency of these two complement types with four verbs in the speech of four children between the ages of 2 and 3. Still missing at age 3 are gerundive complements (e.g., *I like*

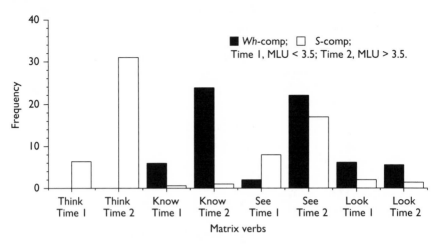

FIGURE 6.1 Mean Frequency of Complement Types

[playing ball]), with the exception of a few structures of the type *I finish/all done eating* (Limber 1973: 178; L. Bloom, Tackeff, and Lahey 1984: 392).

THE DEVELOPMENT OF COMPLEMENTIZERS

English makes use of two major complementizers for clausal subjects and objects—*that,* which introduces a tensed clause, and *for,* which appears with an infinitival clause containing an overt subject. The former element is generally optional, except when the clause that it introduces is in subject position.

(9)   a. That *introducing an object clause:*
              Harry thinks [that/∅ he will win].
        b. That *introducing a subject clause:*
              [That/*∅ he won] surprised Harry.

Like *that, for* is obligatory when it introduces a subject clause.

(10)   [For/*∅ Harry to win] would surprise him.

Depending on the matrix verb, *for* can be obligatory, optional, or forbidden when the infinitival clause occurs in direct object position.

(11)   a. We were hoping [for/*∅ Harry to win].
        b. We wanted [for/∅ Harry to win].
        c. We believed [*for Harry to be intelligent].

Phinney (1981) carried out a simple experiment (box 6.1) to determine when complementizers emerge in children's speech. The results allowed her to divide her subjects into four groups (table 6.3), each of which is arguably in a different

Box 6.1

THE STUDY: Phinney 1981
SUBJECTS: 51 preschool children aged 3;0–6;6 and 34 children in 2nd–4th grades
SENTENCE TYPES: (5 tokens of each type)
    Test 1: Tensed embedded clauses
      a. The bear said [that the turtle tickled the horse].
      b. The cow decided [∅ the sheep pushed the bear].
      c. [That the lion patted the turtle] bothered the rooster.
      d. *[∅ the pig kissed the lion] surprised the dog.
      e. It amused the horse [that the cow touched the lion].
    Test 2: Infinitival embedded clauses
      a. The bear loved [for the pig to tickle him].
      b. The bear wanted [the turtle to kiss him].
      c. The cow hated [. to kiss the horse].
      d. The sheep liked [. to pat the dog].
      e. It amused the pig [for the cow to tickle the dog].
TASK: Imitation

Table 6.3 Phinney's Results

Group	Mean Age	Characteristic	Test Sentence	Response
1	3;7	Sentences containing a complementizer are imitated by either (a) producing a single clause or (b) treating an embedded tensed clause as infinitival. No complementizers are produced.	The bear said [that the turtle tickled the horse].	(a) The turtle tickled the horse. (production of embedded clause only) (b) The bear said to tickle the horse. (substitution of infinitival clause)
2	4;9	Both tensed and infinitival complement clauses are produced, but usually without a complementizer.	The bear said *that* the turtle tickled the horse.	The bear said the turtle tickled the horse.
3	5;0	The complementizer *that* is retained, but *for* is omitted.	The bear said *that* the turtle tickled the horse.	The bear said *that* the turtle tickled the horse.
			It amused the pig *for* the cow to tickle the dog.	It amused the pig the cow to tickle the dog.
4	5;2	Both complementizers are produced, and *that* is present in tensed subject clauses from which it had formerly been omitted (e.g., sentence type (c) in test 1).		

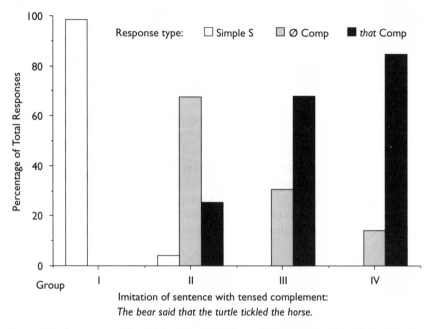

FIGURE 6.2 Response to Tensed Complement Clauses Introduced by *that* (after Phinney 1981 : 156)

stage of development with regard to the ability to produce biclausal constructions. (Recall that because this is a cross-sectional study, no child was observed to pass through the developmental sequence implied by these groupings.) Figure 6.2 demonstrates the four major response patterns for test items containing a *that*-clause. As this bar graph shows, the youngest children (group I) produce only simple sentences, while the second youngest group (group II) produces some complement clauses, but primarily without a complementizer. Only the children in groups III and IV were proficient at producing a tensed complement clause along with the complementizer *that*.

Subsequent work by Thornton (1990) suggests that Phinney's results present an overly conservative view of the age at which children begin producing complementizers (box 6.2). Thornton reports (pp. 83–84) that 15 of the 20 children she studied (including several 3-year-olds) produced biclausal sentences with overt complementizers, as in (12). (Interestingly, 5 of the 15 children used *if* instead of *that*.)

(12)   Is it true *that* you eat flies? (Caroline, 3;7)
       Is it true *if* you're ticklish? (Tyler, 3;9)
       Is it true *if, that* rats get tails off? (Morgan, 3;9)
       Is it true *if* you have a pink mouth? (Kelly 3;10)

Box 6.2

THE STUDY: Thornton 1990

SUBJECTS: 21 children aged 2;10–5;5 (mean age 4;3)

TASK: Production. The experimenter read the children a short story that provided them with an opportunity to ask a question that involved a gap in the embedded clause. For example:

> Experimenter: You know what? I've heard that rats are ticklish. Could you find out if it's true [by asking a puppet rat]?
>
> Expected response from child: Is it true *that* rats are ticklish?

In a related study, Thornton (1990:85) found that children as young as 2;6 sometimes used complementizers in biclausal sentences.

Turning now to the complementizer *for*, this element appears in child speech only after its propositional counterpart (e.g., *She did it for you*) has been acquired. Moreover, as has been claimed for *to* (see earlier discussion), the first uses of *for* in infinitival phrases are semantically related to its use as a preposition (Nishigauchi and Roeper 1987). Hence, just as the preposition *for* is used to express purpose (e.g., *this is for you*), so early uses of complementizer *for* have a purposive meaning. The examples in (13), from the speech of a child between the ages of 2 and 3;6, are cited by Nishigauchi and Roeper (p. 99).

(13)   It's *for* the birds to eat.
       These are matches *for* make a fire.
       This milk is *for* to drink.
       Toys are *for* to play with.
       Grandma has a present *for* me to blow on.

2. Control in Infinitival Clauses

A large number of embedded clause constructions in English resemble the pattern exemplified in (14).

(14)   a.   The boys tried [. to push the car out].
       b.   The teacher told the students [. to work hard].

As indicated by the dot (.), the subject position in the embedded clause is empty. In the vast majority of cases, the NP that **controls** or identifies the missing subject can be singled out by the simple generalization in (15).

(15)   The controller corresponds to an argument of the higher verb—the object if it is transitive, and the subject otherwise.

Thus, the controller in (14a) is the subject of the higher intransitive verb *try*, while the controller in (14b) is the object of the higher transitive verb *tell*.

The best known counterexample to this generalization is found in sentences where the higher clause contains the transitive verb *promise,* as in (16). (Such sentences are not grammatical for all speakers of English, it appears.)

(16)   The teacher promised the students [. to work hard].

Here, the person who makes the promise must also be the person who carries out the action encoded in the infinitival clause. Hence the controller in (16) is the subject NP *the teacher* rather than the object NP *the students.* Perhaps because of its exceptional nature, or perhaps because it is extremely rare in parental speech (Pinker 1984:235), this structure creates great difficulty for language learners.

CONTROL IN COMPLEMENT CLAUSES

A pioneering study (box 6.3) of control in child language was carried out by C. Chomsky (1969). Based on the children's responses, Chomsky proposed four steps in the development of control. (Because this was a cross-sectional experiment, these stages are necessarily hypothetical; no child in the study was observed to actually pass through these steps.)

Box 6.3

THE STUDY: C. Chomsky 1969
SUBJECTS: 9 5-year-olds, 7 6-year-olds, 7 7-year-olds, 8 8-year-olds, 8 9-year-olds, 1 10-
    year-old.
SENTENCE TYPES: (4 tokens of each type)
        object control: Bozo tells Donald [. to hop up and down].
        subject control: Bozo promises Donald [. to hop up and down].
TASK: After first being questioned to ensure that they were familiar with the meaning of
    promise, the children were asked to act out the test sentences with the help of
    toys. A typical stimulus was: 'Bozo tells/promises Donald to hop up and down.
    Make him do it.' Consistent with the instructions, children acted out the meaning
    of the embedded clause rather than the telling or promising action.

Step 1 (10 children): The object NP is always chosen as controller. Chomsky sug-
    gests that this response reflects the operation of the following simple principle.

Minimal Distance Principle
    The controller is the first NP to the left of the infinitival clause.

Since this principle forces selection of the object NP as controller, all responses to
    the *tell* structure are correct, and all those to the *promise* structure are wrong.

Step 2 (4 children): Responses to both structures are mixed, with some subject re-
    sponses and some object responses. Children in this stage apparently realize that
    object control is not always appropriate and are puzzled about how to respond.

Step 3 (5 children): Responses to the *tell* structure are all correct, while responses to the *promise* structure are mixed. Children in this stage have determined that object control is appropriate when the higher verb is *tell* but are still uncertain about what to do when it is *promise.*

Step 4 (21 children): All responses to both structures are correct. Children in this stage have acquired the adult system, associating object control with *tell* and subject control with *promise.*

Although the basic findings of Chomsky's study have been replicated (e.g., Goodluck and Roeper 1978; Hsu, Cairns, and Fiengo 1985; Sherman and Lust 1986; Eisenberg and Cairns 1994), various refinements and extensions have been put forward.

A first refinement to Chomsky's study has to do with the relevance of the Minimal Distance Principle. In an important paper, Maratsos (1974) noted that there was an alternative explanation for the 'minimal distance' phenomenon observed by Chomsky in sentences like (17).

(17)   a. Sue told Mary [. to leave].
       b. Sue promised Mary [. to leave].

Maratsos observed that the preferred controller for young children (i.e., *Mary*) is not only the nearer NP but also the 'addressee' or 'goal' of the 'speaking event' denoted by the higher verb. Perhaps, then, children's responses reflect strategy (18).

(18)   *The 'Goal Strategy'*
       Select the 'goal' of the higher verb as controller.

In order to test this hypothesis, Maratsos designed an ingenious experiment (box 6.4).

Box 6.4

THE STUDY: Maratsos 1974
SUBJECTS: 20 4-year-olds and 20 5-year-olds who had demonstrated their ability to understand passive constructions on a pretest
SENTENCE TYPES: (2 tokens of each type)
>   *subject control:* The monkey promises the dog [. to jump off].
>   *object control:* The turtle tells the elephant [. to get out].
>   *passive:* The bear is told by the elephant [. to get in].
TASK: The children were asked to act out the meaning of the test sentences with the help of toys. Pretest training ensured that children would act out both the main clause action and the complement clause action.

The crucial sentence here is the passive construction, in which the goal of the speaking event (i.e., *the bear*) is not the NP closest to the infinitival clause. Rather,

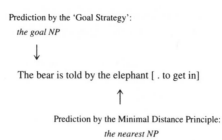

Prediction by the 'Goal Strategy':
the goal NP

↓

The bear is told by the elephant [. to get in]

↑

Prediction by the Minimal Distance Principle:
the nearest NP

FIGURE 6.3

because of the sentence's passive structure, the goal is in subject position and the agent in the *by* phrase is closer to the infinitival clause (fig. 6.3). For this sentence type, then, the Minimal Distance Principle and the 'Goal Strategy' make different predictions. In the 50 instances in which children correctly interpreted the higher verb as passive, they chose the goal NP as controller 48 times. (These results were later replicated by Goodluck 1981.) This provides strong evidence for the view that the acquisition device has opted for a semantically based preference for a goal controller rather than the linearly based Minimal Distance Principle. (Work on control in adult English suggests that it too is guided by semantic principles: see Jackendoff 1972; Nishigauchi 1984; Ladusaw and Dowty 1988.)

A further refinement to Chomsky's work on the emergence of control came from the study of children under age 5. Because the youngest children in Chomsky's study were 5 years of age, some researchers began to explore the possibility that there might be an early developmental stage not manifested in her experimental results. Tavakolian (1978) reports on an experiment that seems to uncover just such a stage (box 6.5). The crucial finding here involves the relatively large number of subject control responses on both the *promise* and *tell* sentences, especially among the 3-year-olds (table 6.4). Tavakolian suggests that there is a period prior to Chomsky's first stage in which children's responses are influenced by the Conjoined Clause Strategy in (19) rather than (or perhaps in addition to) the Minimal Distance Principle.

Box 6.5

THE STUDY: Tavakolian 1978
SUBJECTS: 8 3-year-olds, 8 4-year-olds, 8 5-year-olds
SENTENCE TYPES: (3 tokens of each type)
        object control: The lion tells the pig [. to stand on the horse].
        subject control: The pig promises the rabbit [. to jump over the duck].
TASK: The children were asked to act out the test sentences with the help of toy
    animals.

Table 6.4 Tavakolian's Results (no. of responses out of 24) (from Tavakolian 1978:76)

Element Chosen as Controller	3-year-olds	4-year-olds	5-year-olds
The promise *Sentences*			
Subject	12	11	14
Object	10	13	9
Other	2	0	1
The tell *Sentences*			
Subject	11	9	7
Object	11	14	17
Other	2	1	0

(19)   *The Conjoined Clause Strategy:*
Interpret a string of the type *NP V . . . V . . .* as a coordinate structure of the type *NP V . . . and . . . V . . . .*

According to this strategy, a string such as *Mickey told Bozo to leave* would be interpreted as 'Mickey told Bozo (something) and left'. This leads to the observed response pattern, in which Mickey does both the telling and the leaving.

The existence of a developmental stage characterized by use of the Conjoined Clause Strategy is controversial. As Pinker (1984:242) notes, Tavakolian's data suggest chance performance rather than use of a consistent strategy: among the three-year-olds, for example, responses are almost equally divided between subject control and object control. Indeed, results of this type have been reported in a number of other studies, including a recent experiment (box 6.6) by Eisenberg and Cairns (1994). They report that seven children permitted only the nearest preceding NP to serve as controller and that twelve children allowed either the matrix

Box 6.6

THE STUDY: Eisenberg and Cairns 1994
SUBJECTS: 27 children aged 3;7–5;4
RELEVANT SENTENCE TYPES: (3 tokens of each type)
 NP V [. to VP] patterns:
  arbitrary reference: Ernie says [. to carry Bert]. (2 tokens)
  subject control: Mickey pretends [. to swim]. (10 tokens)
 NP V NP [. to VP] patterns:
  object control: Mickey tells Ernie [. to find Bert]. (6 tokens)
  subject control: Mickey promises Ernie [. to swim]. (2 tokens)
  subject or object control: Bert begs Ernie [. to find Mickey]. (2 tokens)
TASK: The children were asked to act out the test sentences with the help of toy animals.

subject or the object to serve as controller for both *tell*-type and *promise*-type verbs. An additional three children consistently selected entities not mentioned in the sentence as controllers (see also Cairns et al. (1994) and the discussion of McDaniel, Cairns, and Hsu (1990/91) below). No children permitted only subject control.

Other authors have also failed to find evidence for an initial stage characterized by subject control. For instance, Hsu et al. (1989) report a subject control preference in only 4 (mean age 3;7) of the 81 children (aged 3;1–8;0) that they studied.[1] In a study of control in 60 children aged 3 to 10, Phillips (1985) found that the initial stage involved mixed responses rather than subject control. Sherman and Lust (1993) (see also Sherman 1987) report a similar finding (box 6.7), noting that of the 72 children (aged 3–7 years) that they studied, only three gave predominantly subject control responses and they were all over 7 years old. They report (p. 32) that even the 3-year-olds preferred an object antecedent for the understood subject in infinitival patterns; in contrast, the matrix subject was the preferred antecedent for a pronoun subject in a finite complement clause. This suggests that even 3-year-olds realize that the control relation is found in infinitival clauses with understood subjects (not tensed clauses with pronoun subjects), and that it generally links the understood subject with a designated argument in the matrix clause (i.e., an object, if one is available).

Box 6.7

THE STUDY: Sherman and Lust 1993
SUBJECTS: 24 3-year-olds, 24 5-year-olds, 24 7-year-olds
SENTENCE TYPES:

> promise *(subject control) with infinitival complement* (4 tokens):
>> Tom promises Billy [. to eat the ice cream cone].
> tell *(object control) with infinitival complement* (4 tokens):
>> The sister tells the brother [. to draw a picture].
> promise *with finite complement* (4 tokens):
>> Jimmy promises Tom [that he will drink the milk].
> tell *with finite complement* (4 tokens):
>> Jimmy tells Tom [that he will ride the bicycle].

TASKS:

> *elicited imitation:* The children were asked to repeat a sentence presented by the experimenter.
> *comprehension:* The children were asked to "show what happens in the sentence" by acting out its meaning with the help of a set of dolls and props.

The 3-year-olds in Sherman and Lust's study chose the subject as antecedent an average of 1.08 times out of 4 for *promise*-type verbs and 1.04 times out of 4 for *tell*-type verbs, thus failing to distinguish the subject and object control patterns (p. 31). A contrast emerged among the 5-year-olds (1.54 subject responses out of 4 for *promise* vs. 0.54 for *tell*) and became even sharper among the 7-year-olds.

In sum, if the development of control patterns includes a stage prior to those manifested in Chomsky's pioneering work, it seems to involve the same type of mixed responses associated with children in her third stage, not a preference for subject control. In addition, it is possible that at least some preschool children permit the controller to be an entity not named in the sentence—a possibility to which we return below.

CONTROL IN ADVERBIAL CLAUSES

A limitation of Chomsky's study is that the control patterns she investigated all involve an understood subject in an embedded complement (direct object) clause. However, control is also found with adverbial clauses of time and purpose such as (20) and (21).

(20)   Harry criticized Jane [before/after . leaving].
(21)   Harry met the principal [in order . to criticize Jane].

As these sentences help illustrate, adult speakers of English permit only the higher subject to serve as controller for the understood subject of an adverbial clause. This contrasts with the situation in complement clauses, where object control is the more common pattern.

McDaniel, Cairns, and Hsu (1990/91) investigated the development of children's responses to control patterns involving adverbial and complement clauses (box 6.8). Based on this cross-sectional study, they hypothesize four stages in children's ability to deal with these patterns (p. 306). As the following characterization of these stages show, all but the first has a straightforward counterpart in the developmental sequence for control in complement clauses described by C. Chomsky (1969).

Box 6.8

THE STUDY: McDaniel, Smith, and Hsu 1990/91
SUBJECTS: 20 children (12 girls and 8 boys) aged 3;9–5;4 (mean age 4;6)
SENTENCE TYPE RELEVANT HERE: (6 tokens of the first type, 3 of the second)
  adverbial clause: The zebra touches the lion [before . drinking some water].
  complement clause: Cookie Monster tells Grover [. to jump into the water]
TASK: The children were asked to act out the meaning of the test sentences with the help of Sesame Street characters. In a session on a later day, they were asked for their judgments about the interpretation of the test sentences. (The children received prior training and practice in giving such judgments.)

Step 1 (5 children): Three of the children selected a controller not mentioned in the test sentence for both the complement clause pattern and the adverbial clause pattern. Another two children responded in this manner only for adverbial clauses. The average age of these children (4;1) may explain why this step was not observed in Chomsky's study, which involved children aged 5 and over.

Step 2 (7 children): The direct object in the main clause is chosen as a controller. Children responding in this manner interpret the sentence *The zebra touches the lion [before . drinking some water]* by having the lion rather than the zebra drink the water. This parallels the response pattern that Chomsky attributed to the Minimal Distance Principle.

Step 3 (2 children): Responses are mixed, with the controller corresponding sometimes to the higher subject and sometimes to the higher object. A similar intermediate stage is described by Chomsky.

Step 4 (3 children): Emergence of the adult system; responses are uniformly correct.

The existence of these developmental steps was confirmed by McDaniel et al. in a follow-up study reported in the same article—a semi-longitudinal study involving 14 children (age 4;1–4;10) and three test sessions over a six-month period. Goodluck (1987:253) reports that responses in which the controller is taken to be sentence-external (step 1) are even more common in patterns such as (22), in which the clause containing the understood subject is preposed.

(22)   [Before . drinking some water], the zebra touches the lion.

Goodluck observed that the majority of even 5- and 6-year-old children incorrectly take the understood subject of the temporal clause in such patterns to be someone not mentioned in the sentence.

Turning now to the second developmental step reported by McDaniel et al., we must ask why the acquisition device should equate the understood subject of an adverbial clause with the direct object of the higher verb rather than the subject, as in adult speech. One possibility, put forward by Goodluck (1981), Goodluck and Tavakolian (1982), and Hsu, Cairns, and Fiengo (1985), is that the acquisition device is predisposed to interpret missing subjects with respect to a higher NP. Given that adverbial clauses introduced by connectives such as *before* and *after* attach to S, as depicted in (23), only the matrix subject is an eligible controller in adult English, since only it is higher than the missing NP.

(23)   *Adult system: adverbial clause attaches to S:*

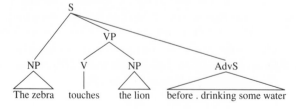

However, if the acquisition device initially attaches adverbial clauses to VP, as illustrated in (24), there are in fact two eligible controllers—the matrix subject and direct object, each of which is higher than the missing subject.

(24)   *Child system: adverbial clause attaches to VP:*

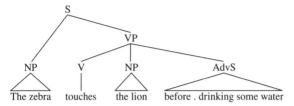

If we assume that the preferred controller is the closest of the higher NPs (cf. the Minimal Distance Principle), this proposal accounts for why an object control response predominates in step 2 of the above developmental sequence.[2] However, before this idea can be accepted, various issues must be resolved, including the question of why the acquisition device posits the wrong structure in the first place and how it can later identify and correct its mistake. For some commentary on these matters, see Goodluck and Behne (1992), Jones (1992), McDaniel, Smith, and Hsu (1990/91), and Sherman and Lust (1993).

CONTROL IN *WH*-COMPLEMENTS

Another important finding of C. Chomsky's (1969) research has to do with the interpretation of subjectless infinitival clauses that begin with a *wh* word. These constructions permit a quite unexpected interpretation, as (25) helps illustrate.

(25)   a. Jane asked Mary [. to make the bed].
       b. The student asked the physicist [how . to measure gravity].

In the first sentence, the strongly preferred controller is *Mary,* the goal argument of the verb *ask.* However, when the infinitival clause begins with a *wh* word, as in (25b), two interpretations are possible: the controller can be either the subject of the matrix clause (*the student*) or an unspecified person (so that the student is asking how in general one goes about measuring gravity).

In her study, Chomsky tested children's understanding of a number of *ask* constructions, including imperative versions of the pattern in (25b).

(26)   Ask X [what . to feed the doll].

Each child was presented with sentences like (26) in the presence of a second child to whom the question could be addressed. Only 14 of the 40 subjects responded correctly to sentences of this sort. The rest chose the goal as controller and often interpreted *ask* as if it were *tell* (thereby instructing the other child what to feed the doll).

LAURA, age 6;5: goal is controller and *ask* is interpreted as 'tell'
Ask Joanne [what . to feed the doll].
    The hot dog.
Now I want you to *ask* Joanne something. *Ask* her [what . to feed the doll].
    The piece of bread.
SAMUEL, age 8;5
Ask Ellen [what . to feed the doll].
    Feed her hamburgers.
All right now, tell Ellen [what . to feed her].
    Again?
M-hm.
    Tomato
Now I want you to *ask* Ellen something. I want you to *ask* her [what . to feed the doll].
    Feed her this thing, whatever it's called.
All right. Now listen very carefully, because I don't want you to *tell* her anything this time. I want you to *ask* her a question. I want you to ask her [what . to feed the doll]. Can you do that?
    Let's see. I don't get it.
Ok, just go ahead and ask her [what . to feed the doll].
    Feed her eggs.

STEVEN B., age 8;8: goal is controller but *ask* has correct interpretation
Ask Lynn [what . to feed the dog].
    What do you wanna feed the dog?
Ask Lynn [what . to put in the box].
    What are you going to put in the box.

STEVEN V., age 8;4
Ask Bryan [what food . to put back in the box].
    What kind of food do you want to put back?

Identical errors occurred in a follow-up experiment in which children had to select a picture like those in figure 6.4 appropriate to the sentence that they had just heard. A child who responded incorrectly would typically match the sentence *The boy asks the girl [what shoes . to wear]* with the picture on the right and would conjecture that the boy was saying something like 'Wear those shoes'. Such a response not only involves telling rather than asking, but also treats the goal argument of the first verb as controller of the infinitival clause, since the girl is the one putting on the shoes. (In contrast, an adult would choose the picture on the left, interpreting *ask* in the sense of 'request information' and treating the agent of the first verb as controller of the infinitival clause.)

Kramer, Koff, and Luria (1972) showed that even many adults have trouble correctly interpreting these structures, a phenomenon which C. Chomsky (1969:

FIGURE 6.4 Sample from the Picture Selection Task (from C. Chomsky 1969:100)

101) had noted in passing. Although the question of an experimental bias has been raised (see, for example, Warden 1981 and C. Chomsky's 1982 response), there may be another explanation for these results. The errors that children make on this particular experiment suggest that they are treating infinitival clauses that begin with a *wh* word in the same manner as they do the more common pattern in (27), which has no *wh* word.

(27)   John asked Mary [. to feed the dog].

Notice that *ask* in this sentence has the sense of 'politely tell'—not 'question'—that the preferred controller is the goal NP in the matrix clause (*Mary*), and that he or she is under some obligation to carry out the action—precisely the properties that the children erroneously attributed to the test sentences in Chomsky's experiment. This suggests that the errors noted by Chomsky are linguistic in origin, reflecting the fact that children have not yet learned that *ask* means 'request information about' when it takes a *wh* complement and that it has special control properties in these patterns.[3]

CONTROL IN '*EASY TO SEE* PATTERNS'

Perhaps the best known experiment in Chomsky's study involved the sentence structure exemplified in (28).

(28)   The doll is easy [. to see __].

In sentences such as this, not only is there no overt subject but the direct object position (marked by __) is empty as well. The sentence has only one interpretation: the missing direct object is taken to 'match' the subject of the higher verb while the understood subject has 'generic' (nonspecific) reference. Hence, the sentence has the interpretation 'It is easy (for anyone) to see the doll.'

Chomsky tested children's knowledge of '*easy to see* constructions' with the help of a blindfolded doll. As each child was shown the doll, he or she was asked: 'Is the doll easy to see or hard to see?'. Note that the correct response here is 'easy to see' since the blindfolded doll was in plain sight of the child. Only if the children incorrectly took *the doll* to be the understood subject of the infinitival verb *see* should they respond by saying 'hard to see'.

Of Chomsky's 40 subjects, 14 (ranging in age from 5;0 to 8;5) gave the incorrect response. Follow-up questions demonstrated that these children had indeed interpreted *the doll* as the missing subject of the infinitival verb rather than the missing direct object. The following exchange involving Eric (age 5;2) illustrates this (C. Chomsky 1969:28).

> Is the doll easy to see or hard to see?
>> Hard to see.
> Will you make her easy to see?
>> OK. [He removes blindfold.]
> Will you explain what you did?
>> Took off this. [pointing to blindfold]
> And why did that make her easier to see?
>> So she can see.

A similar exchange took place with Lisa, aged 6;5 (p. 30).

> Is the doll easy to see or hard to see?
>> Hard to see.
> Will you make her easy to see?
>> If I can get this untied.
> Will you explain why she was hard to see?
>> [to doll:] Because you had a blindfold over your eyes.

A possible problem with Chomsky's study is that the blindfold covering the doll's eyes creates a bias by focusing the children's attention on the doll's inability to see. This in turn might have led them to ignore the structural details of the question in favor of the pragmatically reasonable assumption that the doll's inability to see would be the subject of conversation. However, a number of subsequent experiments that removed this potential bias (e.g., C. Chomsky 1972; Kessel 1970; Cromer 1970, 1972, 1974, 1987; Cambon and Sinclair 1974) confirmed Chomsky's basic finding. One such study (box 6.9) was carried out by Cromer (1970). He found that only 5 of his 40 subjects responded appropriately to all four tokens of the test sentence; 17 subjects answered all four items incorrectly and another 18 made a mistake on at least one of the test sentences. As in Chomsky's study, the principal error involved equating the missing subject of the infinitival verb with the matrix subject. These results confirm that the *easy to see* structure is difficult even when the test sentences do not contain the potential bias found in Chomsky's original task.

Box 6.9

THE STUDY: Cromer 1970
SUBJECTS: 40 children aged 5;3 – 7;5
SENTENCE TYPE RELEVANT HERE: (4 tokens)
    The duck is easy [. to bite ___]
TASK: The children were asked to act out the meaning of the test sentences with the
    help of puppets.

Still other studies (e.g., Morsbach and Steel 1976; Fabian-Kraus and Ammon 1980) report difficulties with the *easy to see* pattern but note an earlier age of mastery than in Chomsky's experiment.

Box 6.10

THE STUDY: Fabian-Kraus and Ammon 1980
SUBJECTS: 21 4-year-olds, 11 5-year-olds, 13 6-year-olds
TASK: The children listened to a short story illustrated with the help of cartoons and
    were then asked a series of questions which tested their knowledge of both the
    story and the *easy to see* construction.
STORIES: 6 different stories and sets of questions of the following sort were used.
    Linus and Charlie are playing tag. Charlie runs after Linus and tags him right away.
        Who won the game?
        Who wasn't running fast enough?
        Who was easy to catch?
        Who was tagged in the end?

The crucial question here (box 6.10) is the third one—to which an adult speaker of English would respond by saying 'Linus'. On the other hand, a child who had not yet mastered this construction might answer 'Charlie' in the belief that *who* in the question corresponds to the missing subject of the embedded verb rather than the missing object (fig. 6.5).

The children were divided into three groups: those with no correct responses, those who responded correctly between 1 and 5 times, and those who gave the

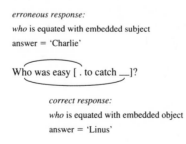

erroneous response:
who is equated with embedded subject
answer = 'Charlie'

Who was easy [. to catch ___]?

correct response:
who is equated with embedded object
answer = 'Linus'

FIGURE 6.5

Table 6.5 Percentage of Children with Each
Score (from Fabian-Kraus and Ammon
1980:407)

Score	4-year-olds	5-year-olds	6-year-olds
0	24	0	0
1–5	62	9	15
6	14	91	85

correct answer for all 6 stories (table 6.5). As these group averages show, most 5-
and 6-year-olds responded correctly to all the *easy to see* structures. This suggests
that mastery of this construction takes place by age 5, somewhat earlier than indicated by the results of Chomsky's pioneering study.

Even if the age of acquisition is somewhat lower than originally estimated by
Chomsky, it is evident that something about the *easy to see* pattern creates a problem for the acquisition device. One possibility is that children err on these structures because of a general tendency to interpret the (matrix) subject as agent. Thus,
in the sentence *The doll is easy to see,* the doll would be interpreted as the one
who does the seeing—giving the principal error type reported by Chomsky and
others. Crucially, however, children who use this strategy should also have trouble
with passive sentences (e.g., *The doll was seen by the dog*), in which the subject
corresponds to the theme rather than the agent. Such difficulties are sometimes
found among younger children (see chap. 10) but are apparently not common
among the older children who participated in the *easy to see* experiments: Cromer
(1970:406) reports that 15 of the 17 children who systematically misinterpreted
the *easy to see* pattern in his study responded correctly to passive structures in
another part of his experiment.

A clue to a possible alternative account for the difficulty of *easy to see* patterns comes from Fabian-Kraus and Ammon's observation that the choice of verb
in the embedded clause influenced children's performance in their experiment
(table 6.6). As they note, the verbs that children found easiest were those that are

Table 6.6 Score for Each Verb in the
Embedded Infinitival Phrase (Fabian-
Kraus and Ammon 1980:408)

Verb	Percentage Correct
find	100
catch	93
save	69
draw	53
watch	33
hear	25

obligatorily transitive, while those that were hardest can be used intransitively. Thus, *find,* which had the highest score, must occur with a direct object (cf. **He found*), while *hear,* which had the lowest score, is often used intransitively (cf. *I can't hear*). The verbs in between seem to vary in terms of their degree of transitivity in the right way: *catch* and especially *save,* with relatively high scores, seem more likely to occur with a direct object, while *draw* and *watch,* with comparatively low scores, can easily be used intransitively.

Why might the likelihood of the verb being transitive affect the children's interpretation of the understood subject in *easy to see* patterns? As I explain in more detail in the next chapter, the key factor seems to be how the computational mechanisms used by the acquisition device treat **gaps**—'open' positions (such as the one after the verb in *easy to see* patterns) in which one normally expects to find an NP. All other things being equal, gaps seem to be treated with increasing disfavor the more distant they are from the element that determines their interpretation. Thus, by this criterion, a subject gap is preferred to a direct object gap, since the former is closer to the element in the higher clause that determines its interpretation (the matrix subject in the case of *easy to see* patterns), as in (29).

(29)

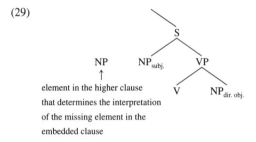

Children's responses to *easy to see* structures during intermediate stages of development are consistent with this tendency in that the missing subject receives an interpretation, but the missing object is ignored (fig. 6.6). In ignoring the missing object, children are in effect treating the embedded verb as if it were intransitive (i.e., objectless). This in turn explains the transitivity effect noted by Fabian-Kraus

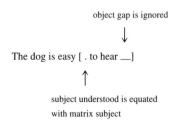

FIGURE 6.6

and Ammon: the strategy depicted in figure 6.6 reanalyzes the embedded verb as intransitive, which is naturally much easier to do in the case of optionally transitive verbs such as *hear* than obligatorily transitive verbs such as *find*. The strategy will thus be applied more frequently to *hear*-type verbs (accounting for the higher error rate) than to *find*-type verbs.

In sum, even after the acquisition device identifies the grammatical properties of *easy to see* patterns (noting that there is an object gap, that it is coreferential with the matrix subject, etc.), children may waiver in their ability to correctly interpret these patterns. Succumbing to the relative difficulty of missing objects versus missing subjects, they commonly interpret the subject gap and ignore the direct object gap, especially in cases where the embedded verb independently permits an intransitive (objectless) interpretation.

Perceived without an object gap, *easy to see* patterns resemble the quite different construction exemplified in (30). (Notice that the matrix predicates here belong to a different semantic class than in the *easy to see* pattern.)

(30)   a. Mary is eager [. to work].
       b. Brian is anxious [. to leave].

In these sentences there is no direct object gap in the embedded infinitival phrase (the verb being truly intransitive), and the 'missing' subject is interpreted as coreferential with the matrix subject. Because such structures do not have a missing direct object in the embedded VP, they should be 'one step' easier than *easy to see* constructions. This prediction seems to be confirmed by the results of a study carried out by Cromer (1970) and described earlier in this section. In addition to patterns such as *The duck is easy to bite,* Cromer's experiment also included four tokens of the type *The duck is eager to bite,* in which the embedded verb must be interpreted intransitively and the embedded subject is coreferential with the matrix subject (see fig. 6.7). Cromer found that the 18 subjects who were at a transitional stage of development averaged 2.18 errors per 4 tokens on the *easy to bite* pattern compared to only 0.29 errors per 4 tokens on the *eager to bite* structure.

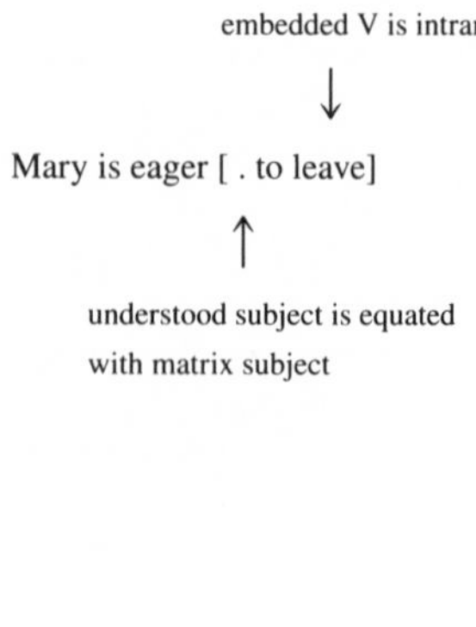

embedded V is intrans.

↓

Mary is eager [. to leave]

↑

understood subject is equated
with matrix subject

FIGURE 6.7

Box 6.11

THE STUDY: Solan 1978
SUBJECTS: 17 children aged 3–5
SENTENCE TYPES RELEVANT HERE: (3 or 4 tokens of each type)
  without object gap: The monkey is eager [. to bite].
  with object gap: The monkey is easy [. to bite __].
TASK: The children were asked to act out the meaning of the test sentences with the
  help of puppets.

Comparable results are reported from a study (box 6.11) carried out by Solan (1978). He found that while all of his subjects correctly interpreted the first sentence type, only 13 also gave the correct response for the second construction. This points toward the greater difficulty of the structural pattern in which the gap is in direct object position. (For an explanation of this phenomenon couched within a different set of assumptions, see Pinker 1984 : 221.)

Still another pattern that may illustrate the same point involves the purpose clause structure illustrated in (31).

(31)   Daisy chooses Pluto [. to read to __].

Here, the embedded clause is missing both a subject and an object (of the preposition). Based on preliminary experimental work, Goodluck and Behne (1992) report that even some 10-year-olds have difficulty with this pattern and that a common error among 5- and 6-year-olds involves ignoring the object gap altogether (thereby taking (31) to mean 'Daisy chooses Pluto as the one who reads'.) This once again suggests that the acquisition device has an aversion to nonsubject gaps.

3. Other Embedded Structures

In addition to complement and adverbial clauses (discussed above) and relative clauses (considered in a later chapter), English contains a number of other sentence types containing embedded clauses. Foremost among these are the **coordinate** or **conjoined** structures exemplified in (32) and the **tensed adverbial** clause structures illustrated in (33). (The italicized elements linking the clauses in these sentences are called **connectives** or **conjunctions.**)

(32)   Harvey should stay in school *or* he should get a job.
       Who stayed *and* who left?
(33)   John ate supper *after* he got home.
       Harry will be furious *if* he reads that.
       Because Sue worked hard, she passed the exam.

Before they acquire connectives, children simply juxtapose clauses to form complex sentences. (Example (34) is cited by Limber 1973:181.)

(34)   You lookit that book; I lookit this book. (age 2;0)

Connectives generally make their appearance sometime after age 2;6. (Examples in (35) from Limber ibid.)

(35)   You play with this one *and* I play with this. (2;8)
        Here's a seat. It must be mine *if* it's a little one. (2;10)
        I want this doll *because* she's big. (2;10)
        When I was a little girl I could go "geek-geek", *but* now I can go "this a chair".
        (2;10)

Bowerman (1979:287) reports that the first connective to appear is *and,* followed by *and then.* The connectives *because, so, when, if, or, but, while, before,* and *after* follow in variable order. A similar scenario emerges from Bloom et al.'s (1980) study of four children during the period from about 1;7 to 3;0 (fig. 6.8). While there are certain shared features of development here (e.g., the early emergence of *and* and *because*), there is also considerable variation among the children in the development of connectives. As Bloom et al. note, *then* was productive early only for Kathryn and Gia, while *where* was an early acquisition only for Kathryn.

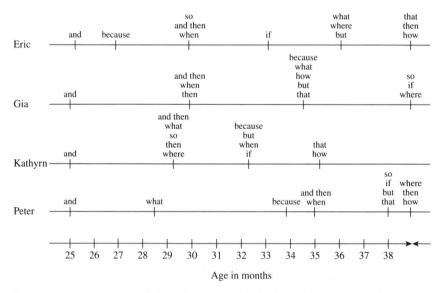

FIGURE 6.8 Developmental Patterns for Connectives in Four Children (from Bloom et al. 1980:242). *Wh* words are counted as connectives when they appear in initial position of embedded questions.

Perhaps the two most difficult connectives to acquire are *before* and *after,* which are infrequent even at age 5 (Bowerman 1979:287). Consider in this respect the four sentences in (36).

(36)   a. Ellie pushed the boat *before* she waved the flag.
      b. *Before* Ellie waved the flag, she pushed the boat.
      c. *After* Ellie pushed the boat, she waved the flag.
      d. Ellie waved the flag *after* she pushed the boat.

As noted by Coker (1978) in her review of the literature, two results are widely reported when children are asked to act out these sentences (with the help of puppets or toys). First, sentences whose clause order reflects the actual order of events are easier than sentences that do not exhibit this property. Hence (36a), for instance, is easier than (36b) since only the former has its component clauses arranged in a way that mirrors the event order: Ellie pushes the boat and then waves the flag. E. Clark (1971:267), who first made this finding, suggests that it reflects a strategy that children use in their own spontaneous speech prior to mastering conjunctions: they talk about events in the order in which they occur.

The second widely reported result, now disputed, is that children do better on *before*-clauses than *after*-clauses. Based on a comprehension study involving 60 kindergarteners (aged 5;3–6;4) and sixty first-graders (aged 6;3–7;7), Coker (1978) concluded that there is no fixed acquisition order for the two connectives. However, she did find that both connectives are acquired as prepositions (e.g., *Sue came before/after Harry*) before they are acquired as conjunctions. See Bowerman (1979:295 ff.) for further discussion.

COORDINATION

The coordination rule for English can be formulated as (37), which simply states that elements of the same category type can be combined to form a coordinate structure of that type (X = any category and * = any number of).

(37)   X → X* and X

Some examples of structures in child language formed in accordance with this rule are given in (38). (These examples are from Lust and Mervis 1980.)

(38) $[_S$ He's light] and $[_S$ he's big].
      $[_{NP}$ The mommy monkey] and $[_{NP}$ the baby monkey] can sit.
      I $[_{VP}$ sit down] and $[_{VP}$ jumped in].

Of special interest from the point of view of language acquisition are structures such as (39), in which each of the two phrases contain a direct object gap.

(39)   [The cat kissed ___] and [the turtle pushed ___] the dog.

The key assumption here is that coordination applies to structural units with identical properties (e.g., Ss, NPs, VPs, etc.). However, the sequence to the left of *and* in (39) (namely, *the cat kissed*) cannot be a structural unit unless there is an object gap, since a subject and a transitive verb by themselves cannot form a phrase. Because coordination applies to units with identical properties, it therefore follows that the element to the right of the conjunction must also contain an object gap. For further discussion of this pattern, see McCawley (1988:55 ff.).

To the extent that direct object gaps are difficult for the acquisition device (recall our discussion of *easy to see* patterns), we can expect structures like (39) to be relatively late acquisitions. (Admittedly, this prediction might also be derived from the fact that such structures are very rare in everyday speech.) The results of an experiment (box 6.12) by Ardery (1980) are particularly relevant here. (Similar results are reported by Tager-Flusberg, de Villiers, and Hakuta 1982.) As the results in table 6.7 help show, the fourth structure (the one containing the object gap) was by far the most difficult. Similar results were obtained from a production task involving the same children: the structures that were easy to comprehend were also easy to produce, but structures containing a gap were rare.

Box 6.12

THE STUDY: Ardery 1980
SUBJECTS: 60 children ranging in age from 2;6 to 6;0
SENTENCE TYPES: (2 tokens of some types; 4 of others)
    coordinate Ss: [The dog ran] and [the cat fell].
    coordinate VPs: The dog [kissed the horse] and [pushed the dog].
    coordinate NPs: [The tiger] and [the turtle] pushed the dog.
    coordinate structures containing a gap: [The cat kissed ___] and [the turtle pushed ___]
    the dog.
TASK: Children were asked to act out the meaning of the test sentences with the help of
    toy animals.

Table 6.7 Results of Ardery's Comprehension Test
(from Ardery 1980:314)

Pattern	Percentage of Children Correct[a]	Mean Age of Those Who Responded Correctly
Coordinate Ss	97	4;3
Coordinate VPs	95	4;5
Coordinate NPs	75	4;9
Coordinate structure with gap	4	5;9

a. 2 out of 2, or 3 out of 4 correct.

An explanatory role for gaps has been posited for other coordinate structures as well. In a study of coordination in natural speech samples from 32 children between the ages of 2;0 and 3;1 (MLU 1.97 to 6.38), Lust and Mervis (1980)—like Ardery—found that the 'predicate coordination' pattern exemplified in (40a) preceded and was more frequent than the subject coordination illustrated in (40b).

(40)   a.   *Predicate coordination:*
           The dog [kissed the horse] and [pushed the tiger].
       b.   *Subject coordination:*
           [The tiger] and [the turtle] pushed the dog.

Lust and Mervis attempt to explain this preference by assuming that the two sentence types contain gaps placed as in (41).

(41)   *Lust & Mervis's Analysis:*
       a.   VP coordination:
           [The dog kissed the horse] and [__ pushed the tiger]. (__ = the dog)
       b.   Subject coordination:
           [The tiger __] and [the turtle pushed the dog]. (__ = pushed the dog).

They suggest that (41a) is easier than (41b) because the gap follows rather than precedes its antecedent. Unfortunately for this analysis, there is no independent evidence of a gap in either of these sentences, and virtually all syntactic theories posit a simple coordinate VP in the former sentence and a coordinate NP in the latter.[4]

(42)   *The standard analysis:*
       a.   VP coordination:
           The dog [$_{VP}$ [$_{VP}$ kissed the horse] and [$_{VP}$ pushed the tiger]].
       b.   Subject coordination:
           [$_{NP}$ [$_{NP}$ The tiger] and [$_{NP}$ the turtle]] pushed the dog.

Evidently, then, there must be some other explanation for the preference noted by Lust and Mervis. (For a possible pragmatic explanation, see Greenfield and Dent 1982.)

4. Conclusion

The acquisition device masters the syntax of multiclausal sentences over a period of several years. The first such structures to be acquired are subjectless infinitival complements, which emerge around age 2 and are followed by a series of other tensed and untensed embedded structures during the next two years. For certain structures at least (e.g., *wh* complements with a missing subject, *easy to see* constructions, and coordinate structures containing a gap), development may continue until age 6 or later.

Of more general interest is the manifestation of a 'computational' phenomenon that will resurface a number of times in the next chapters. As suggested earlier, the acquisition device seems to disfavor gaps in proportion to their relative depth of embedding. Thus, all other things being equal, a missing subject (e.g., *The rabbit is eager . to eat*) is preferred to a missing direct object (e.g., *The rabbit is easy . to catch* __). The next chapter describes a parallel phenomenon in the production and comprehension of *wh* questions.

7

Wh Questions

Linguistic theories differ in their treatment of *wh* questions. In transformational grammar and its variants (e.g., N. Chomsky 1977, 1981), the *wh* word originates in a sentence-internal position and is then moved to the beginning of the sentence, leaving behind a 'gap' in the direct object position. Hence a sentence such as *What should Lucy buy?* is associated with the two syntactic representations in (1). (We consider the positioning of 'auxiliary' verbs such as *should* in the next chapter.)

(1)   a. *Initial or 'underlying' structure:*
          Lucy should buy *what*
     b. *After movement:*
         What should Lucy buy __ ?
          ↖___ '*wh* movement' ___↗

In other theories, *wh* questions are formed directly—without an underlying structure or a movement operation. One way to do this is exemplified in (2), following a suggestion made within the framework of categorial grammar by Bach (1981). (Similar ideas have been developed in generalized phrase structure grammar (Gazdar et al. 1985) and head-driven phrase structure grammar (Pollard 1988).)

(2)

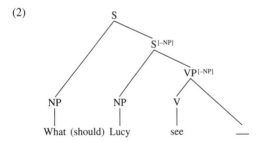

The feature [−NP] signals a 'missing NP'. As depicted in (2), which should be read from the bottom up, this feature is passed from the VP in which it originates to the S category immediately above. This S then combines with the *wh* word, which corresponds to the NP that is 'missing' from the direct object position. The [−NP] feature is thus canceled, resulting in a complete sentence in which the question word is interpreted as the verb's direct object. Because the [−NP] feature is 'passed up' the syntactic structure from the position of the gap, this type of approach to the formation of *wh* questions is often referred to as a **feature-passing** analysis.

1. Early *wh* Questions

Children's first *wh* words are typically *where* and *what,* although they initially seem to understand only *where* (Klima and Bellugi 1966). Based on a 14-month longitudinal study of 7 children (aged 22 mos. at the beginning of the study), L. Bloom, Merkin, and Wootten (1982:1086) report the developmental pattern in table 7.1 for *wh* words in spontaneous speech.[1] (A similar sequence has been observed for English by Johnson 1981:231 and for Korean by Clancy 1989.) A *wh* word was considered to be acquired when it was used correctly in three distinct sentences.

One factor contributing to the early emergence of *where* and *what* questions may be their relative frequency of occurrence: as noted by H. Clark and E. Clark (1977:352), *where* questions made up 80% of the *wh* questions asked of Adam, Eve, and Sarah by their parents. The early predominance of *what* questions over *who* questions may be due to the fact that children are more likely to know the people around them than they are to know all the things they see (L. Bloom, Merkin, and Wootten 1982:1091). They therefore have less reason to use *who* questions. Clancy (1989:337) suggests that the developmental order may also be partly determined by cognitive factors in that early *wh* words correspond to objects and relations that are easily perceivable, while late acquisitions (e.g., *when, why, how*) require an understanding of time and causality.

A striking fact about children's early *wh* questions is that they tend to follow a formulaic pattern consisting of the *wh* word itself, an optional contracted copula, and an NP—i.e., *Wh('s) NP?* (Brown 1968:283; L. Bloom, Merkin, and Wootten 1982:1086–87; Radford 1990:125). The examples in (3), from Radford (ibid.), were produced by children aged 17 to 20 months.

Table 7.1 Developmental Order for
                wh Words

Wh word	Average Age of Acquisition
where, what	26 months
who	28 months
how	33 months
why	35 months
which, whose, when	after 36 months

(3)   What's that?
        What's this?
        What this?
        Who that?
        Where's helicopter?
        Where mummy?

Because of their formulaic character, it seems reasonable to treat these utterances as instantiations of a simple template rather than the product of whatever mechanism (movement or feature passing) forms *wh* questions in the adult grammar.

Independent evidence for this suggestion is offered by Radford (1990:126), who notes that even after children master the system of subject–verb agreement in English, they continue to produce utterances such as (4).

(4)   What colour *is* these? (24 mos.)
        What*'s* these? (26 mos., 28 mos.)
        What*'s* those? (28 mos.)
        Where*'s* my hankies? (28 mos.)
        What*'s* animals' names? (36 mos.)

The fact that children who are otherwise in control of agreement fail to select the appropriate form of the copula verb in these patterns suggests that their *wh* questions are not subject to general grammatical rules—the hallmark of a formulaic pattern.

Further evidence that these children have not mastered the syntax of *wh* questions comes from the fact that they have difficulty responding appropriately to questions that include a direct object *wh* word and a non-copular verb (Klima and Bellugi 1966:201; Radford 1990:129–30). The following examples of inappropriate responses are from Radford (1990:130).

(5)   What have you got?—*Eh?* (20 mos.)
        What are they doing with it?—*Uhm.* (24 mos.)
        What did mummy say?—*Mummy.* (21 mos.)
        What's she [= nana] doing?—*Nana.* (24 mos.)
        What do they [= birds] want?—*Bird.* (20 mos.)
        What are you doing with him [= snake]?—*Snake.* (23 mos.)

2. A Subject–Object Asymmetry

Stromswold (1995) (see also Stromswold 1988) examined *wh* questions in the spontaneous speech of 12 English-speaking children with a view to determining the relative order of emergence of subject and object *wh* words (e.g., *Who will help Sue?* vs. *Who will Sue help?*) Using transcripts of parent–child interactions

Table 7.2 Number of Children in Whom Particular Types
of *wh* Questions Emerged First

Type of Question	Subject Pattern	Object Pattern	Both at the Same Time
Wh questions overall	3	5	4
Who question[a]	4	6	1
What question	0	8	4
Which question[b]	0	5	1

a. One child produced no novel *who* subject or object questions
b. Only 6 children produced *which* questions

that began when the children were aged 1;2−2;6 and ended when they were 2;3−6;0, Stromswold identified about 13,000 utterances in which the children used *who, what,* or *which.* The results (table 7.2) are somewhat indeterminate. Although there seems to be a clear preference for *what* object questions over subject questions, this presumably reflects the fact that inanimate subjects in general are rare in children's speech (see chap. 3) and that even adults rarely use subject *what* questions (Stromswold 1995:36).

Matters are also somewhat complicated for *who* questions. Stomswold reports (p. 31) that children produced significantly more subject questions than object questions (on average 63% of their *who* questions were subject questions). On the face of it, this suggests a preference for subject questions. On the other hand, as Stromswold notes (p. 32), the fact that 6 children produced object *who* questions before subject *who* questions points in the other direction, especially in light of the overall greater frequency of subject questions.

Do experimental studies provide a clearer picture of whether the acquisition device has a preference for subject or object *wh* questions? A study (box 7.1) by Tyack and Ingram (1977) points toward a possible preference for subject questions. They found a strong preference for subject *wh* questions, with performance on object *wh* questions only slightly above 50% for all age groups.[2] (The principal

Box 7.1

THE STUDY: Tyack & Ingram 1977
SUBJECTS: 100 children divided into 5 groups consisting of 20 children each (10 boys
and 10 girls) in the following age ranges:
Group A: 3;0−3;5   Group B: 3;6−3;11   Group C: 4;0−4;5
Group D: 4;6−4;11   Group E: 5;0−5;5
SENTENCE TYPES: (6 tokens of each type)
who subject: Who is helping the boy?
who object: Who is the boy helping ___?
TASK: the children had to answer *wh* questions about the events depicted in a series of photographs.

Table 7.3 Results of the Comprehension Task (percentage correct)

| | AGE GROUPS | | | | | |
TYPE	A	B	C	D	E	MEAN
Subject	72	82	72	90	83	80
Object	52	55	60	60	55	56

error involved interpreting the *wh* word in object questions as it were the subject.) These results (table 7.3) coincide quite closely with those obtained earlier by Ervin-Tripp (1970). Comparable, albeit fragmentary, results are reported by Stewart (1976) for *which N* phrases in subject and object position. However, Stewart and Sinclair (1975, cited by Stromswold 1995:16), report the reverse preference, although their experiment involved older children (aged 5–9) and used the form *whom* rather than *who* for object questions. To complicate matters still further, Cairns and Hsu (1978) report no significant difference in children's ability to comprehend subject and object *who* questions.[3]

Turning now to the production of *wh* questions under experimental conditions, a small study by Wilhelm and Hanna (1992) reports a preference for subject *wh* words.

Box 7.2

THE STUDY: Wilhelm and Hanna 1992

SUBJECTS: 11 children aged 3;4–4;4 (6 boys and 5 girls)

SENTENCE TYPES: (3 tokens of each type)

> *who subject:* Who is helping the boy?
> *what subject:* What is pushing the boy?
> *who object:* Who is the boy helping __?
> *what object:* What is the boy pushing __?

TASK: Two experimenters presented the child with a picture (fig. 7.1) depicting an action involving two participants, one of whom was covered over. The child was then given a prompt such as the following (for the *who* object sentence type):

> Experimenter I (pointing to the picture): The monkey is pushing someone, and I know who.
> Experimenter II: Can you make up a question to find out who?

The experiment began with the two experimenters modeling a series of examples; only one child (the youngest) refused to participate or did not understand what was expected.

The results are depicted in table 7.4. The younger children did poorly on both subject and object questions, getting fewer than half right. The older children also did poorly on the object questions (with a success rate of only 50%) but performed relatively well on the subject questions (70% correct). Interestingly, the most common structural error involved production of a subject question when an object

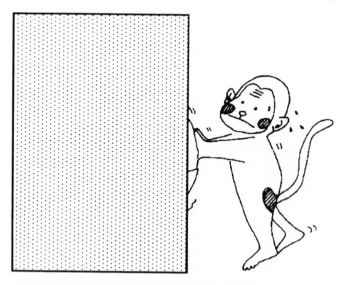

FIGURE 7.1 Sample Picture Used in the Wilhelm and Hanna Study

Table 7.4 Results of the Production Task
(out of 30 tokens)

	AGE GROUPS	
TYPE	3;4–3;6 (5 children)	4;1–4;7 (5 children)
Subject *wh*	12 (40%)	21 (70%)
Object *wh*	13 (43.3%)	15 (50%)

question was called for (21 of 120 responses). The reverse error was extremely rare (3 out of 120 responses). This strongly suggests a preference for subject questions.

A larger study (box 7.3) along the same lines was conducted by Yoshinaga (1996). The results (table 7.5) include a large and statistically significant preference for subject *wh* questions.

Box 7.3

THE STUDY: Yoshinaga 1996
SUBJECTS: 21 children (3 2-year-olds, 9 3-year-olds, 11 4-year-olds)
SENTENCE TYPES: (4 tokens of each type)
       who subject: Who is helping the boy?
       who object: Who is the boy helping __?
TASK: as in the Wilhelm and Hanna study

Table 7.5 Results of the Production Task (percentage correct)

	AGE GROUPS			
TYPE	2-year-olds	3-year-olds	4-year-olds	TOTAL
Subject *wh*	100	97.2	88.6	93.5
Object *wh*	8.3	41.7	79.6	55.4

These results can apparently not be attributed to the effects of experience. Stromswold's (1995:32) analysis of 12 adult-to-child speech samples shows that subject questions are not the most frequent type of *who* question in the speech of all adults (although they are dominant for most). Moreover, Yoshinaga's results also showed a significant preference for subject *what* questions over object *what* questions in the children's scores; yet subject *what* questions were far less frequent than object *what* questions in all 12 adult speech samples studied by Stromswold.

Why should subject *wh* questions be easier than object *wh* questions? A variety of factors may be involved. As can be seen by comparing the two patterns, object *wh* questions differ from subject *wh* questions in undergoing subject–verb inversion and in departing from the usual SVO word order employed in English.

(6)   a. *Subject* wh *question:*
             Who   is helping Mary?
             subject ↑ verb   object
             uninverted aux
        b. *Object* wh *question:*
             Who   is Mary   helping?
             object ↑ subject verb
             inverted aux

It is conceivable that these 'extra' properties of object *wh* questions complicate this pattern, making it more difficult for young language learners to produce and understand. (However, it is worth noting that neither Wilhelm and Hanna nor Yoshinaga marked a response as incorrect based on the presence or placement of the auxiliary verb; the errors that they counted involved producing an object *wh* question when a subject *wh* question was called for, and vice versa.)

A more promising possibility has to do with the 'distance' between the sentence-initial *wh* word and the gap with which it is associated. Regardless of how the *wh* word is linked to the gap (e.g., by a movement transformation or by a feature-passing mechanism), the relationship in object *wh* questions extends over both an S boundary and a VP boundary. This is illustrated in (7), where the categories that intervene between the *wh* word and the associated gap are circled.

(7)   *Movement analysis:*   *Feature-passing analysis:*

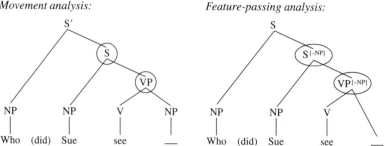

It has long been known that processing difficulty for adults increases with the distance between the gap and its 'filler' (e.g., Wanner and Maratsos 1978; Stromswold 1995:17), and work in grammatical theory has occasionally attempted to make use of this fact as well (e.g., Collins 1994). Let us formulate the relevant generalization as in (8).

(8)   A structure's complexity increases with the number of XP categories (S, VP, etc.) between a gap and the element with which it is associated.

In a movement theory, we can determine complexity by counting the number of XPs that the *wh* word has to move across on its way to the sentence-initial position. In a non-movement theory, we determine complexity by counting the number of times the [−NP] feature appears on an XP. In both types of theory, then, object *wh* questions such as those in (7) have a complexity rating of 2.

In the case of subject *wh* questions, matters are complicated by the fact that it is not clear whether the *wh* word remains in the subject position as in (9a) or whether it moves vacuously to the left as in (9b). (Discussion of this point can be found in Chomsky 1986a:48ff. for the movement analysis and in Gazdar 1981 for the feature-passing analysis.)

(9)   a. Wh *word stays in subject position, hence no gap. Complexity rating = 0:*
             Movement analysis   *Feature-passing analysis*

       b. Wh *word appears in pre-sentential position. Complexity rating = 1:*
             Movement analysis   *Feature-passing analysis*

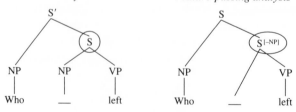

Depending on how these sentences are formed, then, they will have a complexity rating of 1 or 0—in either case, less than the 2 assigned to object *wh* questions. Herein lies a possible explanation for the relative difficulty of object *wh* questions.

If this idea is on the right track, it makes predictions about the relative difficulty of a wide range of other sentences, including those in (10)–(12). Complexity as defined in (8) can be determined in these sentences by counting the number of labeled brackets between the gap and the *wh* word with which it is associated.

(10) What [$_S$ will Sue [$_{VP}$ say __]]? *complexity rating = 2*
(11) What [$_S$ will Sue [$_{VP}$ talk [$_{PP}$ about __]]]? *complexity rating = 3*
(12) What [$_S$ will Sue [$_{VP}$ read [$_{NP}$ a book [$_{PP}$ about __]]]]? *complexity rating = 4*

Note that all three of these sentences have inverted auxiliaries and depart from the canonical SVO word order of English. Of the factors we have been considering, only the distance between the *wh* word and the associated gap predicts a difference in the relative difficulty of these patterns. An experiment (box 7.4) by Hildebrand (1984, 1987) sheds light on whether such a difference is manifested in syntactic development. The results in table 7.6 confirm that Type I is the easiest structure, with a success rate of 83% for the 4-year-olds and 94% for the 6-year-olds. This was better than the Type II pattern (46% correct for the 4-year-olds), which in turn was better than the Type III structure (31% correct).

Box 7.4
___

THE STUDY: Hildebrand 1987
SUBJECTS: 48 children: 12 4-year-olds, 12 6-year-olds, 12 8-year-olds, and 12 10-year-olds
TASK: imitation of sentences containing gaps inside various types of categories. Test sentences were all roughly equal in length.
SENTENCE TYPES:
> *Type I (4 tokens): gap inside an S and a VP:*
> What [$_S$ did the little girl [$_{VP}$ hit __ with the block today]]?
> *Type II (4 tokens): gap inside an S, a VP, and a PP:*
> What [$_S$ did the little boy [$_{VP}$ play [$_{PP}$ with __] behind his mother]]?
> *Type III (3 tokens): gap inside an S, a VP, a NP, and an PP:*
> What [$_S$ did the boy [$_{VP}$ read [$_{NP}$ a story [$_{PP}$ about __]] this morning]]?
___

Table 7.6 Results of the Imitation Task (percentage correct) (from Hildebrand 1984:69)

TYPE	4-year-olds	6-year-olds	8-year-olds	10-year-olds
I	83	94	97	100
II	46	80	86	97
III	31	78	89	89

The types of errors reported by Hildebrand are also revealing. Especially interesting is the fact that 84% of the children's errors on the Type II and III patterns involved restructuring the sentence as in (13) so that the gap no longer occurred within the PP (p. 79), thereby reducing the distance between it and the sentence-initial *wh* word.

(13)   *Restructuring of Type II sentence:*
       What [s did he [vp play [pp with __]]]? → What [s did he [vp play __]]?
       complexity rating = 3   complexity rating = 2

In sum, then, Hildebrand's findings are consistent with the suggestion that the acquisition device is sensitive to the 'structural distance' between a gap and the matching *wh* word, with an increase in the number of intervening XPs leading to greater difficulty.[4]

3. Extraction from Embedded Clauses

If the idea just outlined is right, we would expect patterns in which the sentence-initial *wh* word is associated with a gap in an embedded clause to be particularly difficult in the early stages of acquisition.

(14)   What [s do you [vp think [s he [vp ate __]]]]?

Children's spontaneous speech involves relatively few patterns in which there is extraction from an embedded clause. Stromswold (1995:40) reports finding about 200 such structures among 13,000 *wh* questions in her study of spontaneous speech samples from 12 children (see above). De Villiers, Roeper, and Vainikka (1990:257) report that they uncovered only 16 patterns of this sort in Adam's speech over a three and one-half year period, most of which seem to involve an embedded infinitival clause, as illustrated by (15)–(16).

(15)   What chu like [to have __]? (2;6)
(16)   What he want [to play with __]? (2;6)

The earliest example of extraction from an embedded tensed clause, (17), is from age 2;7.

(17)   What (d')you think [this look like __]?

This suggests that gaps of any type in embedded clauses are relatively difficult compared to those in matrix clauses. Further evidence in support of this conclusion can be found in the results of an elaborate experiment (box 7.5) reported by de Villiers, Roeper, and Vainikka (1990), parts of which are described in more detail later in this chapter. (See also Roeper & de Villiers 1994.) The experiment made use of the potential ambiguity of test sentences such as (18), in

Box 7.5

THE STUDY: de Villiers, Roeper, and Vainikka 1990
SUBJECTS: 25 children aged 3;7−6;11 (12 boys and 13 girls)
SENTENCE TYPES: (2 tokens of each type)
    wh *argument:* Who did the girl ask [to help]?
    wh *adjunct:* When did the boy say [he hurt himself]?
TASK: the children had to answer wh questions after hearing a story (see below) illus-
    trated by pictures.

which *when* could ask about either the time of the saying event or the time of the hurting event.

(18)   When [did the boy say [he hurt himself __] __]?
                                                ↑   ↑
                                    interpretation 1:   interpretation 2:
                                    when asks about   *when* asks about
                                    the time of the   the time of the
                                    hurting   saying

Children heard stories such as the following (accompanied by appropriate illustrations).

> The boy loves to climb trees in the forest. One day he slipped and fell to the
> ground. He picked himself up and went home. That night when he had a
> bath, he found a big bruise on this arm. He said to his Dad, "I must have
> hurt myself when I fell this afternoon." *When did the boy say he hurt
> himself?*

Depending on how children respond, it is possible to determine whether they associate *when* with the embedded verb (answer = 'when he fell from the tree') or the matrix verb (answer = 'when he had a bath').

In the case of the *wh* argument pattern, there is also a potential ambiguity, although it is of a somewhat subtler sort. As (19) helps illustrate, the *wh* word in the test sentence can be interpreted as the object of either the matrix verb *ask* or the embedded verb *help*.

(19)   Who did the girl ask __ [to help __]?
                             ↑   ↑
                    interpretation 1:   interpretation 2:
                    object of *ask*   object of *help*

The subjects were presented with this question in a story such as the following.

> Kermit and Cookie Monster were baking. Big Bird came in and wanted to
> help someone. He wanted to do his favorite kind of baking, but he didn't

know who he should help. So he asked Bert if he could help Kermit. *Who did Big Bird ask to help?*

If the children respond by saying 'Bert', we can infer that they are treating *who* as object of *ask*. If, on the other hand, they answer by saying 'Kermit', then we can infer that they have analyzed the *wh* word as object of the embedded verb *help* (the 'long-distance' (LD) interpretation).[5]

Table 7.7 summarizes the results of this part of de Villiers et al.'s experiment; the LD response corresponds to the intrepretation that associates the *wh* word with the embedded clause. As these results show, children preferred the interpretation in which the *wh* word is associated with the less deeply embedded gap, although they evidently were capable of linking it to the gap in the embedded clause as well.

An interesting and unexpected finding of this research was that the younger children gave the LD response more frequently than the older children (de Villiers et al., pp. 276–77). De Villiers et al. (p. 278) suggest that the younger children may not realize that the matrix verb *ask,* which was used in all their test sentences, permits an NP complement in the indirect question pattern (as in *I asked [John] [to leave]*). (De Villiers et al. note that no instances of this pattern occur in the extensive spontaneous speech samples collected from Adam, Eve, or Sarah; see also note 4.)

There is perhaps another possibility, however. As I explain in more detail in section 5, there is a tendency to link 'unassociated elements' with the most recently heard clause even if this violates grammatical principles. It is conceivable that young children, for whom the length and complexity of the stimulus sentences must be quite demanding to begin with, succumb to this strategy more frequently than older children. Indeed, it is quite possible that the younger children in de Villiers et al.'s study even have difficulty remembering the matrix verb by the time they have finished processing the stimulus sentence: as reported in chapter 6, section 1, Phinney (1981) has found that 3-year-old children often delete the matrix subject and verb when attempting to imitate biclausal sentences.

Overall, then, de Villiers et al.'s results suggest that gaps in embedded clauses are relatively difficult, all other things being equal. However, it is unclear at this time whether there is a developmental stage in which such patterns are actually

Table 7.7 Results of the Long-Distance Study (percentages) (from de Villiers, Roeper, and Vainikka 1990:270)

Sentence Type	LD Interpretation	Non-LD Interpretation
wh argument	32	68
wh adjunct	44	50

ruled out or simply disfavored. Additional research with a wider range of sentence types (including both finite and infinitival embedded clauses) and younger children is needed to shed light on this question.

Is There a Subject–Object Asymmetry in Embedded Clauses?

A further test of the depth of embedding hypothesis involves the contrast illustrated in (20).

(20)   a. *Subject gap in an embedded clause:*
        Who [$_S$ do you [$_{VP}$ think [$_S$ __ saw Mary]]]? *complexity rating = 3*
    b. *Object gap in an embedded clause:*
        Who [$_S$ do you [$_{VP}$ think [$_S$ Mary [$_{VP}$ saw __]]]? *complexity rating = 4*

The two patterns are similar in terms of inversion (both have it in the matrix clause) and canonical word order (neither follows it), but they differ in terms of the depth of the gap associated with the *wh* word: it is separated from the associated *wh* word by three XP nodes in the first case and by four in the second.

Stromswold (1995) observes that 11 of the 12 children whose spontaneous speech she studied (see the discussion in section 2) produced biclausal questions involving the extraction of a *wh* word from the direct object position in an embedded clause; in contrast, only one produced the comparable pattern with extraction from the embedded subject position, and he did so only at age 5;0. On the other hand, Crain and Thornton (1991:333 n.) report that in an experiment designed to test the '*that*-trace effect' (see section 4), children had less difficulty producing embedded clauses with subject gaps than ones with object gaps. (Unfortunately, no scores are given.)

Yoshinaga (1996) used a production task (see the discussion of the Wilhelm and Hanna experiment in section 2 of this chapter) to elicit biclausal subject and object *wh* questions from 17 children aged 3 and 4. The children were far more successful at producing subject *wh* questions than object *wh* questions (75% vs. 51%, respectively)—consistent with the idea that gaps are disfavored in proportion to their depth of embedding. However, it is unclear how this result can be reconciled with Stromswold's findings concerning children's spontaneous speech. One possibility is that there are simply more opportunities in spontaneous speech to produce biclausal object questions: for the independent reason discussed in the next section, extraction of a subject phrase (but not an object) is blocked when the clause begins with the complementizer *that*. Moreover, many (perhaps most) complement clauses in biclausal sentences are infinitival (e.g., *We decided [. to visit Mary]*), in which case the embedded subject is not overt and therefore not able to be questioned.

4. The *that*-Trace Effect

One of the greatest puzzles in the contemporary study of syntax involves the contrast illustrated in (21).

(21) *Subject gap in embedded clause:*
    a. with complementizer *that*
        *Who did Harry say [that __ mistrusted the stranger]?
    b. without complementizer *that*
        Who did Harry say [__ mistrusted the stranger]?

As this contrast shows, a subject gap is not permitted when the complementizer *that* is present: (21a) is ungrammatical even though its counterpart without *that* is acceptable. Strangely, this contrast is found only with subject gaps. As (22) demonstrates, the presence of *that* has no effect on the admissibility of an object gap in an embedded clause.

(22) *Object gap in embedded clause:*
    a. with complementizer *that*
        Who did Harry say [that the stranger mistrusted __]?
    b. without complementizer *that*
        Who did Harry say [the stranger mistrusted __]?

Even more puzzling is the fact that subject gaps are not incompatible with complementizers in relative clauses. Hence (23) is perfectly acceptable, in contrast with (20a).

(23) *Subject gap in relative clause:*
    I know the people [that __ mistrusted the stranger].

The classic statement of the contrasts found in (21)–(23) involves the 'filter' paraphrased in (24), which blocks a string consisting of the complementizer *that* and a subject gap (or 'trace') in a non-relative clause. (There have been numerous attempts to derive this filter from a more general grammatical principle; see Rizzi 1990 for one proposal.)

(24) *The* that-*trace filter* (e.g., Chomsky and Lasnik 1977):
    that __
    except in a relative clause

The acquisition of the *that*-trace filter was investigated (box 7.6) by Phinney (1981). The stories that preceded the test questions were designed in such a way that each question could be answered by interpreting the bracketed S as a complement clause (call this the 'complement clause response') or a relative clause (the 'relative clause response'). This can be illustrated by considering the story asso-

Box 7.6

THE STUDY: Phinney 1981
SUBJECTS: 85 children aged 3;0–6;5, divided into four groups on the basis of their performance on a pretest requiring imitation of sentences with finite and nonfinite
   complement clauses:

   Group I   mean age = 3;7   Group II   mean age = 4;9
   Group III   mean age = 5;0   Group IV   mean age = 5;2

SENTENCE TYPES: (4 tokens of each type)
   i.   *Subject gap with* that:
        Who did the lion know [that __ swam in the pond]?
   ii. *Subject gap without* that:
        Who did the lion believe [__ swam in the pond]?
   iii. *Object gap with* that:
        Who did the dog notice [that the rooster kicked __]?
   iv. *Object gap without* that:
        Who did the horse believe [the lion hugged __]?

TASK: Children responded to questions of the above types after listening to a short
   story.

ciated with sentence type (i), the structure that contains a complementizer followed by a subject gap.

> The lion and the rooster are friends. Yesterday, the lion saw a strange dog
> swimming in the pond. While the lion was away, the rooster went swim-
> ming. *Who did the lion know that swam in the pond?*

One interpretation of the test question treats the embedded clause as complement
of the matrix verb *know*. Because this clause contains both the complementizer
that and a subject gap, it violates the *that* trace filter.

(25)

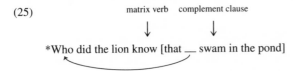

Children who assign the test sentence this interpretation respond by saying 'the
dog', since this is the animal that the lion actually saw swimming in the pond.
   Another interpretation for the test sentence involves treating the embedded S
as a relative clause that has been separated from the element it modifies—the
question word *who*. This *wh* word in turn is interpreted as the direct object of the
matrix verb *know*. (The gap in the relative clause here corresponds to a deleted
relative pronoun.)

(26)

This is the only interpretation for this sentence permitted by the adult grammar, since there is no violation of the *that*-trace filter (recall that this constraint does not apply to relative clauses). Children who choose this interpretation respond by saying 'the rooster', since this is the only animal who is known to the lion and who swam in the pond.

Table 7.8 summarizes the results of Phinney's experiment for the two youngest groups of children. The crucial scores are for the first sentence type, where the complement clause response entails a violation of the *that*-trace filter. In the other three patterns, the complement clause response is compatible with the filter since there is either no *that* (type ii) or the gap is in object position (types iii and iv). Even the youngest children in Phinney's study seem to have acquired the *that*-trace filter, since they systematically avoid the prohibited complement clause response in sentence type (i), but not the other three sentence types. The rate of complement clause responses for sentence type (i) is at 5% or below, compared to scores in the 63 to 89% range for the other sentence types.[6]

Table 7.8 Results of the *that*-Trace Experiment (percentages) (based on Phinney 1981 : 193–96)

SENTENCE TYPE	COMPLEMENT CLAUSE RESPONSE		RELATIVE CLAUSE RESPONSE	
	Group I	Group II	Group I	Group II
i	5	3	36	52
ii	63	84	17	5
iii	78	83	12	16
iv	70	89	17	0

A more recent study by Thornton (1990) (box 7.7, table 7.9) only partly confirms Phinney's finding that very young language learners obey the *that*-trace filter. A large number of questions were elicited, with all but one of the children producing questions with a gap in the embedded clause. The children used the complementizer *that* with an embedded clause containing a subject gap 18% of the time (19 times out of 105), even though this pattern violates the *that*-trace filter. Although this error rate is unexpectedly high (in light of Phinney's results), Thornton notes that the offending pattern was produced consistently by only two children (both age 3;9). Nonetheless, McDaniel, Chiu, and Maxfield (1995:723) note that on a grammaticality judgment task involving 32 children aged 2;11 to 5; 7, the acceptance rate for *that*-trace patterns was 24%, compared to 2% for adults.

Box 7.7

THE STUDY: Thornton 1990
SUBJECTS: 21 children aged 2;10–5;5 (mean age = 4;3)
SENTENCE TYPES:
      i. *Subject gap* (5 tokens):
         What do you think [(*that) __ eats bugs]?
      ii. *Object gap* (4 tokens):
         What do you think [(that) bugs eat __]?
TASK: Production. The experimenter read the children a short story and then prompted them to ask a question that involved a gap in the embedded clause. For example:

Experimenter: In this game, the rat has to guess what Cookie Monster eats. We know that Cookie Monster eats cookies, right? But ask the rat what he thinks.
Expected response from child: What do you think (that) Cookie Monster eats?

Experimenter: In this game, the rat has to guess what is in the box. We know that there are some marbles, right? But ask the rat what he thinks.
Expected response from child: What do you think (*that) is in the box?

Table 7.9 Results of Thornton's *that*-Trace Experiment
(based on Thornton 1990:88)

	With *that*	Without *that*
Embedded clause with subject gap	19[a] (18%)	86 (82%)
Embedded clause with object gap	21 (25%)	62 (75%)

a. Violates the *that*-trace filter.

The *that*-trace filter is just one of several constraints on the occurrence of gaps that have been studied in the literature on syntactic development. The next three sections of this chapter consider a series of experiments that explore the emergence of several other principles of this sort.

5. Complex NP Effects

The contrast between the *wh* questions illustrated in (27) and (28) has been of intense interest to syntacticians for almost three decades.

(27)   Who did John [$_{VP}$ believe [$_S$ that Sue met __]]?
       (cf. John believed that Sue met Mary.)
(28)   *Who did John believe [$_{NP}$ the man [$_S$ that met __]]?
       (cf. John believed the man that met Mary.)

In the first of these sentences, the gap associated with the sentence-initial *wh* word is embedded within a complement clause that is itself embedded within a VP. In (28), in contrast, the gap is embedded within a relative clause which in turn is embedded within an NP. (An NP that contains an S is known as a **complex NP,** following Ross 1967.) The latter type of sentence is ungrammatical, perhaps universally.

The constraint that distinguishes (27) from (28) is stated as in (29). (In more recent work, this constraint is usually subsumed under a more general principle, the Subjacency Condition—see, e.g., N. Chomsky 1981.)

(29)   *The Complex NP Constraint:*
       A *wh* word outside a complex NP cannot be associated with a gap inside it.

For reasons that will become clear in later chapters, it is widely believed that the acquisition device should respect the Complex NP Constraint from the earliest stages of development. An experiment (box 7.8) by Otsu (1981) provides relevant data.

Box 7.8

THE STUDY: Otsu 1981
SUBJECTS: 12 3-year-olds, 12 4-year-olds, 12 5-year-olds, 12 6-year-olds, 12 7-year-olds.
TASK: After a practice session, children were read a story such as the following and
        asked to answer the question at the end while looking at an accompanying picture
        (e.g., fig. 7.2). (There were four such stories.)
           Jim is catching a cat with a net. The cat is climbing a tree with a ladder. What is
           Jim catching a cat that is climbing a tree with ___?

If the child responds to the question in the example story by saying 'a ladder', he or she is treating the gap as part of the relative clause, as in (30), since *with a ladder* describes the climbing.

(30)   Jim is catching [$_{NP}$ a cat [$_S$ that is climbing a tree with a ladder]].

If, on the other hand, the child responds by saying 'a net', then he or she is associating the gap with the higher S, as in (31), since *with a net* describes the catching and not the climbing.

(31)   Jim is catching [$_{NP}$ a cat [$_S$ that is climbing a tree]] with a net.

Of course, only the latter interpretation is consistent with the prohibition against associating a *wh* phrase with a gap embedded inside a complex NP.

Because children could not be expected to perform correctly on this task if they had not already acquired relative clause structures, two diagnostic pretests were given. In the first test, the children used toys to act out the meaning of three relative clause constructions such as (32) (Otsu 1981:67).

FIGURE 7.2 A Sample Picture (from Otsu 1981:65)

(32)   The cow kissed the horse [that jumped over the elephant].

In the second diagnostic test, the children had to repeat four relative clause structures equal in length to the sentences used in the gap interpretation test, as in (33) (p. 70). In each case an accompanying picture was provided.

(33)   Susan is chasing a boy who is hitting a rat with a stick.

The criterion for passing the gap interpretation test was 3 correct answers out of 4; for the diagnostic tests, the criterion for success was 2 out of 3 on the toy manipulation task and 3 out of 4 on the repetition task. Table 7.10 provides information about the number of children passing and failing Otsu's tests. Given that the acquisition device is supposed to respect the Complex NP Constraint from the earliest stages of development, it is reassuring to find that a large number of subjects (21 in all) passed both the diagnostic tests and the gap interpretation test, thereby demonstrating knowledge of the Complex NP Constraint. It is also not surprising to see that 23 children failed both the diagnostic tests and the gap interpretation test: as noted earlier, children who are not familiar with relative clause structures cannot be expected to respond correctly on tasks that presuppose knowledge of such structures.

The nine children in the first row of the fail column represent a more puzzling case, since they failed the diagnostic tests but somehow succeeded on the gap

Table 7.10 Results of Otsu's Tests (number of children)
(from Otsu 1981:82)

GAP INTERPRETATION TEST	DIAGNOSTIC TESTS		
	Pass	Fail	Total
Pass	21	9	30
Fail	7	23	30
Total	28	32	60

interpretation test. Presumably, their success can be attributed either to guessing or to use of a nonlinguistic strategy of some sort. More problematic, however, are the seven children in the second row of the pass column who passed the diagnostic test but failed the gap interpretation test. These children constitute over 10% of the test group (even higher percentages occur in variations of this experiment subsequently reported by Otsu), and their performance cannot simply be ignored.

Crain and Fodor (1984) approached this problem in an interesting way: they gave Otsu's gap interpretation test to adults and found that these subjects made about as many mistakes as did the children in the original study. Crain and Fodor suggest that the errors made by their adult subjects and by Otsu's children can be attributed to the operation of an independently attested processing strategy. They note that in sentences such as (34), there is a strong tendency to associate the italicized PP with the embedded clause rather than with the matrix clause.

(34)   Jim is drawing a monkey that is scratching its head *with a crayon.*

Hence, the preferred interpretation of (34) is that the monkey is using a crayon to scratch its head and not that Jim is using a crayon to draw the monkey.

(35)   a. *favored interpretation* (*with a crayon* is in the embedded S):
          Jim is drawing [$_{NP}$ a monkey [$_S$ that is scratching its head with a crayon]].
       b. *disfavored interpretation* (*with a crayon* is in the higher S):
          Jim is drawing [$_{NP}$ a monkey [$_S$ that is scratching its head]] with a crayon.

This suggests that there are two competing forces in Otsu's gap interpretation task. On the one hand, the processing strategy illustrated in (35) predisposes children (and adults) to interpret the PP (and hence the gap it contains) as part of the embedded clause. On the other hand, the grammar works to block this interpretation, since the gap would then be in a clause that is itself embedded within an NP, in violation of the Complex NP Constraint.

It is conceivable that the processing strategy sometimes overrides the grammatical principle in both children and adults, allowing the deviant interpretation. If Crain and Fodor are right, though, even young children have the Complex NP

Constraint in their grammar—otherwise, there would be nothing to counteract the processing preference and they would never give a correct response.

6. *Wh* Island Effects

Another type of constraint on *wh* structures is illustrated in (36).

(36) a. What [do they know [(that) Mary gave ___ to her brother]]?
      b. *What [do they know [who Mary gave ___ to ___]]?

As expected, the *wh* word in the first of these sentences can be associated with the gap in the embedded clause. In the second sentence, though, this relationship is blocked by the *wh* word at the beginning of the embedded clause (hereafter called the **medial** *wh* word). Because of this blocking effect, the embedded clause in this pattern is sometimes referred to as a ***wh* island.**

There are many subtleties associated with *wh* islands. For one thing, it is known that the *wh* island effect is stronger when the medial *wh* word is an argument (e.g., *what* or *who*) rather than an adjunct (e.g., *how, when,* or *why*). Thus, there is a sharp contrast between (37) and (38).

(37) *Medial* wh *word is the adjunct* how:

What does Harry know [how to explain ___ to the students ___]?

(38) *Medial* wh *word is the argument* who:

*What does Harry know [who to explain ___ to ___ carefully]?

In sentence (37) the sentence-initial *wh* word can be associated with the embedded verb because the medial *wh* word (*how*) is an adjunct. In (38), in contrast, the medial *wh* word (*what*) is an argument, and the sentence-initial *wh* word cannot be associated with *explain*. We can summarize this part of the *wh* island effect as follows:[7]

(39) *The* Wh *Island Condition:*

*[Wh   [$_s$ Wh-argument . . . ___ . . .]]

In a complicated experiment mentioned earlier in this chapter, de Villiers, Roeper, and Vainikka (1990) attempted (box 7.9a) to determine the status of this constraint in early child language. As before, the question and context were designed so that the sentence-initial *wh* word could be associated with either the matrix verb (in which case the response would provide information about who was asked) or the embedded verb (the long-distance (LD) response, providing information about who was helped). A sample story for sentence type II follows the box.

Box 7.9a

THE STUDY: de Villiers, Roeper, and Vainikka 1990
SUBJECTS: 25 preschool children aged 3;7–6;11 (12 boys and 13 girls)
SENTENCE TYPES: (2 tokens of Type I; 4 tokens of Type II)
  Type I-Medial argument:
    Who did the girl ask [what to throw]?
  Type II-Medial adjunct:
    Who did Big Bird ask [how to help]?
TASK: the children had to answer the relevant *wh* questions after hearing a story illustrated by pictures.

Kermit asked Big Bird to help his friend clean up the playroom. Big Bird wanted to know how he should help. He asked Kermit, "How can I help my friend?" And, look, he helped Bert to sweep the floor. *Who did Big Bird ask how to help?*

The answer 'Kermit' (40a) indicates that the child is associating the *wh* word with a gap in the matrix clause while the answer 'his friend' (40b) indicates that the *wh* word is linked to a gap in the embedded clause. In this way, the experimenters were able to use the children's answers (table 7.11) to determine whether they respected the *Wh* Island Condition.

(40) a. *First interpretation; answer = 'Kermit':*

      Who did Big Bird ask __ [how . to help __]?

    b. *Second interpretation; answer = 'his friend':*

      Who did Big Bird ask [how . to help __ __]?

Because a medial *wh* adjunct does not create a *wh* island, the grammar permits either response in this case. However, the medial *wh* argument in sentence type I ensures that *who* can only be associated with the matrix verb in that case; associating it with the embedded verb would violate the *Wh* Island Condition. The children almost never associated the sentence-initial *wh* word with the embedded verb (the LD response) in sentences that contain a medial *wh* argument (type I). In

Table 7.11 Results of the *Wh* Island Study (percentage)
(based on de Villiers et al. 1990:270)

Sentence Type	LD Response	Non-LD Response	Other
I: medial argument	2	70	28
II: medial adjunct	30	63	7

contrast, they did make this association in almost one third of their responses to sentences in which the medial *wh* word is an adjunct (type II). Thus, even pre-school children apparently recognize that a medial *wh* argument creates an island.

A SECOND *WH* ISLAND EFFECT

A second *wh* island effect is illustrated in (41)–(42), where the sentence-initial *wh* word is an adjunct (rather than an argument, as in the previous examples). Note that these sentences are ungrammatical on the interpretation indicated by the arrows, with *when* associated with the embedded clause.

(41)   *Initial* wh *word is an adjunct; medial* wh *word is an argument:*

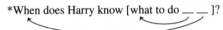

(42)   *Initial* wh *word is an adjunct; medial* wh *word is an adjunct:*

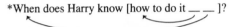

As these sentences show, a sentence-initial *wh* adjunct cannot be associated with an element in an embedded clause, regardless of whether the medial *wh* word is an argument (as in (41)) or an adjunct (as in (42)). We can therefore extend our earlier *Wh* Island Condition (39) by adding part (b), as in (43).

(43)   *The* Wh *Island Condition:*

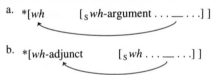

De Villiers et al.'s study included (box 7.9b) the sentence types needed to determine whether preschool children are aware of the second type of *wh* island effect.

Box 7.9b

SENTENCE TYPES: sentences with initial *wh* adjunct (4 tokens of Type III; 2 tokens of the Type IV) [a]

    Type III: Medial argument:
    How did Kermit ask [who to help]?
    Type IV: Medial adjunct:
    When did the boy know [how he hurt himself]?
TASK: the children had to answer the relevant questions after hearing a story illustrated by pictures.

a. Note that the embedded clause is infinitival in sentence type III but finite in type IV.

Table 7.12 Results with a Sentence-Initial Adjunct
(percentage) (based on de Villiers et al.
1990:270)

Sentence Type	LD Response	Non-LD Response	Other
III: medial argument	8	23	69
IV: medial adjunct	6	48	46

Table 7.13 Incidence of Answering
the Medial *wh* Word (based on
Roeper and de Villiers 1992:212)

Sentence Type	Percentage
I	28
II	4
III	68
IV	40

Here, the crucial issue has to do with whether the sentence-initial *wh* word is taken to ask about the embedded verb (a violation of the *Wh* Island Condition) or the matrix verb (a fully acceptable interpretation). Table 7.12 indicates how the children in de Villiers et al.'s experiment responded to these sentences. (We will discuss the status of the responses in the 'other' category shortly.) Once again, the children's responses suggested an awareness of the *wh* island effect, since fewer than 10% of the answers were of the long-distance type, in which the sentence-initial *wh* word is linked with a gap inside the *wh* island.

One other aspect of de Villiers et al.'s study requires comment here. In all, three ungrammatical sentence types (i.e., type I in table 7.11 and types III and IV in table 7.12), a large portion of the children's responses (table 7.13) did not involve associating the sentence-initial *wh* word with either the matrix verb or the embedded verb (see the 'Other' category in the two tables). Rather, the children ignored the sentence-initial *wh* word and answered the medial *wh* word instead. Thus, in response to a sentence such as *How did Kermit ask [who to call]*, they gave a response such as 'Big Bird', thereby answering the *who*-question rather than the *how*-question. De Villiers, Roeper, and Vainikka (1990:281) explain this error type by suggesting that the children are taking the matrix *wh* word to be a 'scope marker' for the medial *wh* word, so that the latter element is interpreted as if it were the sentence-initial *wh* word and therefore required an answer. They claim that a mechanism of this type is attested in adult German, and Thornton (1995:151) reports finding instances of it in the biclausal *wh* questions such as (44) elicited from one of 28 English-speaking children (aged 2;10–5;5) in a production task (p. 146).

(44)   [*What* do you think [*which animal* says "woof woof "]]? (Tiffany, age 4;9)

An additional 3 children systematically produced patterns such as (45), in which a copy of the fronted *wh* phrase appears at the beginning of the embedded clause.

(45)   [*Who* do you think [*who*'s under there]]?
         [*What* do you think [*what* Cookie Monster eats]]?

McDaniel, Chiu, and Maxfield (1995:723) report that on a grammaticality judgment task involving 32 children aged 2;11 to 5;7, patterns such as these were accepted 36% of the time. (An especially intriguing feature of McDaniel et al.'s results is that children who accepted such patterns also accepted sentences containing *that*-trace sequences; see section 4.)

Although these facts point toward a grammatical phenomenon, various considerations suggest the possibility of a processing explanation. First, Stromswold (1995:42) claims that children never produce such patterns in their spontaneous speech. Second, as de Villiers et al. note (p. 278), the children who were most likely to answer the medial *wh* words were the younger participants in the experiment—the very subjects who exhibited a tendency to focus on the second clause in biclausal sentences (see section 3). Third, the one sentence type that rarely triggered an answer to the medial *wh* word was pattern II (see table 7.11)—the only structure in which the sentence-initial *wh* word can be grammatically associated with the embedded verb.

We might therefore suppose that in processing all four sentence types, the young children try to link the sentence-initial *wh* word with the second (embedded) clause. While successful in pattern II, this strategy fails in patterns I, III, and IV, where the embedded clause is an island (fig. 7.3). As a result, the sentence-initial *wh* word cannot be assigned a grammatical relation, and attempts to process it are abandoned. Because they know that they are supposed to answer a *wh* ques-

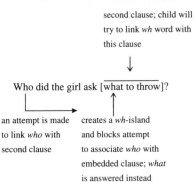

FIGURE 7.3 Strategy That Leads to Answering the Medial *wh* Word

tion to satisfy the experimenter, the children respond to the *wh* word that is already in the embedded clause in these three patterns, thereby answering the medial *wh* word.

7. Adjunct Island Effects

Yet another type of island constraint underlies the contrast between (46) and (47).

(46) a. Who did the man decide [that he should consult __]?
      b. Who did the man decide [to consult __]?
(47) a. *Who did the man decide [after he consulted __]?
      b. *Who did the man decide [after consulting __]?

The crucial difference between these two sentences is that whereas the gap lies within a complement (direct object) clause in (46), it occurs inside an adjunct (modifier) clause in (47). The latter pattern violates the Adjunct Island Condition in (48).

(48) *The Adjunct Island Condition:*

$$*[Wh \qquad [_{Adjunct} \cdots \underline{\quad} \cdots]]$$

As with the other phenomena considered in this chapter, questions arise as to when adjunct island effects emerge in the course of the language acquisition process. This issue is addressed in an experimental study (box 7.10) carried out by

Box 7.10

THE STUDY: Goodluck, Sedivy, and Foley 1989
SUBJECTS: 10 3-year-olds, 10 4-year-olds, 10 5-year-olds
SENTENCE TYPES: (3 tokens of each type)
> Type I—Eat *with adjunct clause:*
>> What did the fox eat *[before singing]*?
> Type II—Ask *with clausal complement:*
>> Who did the zebra ask *[to kiss]*?
> Type III—Ask *with adjunct clause:*
>> Who did the elephant ask *[before helping]*?

TASK: The children were presented 'stories' such as the following:
> The fox ran down to the river. First he ate an ice cream cone. Then he whistled a tune he'd heard on the radio. The fox felt pretty happy. *What did the fox eat before whistling?*
> The answer 'an ice cream cone' indicates that the children associate the gap with the matrix clause, while the answer 'a tune' implies that the gap is associated with the verb in the embedded clause.

Goodluck, Sedivy, and Foley (1989) and replicated by Goodluck, Foley, and Sedivy (1992).

Children's responses for sentence types I and III fell into three categories (table 7.14): (a) those that treated the *wh* word as if it originated in the matrix clause; (b) those that treated the *wh* word as if it originated in the adjunct clause; and (c) 'other'—inappropriate responses that fell into neither of the first two categories. Response type (a) but not (b) indicates respect for the Adjunct Island Condition. As these results show, even the youngest children showed a strong preference for responses that associate the *wh* word with the matrix clause rather than the adjunct clause, as required by the Adjunct Island Condition. Apparent violations of the Adjunct Island Condition are not infrequent, however, especially among three-year-olds (13% and 20% for types I and III, respectively). But, as the authors note (p. 129 n. 6), these responses can plausibly be attributed to the processing preference that seeks to link unassociated elements with the last clause (see previous sections).

Quite a different set of responses was observed for sentence type II, which involves no adjunct island (table 7.15). Here, even the youngest children were able to associate the *wh* word with either the matrix clause (37% of their responses) or the embedded complement clause (43%). Once again, then, we have evidence that a relatively abstract constraint of adult grammar is accessible to the acquisition device from a very early point in the language learning process.

Table 7.14 Interpretation of the *wh* Word in Sentences with Adjunct Clauses (percentage)

	Type I			Type III		
Age (yrs.)	Matrix S	Adjunct S	Other	Matrix S	Adjunct S	Other
3	50	13	36	47	20	33
4	60	7	33	70	7	23
5	90	3	7	100	0	0

Table 7.15 Results of the Comprehension Task for Sentence Type II (percentage)

Age (yrs.)	Upper clause	Embedded clause	Other
3	37	43	20
4	23	53	23
5	53	40	7

8. Conclusion

The major theme of this chapter has been the status of gaps and their relationship to a 'matching' *wh* word elsewhere in the sentence. From the developmental pattern observed in children's speech and from the errors they make, three conclusions can be drawn about how the acquisition device deals with this type of structure. First, there is a preference for sentences without gaps (this is why children's early *wh* questions involve the formulaic copula constructions described in section 1). Second, in cases where a gap must be posited, the acquisition device prefers it to be relatively close to the matching NP (this is why object gaps are more difficult than subject gaps, for example). Finally, for reasons that we will explore in later chapters, the acquisition device does not permit certain gap patterns at all, as shown by the various 'island' effects discussed in sections 4 through 7.

8

Inversion

All languages need a way to distinguish between statements and questions. A syntactic process that is frequently used for this purpose in the world's languages (Greenberg 1963; Steele et al. 1981) is **inversion,** a change in the relative order of a verb and its subject. In English, for example, inversion applies to auxiliary verbs, giving the sentence types illustrated in (1).

(1) Has Harry finished the book?
     Can Lynda win the race?
     What were you doing?

As was the case with the *wh* questions considered in the preceding chapter, syntactic theories differ in terms of their treatment of inversion patterns. In transformational grammar, for example, a movement rule is posited to account for the appearance of an auxiliary verb to the left of the subject (e.g. Akmajian and Heny 1975; N. Chomsky 1986a). On the other hand, many other syntactic theories assume that these patterns are formed directly, with the auxiliary in the initial position to begin with (see, e.g., Gazdar et al. 1985:60ff. for generalized phrase structure grammar; Bach 1983 for categorial grammar; and Pinker 1984:276ff. for lexical-functional grammar).

It is not practical to try to describe or compare these various theories here. Suffice it to note that all approaches treat the inversion pattern as somehow special or unusual in English, acknowledging that it can occur with only a small number of verbs (cf. (2)).

(2) *Goes John?
     *Want they to stay?
     ?*Ought John to leave?

As we will see directly, the special status of inversion also has developmental correlates.

1. The Development of Inversion in *Yes–No* Questions

In the early stages of multiword speech, children do not have auxiliary verbs and hence cannot form questions by inversion. Instead, intonation is used to signal a *yes–no* question, as in the examples in (3) from Klima and Bellugi's (1966) pioneering study of the development of interrogatives in the speech of Adam, Eve, and Sarah.

(3)   Fraser water?
       Mommy eggnog?
       See hole?
       I ride train?
       Sit chair?
       No ear?
       Ball go?

At about the time that children's MLU reaches 3.5 morphemes, auxiliary + verb combinations make their appearance. (As noted by Pinker (1984:261), this is also the point at which other multiverb structures begin to emerge; see chap. 6 for discussion). From the beginning, auxiliaries occur only with 'bare' VP complements, as in (4), just as they do in the adult language (Aldridge 1989:109–11).

(4)   I *can't* see it. (Chrissie, 23 mos.)
       We *could* watch. (Michael, 24 mos.)
       Mummy *will* do this. (Jem, 24 mos.)
       I *will* get it. (Angela, 25 mos.)
       You *can* see yourself. (Elizabeth, 26 mos.)

Structures such as *I can to go there*, in which the infinitival marker *to* is over-generalized to the complement of an auxiliary, are not attested.

Based on a study of spontaneous speech samples from 16 children between the ages of 2 and 5, Kuczaj and Maratsos (1983) report that inversion patterns emerge gradually, occurring earlier with some auxiliary verbs than with others. Table 8.1 summarizes Kuczaj and Maratsos's findings for two children from whom weekly speech samples (30–60 minutes per session) were collected over an extended period. (The criterion for 'acquisition' here is 90% correct use in obligatory contexts.)[1] Three facts are of special interest here. First, the various verbs listed in this table make their first appearance in inverted structures at different points over a period of several months. The auxiliary *can*, for instance, appears in inverted *yes–no* questions in Ben's speech at age 2;10—three months before auxiliary *is*.

Second, the only verbs to occur in inversion patterns are those that can do so in adult speech. As noted by Pinker (1984:273) and Aldridge (1989:109), non-auxiliary verbs are virtually never inverted. The type of error in (5), cited by Erreich, Valian, and Winzemer (1980:163), is extremely rare. (Indeed, this may not be an inversion error at all: as noted in section 1 of chap. 4, young language learners sometimes use a verb-initial order with verbs such as *go* even in declarative sentences.)

(5)   Goes paci[fier] in mouth? [produced sometime between 1;9 and 1;11]

Table 8.1 Age of Acquisition of Inverted
and Non-inverted Verbs
(from Kuczaj and Maratsos
1983 : 442 – 43)

Form	Non-inverted	Inverted
	Abe	
can	2;5	2;11
is (copula)	2;7	3;1
are (copula)	2;9	3;0
is (auxiliary)	3;0	3;0
are (auxiliary)	3;0	3;1
will	3;0	3;1
	Ben	
can	2;6	2;10
is (copula)	2;4	2;8
are (copula)	2;7	2;10
is (auxiliary)	2;7	3;1
are (auxiliary)	2;10	3;0
will	2;10	2;10

Even verbs such as *gotta* and *hafta,* which are semantically similar to the auxiliaries *must* and *should,* are not used by language learners in inversion patterns as in (6) (Kuczaj and Maratsos 1983; Pinker 1984 : 273; Stromswold 1990 : 163).

(6)   * Gotta I go?
       * Hafta they be here?
       * Better she do that?

These facts suggest that the acquisition device quickly identifies the verbs that can occur in the inversion pattern, either because it is extremely conservative or because (as Stromswold 1990 has observed) it recognizes the category of auxiliary verbs from an early point and restricts inversion to members of this class.

A third fact of interest in table 8.1 is that auxiliaries appear first in non-inverted structures. (This is despite the fact that sentence-internal auxiliaries tend to be phonetically reduced and hence less perceptible than their inverted counterparts.) In the speech of Abe, for instance, *can* was used in declarative sentences such as *You can do it* a full six months before it appeared regularly in question structures such as *Can you do it?.* A comparable finding is noted by Davis (1986) for the speech of a child from age 2;9 to 3;6. In the most comprehensive study of this question to date, Stromswold (1990) examined longitudinal speech samples from 14 children, reporting that VP-internal auxiliaries emerge at an average age of 2.94 years compared to 3.17 years for inverted auxiliaries (p. 95).

Still, there may be exceptions among individual children. Bellugi (1971:98) reports that inversion occurred immediately upon the emergence of auxiliary verbs in the speech of Adam, and Aldridge (1989:129) observes that auxiliaries emerged simultaneously in "pre- and post-subject position" for several children that she studied. There are even reports of auxiliaries occurring first in inversion patterns (e.g., Limber 1973:178 and, for a summary, Aldridge 1989:126).

Is it possible to reconcile such seemingly contradictory findings? No developmental study can examine all the utterances produced by a language learner. Typically, the data for a particular child consist of a series of one-hour speech samples that are collected every two to four weeks. Although the data may include thousands of utterances, these constitute only a fraction of the child's total speech production for any particular developmental stage. It is always possible, then, that apparent inconsistencies across children reflect gaps in the developmental record rather than differences in the operation of the acquisition device. This is especially likely in cases where claims are being made about the use of a particular word in a particular structure, as is the case with auxiliary verbs in inversion patterns. Since the studies reporting that auxiliaries appear first in inversion patterns are in a minority, and since none of these reports provides information about the size of the speech sample on which it is based (Aldridge 1989:132), some skepticism is obviously in order. This leaves us with the tentative conclusion that auxiliaries in VP-internal position emerge either before or at the same time as auxiliaries in inversion patterns.

2. The Development of Inversion in *wh* Questions

As with *yes–no* questions, the absence of auxiliary verbs in early *wh* questions precludes the possibility of subject–verb inversion. Based on the results of an imitation task conducted with 20 children ranging in age from 3;2 to 4;10, Kuczaj and Brannick (1979:48–49) conclude that inversion in *wh* questions emerges in a piecemeal fashion. In general, they report, auxiliary placement is mastered first in *where* or *what* questions and somewhat later in questions beginning with *when, who, why,* and *how.* The generality of this developmental pattern has been questioned by Erreich (1984) and Davis (1986), but Stromswold's survey of longitudinal speech samples from 14 children revealed virtually the same order: inversion in early speech was more common with *who, what, where,* and *how* and less frequent with *which, when,* and *why* (1990:197).

De Villiers (1991:162) notes an intriguing generalization about inversion and *wh* words in the speech of four children that she studied. Not only did inversion in *wh* questions emerge at different times for different *wh* words; its appearance with a particular *wh* word took place only after that word had begun to occur in embedded clauses. In the speech of Adam, for instance, inversion did not take place in *what* questions until he had begun to produce sentences such as *I wonder what that is,* with *what* in the embedded clause. It is unclear at this time whether this a general pattern in syntactic development.

The most celebrated generalization about the development of inversion in *wh* questions is undoubtedly Klima and Bellugi's (1966) observation that such patterns emerge only after inversion has appeared in *yes–no* questions. Adam, Eve, and Sarah began to use inversion in the latter type of construction at about the time that their MLUs attained 2.75, as in (7).

(7)   *Sample* yes–no *questions* (MLU 2.75–3.5; from Klima and Bellugi 1966:204):
       Does the kitty stand up?
       Will you help me?
       Can I have a piece of paper?
       Did I see that in my book?

During this same period, however, inversion in *wh* questions was infrequent; see (8).

(8)   *Sample* wh *questions* (MLU 2.75–3.5; from Klima and Bellugi 1966:205):
       Where the other Joe *will* drive?
       Where I *should* put it when I make it up?
       What he *can* ride in?
       Why kitty *can't* stand up?
       Why he *don't* know how to pretend?
       Which way they *should* go?

Table 8.2 summarizes the relative frequency of inverted modals in *yes–no* and *wh* questions in Adam's speech. The crucial figures are from the second line, which show a large proportion of inverted auxiliaries in *yes–no* questions (198 inverted vs. 7 uninverted). In contrast, only a small proportion of the auxiliary verbs in *wh* questions undergo inversion (9 inverted vs. 22 uninverted). By the next sample (at age 3;8), this asymmetry is no longer evident as inversion becomes the dominant pattern in *wh* questions.

Table 8.2 Modal Auxiliaries in Adam's Questions
(from Bellugi 1971:97, 99)

	yes–no QUESTIONS		*wh* QUESTIONS	
APPROX. AGE	Inverted	Uninverted	Inverted	Uninverted
3;0	0	1	0	3
3;5	198	7	9	22
3;8	no data		33	5
4;3	no data		27	4

Klima and Bellugi's finding invites the suggestion that inverted *wh* questions might be harder to produce than *yes–no* questions because they involve an extra departure from the canonical word order of English: both the auxiliary verb and one of the verb's arguments (the *wh* word) appear to the left of the subject. An obvious problem with this line of reasoning, as noted by Bellugi (1971:101), is that it leaves open the possibility that language learners could 'simplify' *wh* questions by retaining inversion but not doing *Wh* Movement. This would yield the structures in (9), which—like the patterns in (8)—involve a single departure from the canonical word order of English.

(9)   *Can I go where?
        *Should I eat what?

However, such structures occur rarely, if ever, in child speech (Brown 1968; Pinker 1984:276; Stromswold 1995:18).

The generality of the asymmetry between *yes–no* questions and *wh* questions with respect to inversion is quite widely accepted (see, e.g., de Villiers 1991:161; Weverink 1991:19). However, relatively few studies have been able to replicate Klima and Bellugi's findings. A preference for inversion in *yes–no* questions was observed by Kuczai and Maratsos (1975:106) in Abe's performance on an imitation task at age 2;9 and by Labov and Labov (1978:6) in their daughter Jesse's speech around age 3;10. (The latter observation is particularly noteworthy since Labov and Labov's data includes ALL *wh* questions asked by Jesse over a two and one-half year period beginning at age 2;2.) On the other hand, Brown (1968:285) questions the typicality of the data summarized in table 8.2, noting that Adam produced far more examples of uninverted *wh* questions than either Eve or Sarah, the other two children that he studied. Johnson (1981:306) introduces a different cautionary note. She reports that in her study of the naturalistic speech of 8 children aged 1;6 to 3;0, inversion was more common in *yes–no* questions than in *wh* questions, but that this could be attributed to the fact that the latter patterns tended not to include an auxiliary verb.

An experiment (box 8.1) by Ingram and Tyack (1979) provides an even more direct challenge to the view that inversion is more likely in *yes–no* questions than in *wh* questions. In analyzing their results, Ingram and Tyack eliminated sentences that were identical to other tokens in the data. Hence, frequent structures such as *What's that?* were counted only once. As the results reported in table 8.3 show, there was no evidence of a stage at which children employed inversion in *yes–no* questions but not *wh* questions. (The subjects are divided into 5 groups based on the length in morphemes of the longest question structure they produced.)

Box 8.1

THE STUDY: Ingram and Tyack 1979

SUBJECTS: 21 children between the ages of 2;0 and 3;11.

TASK: spontaneous production. After an initial interview and screening, parents were instructed to write down every question their child produced until a total of 225 such structures had been collected.

Table 8.3 Questions Containing Auxiliaries
That Exhibit Inversion (percentages)

Group	Longest Utterance	*yes–no*	*wh*
I	7 morphemes	55	77
II	9	81	91
III	11	91	96
IV	13	98	95
V	14+	97	98

Further disconfirmation of the claim that inversion develops later in *wh* questions comes from a study (box 8.2) by Erreich (1984). Across all children, only 36% of the *wh* questions lacked inversion, compared to 51% of the *yes–no* questions. Ten of the children in the study treated inversion as optional in both question types, while an additional five used non-inverted forms only in *yes–no* questions.

Box 8.2

THE STUDY: Erreich 1984

SUBJECTS: 18 children aged 2;5–3;0 with an MLU range of 2.66–4.26

TASK: Production of *wh* and *yes–no* questions was elicited during play sessions by use of the indirect questions below. Structures identical to tokens found elsewhere were not scored.

SENTENCE TYPES: (15–30) tokens per play session)
    Elicitation of yes–no *questions:*
      Ask Anne if she can swim.
    Elicitation of wh *questions:*
      Ask Anne her mommy's name.
      Ask Anne where to put the book.

In sum, there seems to be no universal tendency among English-speaking children to master inversion first in either *wh* questions or *yes–no* questions. Indeed, Stromswold documents variation from child to child in this regard: among the children whose longitudinal speech samples she studied, three inverted more frequently in *yes–no* questions, four produced more inversions in *wh* questions, and six used the inversion pattern with equal frequency in both types of questions (1990:169).

3. Inversion Errors

As already noted, from its earliest manifestations inversion is restricted to auxiliary verbs, with the result that overgeneralizations such as **Jump man* (for *Did the man jump?*) are unattested. However, this does not mean that inversion is not overgeneralized in other ways. Citing Stromswold (1990), Déprez and Pierce (1993:59–60) note that children aged 2 to 4 incorrectly apply inversion in 14% of their *how come* questions, as in (10a), and 10% of their embedded questions, as in (10b). (See also de Villiers 1991; Weverink 1991; Plunkett 1991.)

(10) a. How come is that?
          Why how come is that?
      b. I don't know [who is that].
          I don't know [what is his name].
          I don't know [what do you think it is].

Perhaps the single most discussed inversion error involves the occasional overuse of an auxiliary verb illustrated in (11).

(11) Why *did* you *did* scare me? (3;2) (Stromswold 1990:55)
      Is it*'s* Stan's radio? (2;6) (Kuczaj 1976:423)
      How *can* he *can* look? (4;8) (Menyuk 1969:76)
      What *shall* we *shall* have? (3;2) (McNeill 1970:18)

In these sentences, a single auxiliary verb occurs twice—once to the left of the subject and once to its right. A variant of this error, especially common with irregular verbs, involves 'double tensing', as illustrated in (12). These examples, produced by a child between the ages of 1;10 and 2;6, are from Hurford 1975.

(12) What *did* you *bought*?
      What *did* you *did*?
      Did you *came* home?

Mayer, Erreich, and Valian (1978) propose a grammatical explanation for the double auxiliary patterns. The key assumption is that movement transformations consist of two parts—an initial operation that copies the target element (the auxiliary verb in the case of inversion) into its surface structure position and a subsequent operation that deletes it from its deep structure position, as in (13).

(13) *Inversion via copying and deletion:*
      deep structure: they will go
      after copying: will they will go
      after deletion: will they $\emptyset$ go

On this view, the doubling errors in (12) occur when the deletion component of the inversion transformation fails to apply. (A version of the auxiliary copying proposal was first put forward by Hurford 1975. For commentary, see Kuczaj 1976; Prideaux 1976; Maratsos and Kuczaj 1978; Fay 1978.)

Although recent work in transformational grammar (e.g., N. Chomsky 1993) does indeed adopt the 'copying and deletion' view of movement rules, problems arise with its application to the acquisition facts. As Mayer et al. themselves note (p. 11), copying errors should also occur with '*wh* movement', giving structures such as *What did I see what*. However, such utterances in child language are rare at best. (Goodluck and Solan 1979:87 suggests that only 'local' rules like inversion, which moves an element over an adjacent category, are susceptible to doubling errors, but they offer no explanation for why this should be so.)

What, then, leads children to make doubling errors? Such errors are infrequent and are apparently not typical of any child's question structures.[2] (Stromswold 1990:60 estimates that double tensing errors ocur in no more than 0.4% of children's question structures.) It is therefore unlikely that they reflect an incorrectly *formulated* rule of the grammar. A more probable explanation is that children are having occasional trouble *applying* a particular rule. A detailed proposal about precisely how this happens has been put forward by Nakayama (1987), who identifies a potential processing problem with inversion structures. Nakayama's key observation is that English *yes–no* questions can be formulated with inversion and rising intonation, as in (14a), or with rising intonation alone, as in (14b).

(14)   a. *With inversion and rising intonation:*
            Can he go↑
        b. *With rising intonation alone:*
            He *can* go↑

Nakayama suggests that children sometimes select the inversion option when they start to form a question (hence the sentence-initial auxiliary verb), but subsequently become confused and revert to the second option, which requires the auxiliary verb to occur after the subject. This miscue leads to the duplication of an auxiliary verb that is characteristic of the doubling error.[3] (Nakayama's proposal, which he calls the **Syntactic Blends Hypothesis,** is reminiscent of an earlier suggestion by Prideaux (1976) to the effect that children simultaneously apply the generalization that auxiliary verbs appear after the subject and the generalization that in question structures they appear to the left of the subject.)

A similar explanation presumably accounts for the doubling errors involving inflection that are exemplified in (15). (Such errors are most common when the auxiliary verb is *do* and the main verb is irregular; Maratsos and Kuczai 1978: 341, 343.)

(15)   What did you found? (1;10–2;6) (Hurford 1975:300)
        What did you bought? (1;10–2;6) (ibid.)
        What did you got? (1;10–2;6) (ibid.)
        Did you came home? (1;10–2;6) (ibid.)
        Where does the wheel goes? (4;4) (Menyuk 1969:73)
        Does he makes it? (2;10) (ibid.)
        What does this does? (3;5) (ibid. 90)

Here, tense and/or agreement is incorrectly expressed twice—once on the 'fronted' auxiliary and once on the main verb. Similar errors have been noted in non–question structures, especially those where a negative intervenes between the auxiliary and the 'main' verb (Maratsos and Kuczai 1978). The examples in (16) are all from Kuczaj 1976:426.

(16)   You didn't had some. (3;1)
        She didn't goed. (3;11)
        You don't has much money. (5;0)
        I didn't saw that. (2;9)
        They didn't spilled. (3;0)
        It don't hurts. (2;8)

Nakayama proposes that syntactic blending is most likely to arise when the subject NP is particularly long, thereby creating a greater distance between the sentence-initial and sentence-medial positions that auxiliary verbs can occupy. He designed an experiment (box 8.3) to test this hypothesis; the results are depicted in table 8.4.

Box 8.3

THE STUDY: Nakayama 1987
SUBJECTS: 16 children, aged 3–5 years (mean age: 4;7)
SENTENCE TYPES: 16 sentences, of which only a subset is exemplified here.
      I. *subject containing two adjectives:*
         [The [$_{Adj}$ big] [$_{Adj}$ hungry] dog] is sleeping.
      II. *subject containing a PP:*
         [The boy [$_{PP}$ in the kitchen]] is sleeping.
      III. *subject containing a short relative clause:*
         [The girl [$_S$ who is crying]] is tired of her dolls.
      IV. *subject containing a long relative clause:*
         [The boy [$_S$ who is watching a small cat]] is upset.
TASK: Elicited production. The stimulus sentences were presented in the frame 'Ask
      Jabba if ———.' Pictures were used as props to help ensure the relevance of the
      question that the children were to ask.

Nakayama's findings support three conclusions. First, as the scores in table 8.4 indicate, subject phrases containing relative clauses (types III and IV) create more

Table 8.4 Results of Nakayama's study
(percentages) (from Nakayama
1987:120)

Type	Correct	Incorrect
I	84	16
II	97	3
III	66	34
IV	44	56

problems than subject phrases containing either PPs or adjectives. Since the type III structure is no longer than the type I or II structure, the complicating factor evidently has to do with the presence of a relative clause—presumably because it introduces a second verb into the sentence.

Second, among subject phrases containing relative clauses, the longer ones (e.g., type IV vs. type III) are more difficult (44% correct vs. 66%). This is consistent with Nakayama's hypothesis that the length of the subject phrase contributes to the likelihood of inversion errors.

Third, the length of the VP (which was varied in the sentences used in the experiment) did not significantly affect the children's responses. This is what Nakayama's hypothesis would predict: since only the subject stands between the two positions where an auxiliary verb occurs in the doubling patterns, only it should interfere with the child's production of inversion structures.

Of the mistakes made by the children in Nakayama's study, the largest number (48%) involved the doubling error illustrated in (17).

(17) *'Target' structure:*
Is [the boy who is watching Mickey] happy?
Doubling error:

Is [the boy who is watching Mickey] is happy?
               doubling error

An additional 23% of the children's errors involved the 'restarting strategy' illustrated in (18).

(18) *'Target' structure:*
Is [the boy who is watching Mickey] happy?
Restarting error:
Is [the boy who is watching Mickey], is he happy?
                    ↑
          sentence is restarted here

Here, the child places an auxiliary verb in the sentence-initial position, but restarts the utterance upon reaching the end of the subject phrase (*the boy who is watching Mickey*), this time using a pronominal subject (*he*).

4. Formulating the Inversion Rule

An interesting question arises with respect to the precise manner in which the acquisition device formulates the inversion rule in response to adult sentences such as (1) above, repeated as (19).

(19)   Has Harry finished the book?
       Can Lynda win the race?
       What were you doing?

Since the NP involved in inversion in these cases (e.g., *Harry* in the first example) is both an agent and a subject, either of the generalizations in (20) will give the right result.

(20)   a.   Place the auxiliary verb to the left of the agent.
       b.   Place the auxiliary verb to the left of the subject.

We know that the inversion rule in the adult grammar refers to the notion 'subject' rather than 'agent' since questions with nonagentive subjects, as in (21), permit inversion.

(21)   a.   *Question with theme subject:*
            Was Harry hurt in the accident?
       b.   *Question with expletive subject:*
            Were there many problems?

But how can we know whether the inversion rule used in children's grammars is sensitive to subjects rather than agents? Crain and Nakayama (1987) conducted an experiment (box 8.4) that addresses this issue. The results (table 8.5) point

Box 8.4

THE STUDY: Crain and Nakayama 1987
SUBJECTS: 14 children aged 2;9–4;8 (average age = 3;9)
SENTENCE TYPES: (two tokens of the second type and three tokens of the three other types)
    I. pretest sentences (agentive subject):
      The dog is chasing the cat.
    II. abstract subject:
      Love is good or bad.
    III. expletive subject:
      It is easy to see the little ghost.
    IV. theme subject:
      The big ghost is easy to see.
TASK: elicited production. The test sentences were embedded in the frame 'Ask Jabba if ———'; accompanying pictures provided a natural context for each question.

Table 8.5 Results of the Inversion Test
(from Crain and Nakayama
1987:540)

Type	Correct	Incorrect	Total
I	29	4	33
II	24	2	26
III	36	5	41
IV	38	3	41

Note: For reasons that are not understood, the children
performed less well on type I sentences containing *should*
(17 correct out of 26). These results are not included.

toward an inversion rule that makes reference to subjects. The fact that the children did about equally well on all structure types, including those containing expletive subjects, suggests that the acquisition device formulates the inversion rule in terms of the notion 'subject' rather than 'agent' from an early point in syntactic development.

STRUCTURE DEPENDENCE

A second issue that arises with respect to the formulation of the inversion rule has to do with the choice of verb that is to be placed to the left of the subject in cases where there is more than one auxiliary, as in (22).

(22)   She *will* think that he *can* stay.

The simplest rule would seem to be (23), which we will refer to as the 'linear rule' since the auxiliary verb to which it applies is selected on the basis of linear order.

(23)   *The linear inversion rule:*
        Place the first auxiliary verb to the left of the subject.

This rule correctly accounts for the fact that the inverted form of (22) is (24a), not (24b).

(24)   a. *Inversion of the first auxiliary verb:*

            Will she ___ think that he can stay?

        b. *Inversion of the second auxiliary verb:*

            *Can she will think that he ___ stay?

Crucially, however, if the acquisition device does characterize the inversion process in linear terms, children will make a serious error when they try to form the question equivalent of sentences like (25).

(25)   The main [who *was* reading the book] *is* studying for an exam.

The linear inversion rule gives the ungrammatical sentence in (26).

(26)   *Was the man [who ___ reading the book] is studying for an exam.

Here, the first auxiliary verb (*was*) is placed at the beginning of the sentence in accordance with the linear inversion rule. Yet the result is obviously ill-formed.

  In order to avoid such errors, the acquisition device must apparently formulate the rule in (27), which we can call the 'structural inversion rule' since it refers to a structural feature ('topmost').

(27)   *The structural inversion rule:*
       Place the auxiliary verb in the topmost clause to the left of the subject.

Because the auxiliary verb *was* in (25) is in the embedded relative clause (see (28)), it will not be affected by the structural inversion rule.

(28)

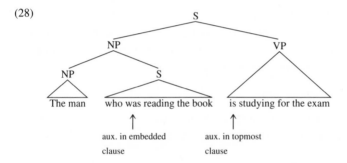

Instead, the auxiliary verb *is,* which is in the highest (or main) clause, will be placed at the beginning of the sentence—giving the grammatical question structure in (29).

(29)   Is [$_{NP}$ the man [$_S$ who was reading the book]] ___ studying for an exam.

Of course, the structural inversion rule also gives the correct result in the case of (22), repeated here as (30), in which the first auxiliary happens also to be in the topmost clause.

(30)   [$_S$ She will think [$_S$ that he can stay]].
              ↑   ↑
          aux. in topmost   aux. in embedded
              clause   clause

Does the acquisition device formulate the more complex structural inversion rule, or does it initially produce the simpler linear rule? No errors like (26) have ever been reported, but this could be because young children spontaneously produce few or no question structures that also contain a relative clause in the subject phrase. In order to determine what really happens here, it is necessary to investigate the structure experimentally. An experiment of the relevant type (box 8.5) was carried out by Crain and Nakayama (1987). They reasoned that if children had formulated the correct inversion rule, they would respond to the test sentence by producing (31) rather than (32).

Box 8.5

THE STUDY: Crain and Nakayama 1987
SUBJECTS: 30 children: 15 aged 3;2–4;7 and 15 aged 4;7–5;11
SENTENCE TYPES: (6 tokens)
    Ask Jabba if the boy who is watching Mickey Mouse is happy.
TASK: elicited production, as in the Crain and Nakayama experiment in box 8.4.

(31) *Inversion of the auxiliary in the topmost clause:*

    Is [the boy who is watching Mickey Mouse] __ happy?

(32) *Inversion of the first auxiliary:*

    *Is [the boy who __ watching Mickey Mouse] is happy?

The results of this experiment are given in table 8.6. Although the children made many errors, none produced sentences such as (32). Instead, one common mistake involved the 'restarting' error illustrated in (33).

(33) *Restarting error* (22% of all errors):
    Is the boy who is watching Mickey Mouse, *is he* happy?
                    ↑
          sentence is restarted here

As noted earlier (see (18)), children who make the restarting error successfully produce the first part of a question—in (33), for example, they produce the aux-

Table 8.6 Results of the Production Task (percentage) (from Crain and Nakayama 1987:529)

Age Group	Grammatical	Ungrammatical
I (3;2–4;7)	38	62
II (4:7–5:11)	80	20

iliary verb *is* followed by the full subject phrase. However, they then restart the utterance, this time using a pronoun as subject (e.g., *is he happy*).

The most common mistake made by the children in Crain and Nakayama's experiment is illustrated in (34). Dubbed the 'prefixing pattern', it is characterized by the presence of a sentence-initial *is* that the authors treat as a question-marking particle rather than a true inverted auxiliary.

(34) Prefixing pattern (58% of all errors):
      Is the boy who is watching Mickey Mouse is happy?

Because the prefixing pattern looks superficially like the doubling error discussed earlier, Crain and Nakayama attempted to verify that it was not the result of duplicating the first auxiliary verb (a variant of the incorrect linear inversion rule above). Since the sentences used in their experiment contain two instances of *is*— one in the embedded clause and one in the main clause—they shed no light on which verb (if either) is being duplicated when the prefix pattern is produced. Hence the need for a second experiment (box 8.6). A total of 6 errors of the type exemplified in (35) were made in response to sentence type I.

Box 8.6

THE STUDY: Crain and Nakayama 1987
SUBJECTS: ten of the children who had produced prefix patterns in experiment 1, administered two weeks earlier
SENTENCE TYPES: (2 tokens of each type)
         Type I: [The boy who *is* happy] *can* see Mickey Mouse.
         Type II: [The boy who *can* see Mickey Mouse] *is* happy.
TASK: the same as in experiment 1

---

(35) **Is* [the boy who *is* happy] *can* see Mickey Mouse?

This error could indicate either that the children use *is* as a question-marking prefix or that they are duplicating the first *is* (the one in the embedded clause). To distinguish between these two possibilities, it is necessary to consider the errors made in response to the second sentence type (i.e., *The boy who can see Mickey Mouse is happy*). If children produce the error in (36), then they are presumably copying the first auxiliary verb and are hence using a variant of the (incorrect) linear inversion rule.

(36) *Can [the boy who can see Mickey Mouse] is happy?

In fact, very few errors of any sort were made. However, the key finding was that *no* errors of the type in (36) were observed. It therefore seems reasonable to conclude that when children produce sentences such as (35), they are treating the initial *is* as an interrogative prefix rather than a copy of the verb in the embedded clause.

Indirect support for this conclusion comes from the fact that unequivocal prefix patterns have been observed in children's spontaneous speech. The sentences in (37), for example, were produced by a 3-year-old (Akmajian and Heny 1975:17).

(37) *Is* Daddy can do it?
      Is you should eat the apple?
      Is the apple juice won't spill?

Since there is no other instance of *is* in these sentences, the sentence-initial element can only be analyzed as a question-marking prefix, consistent with Crain and Nakayama's proposal. (The use of *are* and *do* as question prefixes has been noted in other children; Johnson 1981:105–6.)

The general conclusion that Crain and Nakayama draw from their experiments is that the acquisition device is designed to formulate rules in terms of structural notions such as 'topmost clause' rather than linear notions such as 'first'. This property is called **structure dependence** (e.g., N. Chomsky 1975:30ff.). By assuming that structure dependence is an inherent feature of the acquisition device, it is possible to explain how children avoid the erroneous formulation of the inversion rule (i.e., 'Place the *first* auxiliary verb at the beginning of the sentence') that would significantly impede their mastery of English sentence structure. We return to this point in our discussion of the learnability problem in part II of this book.

5. Conclusion

Inversion patterns make their appearance in child language soon (perhaps even immediately) after the acquisition of auxiliary verbs. Although some children may master inversion in *yes–no* questions earlier than in *wh* questions, roughly parallel development of inversion in both patterns seems to be more common.

From the beginning, the acquisition device formulates an inversion rule that applies to the correctly restricted class of verbs (i.e., to auxiliaries such as *will* and *can*, but not to 'semi-auxiliaries' such as *gonna* and *hafta,* or to regular verbs such as *come* and *go*). Moreover, the requirement of structure dependence is met: the inversion rule is formulated to apply to auxiliary verbs in the topmost clause and to place them to the left of the subject. Possible misformulations in terms of linear order (e.g., reference to the 'first' auxiliary in the sentence) or thematic roles (such as agent) are avoided.

9

Relative Clauses and Clefts

English has a number of different relative clause structures, including the three patterns exemplified in (1).[1]

(1)   a. They bought the car [which Sue recommended __].
        b. They bought the car [that Sue recommended __].
        c. They bought the car [∅ Sue recommended __].

As these sentences show, a relative clause can begin with a relative pronoun such as *which* or *who,* a complementizer such as *that,* or neither. However, all relative clauses share at least two features. First, they combine with a nominal (often called the **head**) whose reference they restrict. In (1), for instance, the relative clause helps narrow down the possible referents of *car* from any member of the set of automobiles to the particular vehicle that Sue recommended. Second, a relative clause contains a gap that is 'matched' with the head. Thus, in (1) it is understood that the thing recommended by Sue is a car rather than a restaurant or a store.

As in the case of *wh* questions, there are two major views on the formation of relative clauses, one employing a movement analysis and the other a feature-passing analysis. According to the former view, the gap in relative clauses is created by movement of a *wh* phrase, as in (2).

(2)   *The movement analysis:*
        a. initial structure
                Max bought the car [that Sue recommended *which*]
        b. *after* Wh *movement:*
                Max bought the car [*which* that Sue recommended __]

Subsequent deletion of *that* gives (1a), while deletion of *which* results in (1b) and deletion of both yields (1c).

In the case of feature-passing analyses, the gap marks the position of a 'missing' NP represented in (3) by the feature [−NP] (see the discussion of *wh* questions in chap. 7). This feature is then inherited upward in the syntactic representation until it can be matched with *the car,* the head of the relative clause.

(3)   *The feature-passing analysis:*

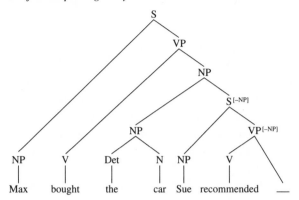

Here, the [−NP] feature associated with the missing NP in the relative clause is inherited by the VP and finally the embedded S. The [−NP] feature is canceled by combination with *the car,* which is thereby identified as the missing NP.

1. Relative Clauses in Child Language

It has sometimes been claimed that children's earliest relative clauses do not have a lexical head (e.g., Limber 1973:181; Hamburger 1980; Flynn and Lust 1980). As illustrated in the examples in (4) from a two-year-old child studied by Hamburger, early relative clauses are claimed either to be headless (the first two examples) or to combine with a *wh* word such as *what* (the latter pattern is often referred to as a 'free relative' in the literature on adult speech).

(4)   Look it [Mommy have on]. (29 mos.)
       Let's see . . . [she's doing]. (30 mos.)
       Look-a wha [I made]. (28 mos.)

The earliest relative clauses with a lexical head come from the speech of children between 2;6 and 3 years of age. The following examples are cited by Hamburger and Crain (1982:248).

(5)   Look at that noise . . . [you're making __ again]. (age 2;7)
       I want something [that the cow(s) eat __]. (age 2;9)

Limber (1973:181) further reports that children initially do not produce relative clause structures within the subject phrase. Sentences such as *The book [that you want] is on the table,* in which the relative clause is part of the subject phrase, are rarely produced even by children as old as 7 years (Menyuk 1969:16, 95). (As

Limber himself notes, complex phrases of any type in subject position seem to be rare; see also chap. 3, section 4.)

However, these claims have been disputed by Y. Kim (1987), based on a study of spontaneous speech samples from three children—Adam (32 biweekly samples collected between 2;8 and 4;0), Eve (10 biweekly samples from 1;11 to 2;3), and Sarah (43 weekly samples from 3;6 to 4;4). Kim reports both that relative clauses with lexical heads emerge before headless and free relatives (p. 94) and that relative clauses modifying subjects are found in children's early speech (p. 48). However, these points remain controversial, in part because of disputes over how to classify the earliest putative examples of relative clauses in children's speech (see, for example, Lee 1991:81 ff.).

Because relative clauses are rather rare in children's speech, it has proven useful to supplement the study of what children say with experiments that probe their mastery of specific relative clause constructions. Experimental research has focused on four structure types, classified according to the grammatical role of both the nominal that the relative clause modifies (the head) and the gap within the relative clause. (In the examples in (6), the head is italicized.)

(6)   *The SS type: subject head, subject gap:*
       The man [that ___ knows us] is waiting outside.

       The SO type: subject head, object gap:
       The man [that we know ___] is waiting outside.

       The OS type: object head, subject gap:
       I saw *the man* [that ___ knows us].

       The OO type: object head, object gap:
       I saw *the man* [that we know ___].

Sheldon 1974 constitutes a good example of the type of experiment (box 9.1) that has been used to study the development of relative clauses. (Sheldon consistently uses the term 'object' to refer to the object of a preposition rather than a direct object.) As the results summarized in table 9.1 show, the children in

Table 9.1 Comprehension of Relative Clauses (Mean no. correct out of 3) (from Sheldon 1974:276)

Group	SS Type	SO Type	OS Type	OO Type
I	1.0	0.18	0.54	1.36
II	1.45	0.73	0.91	1.64
III	2.27	0.64	1.17	1.55
Mean	1.58	0.52	0.88	1.52

Sheldon's study found the SS and OO patterns (mean scores of 1.58 and 1.52) far easier than either the SO or the OS structures (mean scores of .52 and .88). Sheldon concluded from these results that patterns in which the head and the gap have the same grammatical relation (i.e., the SS and OO types) are easier to process than patterns in which different grammatical relations are involved. (She dubbed this suggestion the 'Parallel Function Hypothesis'.)

Box 9.1

THE STUDY: Sheldon 1974
SUBJECTS: Group I: 11 children aged 3;8−4;3; Group II: 11 children aged 4;6−4;11,
    Group III: 11 children aged 5;0−5;5
SENTENCE TYPES: (3 tokens of each type)
    SS type:
        The dog [that __ jumps over the pig] bumps into the lion.
    SO type:
        The lion [that the horse bumps into __] jumps over the giraffe.
    OS type:
        The pig bumps into the horse [that __ jumps over the giraffe].
    OO type:
        The dog stands on the horse [that the giraffe jumps over __].
TASK: Children were asked to act out the meaning of the sentences with the help of toy
    animals. They were given pretest examples to ensure that they understood
    the task.

Sheldon's results were largely replicated (box 9.2) several years later by Tavakolian (1978). (Tavakolian uses the term 'object' to include both direct objects and objects of a preposition.) Table 9.2 summarizes the results. Like Sheldon, Tavakolian found the SS relative clause pattern to be the easiest, followed by the OO type. However, the two studies disagreed on the relative difficulty of the SO and OS types, with Tavakolian finding the former somewhat easier and Sheldon obtaining the opposite result.[2]

Table 9.2 Comprehension of Relative Clauses (total correct out of 24) (from Tavakolian 1978:50−52)

Group	SS Type	SO Type	OS Type	OO Type
I	18	5	1	8
II	16	6	4	9
III	22	4	9	10
Mean	78%	21%	19%	38%

Box 9.2

THE STUDY: Tavakolian 1978
SUBJECTS: Group I: 8 children aged 3;0−3;6, Group II: 8 aged 4;0−4;6, Group III:
     8 aged 5;0−5;6
SENTENCE TYPES: (3 tokens of each type)
          SS type:
               The sheep [that ___ knocks down the rabbit] stands on the lion.
          SO type:
               The lion [that the horse kisses ___] knocks down the duck.
          OS type:
               The lion stands on the duck [that ___ bumps into the pig].
          OO type:
               The horse hits the sheep [that the duck kisses ___].
TASK: Children demonstrated their comprehension of the test sentences by acting out
     their meaning with the help of toys.

The most valuable information about children's interpretation of relative clauses comes not so much from the scores themselves as from the errors that they reflect. In order to comprehend a relative clause structure, listeners must do two things. First, they must identify the grammatical role of the gap within the relative clause and, second, they must determine its reference. As noted above, the gap's role can be inferred from its position, while its reference comes from the nominal with which the relative clause combines (the head). Hence, in (7), it is understood that the gap occurs as the direct object of *hit* and that it corresponds to the sheep, not the horse or the duck.

(7)   *The comprehension of relative clauses:*
       The sheep [that the horse hit ___]   kissed the duck.
             ↑   ↑
          head   gap: role = direct object
                                      reference: determined by *the sheep*

Let us now consider language learners' ability to deal with each of these aspects of relative clause interpretation.

THE ROLE OF THE GAP

Each of the relative clauses in the tasks used by Tavakolian and Sheldon contains two nominals, one overt and one corresponding to the gap. The simplest way to determine whether the appropriate grammatical role is assigned to the gap is to examine children's treatment of the overt NP: once we determine the role that it has been assigned, we can assume that the remaining role is reserved for the gap. So, if the overt NP in the relative clause is assigned the correct role (e.g., subject in the case of *the cat* in (8)), the gap must also be assigned the corrrect role (object).

(8)   overt
                            nominal   gap
       The dog [that *the cat* chased ___] went home.
                              ↑   ↑
                          subject   object

Conversely, if the overt NP is assigned the wrong role in such sentences, it follows that the gap must also be incorrectly analyzed.

Using this technique to reexamine Tavakolian's data, I found that the children had more difficulty interpreting a direct object gap than a subject gap (table 9.3). Children's preference for gaps with the subject relation is also reflected in the type of errors that they make on structures in which the relativized element corresponds to the direct object. The single most frequent error involves interpreting the relativized direct object as subject of the clause.

(9)   *Common Error in the SO type* (31% of responses in Tavakolian's study):
       Test sentence:
           The lion [that the horse kisses ___] knocks down the duck.
                                          ↑
                                     object gap
       Child's interpretation:
           The lion [that ___ kisses the horse] knocks down the duck.
                          ↑
                     subject gap

This pattern of responses and errors is reminiscent of a phenomenon noted in the earlier discussion of *wh* questions (chap. 7): the difficulty of a gap increases with its degree of embedding. Hence, subject gaps are easier than object gaps, since the latter are embedded within VP.

Taking this idea one step further, we can predict that gaps embedded in a PP within a VP should be still harder. Evidence supporting this prediction comes from a study (box 9.3) by de Villiers et al. (1979). They found not only that object gaps were more difficult than subject gaps, but that patterns in which the gap

Table 9.3 Correct Identification of Subject
and Object Gaps (percentages)

SUBJECT GAPS		OBJECT GAPS	
SS Type	OS Type	OO Type	SO Type
91	75	63	45

occurred as object of a preposition (i.e., the SP, OP, and PP types) were the most difficult of all (see also n. 2).

Box 9.3

THE STUDY: de Villiers et al. 1979
SUBJECTS: 114 children: 21 3-year-olds, 37 4-year-olds, 34 5-year-olds, 22 6-year-olds
SENTENCE TYPES: (1 token of each type; P = object of a preposition)
    SS type: The gorilla [that ___ bumped the elephant] kissed the sheep.
    SO type: The turkey [that the gorilla patted ___] pushed the pig.
    OS type: The kangaroo kissed the camel [that ___ shoved the elephant].
    OO type: The turtle hit the pig [that the giraffe touched ___].
    SP type: The giraffe [that the turkey yelled to ___] pushed the zebra.
    OP type: The crocodile touched the gorilla [that the zebra yelled to ___].
    PS type: The turtle shouted to the camel [that ___ pushed the kangaroo].
    PO type: The horse spoke to the turtle [that the sheep touched ___].
    PP type: The kangaroo whispered to the turkey [that the zebra shouted to ___].
TASK: Children were asked to act out the meaning of the sentences with the help of toy animals. They were given pretest examples to ensure that they understood the task.

Still another piece of evidence for the relative ease of subject gaps comes from children's use of 'resumptive pronouns' in place of a gap within relative clauses. Citing unpublished work by Dan Finer, Pérez-Leroux (1995:121) gives the examples in (10) of this phenomenon from a child aged 3;9–3;10.

(10) a. *Resumptive pronoun functioning as subject:*
       He's a little kid [that *he* hurts].
    b. *Resumptive pronoun functioning as direct object:*
       Twenty numbers [that we counted *them*]
    c. *Resumptive pronoun functioning as object of a preposition:*
       I hurt my finger [that Thomas stepped on *it*].

Given the relative difficulty of gaps, we would expect resumptive pronouns (which eliminate gaps) to be more common in object position than in subject position. This seems to be correct. Using a picture description task to elicit relative clauses from 11 children aged 3;5 to 5;5 (mean age 4;10), Pérez-Leroux found no instances of resumptive pronouns in more than 100 subject relative clauses. However, 3 of 9 object relatives had a resumptive pronoun, as did 7 of 26 structures with a relativized object of a preposition. Comparable scores were obtained from Spanish-speaking children for their language.

All other things being equal, we would expect the preference for subject gaps over object gaps to be universal in the early stages of language. Although complications arise in the case of SOV languages (see the discussion of Korean and Japanese below), Demuth (1995) notes the predicted preference in children learning Sesotho (an SVO language of the Bantu family). Based on a 12-month longitudinal study of the spontaneous speech of three children (aged 2 and 3), she reports that subject relatives emerge before object relatives and are far more common in early speech.

Strangely, just the opposite tendency has been reported for English (e.g., Limber 1973:181; Hamburger 1980), as the examples from (5), repeated as (11), help illustrate.

(11)   Look at that noise . . . [you're making __ again]. (age 2;7)
         I want something [that the cow(s) eat __]. (age 2;9)

However, this claim has been disputed by Y. Kim (1987), whose study of transcripts of spontaneous speech produced by Adam, Eve, and Sarah revealed numerous instances of both subject and object gaps in their early relative clauses.

Fox (1987) reports that object relatives are at least as frequent as subject relatives in adult speech, where they fulfill a very special function: they 'anchor' the head noun by linking it to the referent of their subject. Thus, Fox explains, in a sentence such as (12), the head *that girl* is anchored by the referent of *he* in the relative clause, which links it to someone previously mentioned in the discourse.

(12)   What about that girl [that he used to go with __ for so long]?

It is possible that children's early relative clauses fulfill a similar function, which would explain the need for structures with object gaps despite their computational difficulty.

It is also perhaps worth noting that subject relative clauses such as (13a) are syntactically more constrained than object relatives such as (13b) in adult speech in that they require either a relative pronoun or the complementizer *that* in initial position.

(13)   a.   The man [that/who/*∅ __ met Mary] is a friend of ours.
         b.   The man [that/who/∅ Mary met __] is a friend of ours.

This could militate against the production of relative clauses in children's spontaneous speech.

The Reference of the Gap

Turning now to the second aspect of relative clause interpretation, an intriguing developmental phenomenon showed up in children's attempts to determine the reference of the gap in Tavakolian's experiment. For OS relative clauses, 63% of all responses contained the error illustrated in (14). (Sheldon 1974:278 reports this error in 44% of the responses to OS structures in her experiment; see also Hsu, Cairns, and Fiengo 1985:38; Hsu et al. 1989:603).

(14)   *Test sentence and intended interpretation:*

The lion stands on *the duck* [that __ bumps into the pig].

reference determined by *the duck*

Child's interpretation:

The lion stands on the duck [that __ bumps into the pig].

reference determined by *the lion*

As (14) illustrates, children often misinterpret the reference of the gap in the OS pattern, equating it with the higher subject (the lion) rather than higher object (the duck). The frequency of this error is largely responsible for the fact children's scores for OS relative clauses are so low (see tables 9.1 and 9.2), despite their ability to correctly analyze the grammatical role of the subject gap (table 9.3).

Tavakolian (1978) suggests a possible source for this error. Because the OS structure contains a sequence of two VPs, she suggests, the child treats it as if it were a coordinate structure, following the Conjoined Clause Strategy first mentioned in chapter 6, section 2. (See also Lebeaux 1990.)

(15)   *The Conjoined Clause Strategy:*
       Interpret a string of the type *NP V . . . V . . .* as a coordinate structure of the type *NP V . . . and . . . V . . . .*

This strategy has the effect depicted in (16) in the case of OS relative clauses.

(16)   The lion stands on the duck [$_S$ that __ bumps into the pig]
       ⇓
       The lion [$_{VP}$ stands on the duck] and [$_{VP}$ bumps into the pig].

Use of the Conjoined Clause Strategy is probably facilitated in the OS pattern by the fact that the two VPs (in our example, *stands on the duck* and *bumps into the pig*) are separated from each other by an unstressed grammatical morpheme (*that*). It is thus a small step for the child to interpret this element as *and,* thereby deriving a conjoined structure.[3]

Children's use of the Conjoined Clause Strategy may well reflect not only the superficial similarity between certain relative clause constructions and the previously acquired coordinate VP structure, but also a preference on the part of children for the coordinate structure—perhaps because these patterns contain no gap. Compare in this regard the structures in (17).

(17) a. *Coordinate structure* (no gap):
         The lion [_{VP} [_{VP} stands on the duck] and [_{VP} bumps into the pig]].
     b. *OS Relative Clause Structure* (subject gap):
         The lion stands on [_{NP} the duck [_S that __ bumps into the pig]].

Notice that there is no gap in the coordinate structure, but that the relative clause *that bumps into the pig* contains a gap in the position marked by the underscore. As noted previously in this and preceding chapters, gaps seem to create difficulty for young children, who may respond by eliminating them altogether (the Conjoined Clause Strategy) or by minimizing their distance from the matching NP (as when an object gap is reinterpreted as a subject gap in (9) above).

This notwithstanding, it must be noted that there is some disagreement over whether the Conjoined Clause Strategy provides the right explanation for children's errors on relative clause constructions. Lust (1995) is among those who argue against this proposal, suggesting instead that children's mistakes on the OS patterns involve misattachment of the relative clause, as depicted in (18).

(18)

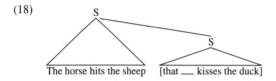

On this view, the bracketed clause in (18) has the same status as the relative clause in (19), which has been 'extraposed' from the subject phrase that it modifies. (Note that the gap in the relative clause is coreferential with the matrix subject— just as it is children's misinterpretation of the OS pattern.)

(19) A man arrived [who __ knew how to fix the car].

A simple way to choose between the two analyses might be to have children imitate OS patterns: the coordination analysis predicts that the complementizer *that* should be replaced by *and,* whereas the misattachment analysis predicts that it should not.

OTHER CONSIDERATIONS

Factors other than the role and reference of the gap may also influence the interpretation of relative clauses. Word order, for example, is known to be important to relative clause interpretation, especially in SOV languages. Based on a comprehension experiment with 30 Korean-speaking children aged 6;3 to 7;3, Clancy, Lee, and Zoh (1986:241) found (among other things) that patterns such as (20a) were significantly easier than (20b).

(20)   a. *Relative clause with subject gap* (78.25% correct):
       [__ oli-lul   nemettuli-n]   thokki-ka   talamcwi-lul ccochaka-ss-ta.
          duck-AC knock.down-REL rabbit-NOM squirrel-AC   chase-PST-DECL
          'The rabbit that knocked down the duck chased the squirrel.'
     b. *Relative clause with object gap* (68.25% correct):
       [Thokki-ka __ nemettuli-n] oli-ka   talamcwi-lul ccochaka-ss-ta.
          rabbit-NOM knock.down-REL duck-NOM squirrel-AC chase-PST-DECL
          'The duck that the rabbit knocked down chased the squirrel.'

This is what one would expect, given the hypothesized preference for subject gaps over objects gaps. However, somewhat surprisingly, children do very poorly on the pattern illustrated in (21), which also contains a subject gap.

(21)   Talamcwi-ka [__ thokki-lul nemettuli-n]   oli-lul   ccochaka-ss-ta.
       squirrel-NOM   rabbit-AC knock.down-REL duck-AC chase-PST-DECL
       'The squirrel chased the duck that knocked down the rabbit.'

However, as Clancy et al. note, another factor intervenes here: the pattern in (21) begins with an NP-NOM NP-AC V sequence (*talamcwi-ka thokki-lul nemettuli-n*) that looks just like an SOV sentence and invites the (incorrect) interpretation 'The squirrel knocks down the rabbit'. This is in fact the most common error made by the children (46% of all responses), suggesting that the superficial resemblance of this relative clause pattern to the SOV template of basic Korean sentences triggers a processing strategy that in turn accounts for the high error rate. An even higher error rate is observed for these patterns in Japanese, where (in contrast to Korean) the verbal inflection used in relative clauses is identical to that found in main clauses (ibid. 247; Hakuta 1982).

It has been suggested (e.g., de Villiers et al. 1979:513) that English children are sensitive to a comparable NP V NP processing strategy (reflecting the SVO character of English). One positive effect of this strategy is that children make relatively few errors determining the grammatical role of the various NPs in OS patterns such as *The kangaroo kissed the camel that shoved the elephant,* in which the sentence-initial NP V VP sequence does in fact correspond to an SVO structure. (Of course, they make many errors of other sorts, as we have already noted.) In contrast, they do comparatively poorly on SO patterns (e.g., *The kangaroo that the camel kissed shoved the rabbit*), in which there is no initial NP V NP sequence.

A different type of processing effect was observed by Goodluck and Tavako-lian (1982) in a study (box 9.4) of the OS relative clause pattern. They found that the first type of relative clause yielded a high percentage of responses (32.5%) in which the gap in the relative clause was coreferential with the higher subject rather than the higher object. This is, of course, a familiar phenomenon and was noted above (see discussion of the Conjoined Clause Strategy). Strangely, however, the number of such incorrect responses was significantly lower (23%) for sentence type II, where the relative clause contained an inanimate direct object, and lower still (20%) for the third sentence type, in which the relative clause was built around an intransitive verb. Goodluck and Tavakolian explain these contrasts by suggesting that an objectless verb is easier to process than a verb with a direct object and that inanimate direct objects are more expected and therefore easier to process than their animate counterparts. As the processing load increases, they propose, so does the incidence of interpretation errors. The possible presence of such processing effects obviously complicates the study of how relative clause patterns develop, but such phenomena must ultimately be taken into account if an accurate picture of the acquisition process is to emerge.[4]

Box 9.4

THE STUDY: Goodluck and Tavakolian 1982

SUBJECTS: 10 4-year-olds and 10 5-year-olds

SENTENCE TYPES: (8 tokens of the first two types, 4 of the third)

> Type I: OS relative clause containing an animate direct object:
>> The dog kicks the horse [that __ knocks over the sheep].
>
> Type II: OS relative clause containing an inanimate direct object:
>> The dog kicks the horse [that __ knocks over the table].
>
> Type III: OS relative clause containing an intransitive verb:
>> The dog kicks the horse [that __ jumps up and down].

TASK: Children were asked to act out the meaning of the sentences with the help of toy animals. They were given pretest examples to ensure that they understood the task.

DESIGN PROBLEMS

As noted at the outset, a major function of a relative clause is to restrict the reference of the head noun by selecting a subset of the set that it denotes. Thus, when someone says *the horse that Jane saw,* it is reasonable to assume that there is more than one horse under discussion, and that the relative clause *that Jane saw* is being used to pick out a particular horse from that set. Surprisingly, however, little attention has been paid to this fact in the language acquisition literature. As Hamburger and Crain (1982:258) observe, many studies (including Tavakolian's) provide only one animal of each type in the group of toys used in the comprehension task. A child who is asked to act out the meaning of *The cow pushed the dog [that kissed the rabbit],* for instance, is typically presented with one cow, one dog, and one rabbit. It is therefore difficult for the relative clause to fulfill its normal restrictive function in this setting.

As Hamburger and Crain further note, this may contribute to the conjoined clause analysis in that structures of the latter type do not presuppose the existence of a set from which a subset is to be chosen. In the sentence *The cow pushed the dog and kissed the rabbit,* for instance, there is no implication that there is more than one animal of any type. (This may be somewhat less of a problem than Hamburger and Crain believe, however: many relative clauses in English serve to 'characterize' the head and do not suppose the presence of a set of entities—e.g., *This man who's coming up the street is a friend of mine* can be felicitously used even when the setting contains only one man.)

Hamburger and Crain attempted to remedy this problem by making use of an experimental design (box 9.5) that provides the child with several potential referents for the head of the relative clause. Hence, a child who was to act out the meaning of the sentence *The cow pushed the dog [that kissed the rabbit]* had to choose among three toy dogs in addition to a cow and a rabbit. Children's performance under these conditions was surprisingly good: of the responses by the 3-year-olds that included acting out the relative clause rather than just the matrix clause, 69% were correct; still higher scores were obtained by the older children (Hamburger and Crain 1982:267). (However, Hamburger and Crain's experiment may have been overly biased in the children's favor: as pointed out to me by Kevin Gregg, their design provided three examplars of the animal corresponding to the relativized nominal (e.g., the dog, in the example above), but only one each of the other two animals; this presumably gives the children an extra clue about the referent of the relativized nominal, allowing them to arrive at the correct interpretation without using grammatical knowledge.)

Box 9.5

THE STUDY: Hamburger and Crain 1982
SUBJECTS: 18 children ranging in age from 3 to 5
SENTENCE TYPES: 10 sentences containing OS relative clauses (in addition to 30 sentences of other sorts not relevant to the present discussion)
        The cow pushed the dog [that ___ kissed the rabbit].
TASK: the children were asked to act out the meaning of the test sentences with the help of toys.

A second problem with many experimental approaches to relative clause structures is that they employ an act-out procedure. The difficulty here is that even adults tend to act out only the matrix S in sentences containing a relative clause. Thus, a natural response to the sentence *The dog that the horse kissed jumped on the camel* is to take a toy dog, assume that it is the animal that the horse kissed, and make it jump on the camel. This type of response occurred 13% of the time among Hamburger and Crain's 4-year-olds and 55% of the time among their 5-year-olds. A similar problem is reported by de Villiers et al. (1979:511).

A more appropriate comprehension task might well involve picture selection.[5] For instance, a child might hear a sentence such as *The dog that the cat is chasing is always in trouble* and then be asked to point to 'the dog'. The child would then have to choose among three alternatives (fig. 9.1): (a) a dog running, (b) a dog being chased by a cat (the correct response), and (c) a dog chasing a cat. This task has the advantage of requiring children to focus on the interpretation of the relative clause, since they cannot point to the right dog without interpreting the modifier *that the cat is chasing*. Moreover, in offering them a set of dogs from which to choose, it also permits the relative clause to fulfill its restrictive function, thereby avoiding the common flaw noted above. Experimentation of this sort could conceivably shed further light on the way in which the acquisition device analyzes relative clauses.

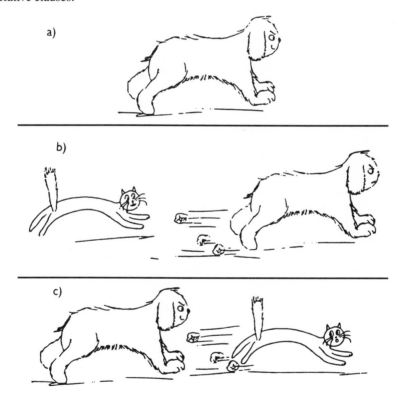

FIGURE 9.1 Picture Accompanying Comprehension Task

2. Clefts and Related Constructions

In addition to *wh* questions and relative clauses, English contains a number of other sentence types whose internal structure includes a gap. One such sentence type involves the **cleft** constructions illustrated in (22).

(22)   It was the blue car [that ___ went through the red light].
       It was the driver of the blue car [that the police arrested ___].

Although the purpose of the bracketed clause in the cleft structures is to highlight a particular NP rather than to restrict its reference, these patterns resemble relative clauses in that they contain a gap that must be 'matched' with the nominal with which they combine. We would thus expect these structures to exhibit the same gap interpretation phenomena associated with *wh* questions and relative clause structures. A first study relevant to this question (box 9.6) was carried out by Lempert and Kinsbourne (1980). As the results depicted in table 9.4 show, children found subject clefts to be significantly easier to understand than object clefts. These results are consistent with earlier findings that children prefer less deeply embedded gaps. Hence, a gap that is embedded within a VP inside an S (as in the object clefts) is more difficult than a gap that is outside the VP (as in subject clefts). Similar results have been reported for French by Hupet and Tilmant (1989).

Box 9.6

THE STUDY: Lempert and Kinsbourne 1980
SUBJECTS: 52 children. Group I: 13 aged 2;5–3;5, Group II: 13 aged 3;7–4;5, Group III: 13 aged 4;6–5;1, Group IV: 13 aged 5;3–6;3
SENTENCE TYPES: (8 tokens of each type)
   Subject cleft: It's the cow [that ___ bumps the horse].
   Object cleft: It's the truck [that the wagon bumps ___].
TASK: Children were asked to act out the meaning of the sentences with the help of toys.

Table 9.4 Results of the Cleft Comprehension Test (percentage correct) (from Lempert and Kinsbourne 1980:374)

Group	Subject Clefts	Object Clefts
I	88	66
II	95	67
III	100	69
IV	100	83
Mean	96	71

We also expect that gaps embedded in a PP within a VP should be harder than those embedded within just a VP, and that gaps embedded within a PP in an NP inside a VP would be harder still. These predictions are borne out by the results of a study (box 9.7) conducted by Hildebrand (1987); see table 9.5. For three of the four age groups, the type I structure is easier than the type II pattern (there is a small difference in the opposite direction for the 6-year-olds); the type III pattern was the most difficult for all age groups. (Both age and sentence type were significant as main effects.)

The effect of embedding on gap interpretation is confirmed by the types of errors made by the children in Hildebrand's experiment. The most common

Box 9.7

THE STUDY: Hildebrand 1987

SUBJECTS: 48 children—12 4-year-olds, 12 6-year-olds, 12 8-year-olds, and 12 10-year-olds.

TASK: elicited production. Children were taught a game in which they had to produce a cleft-like construction in response to a simple declarative sentence and an accompanying picture. The stimulus sentences and pictures were designed to elicit gaps within different types of phrases.

SENTENCE TYPES: (4 tokens of types I and II, 3 tokens of type III)

    Type I: gap inside VP:

    STIMULUS SENTENCE: The boy on the road is pulling a car.

    ACCOMPANYING PICTURE: a car

    EXPECTED RESPONSE: This is the car that the boy on the road is pulling __.

    Type II: gap inside VP and PP:

    STIMULUS SENTENCE: The boy at the table is drawing with a crayon.

    ACCOMPANYING PICTURE: a crayon

    EXPECTED RESPONSE: This is the crayon that the boy at the table is drawing with __.

    Type III: gap inside VP, PP and NP:

    STIMULUS SENTENCE: The boy is reading a story about a girl.

    ACCOMPANYING PICTURE: a story book showing a picture of girl

    EXPECTED RESPONSE: This is the girl that the boy is reading a story about __.

Table 9.5 Results of the Production Task (percentage correct) (Hildebrand 1987 : 74)

Type	4-year-olds	6-year-olds	8-year-olds	10-year-olds
I	78	74	86	95
II	32	80	75	85
III	0	15	45	70

error type (45% of the total) involved omission of the preposition, as illustrated in (23).

(23) *Stimulus sentence:*
     The little boy at the table is drawing with the crayon.
     Expected response:
     This is the crayon [$_S$ that the little boy at the table [$_{VP}$ is drawing [$_{PP}$ with __]]].
     Actual response:
     This is the crayon [$_S$ that the little boy at the table [$_{VP}$ is drawing __]].

In avoiding the preposition, the children were in effect producing a pattern in which the gap lies in the VP rather than a more deeply embedded PP category.

The second most common error also involved converting a type II structure into a type I pattern, this time by reversing the order of the direct object and the preposition, as in (24).

(24) *Stimulus sentence:*
     The little boy is drawing a pencil with a crayon.
     Expected response:
     This is the crayon [$_S$ that the little boy [$_{VP}$ is drawing a pencil [$_{PP}$ with __]]].
     Actual response:
     This is the crayon [$_S$ that the little boy [$_{VP}$ is drawing __ [$_{PP}$ with a pencil]]].

Here again, the gap occurs inside only a VP rather than a more deeply embedded PP. This type of response maintains the length and the lexical composition of the original sentence, changing only those structural features that affect the depth of the gap.

The third most common error had the effect of producing Type II structures instead of the expected Type III patterns, as in (25).

(25) *Stimulus sentence:*
     The little boy is watching a movie about a girl.

     Expected response:
     This is the girl [$_S$ that the little boy [$_{VP}$ is watching [$_{NP}$ a movie [$_{PP}$ about __]]]].

     Actual response:
     This is the girl [$_S$ that the little boy [$_{VP}$ is watching [$_{PP}$ about/with __]]].

This strategy places the gap inside a VP and a PP rather than the expected VP, NP, and PP—thereby minimizing its distance from the matching NP.

All three error types as well as the overall scores from Hildebrand's experiment point toward the same conclusion: the computational mechanisms to which the acquisition device has access disfavor gaps in proportion to their depth of embedding with respect to the element that determines their interpretation.[6]

3. Conclusion

Since both relative clauses and cleft structures are characterized by the presence of a gap that must be associated with an NP outside its clause, we can expect their development to resemble that of other gap-containing constructions. The data reviewed here suggest that this is correct. In particular, we find a systematic resemblance to *wh* questions in terms of both relative difficulty and the types of errors made by language learners. In all cases, the acquisition device prefers structures in which the gap corresponding to the 'missing' element is less deeply embedded, consistent with the notion of computational complexity proposed in chapter 7. This gives a developmental profile characterized by relatively early and error-free acquisition of patterns containing a subject gap vs. those containing a gap in more deeply embedded positions.

10

Passives

One of the most important syntactic processes in human language is passivization, an operation that applies to a transitive verb to bring about the changes stated in (1) in the prototypical case. (An 'oblique' agent in English is marked by the preposition *by;* the parentheses indicate that it can be optionally suppressed.)

(1) agent ⇒ (oblique)
     theme ⇒ subject

Passivization has the effect of reorganizing the relationship between thematic roles and grammatical relations found in active sentences such as (2), where the agent *the boy* serves as subject and the theme *the ball* as direct object.

(2) subject   direct object
     The boy kicked the ball.
     agent   theme

Following passivization (see (3)), the theme functions as subject while the preposition *by* is used to mark the now optional agent.

(3) subject   oblique
     The ball was kicked (by the boy).
     theme   agent

As the above example also illustrates, a passive VP in English includes an auxiliary verb (usually *be,* but sometimes *get*) and the past participle form of a transitive verb. (The past participle of regular verbs such as *kick* takes the suffix *-ed;* however, many verbs have an irregular past participle form: *taken, seen, put,* etc.)

The study of passives is complicated somewhat by the fact that is necessary to distinguish among two subtypes—a verbal pattern as in (4) and an adjectival pattern as in (5) (e.g., Wasow 1978; Bresnan 1982). As its name suggests, the latter pattern has many properties of an adjectival construction: it often expresses a state and is compatible with the negative prefix *un-* and/or degree words such as *very.*

(4) *Verbal passives:*
     *The book was *unput* on the shelf.
     *Harry was very *hit* by the ball.

(5) *Adjectival passives:*
     The island is *uninhabited.*
     The teacher was very *annoyed.*

Most acquisition research focuses on verbal passives, as we will see.

192

Passives of any type are relatively rare in parental speech to children, as a study (box 10.1) by Gordon and Chafetz (1990) helps demonstrate. Passives occurred infrequently in Gordon and Chafetz's data, appearing on average only 36 times per 1000 utterances. (Adjectival passives were about twice as frequent as verbal passives.) The relatively rarity of the passive pattern in adult speech to children raises questions about when and how the acquisition device takes note of its existence and determines its properties.

Box 10.1

THE STUDY: Gordon and Chafetz 1990
SUBJECTS: 3 children in the age ranges 2;3–4;11, 1;6–2;3, and 2;3–5;1
METHOD: A total of 86,655 utterances from the children's parents were examined in search of various types of passives.

---

1. Some Experimental Studies

The passive is one of the most widely studied structures in child language. Rather than attempting an exhaustive review of the literature, I will focus here on a small number of representative studies, beginning with Turner and Rommetveit's (1967) investigation (box 10.2) of reversible and nonreversible active and passive sentences. (A sentence is considered to be reversible if its agent and theme arguments can be switched without affecting the plausibility of its meaning. Hence, *John helped Sue* is reversible since switching the agent and theme NPs gives *Sue helped John,* a sentence whose meaning is still plausible. In contrast, *John painted the house* is not reversible.)

Box 10.2

THE STUDY: Turner and Rommetveit 1967
SUBJECTS: 48 children from five different age groups: nursery school, kindergarten, grade 1, grade 2, and grade 3.
SENTENCE TYPES: (6 tokens of each type)
    Nonreversible active: The bird carries the branch.
    Reversible active: The boy visits the doctor.
    Nonreversible passive: The branch is carried by the bird.
    Reversible passive: The doctor is visited by the boy.
TASKS: *imitation:* repetition of stimulus sentences
    comprehension: matching orally presented sentences with a picture
    production: The children were asked to describe individual pictures. Context was used to encourage production of a passive by establishing the theme NP as the topic of the conversation.

Figure 10.1 summarizes the results of the Turner and Rommetveit study. The results uncovered two major asymmetries in the development of passive construc-

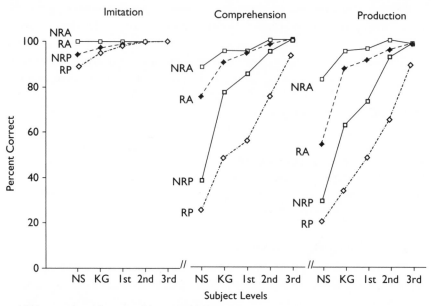

NRA, nonreversible active; RA, reversible active;
NRP, nonreversible passive; RP, reversible passive

FIGURE 10.1 Results of Turner and Rommetveit's Study (from Turner and Rommetveit 1967:654)

tions. First, reversible sentences are uniformly more difficult than their nonreversible counterparts—not a surprising result, given that the former patterns contain no semantic clues about their interpretation, forcing children to rely solely on grammatical features of the sentence. Second, the ability to imitate a structure precedes the ability to comprehend it, which, in turn, emerges before the ability to produce it. In the case of reversible passives, for example, imitation scores reach the 90% level in the kindergarten group, compared to 3rd grade for comprehension and even later for production.

By far the most common error observed by Turner and Rommetveit (94.5% of all incorrect responses) involves **reversal** (6)—treating the theme subject as if it were the agent and the agent in the *by* phrase as if it were the theme.

(6)   The dog was bitten by the cat.

Following a suggestion by Bever (1970), it is widely believed that this error reflects children's reliance on a **Canonical Sentence Strategy** (see (7)) that treats NP V NP sequences as 'agent–action–theme' patterns, consistent with the 'canonical' or most usual correspondences between syntactic positions and thematic roles in English.

(7)   *The Canonical Sentence Strategy:*
       NP V NP = agent action theme

A subsequent study (box 10.3) by de Villiers and de Villiers (1973) sheds light on the use of the Canonical Sentence Strategy by children younger than those in Turner and Rommetveit's experiment. (See note 3 below for mention of a methodological problem with the de Villiers study.) The results are summarized in table 10.1. There are at least two points to note here. First, the children's ability to deal with reversible active structures is obviously more advanced than their ability to deal with comparable passive constructions. Whereas the children in Group II (19.5–27 mos.) can accurately interpret reversible active constructions three quarters of the time, even the most advanced children (Group VI, 26–36 mos.)

Box 10.3

THE STUDY: de Villiers and de Villiers 1973
SUBJECTS: 33 children aged 19–37.5 mos. (mean age = 26.8 mos.). The subjects were
    divided into 6 groups based on MLU.
SENTENCE TYPES: (6 tokens of each type)
    active: Make the dog bite the cat.
    passive: Make the dog be bitten by the cat.
TASK: The children acted out the meaning of the stimulus sentences with the help of
    toys and dolls. The active and passive sentences were presented in different sessions held one week apart.

Table 10.1 Results of the Comprehension Task (percentage correct)
(de Villiers and de Villiers 1973:335)

	MLU	Correct	Reversed	Child as Agent	Refusals
		Active Sentences			
I	1.0–1.5	31	21.4	33.3	14.3
II	1.5–2.0	75.5	5.6	12.2	6.7
III	2.0–2.5	70	11	16.2	2.8
IV	2.5–3.0	81	14.2	2.4	2.4
V	3.0–3.5	85.8	14.2	0	0
VI	3.5–4.0	83.3	13.4	3.3	0
		Passive Sentences			
I	1.0–1.5	28.6	26.2	30.9	14.3
II	1.5–2.0	28.9	30	28.9	12.2
III	2.0–2.5	36.3	43.3	17.6	2.8
IV	2.5–3.0	42.3	41	14.3	2.4
V	3.0–3.5	13.3	86.7	0	0
VI	3.5–4.0	39.4	50	3.3	7.3

Box 10.4

THE STUDY: Baldie 1976

SUBJECTS: 100 children aged 3;0–8;0, evenly divided into 10 age groups at six month
    intervals.

SENTENCE TYPES: (1 token of each type for each task)

　　　reversible passive: The man was helped by the boy.

　　　nonreversible passive: The house was painted by the man.

　　　agentless passive: The large block of ice was melted.

　　　reversible active: The old man pushed the black dog.

TASKS: *Imitation:* repetition of stimulus sentence

　　　Comprehension: selection of a picture (from among 5 possibilities) correspond-
    ing to the stimulus sentence

　　　Production: Formation of a sentence in response to a picture. In order to en-
    courage production of passive sentences, the entity corresponding to the
    theme was emphasized in terms of color and size, while the entity correspond-
    ing to the agent was drawn in outline only. To further encourage the children to
    encode the theme as subject, presentation of the picture stimulus was accom-
    panied by the question 'What has happened to X?'

Table 10.2 Results of Baldie's Experiment (mean no. correct
　　　　　　out of 20) (from Baldie 1976:336)

Age	Nonreversible	Reversible	Agentless
	The Imitation Task		
3;0–3;11	16	14	17
4;0–4;11	18	18	17
5;0–5;11	20	20	20
6;0–6;11	20	20	20
7;0–7;11	20	20	20
	The Comprehension Task		
3;0–3;11	15	10	17
4;0–4;11	20	13	20
5;0–5;11	20	14	18
6;0–6;11	18	18	20
7;0–7;11	19	17	20
	The Production Task		
3;0–3;11	0	1	0
4;0–4;11	1	4	3
5;0–5;11	10	5	5
6;0–6;11	2	9	9
7;0–7;11	6	11	9

correctly understand little more than one third of the passive structures. Second, the incidence of reversals due to the Canonical Sentence Strategy seems to increase with age, peaking in the fifth group, where it is more than twice as common than in the fourth group (86.7% vs. 41%).

Still another study (box 10.4) of the emergence of the abilities required to deal with passive constructions was carried out by Baldie (1976). Table 10.2 summarizes the results of the three types of passive sentences. (The children had no difficulty with any of the active sentences.) Figure 10.2 depicts the developmental

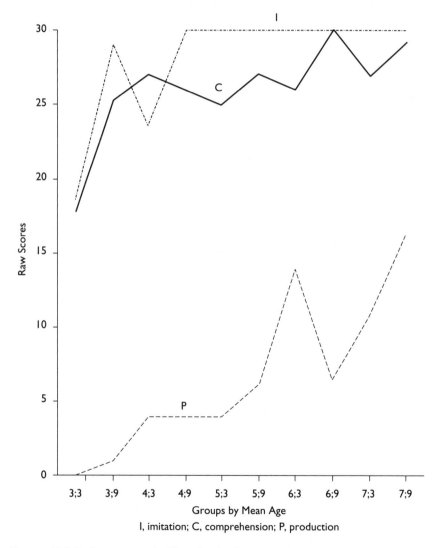

FIGURE 10.2 Performance on the Three Passive Structures (from Baldie 1976:337)

trends in Baldie's subjects. Consistent with what has been found in other studies (e.g., Fraser, Bellugi, and Brown 1963; Turner and Rommetveit 1967), Baldie's results indicate that the ability to imitate passive patterns precedes the ability to understand them accurately. While imitation of the passive form is mastered by the mean age of 4;9, near-perfect performance on the comprehension task is not achieved before age 6. Baldie further reports that it was not until age 7;6 that 80% of the children were able to produce at least one passive sentence on the production task.

With the conclusion that passive patterns are not fully mastered until the early school years apparently secure, the attention of researchers turned to the development of different subtypes of passives, such as those involving non-actional verbs, and to the emergence of the agentive '*by* phrase'.

ACTIONAL VS. NON-ACTIONAL PASSIVES

There is some reason to believe that passive patterns containing actional verbs are acquired before comparable constructions built around non-actional verbs. One indication of this comes from a study (box 10.5) by Sudhalter and Braine (1985) that compared children's ability to comprehend the passive forms of actional and experiential verbs (i.e., verbs denoting cognitive, emotional, and perceptual events such as believing, hating, hearing, and so on.)

Box 10.5

THE STUDY: Sudhalter and Braine 1985
SUBJECTS: 50 preschool children, divided into a younger group (5 3-year-olds and 20 4-year-olds) and an older group (20 5-year-olds and 5 6-year-olds)
SENTENCE TYPES: (6 tokens of each type)
    actional: The orange owl was called by Wally Gator.
    experiential: The orange owl was seen by Wally Gator.
TASK: After hearing the test sentence, the child had to pick the appropriate doll in response to commands such as 'Pick up the animal that called the other'.

As table 10.3 shows, the children perform approximately twice as well on actional verbs as on experiential ones. Similar findings have been noted by Maratsos et al. (1979), de Villiers (1980), Maratsos et al. (1985), and Gordon and Chafetz (1990).

Table 10.3 Results of the Comprehension Test (percentage correct) (from Sudhalter and Braine 1985:465)

Verb Type	Younger Group	Older Group
Actional	54	58
Experiential	26	28.7

In a second experiment (box 10.6), Sudhalter and Braine examined the contrast between actional and experiential verbs in the comprehension ability of older children. Although the children's overall performance was somewhat poorer than might be expected (perhaps because of the task, which required the subjects to choose among written alternatives), scores (table 10.4) were significantly higher for the actional passives than for each subtype of experiential passive. (In contrast, there was no significant difference among the various types of experiential verbs.)

Box 10.6

THE STUDY: Sudhalter and Braine 1985
SUBJECTS: 76 elementary school children: 27 first graders (mean age = 6;5), 19 third graders (mean age = 7;9) and 30 sixth graders (mean age = 10;9)
SENTENCE TYPES: 4 actional verbs and 12 experiential verbs. The experiential verbs were divided into three subtypes (perceptual, cognitive, and affective):
    actional: be pushed
    perceptual: be seen
    cognitive: be believed
    affective: be liked
TASK: Children had to answer questions such as 'Which one believed the other?' about each test sentence. Children responded by circling the appropriate name on an answer sheet. A pretest ensured that even the first-graders were able to recognize and read the names that had to be circled.

Why should experiential passives be harder to understand than actional passives?[1] Frequency in the input may be a factor: Gordon and Chafetz (1990:234) note that actional passives are far more frequent in parental speech to children, constituting more than 90% of verbal passives and almost 60% of adjectival passives. However, other factors may also be involved. For example, Sudhalter and Braine suggest that children consider *by* to be an agent marker and therefore are confused by patterns in which it occurs with an experiencer NP. Another possibility, put forward by Lebeaux (1988), is that children prefer passive constructions in which the referent of the subject is actually affected or changed by the action described in the sentence. Whereas actional passives typically have this property, experiential passives do not. For example, in actional passives such as *John was*

Table 10.4 Results of the Comprehension Test (percentage correct) (Sudhalter and Braine 1985:459)

Grade	Actional	Perceptual	Cognitive	Affective
First	58.3	48.6	36.1	41.6
Third	83.3	65.3	62.5	59.7
Sixth	85	76.6	70	75

hit by the ball and *The ice was melted,* the referent of the subject is tangibly affected by the described action. In contrast, the referent of the subject in experiential passives such as *Ralph was seen by the man* or *Mary is liked by the children* is unaffected to the point where he or she need not even be aware of what has happened.

THE AGENTIVE *BY* PHRASE

Most passives in adult speech to children lack an overt agent (e.g., *The ball was kicked*): Gordon and Chafetz (1990:234) report finding only four passives with overt agents out of more than 85,000 parental utterances. A study (box 10.7) by Horgan (1978) investigated the frequency of agent phrases in passives produced by children. She found that passive structures with an overt agent phrase are very infrequent in children's speech before age 7 (fig. 10.3). When children do attempt to express the agent in a passive pattern, they often employ the prepositions *from* and *with* rather than *by.* The examples in (8) are from Clark and Carpenter (1989).

Box 10.7

THE STUDY: Horgan 1978
SUBJECTS: 54 children aged 2;0–4;2 and 180 children aged 5–13.
TASK: The children were asked to describe pictures.

(8) a. No, he isn't going to get hurt *from* those bad guys. (age 2;7)
     b. It might be stealed away *with* the robbers. (age 4;0)
     c. Daddy, the pigs have been marooned *from* a flood. (age 4;6)

Horgan (p. 69) suggests that children initially treat passives as stative constructions, analogous to *He was tired* and *She is married,* in which the *-ed* form names a property or state rather than an action (see also Borer and Wexler 1987). If correct, this would help explain why a *by* phrase is infrequent in the speech of younger children: as the examples in (9) help show, adjectival structures do not normally permit such phrases.

(9) *He was tired by the teacher.
     *Sue is married by John.

Crucially, however, these structures can occur with other types of PPs, as in (10)—just as children's early passives can.

(10) He was tired from the journey.
     Sue is married to John.

Horgan's suggestion is not without its problems, however. For one thing, it is apparently not true that children's early spontaneous passives are all adjectival (stative) in character. Pinker (1989:315) notes that while all the early passives

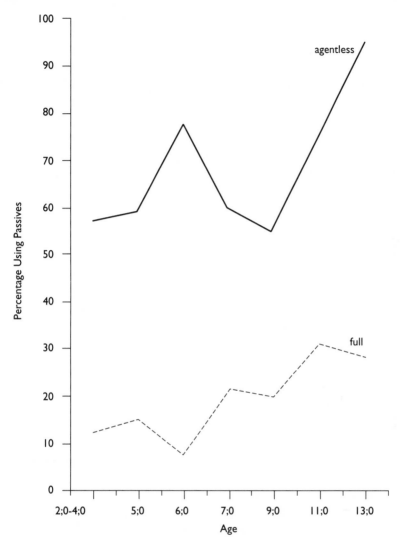

FIGURE 10.3 Children Using Full and Agentless Passives (from Horgan 1978:69)

produced by Eve and Sarah can be analyzed in this way, many of Adam's passives are clearly nonstative, including those cited in (11).

(11)   So it can't *be cleaned?* (3;2)
       When I *get hurts,* . . . (3;3)
       I don't want the bird to *get eated.* (3;7)
       I want to *be shooted.* (3;8)
       Why he gon' *be locked* in a cage? (3;10)
       Mommy, de cow gonna *get locked up.* (4;0)

The claim that children's early passives are almost exclusively agentless is also open to question. Budwig (1990c: 1230) reports that the two children whose spontaneous speech samples she studied used agentive phrases with 30% of their *be*-passives and 48% of their *get*-passives between the ages of 3;6 and 5. Moreover, Pinker, Lebeaux, and Frost (1987:262) found that children in their production study (described below) made frequent use of the *by*-phrase (as much as 85% of the time in one of their experiments).

Finally, it is worth noting that whatever its status in children's spontaneous speech, the preposition *by* has been shown (box 10.8) to be a powerful clue in the comprehension of passive constructions. Stromswold, Pinker, and Kaplan (1985) report that even the advanced children interpreted sentences as active if they did not include *by*.

Box 10.8

THE STUDY: Stromswold, Pinker, and Kaplan 1985
SUBJECTS: 59 children aged 2;9–5;10 (mean age = 4;3).
SENTENCE TYPES: various grammatical and ungrammatical utterances exhibiting some
    or all of the properties of English active and passive sentences (3 tokens each)
    The cow pushes the pig.
    The cow pushed the pig.
    The cow is pushes the pig.
    The cow is pushed the pig.
    The cow pushes by the pig.
    The cow pushed by the pig.
    The cow is pushes by the pig.
    The cow is pushed by the pig.
TASK: Act out with the help of toys.

2. Reassessing the Evidence

The studies reviewed to this point all report a relatively late acquisition time (age 6 or later) for passive structures, and such a conclusion was quite widely accepted for many years. More recently, however, this finding has been called into question based in part on the careful study of children's spontaneous speech. For example, Pinker, Lebeaux, and Frost (1987:202) report that passives occur in the speech of both Adam and Sarah starting at age 3;1. Using a liberal definition of passive (essentially, any past participle accompanied by *be, get,* or *need*), they count 72 possible passives in the speech of Adam prior to age 4;11 and 32 in the speech of Sarah prior to age 5;1. (Since these findings are based on a relatively small speech sample consisting of only one or two hours per month, the actual number of passives in these children's speech would of course have been much higher.) The sentences in (11) above exemplify some of these early passive patterns. Budwig (1990c: 1233–34) offers similar examples (as in (12)) from the speech of Melissa Bowerman's two daughters, and Snyder and Stromswold (1994) report the occurrence of passives as early as age 1;9 in the speech samples of 12 children they studied.

(12)   I want these pancakes to *be sugared.* (Christy, 4;2)
       Do you think that flower's supposed to *be picked* by somebody? (Eva, 2;10)
       She brought her inside so she won't *get all stinked up* by the skunk. (Eva, 4;1)
       I just *got pinched* from these pointed stuff. (Eva, 3;3)
       Does the cream of wheat need to *be cooled?* (Eva, 4;2)
       Hair needs to *be brushed.* (Christy, 4;2)

Pinker et al. note an additional fact in support of the view that even preschool children have a productive rule of passive formation: about a quarter of their passives involve innovations that are not found in the adult language. The examples in (13) of such forms, compiled by Pinker, Lebeaux, and Frost (1987: 204–5), are taken from the speech of a variety of children, including Adam and Sarah. (Budwig 1990c: 1241 reports similar innovations in her two subjects from the age of 3;6.)

(13)   He *get died.* (3;8)
       Is it all *needled?* (3;2)
       It *was bandaided.* (3;4)
       But I need it *watered* and *soaped.* (4;2)
       How *was* it *shoelaced?* (4;4)
       . . . more stuff that she *needs grained.* (4;11)
       I don't want to *be dog-eared* today. (5;6)
       . . . they won't *get staled.* (3;6)
       Why *is* the laundry place *stayed* open all night? (4;3)
       The tiger will come and eat David and then he will *be died* . . . (4+)
       I don't want to *get waved over.* [age unspecified]
       I don't like *being fallen down on.* (4+)

The existence of such sentences suggests that children have a productive rule of passivization from a relatively early age.

The innovations in (13) notwithstanding, Pinker (1989: 289) notes that the scope of the passivization rule seems to be restricted essentially to transitive verbs (including occasional verb–preposition sequences that are analyzed as transitive verbs) in which the theme argument is affected by the agent's action. Children sometimes use an intransitive verb as if it were transitive (e.g., *die* is used to mean 'kill' in the first example in (13)) and they sometimes use a noun as if it were a transitive verb (*bandaid* and *shoelace* in the third and fifth examples). However, like adults, they do not passivize measure verbs, symmetrical verbs, or verbs of pure possession (see (14))—verbs which either are not transitive or do not have theme arguments that are affected by the agent's action.

(14) *Unattested passives in children's speech:*
    a. Measure verb
        *Three ounces is weighed by the letter.
    b. Symmetrical verb
        *Two is equalled by five minus three.
    c. Verb of possession
        *A new car is had by Jerry.

This leads Pinker to conclude that the acquisition device is essentially conservative in nature and that it respects basic constraints on the use of the passive from the outset. We will have occasion to assess the importance of this conservatism for the overall language acquisition process when we examine the learnability problem in later chapters of this book.

The study of children's use of the auxiliaries *be* and *get* in passive constructions provides still further evidence that they have a productive rule of passivization from an early point in syntactic development. Budwig (1990c : 1232) reports that the two children she studied maintained a systematic difference between *be*-passives and *get*-passives. (*Be* passives outnumber *get* passives by a proportion of about 3 to 2 in the speech of these two children (p. 1229).) The key observation here is that, as in adult speech, the principal use of the *get*-passive (65% of the time) is to express actions that have negative consquences for the referent of the subject (e.g., *I just **got** pinched*). In contrast, the *be*-passive tends to be reserved for actions with neutral consequences (74% of its occurrences are associated with this use).

The productive use of passive patterns has been reported at even earlier ages in other languages. In the Bantu language Sesotho, for example, passives are used much more frequently than in English due in part to a constraint that prohibits *wh* words in subject position. Hence, in order to ask the question 'Who cooked the food?', the passive structure 'The food was cooked by who' must be used. (The

Table 10.5 Differences in the Use of *be*- and *get*-Passives (percentages)

FORM	TYPE OF CONSEQUENCE ASSOCIATED WITH THE ACTION DENOTED BY THE VERB			
	Negative	Positive	Neutral	Uncoded
be	18	3	74	6
get	65	6	26	4

following examples are from Demuth 1989:67–68; SM, subject marker; PRF, perfective; PASS, passive; M, mood.)

(15) a. *Active pattern:*
          *Mang o-pheh-ile   lijo?
          who SM-cook-PRF food
          'Who cooked the food?'
      b. *Passive pattern:*
          Lijo li-pheh-il-o-e   ke mang?
          food SM-cook-PRF-PASS-M by who
          'The food cooked by who?'

Demuth reports that passives in Sesotho are acquired by age 2;8, suggesting that adequate exposure to this pattern can quickly overcome any preference for associating the agent with the subject role and the theme with the direct object role. A similar finding has been reported by Pye and Poz (1988) for Quiché Mayan, which also uses passive constructions far more than does English.

STUDIES INVOLVING NOVEL VERBS

A problem inherent in the study of passives and other structures of this sort is that children's ability to produce or comprehend a given sentence may be based on memory rather than a productive grammatical rule. For instance, a child who produces or understands the sentence *I got hurt* may do so because he has heard this utterance (at least the *got hurt* part) in the speech of someone else, not because he has a rule of passivization that can modify the mapping between thematic roles and grammatical relations for a specific class of transitive verbs. How can we know whether language learners have a genuine rule of passivization and what types of verbs (e.g., actional vs. non-actional) it operates on? Children's innovative passives (e.g., *Is it all needled?* and the other examples in (13)) constitute one type of evidence for the existence of a productive rule of passivization. Powerful evidence of another sort comes from the study of novel verbs that are created by researchers and introduced to children in the course of an experiment. Because children cannot have been exposed to these forms previously, it is possible to infer from their responses whether they have a productive rule of passivization and what type of elements it is designed to apply to.

A good illustration of this type of study can be found in the series of production experiments carried out by Pinker, Lebeaux, and Frost (1987), of which a representative example is described in box 10.9.

In the production test, children were given a discourse context that would elicit either an active or a passive form of the new verb. For example, to elicit a passive, the experimenter might say: 'Here's the elephant. Nothing's happening to the

Box 10.9

THE STUDY: Pinker, Lebeaux, and Frost 1987 [experiment 2]

SUBJECTS: 32 children, divided into two groups: one aged 3−4;6 (mean age 3;10) and
the other 4;6−5;6 (mean age 5;1)

MATERIALS: Children were taught four new verb forms: *floose, gomp, jape,* and *pilk.* Two
of the verbs were given actional meanings ('to back into' and 'to slide down the
back of') and two were given non-actional spatial meanings ('to suspend' and 'to
contain').

PROCEDURE: Using toys, the experimenter demonstrated the meaning of a new verb
form. The children's knowledge of that form was then assessed with the help of
production and comprehension tests before moving on to the next form.

In the training session, one action verb was introduced as a passive and the
other as an active. Similarly, one non-action verb was presented as a passive and
the other as an active.

elephant. Now something's going to happen to the elephant. I want you tell me
what's happening.' At that point, the experimenter would use the toys to illustrate
one of the actions for which the child had learned a new verb. (For example, if the
child had previously been taught the verb *gomp* with the meaning 'to back into',
the experimenter might make a tiger back into the elephant.) All new verbs were
tested in both the active and the passive regardless of the voice in which they had
been taught to the child.

On the comprehension task, the experimenter asked the children to act out the
meaning of the novel verbs, saying (for example) 'Can you make it so the elephant
is gomped by the doggy' or 'Can you make it so the doggy gomps the elephant'.
As on the production task, all new verbs were tested in both the active and the
passive regardless of the voice in which they had been taught to the child.

Let us first consider the results from the production task (table 10.6). Since it
is very difficult (if not impossible) to design an experimental situation that is guar-
anteed to elicit passive sentences, there was no expectation that children would
produce these structures 100% of the time. Rather, it was assumed that even a
relatively small number of passive responses would suffice to establish the existence of a productive rule. As these results show, the children were able to use
new passive verbs, especially when they had first been exposed to them in that
form: actional verbs were passivized correctly 38% of the time by the younger
group and 50% of the time by the older group (see the rightmost column). Even
children who had been exposed only to a new actional verb in its active form were
able to produce the passive 25% of the time (second column from the left). Although the scores were much higher for verbs that were taught and elicited in the
active voice (the scores in the leftmost column), Pinker et al. conclude that the
children in their experiment have a productive rule of passive formation (p. 219).[2]

Table 10.6 Proportion of Successful Elicitations on the Production Task
(Pinker, Lebeaux, and Frost 1987:221)

AGE GROUP	TAUGHT IN ACTIVE VOICE		TAUGHT IN PASSIVE VOICE	
	Elicited as Active	Elicited as Passive	Elicited as Active	Elicited as Passive
Actional Verbs				
1 (3–4;6)	69%	25%	38%	38%
2 (4;6–5;6)	100	25	88	50
Non-actional Verbs				
1 (3–4;6)	56	6	38	31
2 (4;6–5;6)	88	25	62	62

Table 10.7 Results of the Comprehension Task (percentages)
(Pinker, Lebeaux, and Frost 1987:223)

AGE GROUP	TAUGHT IN ACTIVE VOICE		TAUGHT IN PASSIVE VOICE	
	Act-out Active	Act-out Passive	Act-out Active	Act-out Passive
Actional Verbs				
1 (3–4;6)	75	56	81	63
2 (4;6–5;6)	100	88	94	81
Non-actional Verbs				
1 (3–4;6)	44	62	56	50
2 (4;6–5;6)	81	88	100	50

Children's performance on the comprehension component of Pinker et al.'s experiment was even more impressive (table 10.7). Children's comprehension of passive verbs was above chance for both groups (especially for actional verbs), although this result was statistically significant only for the older group (p. 223). In sum, the conclusion of more recent work on the acquisition of passive patterns is that even preschool children have a full-fledged passivization rule that resembles its adult counterpart in terms both of the type of structures it can produce and the semantic constraints it obeys (see preceding section). This raises the question of why the results of the experimental tasks reviewed in section 1 of this chapter are so much poorer. Let us first consider the issue of production.

It is widely acknowledged that the failure to elicit a particular structure does not demonstrate that it has not been acquired. This is especially true in the case of passive structures, whose use is often associated with particular discourse and pragmatic conditions (downgrading of the agent, foregrounding of the theme, and so forth) that are hard to replicate in experimental settings. Thus, the failure of Turner and Rommetveit and Baldie (see section 1) to elicit passives in response to questions about pictures cannot in itself establish that children are incapable of producing these structures. These earlier findings must therefore give way to the more recent discovery that preschool children produce passives in their spontaneous speech as well as in experimental situations.

Turning now to children's performance on comprehension tasks,[3] we have already seen that their response to passive structures is routinely influenced by the Canonical Sentence Strategy, repeated in (16), as shown by the frequency of their reversal errors.

(16)   *The Canonical Sentence Strategy:*
        NP V NP = agent action theme

There is independent reason to believe that the relationship between thematic roles and grammatical relations associated with the Canonical Sentence Strategy is preferred by the acquisition device. Even 2-year-olds consistently encode the agent as subject and the theme as direct object rather than vice versa (Angiolillo and Goldin-Meadow 1982), and this set of relationships is the most basic throughout language (e.g. Givón 1984: 139). Not only are passive constructions relatively rare compared to their active counterparts, the agent is overwhelmingly the preferred subject in most (if not all) languages of the world, perhaps reflecting a propensity on the part of speakers to place the instigator of the action in the syntactically most salient position. These expectations about the relationship between thematic roles and grammatical relations apparently become integrated into young children's parser (the mechanism that analyzes and interprets incoming speech) in the form of the Canonical Sentence Strategy. This mechanism then interferes with the recognition of passive patterns under the types of conditions used in most experiments (which use reversible sentences presented without a context), even though the grammatical rule of passivization has been acquired and can be used under more favorable circumstances.

3. Ditransitive Verbs

Unlike many languages, English permits **ditransitive** (or 'double object') verbs—verbs that can take two NP complements, as in (17).

(17)   Harry gave [NP Sue] [NP the book].
        John showed [NP Mary] [NP the new car].

Most ditransitive verbs can also be used as ordinary transitive verbs with one NP complement and one PP complement (the so-called '*to*-dative pattern'), as in (18).

(18)   Harry gave [NP the book] [PP to Sue].
        John showed [NP the new car] [PP to Mary].

The difference between the ditransitive and ordinary transitive pattern is signaled syntactically by the presence or absence of the preposition *to,* a perceptually subtle signal since this element is normally unstressed—a potential problem for the acquisition device.

One of the most intriguing features of double object patterns involves the intricate semantic and morphological constraints that determine which verbs can be used ditransitively. As the examples in (19) show, even verbs that are quite similar in meaning can differ in terms of their ability to occur in double object constructions.

(19) a. Harry gave/*donated the Red Cross some money.
      b. The child threw/?*pushed his father the ball.
      c. Mary told/*said Bob the answer.

Pinker (1989) provides a detailed treatment of the constraints at work here as well as extensive discussion of their emergence in the course of the language acquisition process. In my discussion, however, I will focus on the comprehension and production of double object structures without regard for the lexical constraints that determine which verbs can occur in these patterns. (As noted in chap. 1, the study of lexical properties—including meaning and subcategorization—lies beyond the scope of this book.)

Results from a number of experimental studies (e.g., box 10.10) indicate that the comprehension of ditransitive structures lags behind that of their ordinary transitive counterparts (Waryas and Stremel 1974; Cook 1976; Osgood and Zehler 1981; Roeper et al. 1981). Even at age 10, children's comprehension scores on the ditransitive object pattern are only slightly above 50%, far below the near-perfect scores obtained on the ordinary transitive pattern (see table 10.8). Slightly higher figures (in the 60% range) have been reported by Roeper et al. (1981). In each case, the most common error involves treating the ditransitive pattern as if it contained a regular transitive verb and the preposition *to;* see (20).

Box 10.10

THE STUDY: Cook 1976
SUBJECTS: 90 children between the ages of 5 and 10 (15 in each age group)
SENTENCE TYPES: (8 tokens of each type)
     ditransitive pattern: give NP NP
     ordinary transitive pattern: give NP to NP
TASK: The children were asked to act out the meanings of the test sentences with the help of toys.

(20) *Actual sentence:*   *Child's interpretation:*
     The lion showed the giraffe the bear → The lion showed the giraffe *to* the bear
     agent   goal   theme   agent   theme   goal

In terms of production, however, matters seems to be quite different. As the sentences in (21) illustrate, children are able to *produce* ditransitive patterns at a

Table 10.8 Performance on Cook's Experiment (no. correct out of 120)
(from Cook 1976:436)

Structure	5-year-olds	6-year-olds	7-year-olds	8-year-olds	9-year-olds	10-year-olds
NP NP pattern	37	34	32	48	74	63
NP to NP pattern	106	111	117	120	119	120

much earlier age than the results of comprehension studies would lead one to expect. (The first three sentences are cited by Gropen et al. 1989:215 and the others are from Bloom, Lightbown, and Hood 1975:43 ff.)

(21)   Show Fraser horsie. (Eve, 1;9)
       Give doggie paper. (Adam, 2;3)
       I gave big tiger a bracelet. (Ross, 2;7)
       Daddy give Eric bath. (Eric, 2;1)
       Show Mommy that. (Eric, 2;1)
       Bring Jeffrey book. (Gia, 2;1)
       Mommy give them milk and sugar. (Kathryn, 2)

Moreover, Pinker (1989:284–85) reports (table 10.9) that the ditransitive versions of some verbs are used before their ordinary transitive counterparts. (See also Gropen et al. 1989:213–16.) An even more dramatic finding is reported by Snyder and Stromswold (1994), who studied the emergence of double object and *to*-dative patterns in extensive speech samples from 12 children aged 1;4 to 2;6 at the time of the first recording. They found that 11 of the 12 children acquired the double object pattern before the *to*-dative and that the remaining child acquired both patterns at the same time. (They suggest that earlier reports by Gropen et al. 1989 that neither structure systematically emerges before the other is the result of an overly liberal definition of *to*-datives that wrongly included directional patterns such as *Mommy take me to Delma's*.)

Snyder and Stromswold note that for verbs that allow both patterns, the double object dative is apparently more frequent than the *to*-dative in the speech of adults: in their speech samples, for instance, 73.2% of all adult utterances containing the verb *give* involved the double object pattern. However, Snyder and Stromswold are quick to point out that there was no statistically significant correlation between the relative frequency of *to*-datives in adult speech and the age of acquisition of either *to*-dative or double object patterns by children. They attribute the relatively late acquisition of *to*-datives to the fact that the preposition *to* in these patterns has been 'grammaticized' and no longer denotes the direction of a movement. (Notice that in sentences such as *I showed/explained the answer to Mary,* no movement at all takes place.) Consistent with this idea, Snyder and Stromswold note that the age of acquisition of the *to*-dative pattern is strongly correlated with that of other grammaticized uses of the preposition *to* (e.g., *I read/talked to Mary*) but only

Table 10.9 First Use of Transitive Verbs in the
Speech of Adam and Sarah (ages)

Verb	NP NP	NP PP
Adam		
bring	3;1	
build		4;0
buy	3;3	4;0
cook		3;2
draw	3;4	
drill		4;0
get	2;4	3;2
give	2;3	2;8
hand	2;6	
leave		3;8
make	3;5	3;0
read	4;2	3;2
send		3;3
show	3;0	2;11
sing	3;0	
tell	3;0	
throw		3;0
Sarah		
bring	1;10	2;3
buy		2;0
find		2;2
get	2;0	2;0
give	1;9	2;2
make		2;2
read	1;8	2;0
show	1;9	

weakly correlated with the age of acquisition of directional *to* (e.g., *She went to school*).

How can we reconcile Snyder and Stromswold's findings, which show a preference for double object patterns in children's speech production, with the experimental results reported earlier, which seem to demonstrate a preference for the *to*-dative pattern in comprehension? One possibility is that the two types of study are focusing on different structures—a first pattern in which the postverbal NP is a pronoun (e.g., *I sent **her** a letter*) and a second pattern in which it is a lexical NP (e.g., *I sent **my girlfriend** a letter*). Since pronouns in English tend to be clitics (phonologically dependent elements that must adjoin to a major category such as a verb), it is conceivable that the acquisition device initially does not treat the pronominal pattern as a true double object construction on a par with constructions containing two lexical NPs.[4] Moreover, it is also worth noting (as Kevin

Gregg has reminded me) that the pronominal pattern is likely to be very common in speech to children (e.g., *give me that, show me that*), which might further facilitate its early emergence.

Whereas comprehension experiments have explicitly focused on sentences involving lexical NPs, Snyder and Stromswold's study does not distinguish between the two types of double object patterns. Interestingly, however, Pinker (1984:398) reports that the 'majority' of children's early double object patterns have a pronoun as first object, and it seems reasonable to suppose that the same tendency is present in the speech samples studied by Snyder and Stromswold. Thus, it is conceivable that Snyder and Stromswold's findings pertain to a set of structures quite different from the ones that have been investigated in experimental studies of comprehension. At the very least, it would be interesting to know whether double object patterns involving lexical NPs emerge before their *to*-dative counterparts in Snyder and Stromswold's data.

Another (not necessarily incompatible) possibility is that extraneous factors interfere with children's comprehension of double object patterns, especially those containing two lexical NPs. As documented in the previous section, the ability to produce passive structures in spontaneous speech seems to be well in advance of the ability to comprehend this pattern in many experimental situations—a fact that is often attributed to the Canonical Sentence Strategy. A parallel explanation seems plausible in the case of the ditransitive patterns, as also proposed by Pinker (1984:398, 1989:401).

Let us assume that the association between thematic roles and grammatical relations found in simple transitive patterns (e.g., *The boy ate the apple*) is extended to structures in which the verb takes three arguments. This gives the Extended Canonical Sentence Strategy in (22) in which the first postverbal NP is associated with the theme role, must as it is in simple SVO patterns, and the second postverbal NP is linked to the goal role.

(22) *Extended Canonical Sentence Strategy:*
      NP V NP . . . NP = agent action theme goal

Consistent with this strategy, the erroneous interpretation exemplified in (20), repeated as (23), treats an intended goal–theme sequence in the stimulus sentence (*show the giraffe the bear*) as if it were a theme–goal sequence (*show the giraffe to the bear*).

(23) *Actual sentence:*   *Child's interpretation:*
      The lion showed the giraffe the bear → The lion showed the giraffe *to* the bear
      agent   goal   theme   agent   theme   goal

Indeed, the expectations embedded in the Extended Canonical Sentence Strategy are so strong that they can even override obvious pragmatic clues to a sentence's interpretation. Roeper et al. (1981:49–50) report that children of kindergarten age misinterpret sentences such as (24) almost two thirds of the time by treating *the cow* as the theme and *the spoon* as the goal (recipient).

(24) *Actual sentence:*   *Child's interpretation:*
      The dog gave the cow the spoon. → The dog gave the cow *to* the spoon.
      agent   goal   theme   agent   theme   goal

Thus, instead of having the dog give the spoon to the cow, the children make him give the cow to the spoon. Although pragmatically implausible, this interpretation is consistent with the Extended Canonical Sentence Strategy.

PASSIVIZATION OF DITRANSITIVE VERBS

As the following sentences show, both ditransitive verbs as in (25) and ordinary transitive verbs as in (26) have passive counterparts, although they differ in terms of which argument becomes subject.

(25) *Passive of a ditransitive verb—goal subject:*
      John was given the book (by Sue).
      goal   theme   agent
(26) *Passive of an ordinary transitive verb—theme subject:*
      The book was given to John (by Sue).
      theme   goal agent

I know of no data on children's use of 'ditransitive passives' in spontaneous speech, but at least two studies have examined their ability to understand these patterns. The first study, which I carried out in 1977 (box 10.11), used an act-out procedure to assess children's comprehension of several constructions. The results

Box 10.11

THE STUDY: O'Grady unpublished
SUBJECTS: 25 children aged 6;0–7;6
SENTENCE TYPES:
        ordinary transitive constructions (2 tokens):
            The cow showed the dog to the horse.
        ditransitive constructions (5 tokens):
            The cow showed the dog the horse.
        passive of ordinary transitive verb (3 tokens):
            The horse was hit by the dog.
        passive of ditransitive verb (10 tokens):
            The dog was shown the horse (by the cow).[a]
TASK: The children were asked to act out the meaning of the test sentences with the
        help of toys.

---

a. Half the children heard a version of this structure with an overt *by* phrase and half heard an agentless version.

Table 10.10 Scores on the Comprehension Task

Sentence Type	Percentage Correct
Ordinary transitive verb	80
Passive of transitive verb	86
Ditransitive verb	30.4
Passive of ditransitive verb with overt agent	1.5
Passive of ditransitive verb with understood agent	5.8

(table 10.10) revealed that the comprehension of the passive version of ditransitive verbs lagged far behind all other constructions studied.

The second study (box 10.12), carried out by Roeper et al. (1981), focused on the relationship between passivization and ditransitive verbs. They found that of the 30 children in their study, only 6 had scores of 75% or better on the ditransitive passive patterns. (Of these, three were in 2nd grade and three in 4th grade.) The overall rate of correct responses to this structure was a mere 3.8%.

Box 10.12

THE STUDY: Roeper et al. 1981

SUBJECTS: 10 children in kindergarten, 10 in second grade, and 10 in fourth grade; all children passed a pretest demonstrating their understanding of the passive version of ordinary transitive verbs

SENTENCE TYPE: (12 tokens of each type, with the animacy of the theme and goal systematically varied)

    passive of ditransitive verb:

      {The cow/the spoon} was given {the horse/the glass}.

TASK: The children were asked to act out the meanings of the test sentences with the help of toys.

4. Conclusion

Contrary to the dominant view in the 1960s and 1970s, it is now apparent that the acquisition device constructs a productive rule of passive formation in the preschool years, perhaps as early as age 3 or before. The evidence for this development comes both from children's spontaneous speech and from their ability to deal with novel verbs in experimental situations. Similar observations point to an early age of acquisition for ditransitive patterns.

Children's ability to comprehend both passive and ditransitive constructions is apparently hindered by a set of expectations (in the form of the Canonical Sentence Strategy) about the relationship between thematic roles and syntactic positions. It is unclear at this time precisely how these expectations develop, but it is possible that they reflect inherent predispositions on the part of the acquisition device to favor particular mappings of thematic roles onto structural positions.

Constraints on Coreference

Pronouns are elements whose reference is determined either by another NP (called an **antecedent**) or by the context. In (1), for example, the pronoun *he* can get its interpretation from the antecedent NP *Larry* (or from any other male), while in (2) its reference is contextually determined. (Here and elsewhere, coindexing is used to indicate coreference.)

(1)   Larry$_i$ feels that he$_{i,k}$ should work harder.
(2)   There he goes now.

In recent years, there have been many contributions to the literature on the development of pronouns. The principal goal of this chapter is to survey a representative sampling of these contributions, highlighting the major conclusions and controversies in this important research area.

1. A Directionality Preference

A distinction is often made between two types of pronoun–antecedent relations—**forward** pronominalization, as in (3a), in which the antecedent precedes the pronoun; and **backward** pronominalization, as in (3b), in which the reverse order occurs.

(3)   a. Larry$_i$ feels that he$_i$ should work harder
           antecedent   pronoun
      b. After he$_i$ got home, John$_i$ ate supper.
               pronoun   antecedent

A good deal of evidence indicates that forward patterns of pronominalization are preferred during the early stages of syntactic development. An influential study in this regard (box 11.1) was carried out by Lust (1981). Table 11.1 summarizes the children's scores on Lust's imitation task. As these figures show, both groups of subjects did better on the forward patterns (Types II and IV) than on the backward pattern (Type III). For example, the younger group of children had mean scores of 0.61 and 0.50 out of 2 on the two forward patterns, compared with only 0.21 on the backward pattern. Moreover, whereas these children converted 44% of the backward patterns into forward patterns, as in (4), the reverse modification was made only 1% of the time (pp. 85–86).

Box 11.1

THE STUDY: Lust 1981
SUBJECTS: Group I: 29 children aged 2;6–3;5, Group II: 45 children aged 3;6–5;7
SENTENCE TYPES: (2 tokens of each type)

> *Type I (Redundant structure):*[a]
> Because *Sam* was thirsty, *Sam* drank some soda.
> *Type II (Forward pattern):*
> *Tommy* ran fast because *he* heard a lion.
> *Type III (Backward pattern):*
> Because *she* was tired, *Mommy* was sleeping.
> *Type IV (Forward pattern):*
> Because *Jenna* saw a mouse, *she* ran away.

TASK: Imitation

a. I deliberately ignore a second pattern containing identical NPs because responses to it were not significantly different from those to Type I.

Table 11.1 Results of Lust's Task
(mean no. correct out of 2)
(from Lust 1981 : 81, 84)

Type	Group I	Group II
I (redundant)	0.20	0.88
II (forward)	0.61	1.77
III (backward)	0.21	1.18
IV (forward)	0.50	1.62

(4)   *Test sentence:* Because *he* was thirsty, *Sam* drank some soda (*backward pattern*)
                          ⇓   ⇓
      Response: Because *Sam* was thirsty, *he* drank some soda (*forward pattern*)

Children's preference for forward pronominalization is further confirmed by the performance of both groups on Type I (the redundant pattern containing two identical NPs), which had the lowest scores overall. The most common error (approximately 50% of all responses to this pattern) involved converting the second of the identical NPs into a pronoun (p. 85), thereby creating a forward pattern of pronominalization, as in (5). No children converted the first NP into a pronoun to create a backward pattern of pronominalization.

(5)   *Test sentence:* Because *Sam* was thirsty, *Sam* drank some soda.
                                                  ⇓
      Response: Because *Sam* was thirsty, *he* drank some soda.

The facts just outlined suggest that the acquisition device is subject to the predisposition in (6).

(6)   *The Forward Pronominalization Preference:*
       Forward patterns of pronominalization are preferred to backward patterns, all other
       things being equal.

Why should the acquisition device prefer forward patterns of pronominalization? One possibility is that the processing mechanisms used for sentence comprehension seek to interpret pronouns as soon as possible after encountering them (e.g., Reinhart 1986:140). Under such circumstances forward pronominalization would be favored over its backward counterpart, since the linear organization of this pattern (NP_i . . . $pronoun_i$) makes the antecedent available to aid in the immediate interpretation of the pronoun.

If the preference for forward pronominalization does indeed follow from a deeper computational property (the propensity to interpret pronouns upon encountering them), it should manifest itself in the development of all languages, not just English. Interestingly, it has been suggested (e.g., Lust 1983; Lust and Mangione 1983) that forward patterns of pronominalization are not universally preferred. Rather, it is claimed, directionality preferences are determined by the mechanism in (7).

(7)   *The Principal Branching Direction Parameter:*
       In early child language, the direction of pronominalization accords with the Principal Branching Direction of the specific language being acquired—forward in a principally right-branching language and backward in a principally left-branching language. (Lust and Mangione 1983:147)

A language's principal branching direction is determined by the relative positioning of heads with respect to 'major recursive categories' such as sentential complements and adverbial clauses. Thus, English is a right-branching language since a sentential complement occurs to the right of the head (in italics in (8)).

(8)   Max *believes* [$_S$ that Sally is the best candidate].

In languages such as Korean (see (9)) and Japanese, in contrast, the relative ordering of heads and complements is reversed.

(9)   Chelswu-ka [$_S$ Swuni-ka   aphu-ta-ko]   *mit-nun-ta.*
       Chelswu-NOM Swuni-NOM sick-DECL-COMP believe-PRS-DECL
       'Chelswu believes that Swuni is sick.'

Preliminary results from experiments involving Japanese language learners (Lust 1983; Lust and Mangione 1983) appeared to show a preference for backward patterns of pronominalization. However, a subsequent study (box 11.2) by O'Grady, Suzuki-Wei, and Cho (1986) with monolingual Korean children suggests that the preference for forward pronominalization exists even in 'left-branch-

Box 11.2

THE STUDY: O'Grady, Suzuki-Wei, and Cho 1986
SUBJECT: 96 monolingual Korean children aged 4;1–9;7
SENTENCE TYPES: (3 tokens of each type)
        Korean sentences equivalent to Lust's (1981) Types I, III, and IV
TASK: imitation, as in Lust's (1981) experiment

ing' languages. (O'Grady, Cho, and Sato 1994 report similar results for Japanese.) Table 11.2 list the results of this study for the youngest group of subjects and compares them with the scores of the comparable group in Lust's experiment. (Type II sentences are not considered here since this structure has no direct counterpart in Korean.) As these scores show, the Korean children's performance on the forward pattern (type IV) surpassed their scores on the backward pattern (type III) by a wide margin. Moreover, the redundant Type I structure was frequently converted into a forward NP–pronoun pattern (as much as 78% of the time by some children), just as it is in English. These results are consistent with the view that the preference for forward pronominalization is manifested in the early development of all languages, regardless of branching direction.

Table 11.2 Comparison of Scores for Korean and
English (percentage correct) (based on
O'Grady, Suzuki-Wei, and Cho 1986:412
and Lust 1981:82)

	Korean	English
	(mean age = 4;7)	(mean age = 4;8)
Redundant pattern (= I)	15.2	50
Backward pattern (= III)	37.5	72
Forward pattern (= IV)	88.9	95

2. Constraints on Pronoun Interpretation

The Forward Pronominalization Preference is not a grammatical principle, at least not in adult English. Although it entails that certain patterns of pronominalization are favored over others, it does not categorically rule out any particular type of pronoun–antecedent relation. As the following sentences show, some forward patterns are unacceptable (see (10)) just as certain backward constructions are perfectly natural (see (11)).

(10)   *On John's$_i$ table, he$_i$ put the new book.
(11)   On his$_i$ table, John$_i$ put the new book.
        After she$_i$ returned home, Sally$_i$ had supper.

The search for constraints on pronoun–antecedent relations constitutes one of the major undertakings in contemporary linguistic research, and many different proposals have been made. Several of these employ an important structural relation proposed by Reinhart (1983) and defined in slightly modified form in (12).

(12)   *C-command:*
A c-commands B if the first XP above A contains B.

The best known constraint based on c-command is Principle C, which can be paraphrased as in (13) for the purposes of this chapter.[1]

(13)   *Principle C:*
A pronoun cannot c-command its antecedent.

Principle C rules out all the sentences in (14)–(16), since in each case the first XP above the pronoun (the bracketed S, VP, and NP, respectively) also contains the antecedent.

(14)   *[$_S$ He$_i$ visited John's$_i$ mother].
(15)   *Sue [$_{VP}$ told him$_i$ about John's$_i$ exam].
(16)   *[$_{NP}$ his$_i$ report on John$_i$].

Crucially, however, Principle C does not block acceptable patterns of backward pronominalization such as those in (11), with the analysis in (17).

(17)   On [$_{NP}$ his$_i$ table], John$_i$ put the new book.
After [$_S$ she$_i$ returned home], Sally$_i$ had supper.

Since the first XP above the pronoun in these patterns (the bracketed NP and S, respectively) does not contain the antecedent, there is no violation of Principle C and the sentences are correctly predicted to be grammatical.

THE DEVELOPMENT OF PRINCIPLE C

The question of how and when constraints such as Principle C emerge is among the most difficult and controversial in the entire field of language acquisition research. Pioneering work (box 11.3) by Carol Chomsky (1969) suggests that there may be at least two intermediate stages prior to the emergence of the adult system (table 11.3).

The first stage that can be discerned in Chomsky's results is characterized by the absence of a syntactic restriction on pronoun interpretation. During this stage, children apparently allow a pronoun to get its reference from any other NP in the sentence. Thus even in structures such as *He found out that Mickey won the race,* 9 of the 40 children in Chomsky's study (including 7 of the youngest) took *he* and

Box 11.3

THE STUDY: C. Chomsky 1969

SUBJECTS: 9 5-year-olds, 7 6-year-olds, 7 7-year-olds, 8 8-year-olds, 8 9-year-olds, 1 10-year-old

SENTENCE TYPES: (5 tokens of each type)

> *Type I—Blocked backward:* He found out that Mickey won the race.
>
> *Type II—Permissible backward:* After he got the candy, Mickey left.
>
> *Type III—Permissible forward:* Pluto thinks he knows everything.

TASK: Comprehension was tested by means of a question–answer procedure. Upon hearing the sentence *He found out that Mickey won the race,* for example, the child was asked, 'Who found out?' Toys were used as props, so that the children could respond either by naming or by pointing.

Table 11.3 Major Stages in the Development of Principle C (according to C. Chomsky)

Stage	Principle
1	Pronouns take antecedents.
2	Pronouns cannot precede their antecedents.
3	The adult system (Principle C)

Mickey to be coreferential at least once (p. 107). Ingram and Shaw (1988:401–2) report similar responses by 7 of the 100 children (3;0–7;11) they studied in a comparable experiment. McDaniel, Cairns, and Hsu (1990:126–28) note that 5 of the 20 children (3;9–5;4) in their study acted out at least some sentences in violation of Principle C, although all but two of the children gave responses on a judgment task that suggested some knowledge of this constraint.

According to Chomsky's analysis, the next step in the developmental process involves the formulation of an order-dependent constraint that prohibits a pronoun from preceding its antecedent. Children in this stage not only disallow the pronoun–antecedent relationship in unacceptable sentences such as (18), they also do not accept the pattern in (19).

(18)   *He_i found out that $Mickey_i$ won the race.

(19)   After he_i got the candy, $Mickey_i$ left.

Chomsky placed only 4 children in this stage, these being the only subjects in her experiment who produced no coreferential responses for any of the 5 tokens of either sentence type.

In a third and final major developmental stage, which seems to begin around age 6 or earlier, the acquisition device responds to sentences such as (19) by revising its earlier hypothesis and permitting a pronoun to precede an antecedent that it does not c-command, consistent with Principle C.

Chomsky's second stage is controversial even though subsequent studies have sometimes found evidence of its existence. Using a relatively weak criterion (2 or fewer coreferential responses out of 5), Ingram and Shaw (1988:403) estimate that as many as 26 of their 100 subjects (ages 3;0–7;11) make use of the linear constraint associated with Chomsky's stage 2. Hsu et al. (1989:613, 1991) note that 23 of the 81 children (aged 3;1–8;0) in their act-out experiment "manifested a general tendency to avoid backward coreference," adding that this tendency is most common in 6-year-olds. Solan (1983:121) reports that 6 of 36 children (ages 5–7) he studied with the help of an act-out task produced a coreferential response no more than 1 time out of 5 for backward patterns of pronominalization.

However, in all studies, the evidence for a prohibition against backward pronominalization crucially involves children's failure to select an intrasentential antecedent for the pronoun in sentences such as (19). Since the pronoun–antecedent relationship in such patterns is optional in adult speech, one cannot infer from children's avoidance of coreferential responses that the acquisition device has produced a grammatical rule that prohibits backward coreference. It is conceivable that, like adults, children have a grammar that permits a coreferential relationship in (19), but that this interpretation does not occur to them in the absence of an appropriate context. It is worth noting in this regard that Goodluck (1987) observed broad acceptance of both forward and backward pronominalization among 5-year-olds in an act-out task involving sentences such as those in (20).

(20) a. *Backward pattern:*
          After he jumps up and down, the pirate hits the engineer.
          (sentence-internal antecedent selected 85.1% of the time)
      b. *Forward pattern:*
          The pirate hits the engineer after he jumps up and down.
          (sentence-internal antecedent selected 92.6% of the time)

As Goodluck herself observes (p. 257), children's propensity to select a sentence-internal antecedent (and hence to accept backward pronominalization) in this sort of act-out task may well be related to the fact that they already had to manipulate two dolls just to act out the main clause, making it difficult to select the third doll that would be necessary to indicate a sentence-external antecedent.

This notwithstanding, application of Principle C to the full range of pronominalization patterns found in English may take several years to master. Patterns involving unacceptable forward pronominalization prove especially problematic, and children seem to permit coreference in these cases, (e.g., (10), repeated as

(21)) until age 8 or later (Taylor-Browne 1983; Ingram and Shaw 1988:401; Hsu et al. 1991:352, 1989:615, 619–20).

(21)   *On John's₁ table, he₁ put the new book.

Unfortunately, further discussion of this and other possible substeps in the emergence of Principle C is made difficult by the need to consider technical, theory-dependent issues and details that go beyond the scope of this chapter. I will therefore not try to pursue this matter further here. For relevant discussion, see Solan 1983; Lasnik and Crain 1985; Lust 1986:44ff.; Lust and Clifford 1986; Carden 1986:331ff.; O'Grady 1987:146ff.; and Grodzinsky and Reinhart 1993.

AN ALTERNATIVE VIEW: THE CONTINUITY HYPOTHESIS

In recent years, the existence of intermediate stages in the development of Principle C has been called into question. For instance, Lust, Eisele, and Mazuka (1992:333) claim that reconsideration of the results obtained on earlier experiments supports the conclusion that Principle C is "respected continuously" from the age of 3 onward, consistent with the Continuity Hypothesis (see also Kaufman 1994:193ff.). The key observation on which this conclusion rests is that children of all ages disfavor coreference in sentences violating Principle C compared to sentences that respect this principle. This can best be seen by considering a sampling of the studies that have considered this issue (boxes 11.4–11.7).

Box 11.4

THE STUDY: Lust, Loveland, and Kornet 1980
SUBJECTS: 82 children aged 3;5–7;5 (mean age = 5;6)
RELEVANT SENTENCE TYPES:
   a) *He₁ turned around [when Snuffles₁ found the penny].
   b) When he₁ closed the box, Cookie Monster₁ lay down.
TASK: The children acted out the meanings of the sentences with the help of toys.
RESULTS: The children assumed coreference 14.5% of the time for sentence (a), which
   violates Principle C, compared to 24% of the time for the acceptable sentence (b).
   When the test sentences were presented with a pragmatic context, the proportion of coreferential responses rose to 35% and 59%, respectively.

Box 11.5

THE STUDY: Solan 1983
SUBJECTS: 36 children aged 5;2–8;5
RELEVANT SENTENCE TYPES: (3 tokens of each type)
   a) *He$_{i,k}$ told the horse₁ that the sheep$_k$ would run around.
      *He$_{i,k}$ hit the horse₁ in the sheep's$_k$ yard.
      *He$_{i,k}$ hit the horse₁ after the sheep$_k$ ran around.
      *He$_{i,k}$ hit the horse₁ after the sheep's$_k$ run.

b) After he$_{i,k}$ ran around, the horse$_i$ hit the sheep$_k$.

After his$_{i,k}$ run, the horse$_i$ hit the sheep$_k$.

TASK: The children acted out the meanings of the sentences with the help of toys.

RESULTS: The children assumed coreference 13.5% of the time for the first group of sentences, all of which violate Principle C, compared to 47% of the time for the acceptable sentences in the second group.

Box 11.6

THE STUDY: Crain and McKee 1986

SUBJECTS: 62 children, mean age of 4;2

RELEVANT SENTENCE TYPES:

a) *He$_i$ ate the hamburger when Smurf$_i$ was inside the fence.

b) When he$_i$ stole the chickens, the lion$_i$ was inside the fence.

TASKS: Children were asked to judge whether the situation acted out by the experimenter was a correct interpretation of the stimulus sentence. Thus, the children who have mastered Principle C should respond 'No' if the experimenter has Smurf eat the hamburger in the situation corresponding to sentence (a).

RESULTS: Even the seven youngest subjects (mean age 3;1) responded correctly 79% of the time to patterns such as (a).

Box 11.7

THE STUDY: Grimshaw and Rosen 1990

SUBJECTS: 12 children aged 4−5

RELEVANT SENTENCE TYPES: (2 tokens of each type)

a) *He$_i$ hit Ernie$_i$.

b) *He$_i$ said that Bert$_i$ moved the box.

TASKS: Children viewed a videotaped action sequence depicting either a coreferential or a noncoreferential interpretation of the pronoun prior to presentation of the stimulus sentence. They then had to judge the sentence as it was produced by a puppet frog as 'true' or 'false'. A small discourse context was also provided.

Violation of Principle C in simple sentence: The children were shown a video depicting Ernie hitting himself. The puppet then says: 'Ernie was fighting with Big Bird. He$_i$ hit Ernie$_i$.'

Compliance with Principle C in simple sentence: The children were shown a video of Ernie patting Big Bird. The puppet then says: 'I just saw Ernie do something with Big Bird. He$_i$ patted Big Bird$_k$.'

RESULTS: Children were less likely to accept as true the sentence *He hit Ernie* than the sentence *He patted Big Bird* (37.5% vs. 83.3%). This is crucial since the former sentence can be true only if *he* and *Ernie* were coreferential—in violation of Principle C (recall that the video showed Ernie hitting himself). In contrast, the latter sentence is true on the reading where *he* and *Big Bird* are not coreferential, since Ernie is the one who pats Big Bird in the accompanying video.

These studies all appear to show that despite the existence of errors, children are more likely to reject sentences that violate Principle C than to accept them. On the assumption that the errors that do occur can be attributed to extraneous factors (inattentiveness, memory limitations, confusion over the instructions, a desire to please the experimenter, nervousness, and the like), we are left with the conclusion that the major constraint on pronoun–antecedent relations is in place from an early stage of syntactic development.

There are several reasons for caution, however. For one thing, much of the data used to support claims about early acquisition of Principle C consists of average scores for groups of children. This contrasts with the data reported by Chomsky and by Ingram and Shaw, who consider individual scores. Not surprisingly, it is the latter type of study that has yielded the best evidence in support of intermediate developmental stages. It is possible that a careful examination of the individual scores obtained in the other studies would also uncover evidence for intermediate developmental stages in at least some children.

A second reason to be cautious in evaluating claims about early mastery of Principle C has to do with the type of pronoun–antecedent relations produced by children in their own spontaneous speech. For example, crediting an observation of Joan Maling's, Lust, Eisele, and Mazuka (1992:355) cite the two speech errors by Chris in (22), the first when he was 3;1 and the second when he was 3;3.

(22)   CHRIS: Matt hit me.
       MOM: Where did he hit you?
       CHRIS: He$_i$ hit me in Matt's$_i$ house.

       CHRIS: Kitty ate it.
       He$_i$ ate it all by Kitty's$_i$ self.

I noted the similar violations of Principle C in (23) in the speech of my daughter when she was 33 months old.

(23)   He$_i$'s in MG's$_i$ house.
       She$_i$'s in Mama's$_i$ office.

These are only isolated examples, of course, and no firm conclusion can be drawn from them, since even adults make speech errors from time to time.[2] But they do point to the need for further research in this area. (A study of spontaneous speech that sheds light on a different aspect of the development of coreference is discussed in the next section.)

A third issue that must be considered has to do with the possibility that children's early rejection of unacceptable pronominalization patterns reflects something other than a *grammatical* principle. As the sample test sentences from the various studies reviewed above illustrate, the pronoun typically occurs in the matrix subject position in sentences used to exemplify violations of Principle C.

Since matrix subjects are known to be high in topicality (what the sentence is about) and empathy (the speaker tends to adopt the perspective of their referent), this introduces a potential complication. In particular, it is conceivable that children reject the relevant sentences because they violate the *pragmatic* principle in (24) (see Van Valin 1990 : 178 ff. for a review of several such principles).

(24)   A topic may not be referentially dependent on a component of the comment [the remainder of the sentence].

In order to be sure that a grammatical constraint (i.e., Principle C) rather than a pragmatic restriction such as (24) is operating in early child language, it is necessary to compare patterns in which the c-commanding pronoun is a subject/topic with patterns in which it has some other role (say, direct object). The pairs of sentences in (25)–(27) exemplify this contrast. (I assume that all six of these sentences are ungrammatical on the intended interpretation, as predicted by Principle C; see Solan 1983 : 100 for a similar assumption.)

(25)   a.   *He$_i$ told Mary [that John$_i$ had won].
     b.   *Mary told him$_i$ that [John$_i$ had won].

(26)   a.   *He$_i$ saw Mary in John's$_i$ yard.
     b.   *Mary saw him$_i$ in John's$_i$ yard.

(27)   a.   *He$_i$ saw Mary after John's$_i$ party.
     b.   ?*Mary saw him$_i$ after John's$_i$ party.

Since the pronoun c-commands the intended antecedent in both the (a) and (b) patterns, all six sentences violate Principle C. In addition, the (a) sentences (but not their (b) counterparts) violate our putative pragmatic constraint, since the pronoun is a subject/topic. If Principle C is in fact operative in the early stages of syntactic development, we therefore expect children to reject both patterns, especially in comparison to fully grammatical sentences such as those in (28), from Solan (1983).

(28)   a.   After he$_{i,k}$ ran around, the horse$_i$ hit the sheep$_k$.
     b.   After his$_{i,k}$ run, the horse$_i$ hit the sheep$_k$.

Some information about the status of the relevant sentences can be found in the study by Solan (1983), box 11.5 above, but the data are far from transparent. Since the youngest subjects in Solan's study were 5 years old, his data obviously do not allow us to draw conclusions about what happens at the earliest stages of syntactic development. However, it does raise questions about whether Principle C is operating in older children in the expected manner. Especially noteworthy is the fact that for sentence types (26) and (27), coreference is permitted a much higher percentage of the time in the (b) patterns than in the (a) patterns. This is especially evident for the 6- and 7-year-olds in the case of sentence type (26) and for all three groups in the case of sentence type (27). In all these cases, the percentage of

Table 11.4 Coreferential Responses (percentage)
(from Solan 1983 : 106, 118)

Sentence Type	5-year-olds	6-year-olds	7-year-olds
25a	17	22	0
25b	17	17	6
26a	17	25	6
26b	14	44	22
27a	8	28	14
27b	42	42	33
28a	44	28	36
28b	47	61	64

coreferential responses (above 40%) approaches the range found with the patterns in (28), which do not violate Principle C. (Hsu et al. 1991 : 345 report mean scores above 40% for patterns equivalent to Solan's (25b) among 16 3-year-olds and 15 4-year-olds whom they tested using an act-out experiment. However, their test sentences did not include the equivalent of (25a), so it is difficult to draw firm conclusions from this result.)

In sum, in contrast with the (a) patterns, the (b) patterns in (25)–(27) have the pronoun in the direct object position rather than the subject position. The pragmatic principle proposed in (24) above is thus not applicable, although Principle C should be since the pronoun still c-commands its antecedent. These sentences therefore provide a purer test of Principle C effects than do the (a) sentences. Significantly, judgments of coreference in the (b) patterns seem to rise sharply, contrary to what we would expect if Principle C were in fact operating at these and earlier stages of syntactic development.

3. Reflexive Pronouns

A distinction is usually made between two classes of pronouns: **pronominals** such as *he, they, him,* and *them* and **reflexives** such as *himself* and *themselves*. The two types of pronouns are characteristically interpreted in very different ways. The reflexive pronoun in (29), for example, must take the NP *Harry* as its antecedent, while the pronominal *him* refers either to John or to some person not mentioned in the sentence.

(29) a. John$_i$ knows [$_S$ that Harry$_k$ admires himself$_k$].
      b. John$_i$ knows [$_S$ that Harry$_k$ admires him$_i$].

Another contrast is illustrated in (30), where the reflexive pronoun can refer only to Bob's friend, but the pronominal *him* can be interpreted either as Bob or as some third person (but not as Bob's friend).

(30) a. [Bob's$_i$ friend]$_k$ admires himself$_k$.
      b. [Bob's$_i$ friend]$_k$ admires him$_i$.

Most syntactic analyses assume that reflexive pronouns obey some version of the constraint paraphrased in (31), first proposed by N. Chomsky (1981).[3]

(31) *Principle A:*
A reflexive pronoun must have a more prominent antecedent in its minimal domain.

For the purposes of this discussion, we can take the 'minimal domain' mentioned in (31) to be the smallest S containing the reflexive. This explains why the antecedent for *himself* in (29) must be *Harry:* this is the only NP in the embedded S that contains the reflexive pronoun. Simplifying slightly, we can take the 'more prominent' antecedent to be an NP that is higher in the tree structure (i.e., an NP that c-commands the reflexive). This latter requirement explains why the reflexive pronoun in (30a) can take the subject as its antecedent, but not the possessor NP that is embedded inside the subject; see (32).

(32)

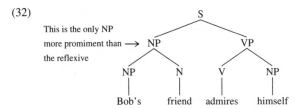

For ease of exposition, I will henceforth refer to the part of Principle A that requires an antecedent in the same clause as the **Locality Requirement** and to the part that requires a more prominent antecedent as the **Prominence Requirement.**[4]

We have already noted that pronominals tend to have interpretations that contrast with those associated with reflexive pronouns. Chomsky's theory accounts for this fact by making pronominals subject to the constraint paraphrased in (33).[5]

(33) *Principle B:*
A pronominal must not have a more prominent antecedent in its minimal domain.

Assuming the minimal domain to be to the smallest S containing the pronoun, we predict that *him* cannot refer to Harry in (29b), repeated as (34). (Coreference with *John* is possible since this NP, although more prominent, is not in the same minimal clause.)

(34) John$_i$ knows [$_S$ that Harry$_k$ admires him$_i$].

Furthermore, the pronominal in (30b), repeated as (35), can be coreferential with *Bob,* which is embedded in the subject phrase and hence not more prominent (although it is in the same clause).

(35)   [Bob's$_i$ friend]$_k$ admires him$_i$.

However, it cannot be coreferential with *Bob's friend,* a more prominent NP in the same clause.

A number of studies have examined the question of when children come to know the principles that underly the contrast between reflexives and pronominals. One such study (box 11.8) was carried out by Jakubowicz (1984).

Box 11.8

THE STUDY: Jakubowicz 1984
SUBJECTS: 7 3-year-olds, 10 4-year-olds, 11 5-year-olds
SENTENCE TYPES:
> *Reflexive:* John said that [$_S$ Peter washed *himself*].
> *Pronominal:* John said that [$_S$ Peter washed *him*].
TASK: Children were asked to act out the meaning of the test sentences with the help of
>   puppets.

Jakubowicz's sentences were designed to determine whether children know that reflexive pronouns, but not simple pronominals, are subject to the Locality Requirement. As figure 11.1 shows, all three groups of children did very well on the sentences containing a reflexive pronoun (scoring above 90%). In contrast, results for the sentences containing ordinary pronominals were much poorer, with children in the youngest group incorrectly linking the pronoun to the subject NP in the same clause more than 50% of the time. Results similar to these have also been reported by Read and Hare (1979), Otsu (1981), and Solan (1987; box 11.9), among others (see Kaufman 1994 for a review).

Box 11.9

THE STUDY: Solan 1987
SUBJECTS: 19 children with a mean age of 4;10, 18 children with a mean age of 6;0
SENTENCE TYPES: (4 tokens of each type)
> *Reflexive:* The dog said that [$_S$ the horse hit *himself*].
> *Pronominal:* The dog said that [$_S$ the horse hit *him*].
TASK: The children were asked to act out the meaning of the test sentences with the
>   help of toys and pictures.

Overall, the children in Solan's study averaged scores of 95% on sentences containing a reflexive pronoun but only 49% on sentences containing an ordinary pronominal. (Once again, their errors on the latter pattern involved linking the pronoun with the subject NP in the same clause.)

Jakubowicz (1984) also reports on an experiment (box 11.10) designed to determine whether children know that reflexive pronouns differ from pronominals

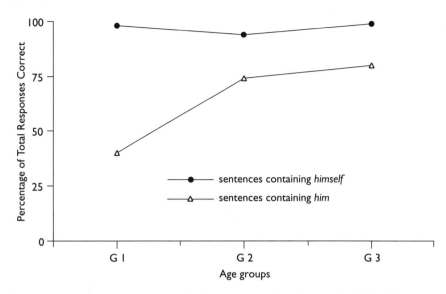

FIGURE 11.1 Performance on the Locality Requirement (from Jakubowicz 1984: 167)

with respect to the Prominence Requirement. The results of this experiment are depicted in figure 11.2. Once again, the reflexive pronouns were interpreted with a high degree of success (close to 90%), but the ordinary pronominals were often incorrectly associated with the more prominent NP in the same clause, especially by children in the two younger groups.

Box 11.10

THE STUDY: Jakubowicz 1984
SUBJECTS: 9 3-year-olds, 12 4-year-olds, 10 5-year-olds
SENTENCE TYPES:
  Reflexive:
    John said that [ₛ [Dave's friend] washed *himself*].
    John said that [ₛ [the friend of Dave] washed *himself*].
  Pronominal:
    John said that [ₛ [Dave's friend] washed *him*].
    John said that [ₛ [the friend of Dave] washed *him*].
TASK: act out, as in the previous experiment. If children have acquired the Prominence Requirement, they should choose *Dave's friend* (or *the friend of Dave*) as the antecedent for the reflexive pronoun but not for the simple pronominal.

Results roughly comparable to those reported by Jakubowicz were obtained in a larger study (box 11.11) by Wexler and Chien (1985). Although the scores were

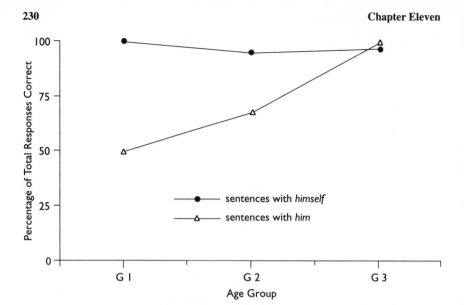

FIGURE 11.2 Performance on the Prominence Requirement (based on Jakubowicz 1984:171)

in general lower than in Jakubowicz's experiment (fig. 11.3), the reflexive pronouns were interpreted correctly more often than the ordinary pronominals.

Box 11.11

THE STUDY: Wexler and Chien 1985
SUBJECTS: 129 children aged 2;6–6;6. The children were divided into 8 groups at 6-
    month intervals, with a minimum of 15 per group.
SENTENCE TYPES: (8 tokens of each type)
        Reflexive: Cinderella's sister points to *herself.*
        Pronominal: Cinderella's sister points to *her.*
TASK: Selecting which of two pictures correctly depicts the situation described by the
    test sentence. One picture depicted the situation appropriate for a reflexive pro-
    noun and the other the situation appropriate for an ordinary pronominal.

The tendencies just reported seems not to be universal, since McKee (1992) reports that even 3-year-olds have relatively little difficulty interpreting the (clitic) pronominals used in Italian. However, there is a striking degree of agreement among experiments investigating the comprehension of pronouns by English-speaking children. As seen in the studies reviewed above, children initially have much more success interpreting reflexive pronouns than simple pronominals. Moreover, exactly the same error is reported for each experiment: in interpreting pronominals, children under age 6 tend to select as antecedent a more prominent

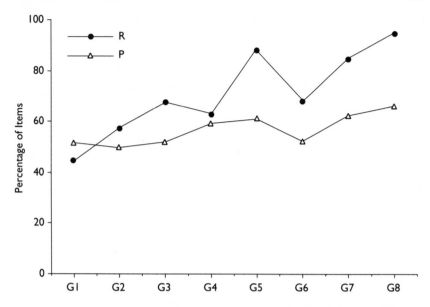

FIGURE 11.3 Comprehension of Reflexives and Pronominals (from Wexler and Chien 1985:143)

NP in the same clause. In other words, they interpret pronominals as if they were reflexives and had to obey the Locality and Prominence Requirements. Thus, in response to a sentence such as *John said that Peter washed him,* typical 4-year-old children make the puppet named Peter wash himself. Similarly in response to the clause *Dave's friend washed him,* they have the puppet corresponding to Dave's friend wash himself.

EXPLAINING THE ASYMMETRY

Why does the acquisition device make such errors? One proposal, put forward by Jakubowicz (1984:175) and Solan (1987:201), is the two-part suggestion that Principle A, with its Prominence and Locality Requirements, is innately 'built into' the acquisition device (which accounts for why children do so well on reflexives) and that ordinary pronominals are initially mistaken for reflexives (which accounts for why children do so poorly in interpreting them). A problem with the second part of this suggestion is that children use pronominals in many contexts where reflexive pronouns cannot occur. For example, they produce sentences such as *He gone* and *I saw him,* in which there is no sentence-internal antecedent. Since children apparently do not use reflexives in such contexts (cf. **Himself gone* and **I saw himself*), they cannot be failing to distinguish between pronominals and reflexives (Wexler and Chien 1985:147; Lust 1986:79). Also problematic is the fact that children's scores on Principle B sentences tend to hover around 50%. Were they consistently applying Principle A to pronominals, their success rate should actually be much *LOWER* (essentially zero, in fact), since this principle would consistently give the wrong result.

Chien and Wexler (1990) and Grodzinsky and Reinhart (1993) offer a very different interpretation of children's poor performance on the sentences designed to test knowledge of Principle B. Following a proposal by Reinhart (1984), they make a sharp distinction between two types of potential antecedents—true referring NPs (e.g., names such as *Harry* and *Sue*), which are used to refer to specific individuals, and quantified NPs (*everyone* and *someone*), which have no such referential function. They further suggest that there are two ways that a pronoun and an NP can come to have the same reference—one via a grammatical mechanism and the other via a pragmatic mechanism.

The grammatical mechanism is **binding,** a relation that holds between a pronoun and a more prominent (i.e., 'c-commanding') antecedent that can be either a true referring NP or a quantified NP; see the examples in (36).

(36)   a. Harry$_i$/Everyone$_i$ thinks that he$_i$ deserves to win.
       b. Paul$_i$/Someone$_i$ lost his$_i$ wallet.

In contrast, the pragmatic mechanism (which we can simply call **coreference**) requires a referring NP as antecedent, and there is no requirement that this element be more prominent in the tree structure; see the examples in (37).

(37)   a. Harry$_i$ thinks that he$_i$ deserves to win.
       b. Paul$_i$ lost his$_i$ wallet.
       c. Even his$_i$ friends wouldn't support Harry$_i$.

Since the antecedent c-commands the pronoun in the (a) and (b) sentences of (36) and (37), it is possible to have either binding or simple coreference. On the other hand, when the antecedent fails to c-command the pronoun (as in (37c)), only coreference is possible (see table 11.5). This is why the pronoun in such a pattern can take a referring NP as its antecedent, but not a quantified NP, as in (38).

(38)   *Even his$_i$ friends wouldn't support everyone$_i$.

Table 11.5 Two Pronoun–Antecedent Relations

Relation	C-command Necessary?	Type of Antecedent	Examples
Binding	yes	quantified NP, or referring NP	36a,b 37a,b
Coreference	no	referring NP only	37a,b,c

A crucial claim of this theory is that Principles A and B regulate the binding relation but not the coreference relation. (The coreference relation is subject to a pragmatic principle whose content need not concern us here.) If this is right, then it is obvious that in order to investigate the emergence of Principles A and B, researchers must focus on the binding relation. Unfortunately, all the experiments considered to this point use test sentences containing referring NPs, which can be involved in either the binding relation or the coreference relation, as we have just seen. To be certain of assessing children's knowledge of Principles A and B, it is necessary to employ test sentences in which the antecedent is a quantified NP, since NPs of this type can *only* participate in the binding relation (see above). Chien and Wexler (1990) carried out just such a study (box 11.12).

Box 11.12

THE STUDY: Chien and Wexler 1990
SUBJECTS: 177 children aged 2;6−7;10, and 20 adults. Child subjects were divided into
      4 groups: I: 48 subjects under age 4; II: 45 subjects aged 4−5; III: 44 subjects aged
      5−6; IV: 40 subjects aged 6−7; an adult control group
RELEVANT SENTENCE TYPES: (6 tokens of each type)
      Pronominal with referring NP as potential antecedent:
      Mama Bear is touching her.
      Pronominal with quantified NP as potential antecedent:
      Every bear is touching her.
TASK: Children were presented with a picture and a short story before being asked a
      question that tested their knowledge of Principle B. (Control sentences were used
      to ensure that the children understood quantified NPs.)

Figure 11.4 provides an example of the type of pictures that accompanied sentences containing a referring NP. (Since these sentences may involve either coreference

This is Mama Bear; this is Goldilocks.
Is Mama Bear <u>touching</u> her?

This is Mama Bear; this is Goldilocks.
Is Mama Bear <u>touching</u> her?

FIGURE 11.4 Sample Test Items (Chien and Wexler 1990:262)

These are the bears; this is Goldilocks.
Is every bear <u>touching</u> her?

These are the bears; this is Goldilocks.
Is every bear <u>touching</u> her?

FIGURE 11.5 Sample Test Items (Chien and Wexler 1990:263)

or binding, they cannot provide unambiguous information about children's knowledge of Principle B, but they are useful for purposes of comparison.) Figure 11.5 illustrates the pictures and sentences used to test children's understanding of a binding relation involving a quantified NP and a pronoun. A response of 'Yes' to the first question and 'No' to the second indicates an understanding of Principle B in these cases.

Figure 11.6 summarizes children's responses on sentences containing a referring NP. As these results show, all the children tended to respond appropriately when the question associated with the picture could be answered 'yes' (what Chien and Wexler call a 'match'). However, the three younger groups had difficulty when the appropriate answer is 'no' (the 'mismatch' condition). Under these circumstances, the rate of correct responses fell to between 40% and 60%, versus 80% and above for the older two groups. The failure to respond appropriately in these cases suggests a deficit in children's understanding of how pronouns are used, since by responding 'yes' they seem to be treating the plain pronominal as coreferential with the subject NP in the same clause. (This is, of course, the same phenomenon noted in earlier studies of pronoun interpretation.)

Figure 11.7 summarizes the results for the sentences in which a quantified NP serves as antecedent. As before, all the children did very well on sentences that matched the picture. But on the mismatches, a crucial difference emerges. In contrast to what was observed in cases where the antecedent is a referring NP, the children in Group III did quite well on the mismatches—scoring above 80%, which suggests mastery of Principle B.

Interestingly, a parallel set of test sentences revealed that these children have also just mastered Principle A. This allowed Chien and Wexler to conclude that

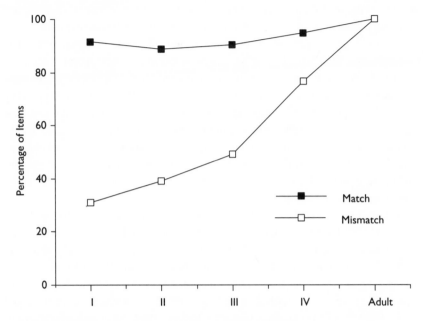

FIGURE 11.6 Results with a Referring NP as Antecedent (from Chien and Wexler 1990:273)

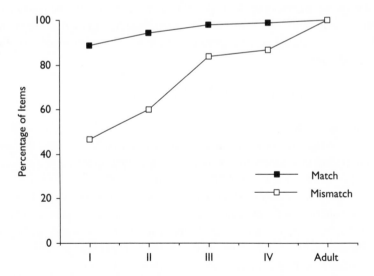

FIGURE 11.7 Results with a Quantified NP as Antecedent (from Chien and Wexler 1990:273)

the two principles do in fact emerge at the same time, contrary to what had previously been believed. Crucially, though, the similarity shows up only in sentences in which the pronoun takes a quantified NP as its potential antecedent (compare figs. 11.6 and 11.7). In sentences containing a referring NP, Chien and Wexler claim, children's performance is hampered by the fact that the pronoun-antecedent relation must be ruled out twice—once by the grammatical principle (Principle B) governing binding relations, and once by the pragmatic principle regulating coreference relations. (Recall that, unlike quantified NPs, referring NPs can participate in either binding relations or coreference relations.) Since children know how to use Principle B (as shown by their performance on the patterns containing quantified antecedents), the problem presumably lies with the pragmatic constraint on coreference.

Although there have been replications of Chien and Wexler's results (see Kaufman 1994:188 for a review), other studies have not found the predicted asymmetry (Grimshaw and Rosen 1990:212; McKee 1992:47; and especially Kaufman 1994:186). Chien and Wexler's conclusion is also controversial for conceptual reasons: it contradicts the 'commonsense expectation' that referential antecedents should be easier to deal with than their quantified counterparts (Grimshaw and Rosen 1990:213–14). An observation by Koster (1994:220) supports this intuition and provides a possible explanation for Chien and Wexler's results. Reviewing experimental work by Chien and Wexler (1991) and an unpublished paper by C. Jakubowicz, Koster observes that children resist linking pronouns to a quantified antecedent in sentences such as (39), even though this binding relationship is perfectly grammatical (since the pronominal and its antecedent are not in the same minimal clause).

(39)   [Every bear$_i$ wants [Ernie to wash him$_i$]].

As Koster notes, this suggests that children generally do not accept a quantified NP as antecedent for a pronominal under any circumstances, and that this predisposition (rather than access to a revised version of Principle B) is responsible for the results reported in Chien and Wexler's original study.

Grimshaw and Rosen (1990) also dispute Chien and Wexler's conclusion with regard to patterns containing quantified antecedents, but they agree with the contention that Principle B is not acquired later than Principle A. Although they focus their attention on issues involving methodology and data interpretation, their paper includes a small illustrative experiment (box 11.13) involving referring NP antecedents. For the grammatical interpretation of the sentence type *Ernie patted him*, the children were presented with the stimulus in (40).

Box 11.13

THE STUDY: Grimshaw and Rosen 1990
SUBJECTS: 12 children (5 girls & 7 boys) aged 4–5
RELEVANT SENTENCE TYPES (2 tokens):
    *Ernie$_i$ hit/patted him$_i$.
TASKS: After viewing a videotaped action sequence, children had to decide whether a
    sentence describing the video was 'true' or 'false'. A small discourse context was
    provided.

---

(40) Videotaped scene: Big Bird pats Ernie.
      The frog's utterance: I just saw Big Bird do something with Ernie.
                             Big Bird$_i$ patted him$_k$.

For the ungrammatical interpretation of the same structure, the stimulus in (41)
was provided.

(41) Videotaped scene: Big Bird hits himself.
      The frog's utterance: Big Bird was standing with Ernie.
                             Big Bird$_i$ hit him$_i$.

Grimshaw and Rosen found that children judged the ungrammatical sentence (*Big Bird hit him*, describing a situation in which Big Bird hit himself) to be 'true' an average of 0.83 times out of 2 (41.5%). (Recall that each child responded to two tokens.) In contrast, they accepted uses of the same structure (e.g., *Big Bird patted him*) to describe a situation in which Big Bird patted Ernie an average of 1.67 times out of 2 (83.5%)—about twice as often. This suggests that children are able to correctly interpret pronouns even in sentences where the antecedent is a referring NP.

Why then do children make so many errors involving pronoun interpretation? (Even in Grimshaw and Rosen's study, 8 of the 12 children accepted one of the two ungrammatical sentences.) Grimshaw and Rosen suggest a number of possibilities.

- Children are biased toward giving 'yes' answers on grammaticality judgment tasks (p. 196). They thus tend to accept both *John$_i$ saw himself$_i$* and *John$_i$ saw him$_i$*, which is the correct response in the former case but not the latter. (For a discussion of judgment biases in general, see Birdsong 1989: 101 ff.)

- For pragmatic reasons, children prefer to find an antecedent for each pronoun that they hear (p. 201). If they are presented with sentences such as *John$_i$ saw himself$_i$* and *John$_i$ saw him$_i$* in isolation, they can comply with this preference only if they select *John* as the antecedent in each case. This preference leads to a grammatical response in the first sentence but not in the second.

- Some errors may be traceable to a misanalysis of the sentence's structure. For example, children are known to make mistakes on sentences such as *Cinderella's sister pointed to her,* by associating *her* with the more prominent NP *Cinderella's sister.* However, Grimshaw and Rosen (pp. 204–6) raise the possibility that these children may be misanalyzing the possessor construction, noting that a study of comparable sentences in Dutch found that children frequently treated the possessor as if it were the subject of the sentence (i.e., they treat Cinderella as the one who does the pointing). Under such circumstances, it is no longer clear that a violation of Principle B actually occurs, since the selected antecedent (the sister) may not be more prominent in the syntactic structure the children assign to the sentence.

Not all the test sentences used in studies of pronoun interpretation are open to these particular criticisms, however. For example, sentences such as (42) provide an intrasentential antecedent for the pronominal, while sentences such as (43) avoid the prenominal possessive whose interpretation may be difficult on independent grounds.

(42)   John said that Peter washed him.
(43)   John said that the friend of Dave washed him.

Both these sentence types were employed in the Jakubowicz study (see box 11.10), and the younger children had the usual difficulty with both, interpreting the pronominal *him* as if it were a reflexive.

A further consideration that must be taken into account when evaluating experimental work on coreference involves the relationship between the test sentences and the context in which they occur. Starting with Sperber and Wilson's (1987) idea that each sentence in a discourse must be 'relevant', Foster-Cohen (1994) observes a variety of problems with the design of experiments that have been used to test children's knowledge of Principle B. Reconsider in this regard the method employed by Grimshaw and Rosen to investigate this aspect of syntactic development; cf. (44)–(45).

(44)   Videotaped scene: Big Bird pats Ernie.
       The frog's utterance: I saw Big Bird doing something with Ernie$_j$.
                                 Big Bird$_i$ patted him$_j$.

(45)   Videotaped scene: Big Bird hits himself.
       The frog's utterance: Big Bird was standing with Ernie$_j$.
                                 Big Bird$_i$ hit him$_i$.

As explained earlier, children are supposed to accept the first sentence but reject the second. However, as Foster-Cohen notes (p. 252), the two types of stimuli differ dramatically in terms of the relevance of Ernie, who is mentioned in the focus position of the lead-in sentence and can therefore be expected to be relevant in what follows (i.e., the test sentence). This expectation is met in the first case, where Ernie is in fact the referent of the pronoun *him*. However, in the second scenario Ernie is not relevant, since the test sentence makes no reference to him on the intended interpretation. Foster-Cohen suggests that this confuses the children, detracting from their ability to process the test sentence and depressing their scores. (Whereas children correctly accept the first test sentence 83.5% of the time, they succeed in rejecting the ungrammatical second test sentence only about half as often.)

Yet another type of confounding factor involves processing considerations. All things being equal, it seems reasonable to suppose that the mechanisms responsible for sentence processing prefer to match pronouns with an antecedent that is in the same minimal clause (so as to reduce memory load; see Solan 1983:119) and that is relatively high in topicality (what the rest of the sentence is about). The former preference duplicates the Locality Requirement, while the latter overlaps heavily with the Prominence Requirement, since it singles out subjects as the most likely antecedents, these being the elements highest in topicality and easiest to emphathize with (Givón 1984:138; Kuno 1987:159).

Among the consequences of these processing preferences is a pattern of interpretative tendencies identical to those reported in the experiments we have just reviewed. In attempting to associate pronouns with prominent antecedents in the same clause, children correctly interpret most sentences containing reflexive pronouns (whose antecedents tend to have just these properties). However, this same tendency has a detrimental effect on the comprehension of pronominals, contributing to an interpretation in which they are treated as if they were reflexive pronouns. Interestingly, in languages where a reflexive pronoun can have an antecedent either inside or outside the minimal clause containing it, children's initial preference is for the nearer antecedent (Hermon 1992, 1994; see chap. 13 for further discussion). A Chinese example cited by Hermon (1992:166) is given in (46).

(46) more distant   nearer (and preferred)
      antecedent   antecedent
         ↓   ↓

      [Xiao-houzi   shuo [Xiaohua gei ziji yi-zhang   tiezhi]]
      little   monkey say   Xiaohua give self one-CLASS sticker
      'The little monkey says that Xiaohua gives self a sticker.'

This is expected, given the processing considerations just outlined.

This is not to say that English-speaking children have no understanding of Principles A and B. If this were so, they presumably would rely solely on the processing considerations just outlined and thereby misinterpret virtually all pronominals as reflexives—which does not happen. (Recall that children's scores on pronominals tend to hover around 50%.) However, it does seem plausible to suppose that processing considerations facilitate reflexive-like interpretations, thereby boosting performance on reflexive pronouns and interfering with the interpretation of plain pronominals.

One way to avoid at least some of the problems we have been considering is to examine coreference in children's spontaneous speech. Because speakers know what they wish to say and provide at least part of the context themselves, their use of grammatical principles is less likely to be influenced by extraneous factors relating to expectations about what others intend. Moreover, since they themselves choose the form of the pronoun, nothing prevents them from reserving the reflexive for cases where there is a local antecedent. Very little work has been done in this area, but a recent study by P. Bloom et al. (1994) is especially promising. The study (table 11.6) focused on three children's use of the first person pronominal *me* and reflexive *myself* in six speech samples over a three-year period. Bloom and his colleagues concentrated on children's use of *me* and *myself* in direct object position (e.g., *NP hit me/myself*), since this is the context in which these two elements contrast most clearly. (The study was restricted to first person pronouns because of the difficulty of determining the intended referent of third person pronouns such as *him* and *himself* in tape recordings.) They were able to identify 2,834 such contexts for *me* and 75 for *myself*. As the data represented in table 11.7 show, errors of any type were extremely rare. Even the speech samples collected

Table 11.6 Subjects in Bloom et al.'s Study

Child	Age Range	Total Number of Utterances Examined
Abe	2;4–4;11	20,950
Adam	2;3–5;2	46,803
Sarah	2;3–5;1	39,426

Table 11.7 Children's Use of *me* and *myself* in Direct Object Position

Sample Context	*me*	*myself*
John hurt __: [correct form = *me*]	2830 [99.7%]	8 [0.3%]
I hurt __: [correct form = *myself*]	4 [5.6%]	67 [94.4%]

when the children were 2 or 3 years old showed predominantly correct usage of *me* and *myself* (99.8% for the former item and 93.5% for the latter).[6]

Even taking into account the fact that Bloom et al.'s study is restricted to first person singular pronouns, the results strongly suggest that children know the essence of the contrast between reflexive and plain pronominals from a very early age. If this is so, then the difficulties reported in the comprehension experiments reviewed earlier do not entail a grammatical deficit; rather, they must reflect difficulties in overcoming the contextual, pragmatic, and processing factors that frequently interact with syntactic principles in actual language use.

4. Conclusion

The development of pronoun–antecedent relations is one of the most complicated and intricate phenomena in the entire language acquisition process. Certain aspects of pronoun–antecedent relations, such as the constraints on forward pronominalization (needed to rule out *Near John$_i$, he$_i$ dropped a knife* and similar patterns), may require a lengthy period of development extending well into the early school years. However, recent research suggests that the acquisition device identifies at least the basic principles of pronoun interpretation (e.g., the constraint embodied in Principle C as well as the distinction between reflexives and pronominals) at a relatively early point in syntactic development (perhaps even by age 3), although extraneous factors such as processing preferences and pragmatic considerations may interfere with their use in certain situations. Efforts to identify the precise contribution of these and other factors to pronoun interpretation continue, offering the promise of new insights into this perplexing phenomenon.

PART II

Theories of Learnability and Development

The Learnability Problem

As noted in the first chapter, the study of syntactic development is oriented around two research themes. One, pertaining to development, is concerned with the description of child language, including the times at which particular constructions are acquired, the errors that are made at intermediate stages, and the path that is followed on the way to acquiring the final linguistic system. The other, the learnability problem, deals with how the acquisition device is able to construct the right grammar for a language in response to experience of a particular sort. Put another way, research into development is primarily concerned with describing and explaining *when* and *in what manner* the acquisition device does its work, while study of the learnability problem focuses on *how* it does it.

Thus far in this book, we have dealt almost exclusively with developmental issues. The time has now come to consider the learnability problem.

1. The Traditional View

An early view of language acquisition that has served as a useful foil for recent work is that the ability to form and interpret novel utterances is based largely on analogical reasoning. For example, Paul (1891:97) maintained that the creation of novel forms is "formation by analogy," while Bloomfield (1933:275) claimed that "a regular analogy permits a speaker to utter speech-forms which he has not heard; . . . he utters them on the analogy of similar forms which he has heard." More recently, a variant of this view has been adopted by Derwing (1973:239), who observes:

> Once we have already taken into consideration such sentences as 'Cows eat grass', 'Horses eat oats' and 'Pigs eat garbage', we should not be astounded to find that a grammar adequate for these should also predict the occurrence of 'Horses eat grass'.

According to this and similar views, then, the acquisition device can essentially be reduced to the mechanism of analogy, whose operation allows the learner to extrapolate from limited experience to an unlimited number of novel sentences.

A serious problem with this idea is that apparently similar sentences in the child's experience often exhibit very different properties—contrary to what analogy would lead us to expect. As noted by Baker (1979:561), for instance, the very analogical reasoning described by Derwing will lead to erroneous predictions in cases such as (1).

(1)   a. It is likely that John will be delayed.
       b. It is probable that John will be delayed.

       c. John is likely to be delayed.
       d. *John is probable to be delayed.

Since (a) and (b) look alike and since (c) is a grammatical variant of (a), it seems reasonable to conclude that, by analogy, (d) should be acceptable as a variant of (b). But analogy gives the wrong result here, since sentence (d) is in fact unacceptable.

A similar problem arises in the case of the sentences in (2)–(3), from Lightfoot 1982:55 ff.

(2)   I met the student from France.
(3)   I met the student of French.

As (4) shows, *student* can be 'replaced' by the indefinite pronoun *one* when it is followed by a *from* phrase.

(4)   I met the student from France and Sue met the *one* from Spain. (*one* = student)

By analogy, a similar substitution should be possible with the *of* phrase in (3), yielding (5).

(5)   *I met the student of French and Sue met the *one* of Spanish. (*one* = student)

Crucially, however, this sentence is ungrammatical. Once again, reasoning by analogy gives a wrong result. Examples such as these can be multiplied indefinitely, each time illustrating the failure of analogy as a general language learning strategy.

This is not to say that analogy has no role to play in language acquisition. Children do in fact make errors that may reflect the operation of analogy in some instances. For instance, I observed my 3-year-old daughter say that a bee had just 'beed out of the room', arguably by analogy with 'The fly flew out of the room'. At the same time, though, there is no indication of a general reliance on analogical reasoning; for instance, children seem not to make errors in the use and interpretation of *one* (see chap. 3 for some discussion).

How then does the acquisition device work? Because we have no way of observing the inner workings of the human mind, the acquisition device cannot be studied directly. Rather, we must attempt to infer its properties from what we know about the task that it performs. The earlier chapters of this book provided numerous examples of how specific developmental phenomena can be used to draw inferences about particular properties and preferences of the acquisition device (see chap. 16 for a brief summary). As we will now see, the investigation of the learnability problem can also shed light on the nature of the acquisition device.

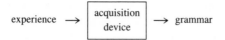

FIGURE 12.1 The Acquisition Process

As first noted in chapter 1, the acquisition device can be seen as a 'function' that takes as its input experience and yields as its output a grammar (fig. 12.1). This state of affairs points toward a promising research strategy: by carefully studying both the grammar that is the output of the acquisition process and the type of experience that is its starting point, it should be possible to draw some important inferences about the device that provides the bridge between the two. (This is, of course, the standard operating procedure of all science: make use of observable facts to draw inferences about the existence and nature of invisible entities and mechanisms that can explain those and other facts.)

In the remainder of this chapter, I focus on some salient properties of both the experience that serves as input to the acquisition device and the grammar that constitutes its output. The next two chapters then address the question of what type of acquisition device is needed to guarantee the success of language learning with such a starting point and end point.

2. The Nature of the Grammar

This is not the place to attempt a comprehensive discussion of contemporary syntactic theory or of the many competing theoretical frameworks that are contributing to the study of human linguistic competence. Instead, I will be content to outline what I believe is a plausible set of assumptions about the nature of the syntactic component of the grammar. These assumptions are not the product of any particular approach to grammatical analysis; rather, they represent a sort of 'synthesis' of proposals and discoveries put forward in many different frameworks over a period of several decades. For the sake of discussion, I will divide the syntactic knowledge necessary for language use into three parts.

The first and arguably most basic component of syntactic knowledge relates to word-level properties, especially those pertaining to membership in a syntactic category (N, V, etc.). I discuss the nature of these categories at greater length in a later chapter. For now it suffices to assume that such categories exist and that the contrasts they represent are relevant to sentence formation. (We might also include in this component of syntactic knowledge information about a word's meaning and subcategorization, two types of lexical properties that fall beyond the scope of this book.)

A second component of syntactic knowledge provides a set of mechanisms for combining words into larger phrases and, ultimately, sentences. Although these mechanisms are themselves finite, they have the capacity to form an unlimited number of sentences, including utterances that have not previously been heard by the language user. It is widely believed that the sentences generated by these mechanisms have a well developed hierarchical structure of the sort illustrated in (6).

(6)

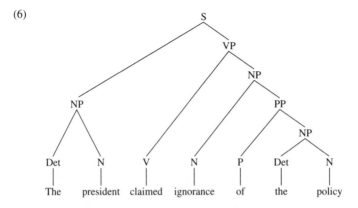

Consistent with the structure depicted in (6), I assume that the mechanisms responsible for sentence formation generally operate on pairs of elements, forming representations with a binary architecture. (Binary branching is quite widely assumed in current syntactic work; see, for example, Kayne 1983:227 n.; Bach 1988:22; Larson 1988:381.)[1] I further assume that, like words, the phrasal constituents of syntactic structure are assigned to categories (NP, VP, PP, etc.), in accordance with their combinatorial properties. Finally, I assume that the syntactic representations for transitive sentences manifest a 'subject–object asymmetry' in that the verb combines directly with its 'direct object' argument but not with its 'subject'. (Note that in (6) the subject combines not with the verb *claim*, but rather with the phrase consisting of the verb and its direct object.)

The third and final component of syntactic knowledge assumed here consists of principles formulated with reference to syntactic representations of the sort depicted in (6). The most obvious candidates for membership in this component are the 'binding' constraints that restrict the relationship between a pronoun and its antecedent (chap. 11) and the constraints that regulate the relationship between a 'gap' and the 'displaced' element with which it is associated (so-called 'island constraints'; see chap. 7). As we have already seen, both types of constraint make reference to configurational features of the syntactic representation—the former to c-command (and perhaps precedence) and the latter to notions such as 'complex NP', 'adjunct', and '*wh* island'.

Table 12.1 summarizes the properties of the grammar assumed here. Although these do not of course constitute a complete inventory of grammatical mecha-

Table 12.1 Components of the Grammar Resulting from
            the Acquisition Process

Component	Contents
Categorial	Inventory of syntactic categories (N, V, A, etc.)
Structure-building	Architectural properties that give binary branching, the subject–object asymmetry, and so on
Constraints	Principles restricting pronoun interpretation and gap placement (for example)

nisms (for example, nothing has been said here about inflection or subcategorization), they constitute a reasonable sampling of the types of core phenomena on which learnability research focuses. Our next task is to consider the input that comes from children's early linguistic experience with a view to determining what information, if any, it provides about the mechanisms summarized in table 12.1.

3. The Nature of Experience

The priority of research into the role of experience in language learning is to identify those properties of the child's environment that are required for the acquisition device to function properly. To date, research into the relevance of experience to linguistic development has focused on **motherese,** the particular form of speech used with young children by their caregivers (usually their mothers); some of its properties are listed in table 12.2, from Owens 1984:224.

A particularly strong version of the claim that caregiver speech is relevant to language learning can be stated as (7), the **Motherese Hypothesis** (see, e.g., Gleitman, Newport, and Gleitman 1984:45).

(7)   *The Motherese Hypothesis:*
      The special properties of caregiver speech are required for language acquisition to occur.

The attractiveness of the Motherese Hypothesis stems from the fact that caregiver speech has many properties that are evidently of potential value to the acquisition device (Snow 1972:561; Levelt 1975:15; Brown 1977:20; Cross 1977:152). For instance, the slow, careful articulation that is typical of motherese should make utterances easier to perceive. Its relatively restricted vocabulary should allow learners with limited lexical resources to comprehend sentences addressed to them. The proliferation of short, simple sentences with frequent repetitions should give children ample exposure to structural patterns that are easy to process and to use. The efforts by mothers to elicit responses from their children and to maintain a conversation with them should provide a valuable opportunity for practicing emerging linguistic skills. And so on.

Table 12.2 Some Properties of Motherese, Compared with Ordinary Speech

Paralinguistic
Slower speech with longer pauses between utterances and after content words
Higher overall pitch; greater pitch range
Exaggerated intonation and stress
More varied loudness pattern
Fewer disfluencies (1 disfluency per 1000 words vs. 4.5 per 1000 for adult-to-adult speech)
Fewer words per minute

Lexical
More restricted vocabulary
Three times as much paraphrasing
More reference to the here and now

Semantic
More limited range of semantic functions
More contextual support

Syntactic
Fewer broken or run-on sentences
Shorter, less complex utterances (approx. 50% are single words or short declaratives)
More well-formed and intelligible sentences
Fewer complex utterances
More imperatives and questions (approx. 60% of total)

Conversational
Fewer utterances per conversation
More repetitions (approx. 16% of utterances repeated within 3 turns)

Moreover, it is known that given a choice between motherese and regular adult-to-adult speech, infants prefer the former. Fernald (1992) has found that children aged 4 months (and perhaps younger) will turn the heads more frequently toward speech that has the prosodic properties of motherese than toward speech with adult-to-adult prosody.

The major problem with the Motherese Hypothesis is that it has not been possible to demonstrate that the acquisition device actually *needs* particular properties of caregiver speech in order to operate successfully (e.g., Ferguson 1977:233). At the very least, we would expect that if the Motherese Hypothesis is correct, then certain key properties of caregiver speech should be universally available to all language learners. However, matters seem not to be so straightforward. Reviewing the literature on mother–child interactions in a variety of cultural and linguistic settings, ranging from white middle class families in New England to black mill workers in Trackton, South Carolina, to Kaluli-speaking communities in Papua New Guinea, Peters (1983:31–32) notes some very fundamental differences (listed in table 12.3) both in how mothers speak to children and in how they view

Table 12.3 Cross-cultural Variation in Maternal Speech and Attitudes

---
1. Rights of the child to participate in conversation

---
a. Children are born with such rights: middle-class English-speaking
b. Children must achieve such rights through the acquisition of sociolinguistic competence: Trackton
c. Children must achieve such rights through the acquisition of age and status: Samoa, Luo

---
2. Modification of talk to babies

---
a. Talk to babies must be modified in order to promote comprehension: middle-class English-speaking
b. Talk to babies should not be modified: Kaluli
c. Caregivers don't talk to babies: Trackton

---
3. Meaning of babies' early vocalizations

---
a. They are interpretable: middle-class English-speaking
b. They are of no consequence: Trackton, Samoa

---
4. Response to babies' vocalizations

---
a. They should be repeated and expanded when possible: middle-class English-speaking
b. They should be accepted but not modified: Kaluli (?)
c. They should be ignored: Trackton, Samoa (?)

---
5. Language skills that adults believe should be explicitly taught

---
a. Labels for people and things: middle-class English-speaking, Luo, Kaluli (to a lesser extent)
b. Appropriate ways to interact socially: Kaluli, middle-class English-speaking (a limited set of routines), Samoa (calling-out routines)
c. People's names: Samoa
d. None: Trackton

---
6. Language teaching mechanisms

---
a. Question-and-answer routines: middle-class English-speaking
b. Direct instructions to 'say X': Kaluli, middle-class English-speaking (to a lesser extent: social routines and names), Samoa (calling-out routines)
c. Children will talk when they have something to say: Trackton

---

children's speech (see also Schieffelin and Ochs 1986:173; Lieven 1994). Particularly important here is the observation that children in some communities are not seen as potential conversational partners (point 1) and that no special effort is made to engage them in speech or to facilitate language learning for them (points 2, 5, and 6). Indeed, as Lieven (1994:62) notes, there are cultures in which children are spoken to relatively little before they themselves can produce multiword speech. This suggests that motherese is not necessary for the successful operation of the acquisition device.

Two additional points must be stressed at this time. First, the findings just reported do not entail that experience is unnecessary or irrelevant to the acquisition process: as noted by Lieven (1994:61), children growing up in these cultures are almost always in the company of a caregiver and are exposed to a great deal of language use in appropriate social settings even if the speech is not directed specifically to them. (For instance, Schiefflin 1985:531 reports that in Kaluli culture, adults direct very little talk to preverbal children, but they do frequently talk about them and their activities in their presence.)

Second, the fact that motherese is *unnecessary* for syntactic development does not preclude the possibility that the acquisition device might find it *helpful* in certain respects. In fact, there are a number of well-known cases where a particular characteristic of maternal speech has been positively correlated with rate of grammatical development in some specific area. For example, both Newport, Gleitman, and Gleitman (1977) and Furrow, Nelson, and Benedict (1979) have found a high positive correlation between mothers' use of *yes–no* questions and children's acquisition of auxiliary verbs: the more *yes–no* questions produced by the mothers, the faster auxiliaries emerge in the speech of their children. Of course, there is a simple and reasonable explanation for this correlation. Since *yes–no* questions make the auxiliary verb salient by placing it in sentence-initial position where it is stressed and uncontracted (e.g., *Will you go?*), it is not surprising that frequent exposure to these structures might facilitate the acquisition of these lexical items. (Nonetheless, it is worth noting that this correlation was not manifested in some subsequent studies—e.g., Scarborough and Wyckoff 1986. For some further discussion of these issues, see Shatz, Hoff-Ginsberg, and Maciver 1989; Yoder and Kaiser 1989; Pine 1994; Richards 1994.)

At the same time, however, it is important to note that many of the reported correlations between maternal speech and language development seem entirely unmotivated and are almost certainly spurious. For example, Furrow, Nelson, and Benedict (1979) report that mothers' use of copulas is negatively correlated with children's acquisition of NPs (i.e., the fewer copulas used by the mother, the more quickly the child learns NPs) and that maternal use of verbs correlates negatively with children's acquisition of these elements (that is, the fewer verbs used by the mother, the faster the child acquires verbs). As noted by Gleitman, Newport, and Gleitman (1984:50), whenever small speech samples are subjected to statistical analysis (the case in much of the motherese literature), some spurious correlations are likely to emerge. In fact, they report (p. 64) that in their study of 6 mother–child pairs (child age: 18–21 mos.), they found a very high positive correlation between the unintelligibility of maternal utterances and the number of verbs used in the children's sentences!

Moreover, as noted by Newport, Gleitman, and Gleitman (1977:146), even those correlations that do make sense involve relatively peripheral, language-specific features of syntactic development. No feature of caregiver speech has ever been causally linked to the emergence of binary branching, the subject–object asymmetry, or constraints on binding, for example. Indeed, there are even some cases where motherese arguably *impedes* syntactic development: as is explained later in this chapter and in the next chapter, certain syntactic phenomena are manifested only in relatively long and complex sentences—the very type of structure that is rare in caregiver speech.

If motherese is not a 'teaching language' and is not necessary for syntactic development, what then is its function? Why is it so widely used, especially in Western cultures? One very plausible idea, put forward by Cross (1977:182), is that it serves to increase the comprehensibility of adult utterances, thereby enhancing communication with the child. In other words, middle-class North American mothers speak to children the way they do simply because they want to be understood. (And short, clearly articulated utterances about the here and now are indeed relatively easy to understand.) This practice may affect particular features of syntactic development (sometimes favorably, sometimes not), but these are incidental (and unintended) consequences of its primary function. We return to this point below in our discussion of the type of linguistic experience that *is* crucial to the operation of the acquisition device.

POSITIVE AND NEGATIVE EVIDENCE

What other types of information might facilitate the operation of the acquisition device? As noted in chapter 1, when linguists try to construct the grammar of a language, they invariably seek out **negative evidence**—information about the ungrammaticality of particular sentences. (In analyzing '*one* substitution', for example, linguists need to know that the utterance **I saw a student of French and one of Spanish* is ungrammatical.) However, it seems that the acquisition device must rely on information that it can cull from sentences that it encounters in the speech of others—so-called **positive evidence.** (The terms 'positive' and 'negative' evidence were first introduced by Gold 1967.) Negative evidence, despite its potential usefulness, appears not to be available to language learners. Let us consider this point in more detail.

In theory, there are two ways that the acquisition device could gain access to negative evidence: it could somehow infer on its own that particular sentences are ungrammatical because they are never encountered, or it could be provided with this information through feedback from a mature speaker of the language. (The term **indirect** negative evidence is sometimes used for the former situation and **direct** negative evidence for the latter.) Interestingly, neither scenario seems plausible given what is currently known about the nature of the acquisition device and the type of information to which it has access.

Consider first the possibility that the acquisition device somehow notices that certain sentences are never heard. As mentioned in chapter 1, there is no limit on

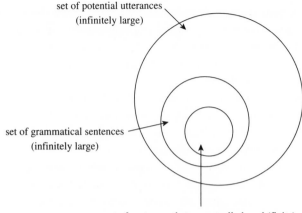

FIGURE 12.2 Grammatical and Ungrammatical Sentences

the number of grammatical sentences that a language allows. This means that no matter how many well-informed sentences are actually observed by the acquisition device during the months crucial to language acquisition, there will always be an unlimited number of grammatical sentences that will not be heard. And, of course, there will also be an unlimited number of *un*grammatical sentences that are not heard (see fig. 12.2). Thus, even assuming that the acquisition device somehow keeps track of all the sentences to which it is exposed,[2] it would not be a simple matter to draw any conclusions about the grammaticality or ungrammaticality of sentences it did not encounter. (However, as we will see in the next chapter, an acquisition device with the right internal structure may be able to infer certain specific types of information from the failure to encounter a particular sentence type.)

Feedback from adults constitutes an equally unlikely source of negative data for the acquisition device. Such feedback does occasionally occur, as the examples in table 12.4 from the speech of Adam and his mother illustrate. However, it generally agreed that corrections of this sort are not as useful to the acquisition device as they might initially appear to be.

Table 12.4 Some Maternal Responses to Adam's Speech around Age 3;11
(from Bellugi 1968 : 106)

Adam	Mother
I can't punch no more.	You can't punch any more?
I don't have no more.	You don't have any more?
I don't want no people to recognize me.	You don't want anyone to recognize you?
Have no paint on.	It doesn't have any paint on?

The classic study of speech corrections was carried out by Brown and Hanlon (1970), who examined transcripts of mother–child interactions for three children ranging in age from 21 to 43 months. Brown and Hanlon found that there was no consistent difference in parents' reaction to children's well-formed and ill-formed utterances in terms either of explicit approval/disapproval or of replies indicating comprehension or lack thereof. Rather, parents paid attention to the truth of what their children said. This led to exchanges in which parents responded approvingly to utterances such as *That broken* (Hirsh-Pasek, Treiman, and Schneiderman 1984: 85) and *He a girl* (said of the child's mother; Brown and Hanlon 1970: 47). Along similar lines, Maratsos (1983: 732) recounts that a parent assented to the statement *Her curl my hair* by saying 'Uh huh', but responded to the grammatical utterance *There's the animal farmhouse* with the correction 'No, that's a lighthouse.' Demetras, Post, and Snow (1986) report similar findings in their study of maternal responses to the speech of four 2-year-olds.

A larger-scale study of parental corrections was carried out by Hirsh-Pasek, Treiman, and Schneiderman (1984), who analyzed a half hour of conversation for forty mother–child pairs. (There were 10 2-year-olds, 10 3-year-olds, 10 4-year-olds, and 10 5-year-olds.) They found that there was no correlation between the grammaticality of a child's utterance and the likelihood that the mother would express approval or disapproval. (Approvals included statements such as 'Right' or 'Good', while disapprovals consisted of comments such as 'No, that's wrong' or 'That's not right'.) As table 12.5 helps show, mothers disapproved of children's well-formed and ill-formed utterances with roughly equal frequency (16% vs. 13.6%). This reflects the fact, noted by Brown and Hanlon, that mothers respond to the content of children's utterances rather than their form.

While maternal expressions of approval or disapproval were unrelated to the form of children's utterances, Hirsh-Pasek et al. did observe an interesting correlation (table 12.6) between the grammaticality of a child's utterance and the likelihood of it being repeated by the mother. (The authors grouped together 'strict repetitions', which retained the exact wording of the child's utterance, and 'loose repetitions', which deleted, modified, or supplemented the original utterance in various ways.) The key finding (fig. 12.3) was that mothers of the 2-year-olds were twice as likely to repeat the child's utterance when it was ill-formed (26.3% of the

Table 12.5 Rates of Maternal Approval and Disapproval of Children's Utterances (Hirsh-Pasek et al. 1984: 85)

	Approval	Disapproval
Well-formed	147	29 (16%)
Ill-formed	38	6 (13.6%)

Table 12.6 Maternal Repetitions of Children's Utterances
(from Hirsch-Pasek et al. 1984:86)

	Repeated	Not Repeated	Percentage Repeated/Not Repeated
2-year-olds:			
well-formed	42	307	13.7/86.3
ill-formed	42	160	26.3/73.7
3-year-olds:			
well-formed	45	219	20.5/79.5
ill-formed	10	66	15.2/84.8
4-year-olds:			
well-formed	30	261	11.5/88.5
ill-formed	6	57	10.5/89.5
5-year-olds:			
well-formed	32	462	6.9/93.1
ill-formed	6	44	13.6/86.4

time) as when it was grammatical (13.7% of the time). There was no comparable correlation for the other age groups. Since a mother's repetition—when it occurred—virtually always included a correction of her child's error, the authors suggest (p. 87) that this type of response might provide children with a source of information about the ungrammaticality of particular sentences.

However, this cannot be right. As the data in table 12.6 show, the percentage of ungrammatical sentences that were not repeated ranged from 73.7% (for the 2-year-olds) to 89.5% (for the 4-year-olds). Moreover, the percentage of gram-

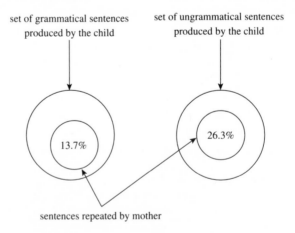

FIGURE 12.3 Repetition of Grammatical and Ungrammatical Sentences by Mothers of 2-year-olds

matical sentences that were repeated, often with various changes, ranged from
6.9% (for the 5-year-olds) to 20.5% (for the 3-year-olds). In other words, despite
the statistical tendencies noted by Hirsh-Pasek et al., parents are in fact responding
inconsistently to well-formedness—sometimes repeating a grammatical sentence
and ignoring an ungrammatical sentence, and vice versa. (Marcus 1993 refers to
such patterns of parental response as **noisy feedback.**) If the acquisition device
were to assume that a parental repetition signals ungrammaticality while the lack
of repetition entails grammaticality, it would end up concluding that a sizeable
percentage of children's grammatical sentences are ill formed and that a large proportion of their ungrammatical utterances are acceptable—thereby doing more
harm than good.[3] This suggests that the acquisition device cannot rely on repetitions or other types of parental responses for information about the possible ungrammaticality of sentences. (A similar point is made by Bowerman 1987:457;
see Marcus 1993 for an insightful critique of research on parental feedback in
general.)

Other studies of parental feedback in language learning have yielded data consistent with this conclusion (see, e.g., Demetras, Post, and Snow 1986; Bohannon
and Stanowicz 1988; Morgan and Travis 1989). In all cases studied to date, parental responses provide noisy feedback at best: there are occasional statistical
differences in terms of how some parents respond to children's grammatical and
ungrammatical sentences, but these differences are neither consistent enough nor
specific enough to constitute a reliable source of information for the acquisition
device.

As if these problems were not serious enough, there is a second reason for
believing that parental feedback does not significantly enrich the data on which
the acquisition device operates. As has been noted in a number of studies, the few
attempted corrections that have been observed in actual adult–child conversation,
as in (8)–(10), seem in general to have little or no effect.

(8)   *From McNeill 1966:68:*
      CHILD: Nobody don't like me.
      MOTHER: No, say 'nobody likes me.'
      CHILD: Nobody don't like me.
      [eight repetitions of this dialogue]
      MOTHER: No, now listen carefully; say 'nobody likes me.'
      CHILD: Oh! Nobody don't likes me.

(9)   *From Jean Berko Gleason, cited by Cazden 1972:92:*
      CHILD: My teacher holded the baby rabbits and we patted them.
      ADULT: Did you say your teacher held the baby rabbits?
      CHILD: Yes.

ADULT: What did you say she did?
CHILD: She holded the baby rabbits and we patted them.
ADULT: Did you say she held them tightly?
CHILD: No, she holded them loosely.

(10) *From Braine 1971:161:*
CHILD: Want other one spoon, daddy.
FATHER: You mean, you want the other spoon.
CHILD: Yes, I want other one spoon, please Daddy.
FATHER: Can you say 'the other spoon'?
CHILD: other . . . one . . . spoon.
FATHER: Say 'other'.
CHILD: other.
FATHER: 'spoon.'
CHILD: spoon.
FATHER: 'other spoon.'
CHILD: other . . . spoon. Now give me other one spoon?

As these examples help illustrate, children appear unable or unwilling to take account of corrections and advice about how to speak even when they are provided with explicit feedback.

A more systematic study of this issue was conducted by Morgan, Bonamo, and Travis (1995), who examined in detail the emergence of determiner use in the speech of Adam, Eve, and Sarah from the time these morphemes first made their appearance until they were used correctly 90% of the time. (Recall that in English singular count nouns must be accompanied by a determiner.) Although parents recast more than 35% of the children's determinerless NPs (e.g., saying 'Yes, the man is here' in response to the child's *Man is here*), Morgan and his colleagues found no evidence that the recasts triggered an immediate modification in the child's grammar, and they found no correlation between the frequency of recasts and the rate at which children's determiner use increases. They report similar results for the use of inverted auxiliaries in *wh* questions.

These findings notwithstanding, it is possible that parental responses are at times helpful to the acquisition device in limited ways. It has been shown, for example, that children are sometimes aware of the new information provided by parental recasts: in a study of one-hour speech samples from 12 mother–child dyads (child average age = 22.8 mos.), Farrar (1992) found that the children were significantly more likely to imitate a grammatical morpheme (such as plural *-s*, *the*, *-ing*, etc.) when it occurred in a recast of one of their own utterances than when it occurred in other types of parental discourse. (Thus, they were more likely to accurately repeat *The dog is running* when they heard it as a recast of their *The dog running* than when they encountered it in some other context.) This opens the possibility that children might on occasion be able to use the information contained in recasts to modify their grammar.

One scenario for how this might happen is sketched by Bohannon, MacWhinney, and Snow (1990), who assume that the acquisition device includes the principle in (11), as proposed by Clark (1987).

(11)   *The Principle of Contrast:*
    Every two forms must contrast in meaning.

Consider now the case of a child who utters the sentence *The doggie eated it all* and then hears his mother respond 'Oh, he ate it all, did he?' Assuming that the child realizes that his mother's *ate* has exactly the same meaning as his *eated,* the Principle of Contrast would be triggered, eliminating the immature form.[4] (This scenario, while plausible, leaves open the question of the precise criteria relevant to determining whether two meanings are the same or different—not a trivial issue.)

On this view, then, the Principle of Contrast provides a way for parental feedback to be useful to the acquisition device—but not as negative evidence (i.e., not as direct feedback about the ungrammaticality of the child's utterance). Rather, it constitutes an especially useful bit of *positive* evidence, providing the acquisition device with an instance of a form from adult speech that apparently has the same meaning as a form in the child's speech. This is enough to trigger the Principle of Contrast, with the consequences noted above.

A rarely noted point about parental feedback—direct or indirect, deliberate or incidental—is that it focuses on relatively peripheral, language-particular aspects of the child's grammar (such as double negatives or irregular inflection, as in the example just considered). It is hard to even imagine a situation in which a parent would have the opportunity (let alone the know-how) to provide feedback that would help a child discover the existence of syntactic categories, binary branching, or the subject–object asymmetry. Yet these are (by most counts) the most central and universal features of the syntax of human language. Clearly something other than parental feedback must be responsible for their emergence.

THE INTERPRETABILITY REQUIREMENT

We have just seen that the acquisition process cannot rely on negative evidence. Then what type of information does it require? It is clear that mere exposure to language cannot be enough. Children (or adults) whose only exposure to Urdu is through radio broadcasts could hardly be expected to learn that language. Not only would they never be able to learn the meaning of individual words, they could not know which words were nouns and which were verbs, which position in sentence structure is occupied by the subject and which by the direct object, whether adjectives and adverbs precede or follow the element that they modify, and so forth.

As explained in chapter 1, a grammar determines the relationship between form and meaning in the sentences of a language. Not surprisingly, exposure to information about this relationship seems to be a minimal requirement for linguistic development: the acquisition device must encounter forms being used to express an identifiable meaning. We can formulate this requirement as in (12). (Similar proposals have been put forward by Macnamara (1972), Wexler and Culicover (1980:78), Gleitman (1981:115), and Pinker (1984:29), among others).

(12)   *The Interpretability Requirement:*
       The acquisition device requires exposure to utterances whose meaning can be independently determined.

At first glance the Interpretability Requirement seems paradoxical since it requires learners to identify the meanings of sentences uttered in a language that they do not yet know. If a child does not speak English, for example, how is he or she to determine that in the sentence *That dog is running* the first two words refer to a particular dog and the last two words to a type of motion, and that the whole sentence says of the dog that it is moving in that way?

To begin, we must admit that the acquisition device will encounter many sentences that cannot be interpreted in the required way. In fact, it is even possible that the *majority* of sentences encountered in the early months of language acquisition are of this type. But this need not undermine the Interpretability Requirement, which demands only that the acquisition device be exposed to *some* utterances whose meaning can be independently determined. For this weaker requirement to be satisfied, two relatively straightforward conditions have to be met.

First, language learners must have at least a rudimentary vocabulary of 'content' words (e.g., nouns and verbs) before the process of actual syntactic development begins. Precisely how this happens need not concern us here, but it seems reasonable to assume that the relevant learning takes place during the one-word stage. As we have already seen (chap. 2), this presyntactic stage is marked by the development of a rudimentary set of words naming objects, actions, and properties in the child's environment.

Second, there must be occasions on which a sentence consisting of previously learned words is encountered in a context where its meaning can be inferred without knowledge of the language's syntactic rules. (For example, a child who already knows the meaning of the words *boy, dog,* and *pat* might be exposed to a sentence such as *The boy is patting a dog* in a context where it is clear that a patting action is taking place, with the boy as the one doing the patting and the dog as the one being patted.)

It is difficult to know with any certainty how frequent such types of experience are. Snow (1977:41) claims that caregiver speech is largely limited to discussion of "what the child can see and hear, what he has just experienced or is just about to experience, what he might possibly want to know about the current situation." This point is further underlined by Dan Slobin (cited by Wexler and Culicover 1980:79), who reports that

> in real life, there is little reason for a preschool child to rely heavily on syntactic factors to determine the basic . . . meaning of sentences which he hears. Judith Johnston and I have gone through transcripts of adult speech to children between the ages of two and five, in Turkish and English, looking for sentences which could be open to misinterpretation if the child lacked basic syntactic knowledge, such as the roles of word order and inflections. We found almost no instances of an adult utterance which could possibly be misinterpreted. That is, *the overwhelming majority of utterances were clearly interpretable in context, requiring only knowledge of word meanings and the normal relations between actors, actions, and objects in the world.* [emphasis added]

Such estimates are perhaps overly optimistic. As Gleitman (1990:15) observes, there are many instances in which the caregiver's utterances do not match up well with the child's attentional focus. Taking a commonplace example, she notes that 'Eat your peas!' is not uttered when the child is in the process of eating his peas; rather, it is likely to be uttered when his mind is occupied with something entirely different. There are also many instances in which the caregiver's utterances do not coincide with his or her own actions: as a mother opens the door upon arriving home from work, for example, she is more likely to say to her child 'What did you do today?' than 'I'm opening the door'.

Responding to these points, Pinker (1994a:39) acknowledges that an utterance's meaning often cannot be inferred from simultaneous sensory experience, proposing instead that "the child keeps an updated mental model of the current situation, including the likely communicative intentions of other humans." When a parent issues an imperative such as 'Eat your peas' and takes steps to enforce it, Pinker proposes, "the child cannot be in much doubt that the content of the [utterance] pertains to the parent's wishes, not the child's current activities." [5]

A likely advantage of motherese (in societies where it is used) is that it provides children with a large set of utterances that satisfy the Interpretability Requirement. (Recall that, as observed earlier, the properties of motherese seem designed not to teach the language but rather simply to facilitate communication—i.e., to enhance the interpretability of adult utterances to children.) However, even in societies where speech to children is not significantly modified (see table 12.3), a significant portion of the sentences to which language learners are exposed satisfies the Interpretability Requirement. As observed by Lieven (1994:68), children being raised in these cultures "are hearing or actively being provided with a sub-stantial number of utterances for which they can make some pairing with meaning."

In sum, then, it seems reasonable to suppose that all children encounter sentences whose meaning can be inferred independent of syntactic knowledge by reference to the meanings of the component lexical items and an understanding (in Pinker's sense) of the situation in which they are uttered. This in turn allows us to adopt as a working hypothesis the view that (at least in the early stages of syntactic development) the experience crucial to the operation of the acquisition device consists of a phonetic form (the utterance) and a semantic representation depicting the meaning of its component parts and their relationship to each other.

In order to illustrate more precisely the use to which this sort of information is put by the acquisition device, it is necessary to have a system of notation capable of representing those aspects of meaning relevant to grammatical development. For expository purposes, I will follow Pinker (1984) in using a modified version of the notation employed within Lexical-Functional Grammar (e.g., Bresnan 1982) for representing the relationship between a predicate, its arguments and modifiers, as well as grammatically relevant semantic features such as tense, as-pect, definiteness, number, gender, and so forth. Hence, exposure under the right conditions to the sentence *The boy is patting a dog* will yield data of the sort shown in Figure 12.4. (For purposes of illustration, I assume that children and

The sentence's form:	*The sentence's meaning:*	
[the boy is patting a dog]	PREDICATE	PAT ⟨agent, theme⟩
	TENSE	present
	ASPECT	progressive
	AGENT	BOY
		[+def]
	THEME	DOG
		[−def]

Possible situational context:

FIGURE 12.4 An Utterance Meeting the Interpretability Requirement

caregivers perceive the situation being described in the same way, that the phonetic
string has been successfully segmented, and that semantic concepts can be matched
with the corresponding words and morphemes in a fairly direct fashion; see Gleitman 1981:115–16; Gleitman and Wanner 1982:10, 12.) The first line of the semantic representation contains the predicate corresponding to the verb *pat* as well
as information about the two arguments that it takes (an agent and a theme). The
next two lines specify the tense and aspect of the sentence, while the last two lines
identify the verb's two arguments and indicate their status with respect to the semantic feature of 'definiteness'.

Deficiencies in Experience

If the line of reasoning adopted so far is correct, then figure 12.4 illustrates the
type of experience that characteristically serves as input to the acquisition device.
Any less information (e.g., exposure only to an utterance's form) would be too
little, while richer types of data (e.g., feedback about the grammaticality of hypothetical sentences) are more than we can reasonably expect to be available.

There is a huge amount of information in this sort of experience—information
about word order, about the language's inflectional system, about the number and
type of arguments associated with a particular predicate, and so on. In other respects, however, experience of this type is strikingly deficient: in particular, it
contains no information about syntactic categories (e.g., N, V, etc.), binary
branching, the subject-object asymmetry, or the constraints on form and interpretation that apply to syntactic representations. Yet, contemporary syntactic theories
agree that the adult grammar forms sentence structures with a particular binary
architecture and that higher-level constraints (such as those on pronoun interpretation and gap placement) operate on these representations. This apparent paradox
illustrates the extent to which experience can be an incomplete source of information about the grammar that the acquisition device must ultimately produce. In
the words of N. Chomsky (1972:78):

> If we contemplate the classical problem of psychology, that of accounting
> for human knowledge, we cannot avoid being struck by the enormous dis-
> parity between knowledge and experience—in the case of language, be-
> tween the generative grammar that expresses the linguistic competence of
> the native speaker and the meager and degenerate data on the basis of which
> he has constructed this grammar.

The technical way to describe this state of affairs is to say that the data of experience **underdetermine** the grammar.

Matters are further complicated by the fact that experience provides children
with no reliable feedback about the grammaticality of their utterances (negative
evidence). Thus, in addition to the lack of information about the composition and

organization of syntactic representations, the acquisition device must confront a second major difficulty: should it make an error in building the complex cognitive system responsible for sentence formation, it cannot rely on external corrections to help discover and remedy its mistake.

How, then, can language acquisition take place? How can the acquisition device construct a grammar of the appropriate type in the absence of the relevant experience and feedback? The answer most widely accepted today is that the acquisition device must itself supply the information about syntactic categories, hierarchical structure, and higher-level constraints that is missing from experience. Put another way, the necessary information must somehow be 'built into' the acquisition device, presumably as part of its inborn structure. The next two chapters outline specific proposals about this inborn structure and its role in the language acquisition process.

4. Conclusion

As explained at the outset, the learnability problem is concerned with the question of how the acquisition device is able to construct a grammar of a particular sort in response to the type of experience available to young children. Although the acquisition device cannot itself be directly observed, inferences about its properties can be drawn from careful study of the experience on which it operates (its input) and the cognitive system that it ultimately yields (its output, the grammar for a human language).

A central claim of this chapter is that the experience on which the acquisition device operates involves a representation of an utterance's phonetic form and its meaning, as illustrated in figure 12.4, consistent with the Interpretability Requirement. This experience provides useful information about countless features of language (its lexical items and their properties, its inflectional system, its word order, and so on). But (even when it involves 'motherese'), it says nothing about syntactic categories, constituent structure, or the constraints that apply to the resulting representations—although these are all indispensable components of the grammar that must be acquired. Nor does experience include feedback from adults (negative evidence) that could quickly redirect the acquisition device when an intermediate grammar produces an ill-formed sentence.

So understood, the learnability problem is indeed daunting. But this only underlines the need to focus research on the acquisition device, which, by definition, provides the needed 'bridge' between experience and the final grammar. The learnability problem can thus be reduced to the problem of determining the precise nature and extent of the information that must be supplied by the acquisition device in order to close the gap between children's experience and the grammar that must eventually be acquired.

UG-Based Theories of the Acquisition Device

As explained in the previous chapter, there is a widespread consensus that sentence formation and interpretation involve the construction of representations that include syntactic categories organized into particular hierarchical configurations to which important constraints on the placement of gaps and the interpretation of pronouns must refer. Yet, the experience that serves as input to the acquisition device (i.e., phonetic forms paired with meanings) provides no direct information about syntactic categories, the details of hierarchical structure, or the specific principles governing gaps and pronouns. It therefore falls to the acquisition device to bridge the gulf between experience and the adult grammar. Determining precisely how this is done has been one of the major objectives of linguistic theory for the past three decades (see N. Chomsky 1965:25 for an early statement of this goal).

The dominant view among linguists and psychologists is that the demands of language acquisition justify a view of the mind that philosophers often refer to as **nativism** (or **rationalism**). The central thesis of nativism is that certain types of knowledge are **innate** (inborn) in the sense that they are the product of the genetic endowment rather than learning through experience. (As observed by Braine 1994:11, the term 'knowledge' is used rather broadly in the contemporary literature to include mental structures and mechanisms as well as content; see Jerry Fodor 1983 for discussion of different types of nativism.)

A unique feature of most contemporary nativism within linguistics is the view that the acquisition device includes an innate **Universal Grammar** (UG) that provides learners with the categories and principles essential to human language. By specifying in advance many of the properties that any language must have, UG offers a powerful solution to the problem presented by the gap between the experience to which learners have access and the grammar that they must ultimately acquire.

To date, the vast majority of acquisition research on the learnability problem has adopted the type of UG associated with work in 'Government and Binding theory' (now sometimes called 'Principles and Parameter theory'), a variety of transformational grammar. Among the few exceptions to this tendency are Pinker (1984), who couches his proposals in the framework of Lexical-Functional Grammar (e.g., Bresnan 1982), and Janet Fodor (1992), who uses phrase structure grammar (e.g., Gazdar et al. 1985). This chapter outlines a synthesis of various proposals on the role of UG in overcoming the learnability problems described in the previous chapter. (In keeping with the practice adopted throughout this book, an effort will be made to avoid theory-internal technical details that are unnecessary for the point under consideration.)

1. Universal Grammar

We will begin by examining the relevance of UG to the development of word-level syntactic categories, and then turn our attention to its role in the emergence of phrase structure and of constraints on pronoun interpretation and gap placement.

SYNTACTIC CATEGORIES

A long-standing assumption of most work on syntactic description is that the languages of the world classify their words in terms of a relatively small number of syntactic categories. Although there is no consensus on a comprehensive inventory of syntactic categories, at least the options outlined in table 13.1 must be permitted. Not all these categories are found in all languages. For example, it has been claimed that Hausa and Telugu have no adjectives (Dixon 1982), that Jacaltec has no prepositions (Day 1973), that Nootkan has neither adjectives nor prepositions (Jacobsen 1979), that Japanese lacks complementizers (Fukui 1986), and so on. Indeed, nouns and verbs are arguably the only two syntactic categories that are found in every human language. However, we will set aside this possibility for the moment and concentrate here on how the acquisition device is able to construct a grammar with the full categorial inventory in table 13.1.

To begin, let us assume that the acquisition device requires that every word it encounters be classified in terms of the categories given by UG. This has two immediate advantages from the point of view of learnability: it alerts the language learner to the existence of syntactic categories, which are not directly represented in experience (see previous chapter), and it makes available a relatively small set of classificatory options, thereby limiting the possibilities that must be considered. How, though, is a learner to decide which items belong to which category? In particular, how is a child learning English to know that *dog* is noun and *pat* a verb, rather than vice versa?

Table 13.1 The Syntactic Categories of Universal Grammar

Lexical Categories	Non-Lexical (Functional) Categories
Noun (N)	Determiner (Det)
Verb (V)	Auxiliary (Aux)
Adjective (A)	Degree word (Deg)
Preposition/Postposition (P)	Complementizer (Comp)
Adverb (Adv)	Pronoun (Pro)
	Conjunction

To date, the most widely accepted solution to this problem comes from Pinker (1984). The key to his proposal, which builds on earlier work by Grimshaw (1981), involves what has come to be called **semantic bootstrapping,** the use of semantic information to draw inferences about syntax. In the case at hand, this involves identifying a word's syntactic category through its semantic properties. According to this idea, the acquisition device includes not only an inborn inventory of syntactic categories, but also a set of prototypical correspondences between those categories and particular semantic notions (table 13.2). Thanks to this set of correspondences, the acquisition device is often able to determine a word's syntactic category from its meaning. Thus, words such as *boy* and *ball* in *A boy kicked the ball* can be classified as nouns, since they refer to a person and a thing, while *kick* can be identified as a verb, since it encodes an action.

Not all words can be categorized on the basis of semantic bootstrapping. As Pinker acknowledges, the correspondences proposed in table 13.2 will not help the acquisition device categorize a verb such as *need* or *contain* (which do not denote an action) or a noun such as *bath* or *anger* (which do not denote things). Pinker suggests (p. 42) that categorization must therefore proceed in two steps (fig. 13.1). In the first step, words denoting concepts that are innately associated with a particular syntactic category are classified in accordance with the help of semantic bootstrapping. In the second step, the acquisition device takes note of the distributional properties of these words (e.g., their positioning and morphological markers) and uses this information to categorize hitherto unclassifiable words.

Imagine, for example, that the acquisition device uses semantic bootstrapping to categorize action-denoting words such as *kick* and *jump* as verbs. It will then note that members of this category form their past tense by adding the suffix *-ed,* that they express the progressive aspect with the help of the suffix *-ing,* and so on.

(1)   a. The boy kick*ed* the ball.
       b. The dog is jump*ing* up and down.

Thanks to these morphological clues, verbs whose meaning does not allow categorization by means of semantic bootstrapping can be assigned to the appropriate

Table 13.2 Some Syntax–Semantic Pairings (based on Pinker 1984:41)

Category	Corresponding Semantic Notion
Noun	Person or thing
Verb	Action or change of state
Adjective	Perceptible physical property or attribute
Preposition	Spatial relation, path, or direction

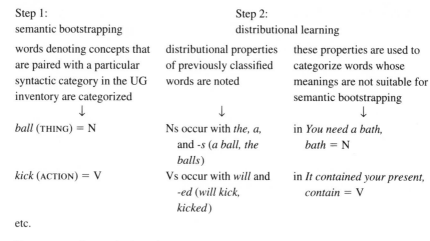

Step 1: semantic bootstrapping	Step 2: distributional learning	
words denoting concepts that are paired with a particular syntactic category in the UG inventory are categorized ↓	distributional properties of previously classified words are noted ↓	these properties are used to categorize words whose meanings are not suitable for semantic bootstrapping ↓
ball (THING) = N	Ns occur with *the, a,* and *-s* (*a ball, the balls*)	in *You need a bath,* *bath* = N
kick (ACTION) = V	Vs occur with *will* and *-ed* (*will kick, kicked*)	in *It contained your present,* *contain* = V
etc.		

FIGURE 13.1 Categorization of Words

category. For instance, *contain* can be categorized as a verb on the basis of its use in a sentence such as (2), where it occurs with the past tense suffix.

(2)   This box *contained* your birthday present.

This use of morphological and/or positional properties of previously categorized words to classify new words is called **distributional learning.**

For the categorization procedure just outlined to be viable, two conditions must be met. First, children must have the ability to use distributional clues to categorize words with nonprototypical semantic properties. As noted by Pinker (p. 59), there is good evidence that this condition is met. For example, Katz, Baker, and Macnamara (1974) have shown that girls as young as 17 months tend to treat a novel name for a doll as a common noun if it is preceded by a determiner (e.g., 'This is a zav') and will therefore apply it to other entities of the same type; in contrast, if there is no determiner (e.g., 'This is Zav'), they treat the novel noun as a proper name that cannot be applied to other entities. Gordon (1985, 1988) shows that children as young as 2 years of age can use distributional clues (e.g., the presence or absence of the determiner *a*) to distinguish between 'count' nouns such as *cloud* and 'mass' nouns such as *air.* In an earlier experiment, Brown (1957) showed children a picture depicting a pair of hands performing a kneading-like action on a mass of red confetti-like material that was overflowing from an unusual blue-and-white striped container. He found that children between the ages of 3 and 5 match the nonsense word *sibbing* with the action, *the sib* with the container, and *some sib* with the substance. Such findings indicate that children make use of the clues provided by affixes and determiners to classify words as verbs and nouns—the very ability required for distributional learning in Pinker's system.

Second, if children are to initially identify syntactic categories on the basis of their semantic properties and then use this information to identify distributional cues that can be used for less transparent cases, they must be exposed to the right type of 'input'. In particular, their early experience must provide a generous number of sentences that exhibit correspondences between semantic types and syntactic categories compatible with the inborn mappings needed for bootstrapping. This will allow the acquisition device to categorize a representative sampling of words and to identify distributional properties that can then be used to classify words whose meanings do not lend themselves to classification on semantic grounds.

This condition seems to be met: Pinker reports that the speech produced by the parents of Adam, Eve, and Sarah when the children's MLU was between 1.5 and 2 had the desired properties. Eighty-eight percent of actions were encoded as verbs, physical objects were always encoded as nouns, virtually all physical properties were encoded by adjectives, and virtually all spatial relations were expressed as prepositions (Pinker 1984:61–62, 1985:433–34; see also Macnamara 1982:124). Even higher correlations were observed by Rondal and Cession (1990) in their study of maternal speech to 18 children (aged 1;8–2;8): not only were all persons and things encoded as nouns (as in Pinker's data); *all* actions were encoded as verbs and *all* physical properties were encoded as adjectives.[1] However, less than perfect correlations were observed by Nelson, Hampson, and Shaw (1993) in their survey of maternal speech to 45 children under age 2. They report (table 13.3) that mothers quite frequently encoded actions as deverbal nouns (e.g., *a bite, a drink, some help, the work*), contrary to the correlations stipulated by the semantic bootstrapping hypothesis. The danger here is that the acquisition device might be misled into thinking that a word such as *walk* in the sentence *I took a*

Table 13.3 Maternal Use of Deverbal Nouns in 30 Hours of Mother–Child Interaction (from Nelson et al. 1993:76)

Word	Frequency	% Use as an N[a]	% Use as a verb[a]
call	118	14	86
drink	110	41	57
kiss	73	59	38
walk	36	31	69
work	67	34	66

a. The data includes only uses that could be unambiguously classified.

walk is a verb because it denotes an action. The mechanisms for distributional learning might then conclude that the morpheme *a* occurs with verbs, which in turn would have disastrous consequences for the categorization of other words that occur with this item (e.g., *a book, a man,* etc.).

There is reason to believe that the acquisition device avoids this sort of error. Not only are categorization mistakes extremely rare (chap. 3, section 4), children's early language suggests that they are able to use the semantic bootstrapping strategy in the intended way: their first nouns refer to concrete objects, early verbs name actions and changes of state, and adjectives describe physical attributes (Pinker 1984 : 57). However, it is unclear at this time precisely how the acquisition device manages to avoid the pitfalls presented by words in the input that contradict the correspondences on which semantic bootstrapping operates.

One possibility, of course, is that the particular syntax–semantic correspondences proposed by Pinker are wrong and need to be modified. (See P. Bloom 1994 for some discussion along these lines with regard to the noun category.) Another possibility, put forward by Pinker (1987), is that semantic correspondences are part of a larger network of 'mutually predictive' cues for category membership that might also include (in the case of nouns) susceptibility to stress and compatibility with affixes that mark definiteness, number, and case, among others. In theory, this network could avoid miscategorization errors in the case of deverbal nouns by noting (for example) that *walk* is 'inflected' for indefiniteness in *I took a walk*—a sign of nounhood despite the word's actional meaning.

HIERARCHICAL STRUCTURE

As explained in chapter 12, the words making up sentences are not only assigned to syntactic categories but are also organized into hierarchically structured, binary-branching syntactic representations. According to one widely held view, phrase structure complies with the schema depicted in figure 13.2. (The X-bar schema is not intended to specify the relative order of elements; the fact that the head precedes rather than follows its complement in figure 13.2 is thus irrelevant.)

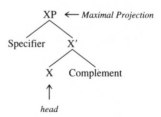

FIGURE 13.2 The X-bar Schema (e.g., Sells 1985 : 28)

As this diagram indicates, a phrase can be divided into three subcomponents—a head (the word around which the phrase is organized), a complement (which combines directly with the head), and a specifier (which combines with the intermediate X′ unit to form the complete phrase or 'maximal projection'). (Radford 1988 offers a more detailed introduction to these notions and the facts that support this view of phrase structure; see also the glossary at the end of this book.) The NP and AP in (3) exemplify structures whose internal organization complies with the X-bar schema.

(3)   a.

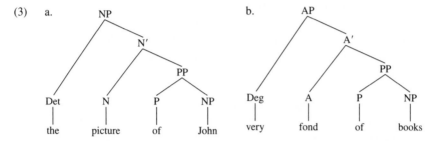

In (3a), for instance, the head of the phrase is the N *picture,* the PP *of John* occupies the complement position, and the determiner *the* functions as specifier.

In order to assimilate sentence-sized units to the X-bar schema, a certain amount of abstraction is required. It is often assumed (e.g., Chomsky 1986a) that sentences take as their head the morpheme carrying information about tense. Although this morpheme frequently corresponds to an inflectional affix and is therefore dubbed 'I' (for 'inflection'), it can also be a modal auxiliary verb such as *will, can, may,* and so on.[2] As illustrated in (4), the category I takes VP as its complement and the subject of the sentence as its specifier.

(4)

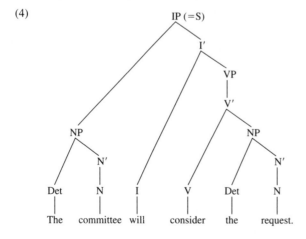

Here *will* is the I category, the VP *consider the request* occurs in the complement position, and the subject NP *the committee* is found in the specifier position.

How do children come to have the structure-building system needed to generate representations of this sort? The key claim of UG-based approaches to syntactic development is that the X-bar schema must be an inborn component of the acquisition device, since experience provides insufficient information about the details of hierarchical structure. To better understand this point, let us consider the paucity of information about hierarchical structure found in a sentence's semantic representation and phonetic form.

By itself, a sentence's semantic representation cannot support any detailed conclusions about its hierarchical structure. Consistent with the notational practice adopted in the preceding chapter, we will assume semantic representations such as (5).

(5)   [the boy will make a snowman]

PREDICATE	MAKE ⟨agent, theme⟩
TENSE	future
AGENT	BOY
	[+def]
THEME	SNOWMAN
	[−def]

While the acquisition device might be able to infer from (5) that *the boy* forms a structural unit since the information associated with the noun and the preceding determiner is grouped together in the semantic representation, there is nothing to indicate the internal structure of this phrase. Thus, any of the representations in (6) are compatible with the information contained in the semantic representation. (In fact, only the first is thought to be correct.)

(6)   a.   b.

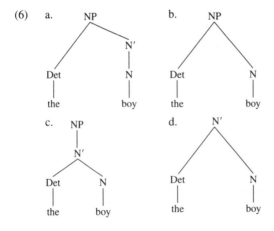

c.   d.

Further difficulties stem from the fact that there is nothing in the semantic representation to indicate that, as shown in (7), the morpheme marking tense is the head of S, that it takes a phrase consisting of the verb and the theme argument as complement, or that it takes the agent phase as its specifier.

(7)   *Syntactic representation required for (5):*

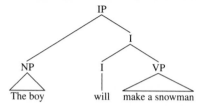

Is a sentence's phonetic form any more informative? Morgan (1986) suggests that suprasegmental information may be useful for determining the boundaries of syntactic phrases. In a study of 34 mother–child dyads (child's age = 1;10–4;5), he examined the way in which the mothers pronounced pairs of sentences such as those in (8) and (9) while reading stories to their children.

(8)   It was [too big]—two feet around.
       It was [too big to see around].

(9)   He climbed [to the top], and he stared.
       He climbed [to the top of the stairs].

Morgan found that phrase boundaries tend to be reliably marked by lengthening of the final vowel, pauses, or both (p. 120). Thus, the pronunciation of the word *top* is different in the two sentences in (9), where it comes at the end of a phrase in the first case but not the second.

In another study (box 13.1), Morgan tested children's ability to remember and repeat syllable sequences that were intonational phrases and those that were not.

Box 13.1

THE STUDY: Morgan 1986: 124 ff.
SUBJECTS: 20 children aged 3–5 years.
TASK: With the help of examples and a puppet game, children were trained to produce either (a) the final phonological phrase in a string of nonsense syllables, or (b) the final phonological phrase plus the preceding syllable.
TEST UTTERANCES: brackets enclose the phonological phrase; the syllables that are to be repeated are italicized; 20 such strings were employed.
    (i) *Sequence to be repeated is a phonological phrase:*
       NEP [*MIP BOT DEM*]
    (ii) *Sequence to be repeated is not a phonological phrase:*
       NEP *MIP* [*BOT DEM*]

He found a dramatic difference between the two types of stimuli. Whereas the children exposed to strings such as (i) had an average of 8.9 correct responses out of 10, children who had to repeat a sequence of syllables that did not make up a phonological phrase, such as (ii), had a mean score of only 0.1.

However, information of this sort is of limited value to the acquisition device. Like the information derivable from a sentence's semantic representation, suprasegmental clues are relevant to only the most general features of syntactic structure. At best, they may indicate a phrase's boundaries—but not its internal structure (such as the number of structural levels within the phrase) or the identity of its head. At worst, they may provide unreliable or inconsistent information. In (10), for example, the sequence to the right of the break (#) is a syntactic unit, but the sequence to the left is not.[3]

(10)   a.   [s John [vp showed the book # [pp to three different people]]].
        b.   [s Harry [vp believed the promise # [s that reforms would take place]]].

In many other sentences, such as (11), in contrast, the words on both sides of an intonation break make up structural units.

(11)   [He bowed politely] # [before leaving the room].

There are even patterns such as (12), in which the words to left of the intonation break form a structural unit but those to the right do not (assuming that time modifiers adjoin to S rather than VP).

(12)

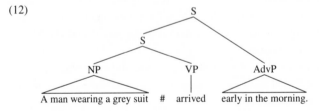

It is therefore not clear what information the acquisition device could confidently draw from the presence of an intonation break (except, perhaps, that the words on at least one side form a structural unit). This compromises the usefulness of such cues as indicators of syntactic structure, suggesting that at the very least they must be subordinate to other types of information. (For further remarks along these lines, see Pinker 1987:404, 1994a:387.)

In sum, we are left with the conclusion that neither a sentence's semantic representation nor its phonetic form reveals the details of its syntactic structure. By the logic outlined in the previous chapter, we must therefore assume that the acquisition device bridges the resulting gap between experience and the adult grammar by providing the necessary information (in the form of the X-bar schema) about the hierarchical structure of phrases and sentences.

Even this is not enough, however. In addition to ensuring that specifiers are attached under maximal projections and that complements are attached as sisters of the head, the acquisition device must also be able to determine which argument of the head is realized as subject (the NP immediately under S) and which as direct object (the NP that combines directly with a transitive verb). In the sentence *The dog ate the food,* for example, the verb's agent argument occurs as subject and its theme as direct object; see (13). (For ease of exposition, I use more traditional structures here, ignoring the I category and eliminating intermediate bar levels.)

(13)

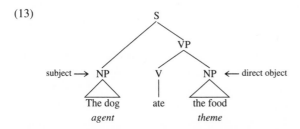

But how does the acquisition device determine this? Why doesn't it treat the theme as subject and the agent as direct object, forming structures of the sort in (14)?

(14)

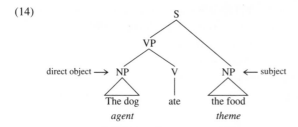

One possibility, put forward by Pinker (1984), makes use of semantic bootstrapping. The acquisition device, he suggests, includes the correspondences in table 13.4 between grammatical relations and thematic roles. Given these correspondences, the acquisition device will identify the agent in *The dog ate the food* as the subject and the theme as the direct object, thereby forming the correct syntactic representation depicted in (13).

As with the parallel proposal put forward for syntactic categories, semantic bootstrapping does not allow the classification of all arguments encountered by the acquisition device. For example, the two NPs in sentences such as *This box*

Table 13.4 Some Pairings of Grammatical
Relations and Thematic Roles
(based on Pinker 1984:41)

Grammatical Relation	Corresponding Thematic Role
subject	agent
direct object	theme
indirect object	recipient/goal

contains a gift or *Mary is a doctor* cannot be classified by semantic bootstrapping, since neither bears a thematic role typical of a subject or a direct object (i.e., neither is an obvious agent or a theme). As before, though, distributional learning offers a promising supplementary strategy (see fig. 13.3). By using semantic bootstrapping for patterns that contain NPs with the relevant thematic roles, the acquisition device can link at least a sampling of NPs with the appropriate grammatical role. This information can then be used to identify characteristic distributional properties of subjects and direct objects (e.g., the basic order in English is subject–verb–object), which in turn can be employed to analyze grammatical roles in patterns where semantic bootstrapping is not applicable. (Other potentially useful distributional properties in English include the ability of the subject to trigger agreement in the verb and the fact that subject pronouns occur in the nominative form and object pronouns in the accusative.)

As was the case with word-level syntactic categories, the viability of the bootstrapping proposal depends on an appropriate input. In particular, it should be the case that in an overwhelming majority of sentences heard by children, agents are encoded as subjects and themes as direct objects. These correspondences are found in most active, transitive sentences, but not in passive constructions, in which the theme is subject rather than direct object and the agent occurs (if at all) with a preposition (see chap. 10). If the acquisition device were to use passive

semantic bootstrapping		distributional learning
NPs whose thematic roles are paired with particular grammatical relations are analyzed	distributional properties of previously identified grammatical roles are noted	these properties are used to determine the grammatical role of NPs whose thematic roles are not suitable for semantic bootstrapping
↓	↓	↓
In *A boy patted a dog*: *a boy* (agent) = subject *a dog* (theme) = direct object	The subject is preverbal; The object is postverbal	in *This box contains a gift*: *this box* = subject *a gift* = direct object

FIGURE 13.3 Identification of Grammatical Roles

sentences as the basis for its initial generalizations, it would incorrectly identify the preverbal NP as direct object (since it is the theme) and the agentive NP following *by* as the subject; see (15).

(15)   *How the semantic bootstrapping system might misanalyze a passive:*
        Assumed correspondences: *agent = subject; theme = direct object*
        passive sentence: The ball was kicked by the boy.
        thematic roles: *theme*   *agent*
                                              ⇓   ⇓
        inferred grammatical roles: dir. obj.   subject
                                              ⇓   ⇓
        distributional properties: (preverbal)   (follows *by*)

The incorrectly inferred distributional clues might then be used to misanalyze a wide range of other sentences, ultimately yielding the wrong grammar for English.

At first glance, the problem seems to be defused by reports that agents are encoded as subjects 100% of the time in various maternal speech samples (Pinker 1984:61; Rondal and Cession 1990:716; see the description of these studies earlier in this chapter). However, this state of affairs cannot be typical of maternal speech. If it were, the acquisition device would lack the information needed to acquire passive structures such as *The ball was dropped by the child* (note the nonsubject agent). Yet Pinker, Lebeaux, and Frost (1987) report that children begin producing such structures around age 3 (see chap. 10).

Although the input to the acquisition device must therefore include examples of passive patterns, there may still be ways to ensure against their misuse by the semantic bootstrapping mechanisms. Pinker (1987) suggests that correspondences between semantic roles and grammatical relations may be only one factor in a network of diagnostic clues that the acquisition device employs to identify subjects and objects. (Recall the parallel proposal for word-level syntactic categories.) Other clues in Pinker's proposed network include relative order (in almost all languages, subjects precede objects regardless of where the verb occurs), agreement (if the verb agrees with only one NP, that NP must be the subject), subject drop (subjects are more likely than objects to be suppressed in human language), and 'control' (infinitival verbs can have 'understood' subjects that are coreferential with an element in the next highest clause—as in *John decided [. to leave]*, where *John* is the understood subject of *leave*).

CONSTRAINTS ON GAPS AND PRONOUNS

A great deal of work in contemporary syntactic theory is concerned with the formulation of principles governing the interpretation of pronouns and the placement of gaps. Two such principles are restated as (16)–(17) from earlier discussion (see chaps. 8 and 11, respectively).

(16)   *The* Wh *Island Condition:*

       *[*Wh*   [*ₛ *Wh*-argument . . . ___ . . .]]

(17)   *Principle C:*
       A pronoun cannot c-command its antecedent.

The *Wh* Island Condition rules out structures such as (18), in which the sentence-initial *wh* word is associated with a gap in the embedded clause that itself begins with a *wh* argument.

(18)   *wh* argument
                                      ↓

       *Who did John wonder [what you gave ___ to ___]

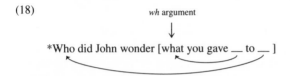

Principle C is motivated by the unacceptability of sentences such as (19), in which the pronoun c-commands its antecedent.

(19)   *He$_i$ believes John's$_i$ teacher.

Constraints such as the *Wh* Island Condition and Principle C present especially challenging learnability problems. This is because there seems to be no way to induce their existence without negative evidence—information about the ungrammaticality of structures such as (18) in the case of the *Wh* Island Condition and the unacceptability of sentences such as (19) in the case of Principle C. (Recall that, as explained in chap. 12, children do not receive reliable information about the ungrammaticality of particular sentences.) Thus, learners apparently have no way of knowing that these constraints are even needed, let alone a way to determine their precise formulation.

A further problem stems from the fact that the notions needed to formulate syntactic principles are often abstract and esoteric. Principle C, for example, makes crucial use of the c-command relation, which is neither directly encoded in a sentence's phonetic form nor manifested in its semantic representation. The same is true of the notions presupposed by the Empty Category Principle, the general constraint in (20), explicated in (21), proposed by N. Chomsky (1986a: 16) to account for the placement and interpretation of gaps. (The *Wh* Island Condition is partly subsumed by the Empty Category Principle in Chomsky's theory.)

(20)   *The Empty Category Principle:*
       An empty category [gap] must be properly governed.

(21) *Definitions:*

Proper Government: α properly governs β iff α theta-governs or antecedent-governs β.

Theta government: α theta-governs β iff α is a zero-level category that theta-marks β, and α, β are sisters.

Antecedent government: α antecedent-governs β iff α governs β and is co-indexed with it.

Government: α governs β iff α c-commands β and every barrier for β dominates α.

Barrier: γ is a barrier for β iff (a) or (b):

(a) γ immediately dominates δ, δ a blocking category for β

(b) γ is a blocking category for β, and γ is not IP (S)

Blocking Category: γ is a blocking category for β iff γ is not L-marked and γ dominates β

L-marking: α L-marks β if α is a lexical category that theta-governs β.

Given the exquisite abstractness and complexity of these notions, it is difficult to see how they could ever be learned by children—even if information about the ungrammaticality of the relevant sentence types were somehow available.

These problems notwithstanding, the principles regulating pronoun interpretation and gap placement are apparently mastered by age 5, if not earlier. How is this possible? The only plausible answer seems to be that the syntactic principles in question are somehow 'built into' the acquisition device, presumably as part of UG, and therefore do not have to be learned at all. In the words of N. Chomsky (1977:65):

> Suppose that we find a particular language has the property P. . . . Suppose, furthermore, that P is sufficiently abstract and evidence bearing on it sufficiently sparse and contrived so that it is implausible to suppose that all speakers, or perhaps any speakers, might have been trained or taught to observe P or might have constructed grammars satisfying P by induction from experience. Then it is plausible to postulate that P is a property of [the acquisition device].

This justification for the innateness of a grammatical property or principle is known as the **argument from the poverty of the stimulus.**

The central thesis of our discussion to this point has been that a great deal of syntactic information is available to the language learner independent of experience, as part of the Universal Grammar that is an integral part of the inborn acquisition device. This raises the question of whether any significant syntactic facts about a language remain to be learned. We address this question in the next section.

2. Parameters

Universal Grammar was originally conceived as an inborn system of categories and principles common to all human languages (e.g., N. Chomsky 1965, 1972). However, subsequent work revealed that UG permitted significant crosslinguistic variation and that many of its principles include **parameters** that make available options of various sorts.

As an illustration of a very simple type of parametric variation, consider again the X-bar schema, repeated as figure 13.4.

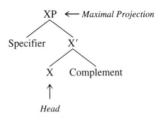

FIGURE 13.4 The X-bar schema (based on Sells 1985:28)

As noted in section 1, the X-bar schema stipulates the point of attachment of heads, specifiers, and complements in phrase structure, but is neutral with respect to their relative linear order, which can differ from language to language. For example, heads precede their complements in English, but follow them in Japanese (table 13.5). These facts are accommodated within UG by adding to the X-bar schema a parameter for head–complement order, as in (22). (Further adjustments are required to account for the placement of specifiers, but this can be ignored for now.)[4]

(22)   *The parameter for head–complement order:*
        Option (a): head-initial [e.g. English]
        Option (b): head-final [e.g. Japanese]

According to this view, then, UG stipulates that complements are attached as sisters of the head, but children must learn the relative ordering of the two elements

Table 13.5 Variation in Head–Complement Order

English	Japanese
[$_{VP}$ read the book]	[$_{VP}$ hon-o yonda]
	book-AC read
[$_{NP}$ pictures of John]	[$_{NP}$ John-no syasin]
	John-of picture
[$_{PP}$ with John]	[$_{PP}$ John-to]
	John-with

from experience. Thus, of the options in (23), only the first two need be considered by the acquisition device, the others being inconsistent with the genetically given X-bar schema.

(23)   a.   b.   c.   d.

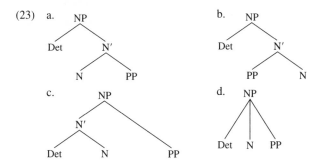

This yields a quite plausible view of syntactic development in that those properties of phrase structure that are not directly manifested in experience (hierarchical relations) are inborn and hence universal, while those properties that are directly observable in the speech of others (word order) are learned and subject to variation from language to language. In the words of N. Chomsky (1975: 39), "learning is primarily a matter of filling in details within a structure that is innate."

A second and much more intricate example of parameterization involves the principle of UG that constrains the interpretation of reflexive pronouns. As noted in chapter 11, English reflexive pronouns require an antecedent that occurs in the same clause. This is why *himself* is interpreted as coreferential with *Harry* but not *Sam* in (24).

(24)   antecedent (NP in the same clause)
                                    ↓
        [Sam$_i$ believes [that Harry$_j$ overestimates himself$_{*i,j}$]]

In contrast, languages such as Japanese allow the reflexive pronoun to select an antecedent inside or outside the same clause. Thus, (25) is ambiguous.

(25)   antecedent in antecedent in
       higher clause same clause
             ↓   ↓
       [$_S$ Sam-wa$_i$ [$_S$ Harry-ga$_j$ zibun-o$_{i,j}$ tunet-ta to]   it-ta]
          Sam-TOP   Harry-NOM   self-ACC pinch-PST-that say-PST
       'Sam$_i$ said that Harry$_j$ pinched (him)self$_{i,j}$.'

These facts suggest that the relevant principle of UG (Principle A) must allow at least two options when it comes to the domain within which a reflexive pronoun must find its antecedent. (There may also be intermediate possibilities; see, e.g., Wexler and Manzini 1987.)

(26) *Principle A:*
      A reflexive pronoun must have a higher antecedent in some domain.
      The domain parameter:
      Option (a): domain = the smallest clause containing the reflexive pronoun.
      Option (b): domain = the sentence containing the reflexive pronoun.

The first option forces selection of *Harry* as antecedent in (24), since this is the only other NP in the smallest clause containing *himself* (i.e., the embedded clause). This is the correct result for English. In contrast, option (b)—which is appropriate for Japanese—permits either of the two NPs in (25) to serve as antecedent for the reflexive.

This raises the question of how the acquisition device determines which option to select for the particular language that it is acquiring. The case of English is particularly interesting, since the sentences encountered by the acquisition device are consistent with both parameter settings. To see this, consider the sentences in (27).

(27)   a. [Harry$_i$ admires himself$_i$.]
       b. [I$_i$ believe [that Harry$_j$ overestimates himself$_{*i,j}$].]

The reflexive pronoun in these examples is coreferential with the NP *Harry*. Crucially, this NP is in *both* the same minimal clause as its antecedent (option a) *and* the same sentence (option b). (Any time *x* is in the same clause as *y*, it is necessarily also in the same sentence.) Under such circumstances, which option is the acquisition device to select?

Somehow, it must pick option (a), since selection of option (b) would lead children to treat sentences such as (28a) as grammatical and (28b) as ambiguous.

(28)   a. *[Sam$_i$ believes [that I overestimate himself$_i$].]
       b. [Sam$_i$ believes [that Harry$_j$ overestimates himself$_{*i,j}$].]

Not only would this be incorrect; nothing in experience would alert the acquisition device to its error. True, children will never hear an adult use a sentence such as (28a). But the acquisition device cannot conclude from this fact that such sentences are ungrammatical, since there are countless grammatical sentences that are never heard (see chap. 12). Moreover, even if children occasionally produced a sentence in which *himself* referred to an NP outside its clause, there is little chance that the error could be corrected. As noted in the previous chapter, parents typically ignore children's mistakes, and children typically resist those few corrections that are attempted. In other words, given the general unavailability and unreliability of negative evidence, the initial selection of option (b) would seriously

Set of sentences permitted by option (a)
(the antecedent must be in the same clause as the reflexive)

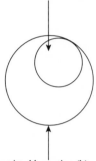

Set of sentences permitted by option (b)
(the antecedent must be in the same sentence as the reflexive;
it may or may not be in the same clause)

FIGURE 13.5 The Relative Restrictiveness of Options (a) and (b).

compromise the ability of the acquisition device to arrive at the correct grammar for English.

How can this be avoided? A key part of the solution to this problem lies in the fact that the two options permitted by the domain parameter are related to each other in a rather special way. As illustrated in figure 13.5, the set of grammatical sentences permitted by option (a) is a **subset** of those permitted by option (b). (This is called the 'subset relation'.) Whereas option (a) only permits grammatical sentences in which the reflexive pronoun has an antecedent in the same minimal clause, option (b) permits sentences in which the antecedent is inside or outside this clause (as long as it is in the same sentence).

Let us now assume that the acquisition device obeys principle (29), versions of which have been proposed by Berwick (1985:37) and Wexler and Manzini (1987:61), among others.

(29) *The Subset Principle:*
      The acquisition device selects the most restrictive parametric value consistent with experience.

We have already seen that experience alone cannot tell the acquisition device which value of the domain parameter is appropriate for English (see the discussion of (27) above). The Subset Principle remedies this indeterminacy by correctly forcing selection of the more restrictive option (a).

Matters are quite different in Japanese. The sentences encountered by the acquisition device in learning that language will include patterns such as (30), in which a reflexive pronoun is unambiguously coreferential with an NP in a higher clause.

(30)   antecedent is in higher clause
        ↓

        Kensan-wa$_i$ [momo-no ki-ga   zibun-no$_i$ uti-ni   aru-to] it-ta.
        Kensan-TOP peach-GEN tree-NOM self-GEN house-at be-that say-PST
        'Kensan said that there was a peach tree at self's house.'

This automatically excludes option (a) for Japanese, leaving the more liberal option (b) as the only setting of the domain parameter that is consistent with experience.

As the data from English show, the intuitive idea underlying the Subset Principle is simply that the acquisition device must not overgeneralize by selecting a parameter value that permits a wider range of sentences than the language in question actually allows. Rather, it should select the most restrictive option consistent with experience, thereby avoiding the need for subsequent corrections and adjustments.

As conceived by Wexler and Manzini, the Subset Principle is not part of Universal Grammar per se. Rather, it belongs to the 'learning module', a separate component of the acquisition device that in their view interacts with UG to ensure that experience selects the appropriate parametric values in cases where more than one option is available.

It is unclear at this time whether parameter setting always complies with the Subset Principle. If it does, then at the very least each parameter of UG will have to obey the requirement in (31).

(31)   *The Subset Condition* (Wexler and Manzini 1987:60):
        For every given parameter and every two given values of it, the languages defined by the values of the parameter are one a subset of another.

This is another way of saying that the sets of sentences permitted by any two values of a parameter must enter into a subset relation with each other. (If they didn't, the Subset Principle would not be able to operate.) Although the Subset Condition is satisfied in the case of the domain parameter (as we have seen), matters may not always be so straightforward. For instance, the two values of the parameter for head-complement order are equally restrictive, one allowing only head-initial phrases and the other permitting only head-final patterns—neither of which is a subset of the other. The Subset Principle is thus inapplicable. This need not create a learnability problem (since an incorrect setting would quickly run up against counterexamples in experience), but it does suggest that the parameteric options permitted by UG are not all of the same type. In section 3, we will consider a more serious counterexample to the Subset Principle.

LEXICAL PARAMETERS

An interesting feature of the domain parameter is that it seems to hold for particular lexical items rather than for the language as a whole. This can be seen by considering sentence (32), in which a pronominal rather than a reflexive occurs in the embedded clause.

(32) [$_S$ Mamorusan-wa$_i$ [$_S$ Kensan-ga$_k$ kare-o$_{i,*k}$ tunet-ta to]   it-ta]
      Mamorusan-TOP   Kensan-NOM him-ACC pinch-PST-that say-PST
      'Mamorusan$_i$ said that Kensan$_k$ pinched him$_{i,*k}$.'

The relevant constraint here is Principle B, which we paraphrase as in (33).

(33) *Principle B:*
      A pronominal cannot have a higher antecedent in the same domain.

As shown by the co-indexing in (32), the domain relevant to the operation of Principle B in Japanese consists of the smallest clause containing the pronoun, not the entire sentence as was the case with Principle A. (This is why *kare* 'him' can corefer with *Mamorusan,* which is in a higher clause, but not with *Kensan,* which occurs with it in the embedded clause.) Evidently, the domain parameter in Japanese is set independently for the reflexive *zibun,* which selects option (b), and the pronominal *kare,* which selects option (a). We thus say that the parameter in question is **lexical,** since its value is determined for individual words rather than for the language as a whole.

It is sometimes suggested that all parameters of UG are lexical. (Wexler and Manzini 1987:55, leading proponents of this view, call this the **Lexical Parametrization Hypothesis.**) This is an attractive idea, since it would limit syntactic variation among languages to the properties of individual words, which are known to differ from each other in any case. Unfortunately, however, at least some of the parameters that have been proposed in the literature on UG seem not to be lexical. For instance, the word order parameter applies not to particular words (it is not as if one verb occurred before its complement and another verb after it), but rather to all head categories in a language (but see note 4).

A further problem with the Lexical Parametrization Hypothesis, pointed out by Paul Bloom (pers. comm.), is that it does not explain why (for example) all pronominals in a particular language (e.g., *I, me, you, he, him, she, her, they,* and *them* in English) have the same domain. If in fact parameters are set on a word-by-word basis, the English situation should be somewhat unusual and we would expect to find languages in which the domain varied from pronoun to pronoun. In fact, this does not happen, suggesting that the Lexical Parametrization Hypothesis has missed an important generalization about the nature of parametric variation in human language.

DEFAULT PARAMETER SETTINGS

Thus far we have been assuming that all values for a particular parameter are initially available to the acquisition device, which then selects the most restrictive option consistent with experience in accordance with the Subset Principle. However, there is another possibility, namely that UG itself specifies an initial or **default** setting for its parameters. (Such settings are sometimes referred to as **unmarked,** which is another way of saying that they are more basic or more expected.) Consider once again the domain parameter for Principle A, repeated as (34).

(34) *Principle A:*
      A reflexive pronoun must have a higher antecedent in some domain.
      The domain parameter:
      Option (a): domain = the smallest clause containing the reflexive pronoun.
      Option (b): domain = the sentence containing the reflexive pronoun.

If option (b) were the initial setting, the facts for Japanese would follow straightforwardly but a problem would arise for English. This is because option (b) is too permissive for English, allowing ungrammatical sentences in which the reflexive pronoun refers to an NP outside its clause. As explained above, there is apparently no reliable way for the acquisition device to identify or correct such an error.

No such problems arise when option (a) is treated as the unmarked case. Children learning English will have no correction to make, since their language does in fact use this option. Of course, children learning Japanese will have to make an adjustment, but the needed information will be readily available to them. All that is required is exposure to structures such as (35) (repeated from (30)) in a context where it is clear that the matrix subject serves as antecedent for the reflexive pronoun.

(35) Kensan-wa$_i$ [momo-no ki-ga   zibun-no$_i$ uti-ni   aru-to] it-ta.
      Kensan-TOP peach-GEN tree-NOM self-GEN house-at be-that say-PST
      'Kensan said that there was a peach tree at self's house.'

This establishes the inadequacy of option (a) and allows the domain parameter to be reset to option (b) on the basis of positive evidence—i.e., sentences that are part of the child's experience.

If the idea of default parameter settings is right, the Subset Principle (or something like it) is part of Universal Grammar itself rather than an independent learning module. Its function, on this view, is not to guide the learner's' hypothesis formation process but rather to determine the default value of parameters, selecting the most restrictive option as the universal initial choice.

As the preceding example illustrates, 'learning' in this approach is 'error-driven' (Wexler and Culicover 1980:99ff.; Berwick 1985:102ff.; R. Clark 1992: 114). So long as the default parametric option is correct (e.g., option (a) of the domain parameter in the case of English), experience provides no counter-examples and the acquisition device simply retains its initial hypothesis. However, where the default option is overly restrictive (e.g., option (a) of the domain parameter in the case of Japanese), the acquisition device will eventually discover its error by taking note of sentences such as (35), which it presumably analyzes in (36).

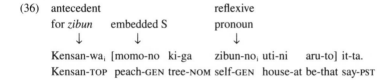

(36) antecedent   reflexive
      for *zibun*   embedded S   pronoun
       ↓   ↓   ↓
      Kensan-wa$_i$ [momo-no ki-ga   zibun-no$_i$ uti-ni   aru-to] it-ta.
      Kensan-TOP peach-GEN tree-NOM self-GEN house-at be-that say-PST

Because *zibun* 'self' in this pattern clearly has an antecedent outside the minimal S containing it, the acquisition device recognizes that it cannot maintain option (a) as its parameter setting for Japanese. It can then revise its hypothesis accordingly, thereby 'learning' that Japanese employs option (b) for the domain parameter.[5]

Note that nothing in this illustration violates the assumption that negative evidence is unavailable to language learners. The acquisition device corrects its mistake solely on the basis of positive evidence (exposure to a sentence that it predicted not to be possible), with no use of parental correction or similar feedback.

Recent experimental work has uncovered developmental data that might support the default setting hypothesis. As noted by Hermon (1992, 1994), evidence from a variety of languages (Chinese, Korean, Danish, and Icelandic) that adopt the more liberal option (b) of the domain parameter suggests that children initially exhibit a strong preference for an antecedent in the same clause. In the case of Korean, this preference apparently reaches 100% between the ages of 4 and 6 (Lee and Wexler 1987, cited by Hermon 1992:167)—suggesting that there is a default setting for a local antecedent. However, there are also problems with this conclusion, including the fact that even some adults apparently exhibit it in comprehension tests (suggesting a processing effect) and the fact that some very young children fail to manifest it.

3. The Data Required for Parameter Setting

One advantage of UG-based approaches to language acquisition is that, in principle at least, they require relatively limited types of experience for syntactic development to occur. Because so much of the final grammar is given in advance, the primary task of the acquisition device is to determine the appropriate value for various parameters. As the examples in section 2 illustrate, parameter setting can be triggered by utterances that are actually encountered in the child's environment (positive evidence). For instance, the data required to set the word order parameter consists of sentences in which heads (Vs, Ns, Ps, etc.) are either preceded or followed by a complement. Since such sentences are plentiful in the speech of adults, the acquisition device should have no trouble finding the information that it needs to select the correct parametric value.

Determining the value of at least some parameters may be even simpler if UG includes default settings. Consider once again the possibility that option (a) of the domain parameter associated with Principle A, repeated yet again as (37), is the default value.

(37) *Principle A:*
      A reflexive pronoun must have a higher antecedent in some domain.
      The domain parameter:
      Option (a): domain = the smallest clause containing the reflexive pronoun.
      Option (b): domain = the sentence containing the reflexive pronoun.

If the language being acquired is of the English type, the initial setting for the domain parameter (option (a)) is already correct and no learning at all is required. On the other hand, if the language being acquired is of the Japanese type, the initial parameter setting must be revised, but the required experience consists of relatively simple sentences (i.e., sentences such as (35)) that will eventually be encountered in the child's environment.

N e g a t i v e   E v i d e n c e

Matters may not always be so simple, however. To see this, we need only reconsider the subject drop parameter in (38).

(38) *The 'subject drop' parameter:*
      Option (a): subject drop is permitted.
      Option (b): subject drop is not permitted.

Of the two settings for the subject drop parameter, the second is apparently the least restrictive since it allows sentences with overt subjects, but not sentences with null subjects. In contrast, the first option allows both sentences with overt

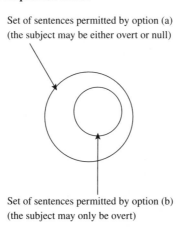

Set of sentences permitted by option (a)
(the subject may be either overt or null)

Set of sentences permitted by option (b)
(the subject may only be overt)

FIGURE 13.6 The Options Permitted by the Subject Drop Parameter

subjects and sentences with null subjects.[6] Given this state of affairs, we would expect option (b) to be the initial parameter setting. In the case of English, this option correctly blocks null subjects and can be retained by the acquisition device. In the case of Italian, by contrast, option (b) must eventually be rejected in factor of option (a), since this language allows null subjects. However, the acquisition device should have no trouble making this adjustment, since it will quickly encounter sentences containing null subjects in this language.

Here, though, the developmental facts have sometimes been taken to point to a very different scenario. For example, it has been claimed (e.g., by Hyams 1986, 1992) that even children acquiring English initially drop subjects. This is a controversial and problematic hypothesis, as we have seen (chap. 5), but let us assume for the sake of argument that it is correct. Among other things, this would suggest that the more permissive option (a) is the initial parameter setting, contrary to the Subset Principle. This then raises the question of how the acquisition device is able to correct its mistake and reset the subject drop parameter at option (b) for languages like English.

We have already seen that negative evidence is not in general available to the acquisition device, but there may be an interesting exception to this state of affairs. In particular, N. Chomsky (1981:9) has suggested that

> [a] not unreasonable acquisition system can be devised with the operative principle that if certain structures or rules fail to be exemplified in relatively simple expressions, where they would be expected to be found, then a (possibly marked) option is selected excluding them in the grammar, so that a kind of "negative evidence" can be available.

Taking this idea as his starting point, Lasnik (1989:91) proposes that the acquisition device could reset the subject drop parameter to option (b) by simply noting that sentences such as *Left early* do not occur in the speech to which it is exposed. (As noted in the previous chapter, information of this sort is known as 'indirect negative evidence'.)

Unlike the view considered and rejected in the preceding chapter, Lasnik's proposal does not require the acquisition device to keep track of all the sentences that it hears and to assume that all sentences not encountered are ungrammatical. Rather, UG directs the acquisition device to be 'on the lookout' for a very particular sentence type (a sentence with no overt subject). The failure to discover the sought-for sentence within a specific period of time then leads to parameter resetting, resulting in the prohibition of the subject drop option in the case of English. In this way, negative evidence could have a limited role to play in the language acquisition process.

Reliance on indirect negative evidence involves a significant departure from the simple parameter-setting model originally envisioned by UG-based theories of learnability (see, e.g., Valian 1990:114). Particular parametric values must now sometimes be innately associated with the absence of particular patterns, and new mechanisms must be posited within the acquisition device to take note of and evaluate 'missing' stimuli. It is not yet clear whether such extensions to the power of the acquisition device are necessary.

Designated Triggers

Among the many perils that the acquisition device must confront in the course of parameter setting is the existence of potentially misleading experience. Consider in this regard the status of the sentences in (39) with respect to Principle B (which requires that a pronominal not have a higher antecedent within the same minimal domain).

(39)   a.   I'm gonna make me a sandwich.
        b.   John$_i$ saw a snake near him$_i$.

Discussing these sentences, Janet Fodor (1994) notes that they could easily mislead the acquisition device into believing that English permits pronouns to have an antecedent within the same minimal clause (an option that is permitted in some languages). Fodor proposes an interesting way out of this problem, namely that UG associates with each parametric value a **designated trigger**—a particular sentence type that alone can license parameter setting. In the case of Principle B, she suggests, the designated trigger would be a sentence in which a pronominal direct object in a simple transitive clause is coreferential with the subject of that clause (e.g., *John$_i$ kicked him$_i$*). Nothing other than exposure to such a sentence would lead the acquisition device to conclude that a pronominal can have an antecedent in the same clause in 'core' sentences of the language. Since no English sentences, including those in (39), are of the right type, there is no danger of the wrong parametric option being selected. (The acquisition device must still deal with the sentences in (39) in some way, of course. The pattern in (a) is probably just an exception, but the pattern in (b) may ultimately fall under UG; see, e.g., Hestvik 1991.)

A second example of potentially misleading experience is offered by Valian (1990), who objects to the conventional model of parameter setting on the grounds that it assumes an overly optimistic view of the data to which the acquisition device is exposed. Valian focuses her remarks on the parameter in (40), repeated from (38), that determines whether a language allows finite verbs to have null subjects.

(40)   *The 'subject drop' parameter:*
       Option (a): subject drop is permitted.
       Option (b): subject drop is not permitted.

As we saw in chapter 5, languages such as Italian select option (a), while English chooses option (b); see (41a) and (41b) respectively. (Following tradition within Government and Binding theory, we represent a missing subject as *pro*.)

(41)   a. *pro* ha visto Piero. (Italian)
          '[S/he] has seen Peter.'
       b. **pro* has seen Peter.

Valian notes that there are problems with assuming that either value of this parameter is adopted as the default. If option (b) is the default, two dangers arise. First, children learning English might be misled into thinking that this is the wrong value for their language because of the existence of imperatives (e.g., *eat your supper*) and incomplete utterances (e.g., *Looks good, Seems OK*), which lack overt subjects. On the other hand, children learning Italian might be tempted to analyze bona fide subjectless sentences in their language as imperatives or incomplete utterances in order to make them compatible with the default setting (i.e., option (b)).

A different problem arises if option (a) is the default value of the subject drop parameter. Under this scenario, it would be difficult for children learning English to realize that this is the wrong option for their language. Not only might they be misled by imperatives and incomplete utterances into confirming this option; they could conclude nothing definitive from the many sentences with overt subjects that they encounter. This is because option (a) of the subject drop parameter does not rule out sentences with overt subjects; it simply indicates that an overt subject need not be present. As the parameter-setting process is traditionally understood, then, no amount of exposure to sentences with overt subjects can ever demonstrate the inadmissibility of sentences without overt subjects.

Valian suggests that these problems can be overcome if UG makes available both values of the subject drop parameter from the outset and if the acquisition device is able to weigh the relative merits of each against input that has been 'filtered' to exclude irrelevant data, especially incomplete sentences formed by deleting the utterance-initial element (e.g., *Looks good*). The details of Valians's proposal remain to be worked out (see John Kim 1993 and Valian 1993 for further discussion), but one way to implement it would be to assume that the subject drop parameter is linked to a designated trigger—namely, subjects in embedded clauses. As noted by Roeper and Weissenborn (1990) (see chap. 5), only true subject drop languages allow null subjects in tensed embedded clauses, as in (42b).

(42)   a. *English:*
           *John knows that [*pro* must go].
        b. *Spanish:*
           Juan sabe que [*pro* debe ir].
           'John knows that [he] must go.'

Assisted by such a link between the parameter and the relevant type of triggering stimulus, the acquisition device could avoid potentially misleading experience of the type noted by Valian and select the correct parametric option.

DEGREE-0 LEARNABILITY

An issue that has received considerable attention in the literature on learnability concerns the character of the sentences that can trigger parameter setting. These sentences must obviously be simple enough to be processed by young children and common enough to be encountered in the course of 'normal' linguistic experience (which may vary from child to child and community to community, as we have seen). Lightfoot (1989, 1991, 1994) puts forward a particularly daring proposal in this regard, suggesting that all the data required by the acquisition device occurs in unembedded domains—i.e., main clauses. Put another way, the acquisition device should never require sentences that are more than one clause in length. This is known as **degree-0 learnability** because 'zero' degrees of embedding are required. Previous proposals (e.g., Wexler and Culicover 1980) had suggested that the acquisition device might require information from sentences with a many as two levels of embedding in order to set all the parameters of UG ('degree-2 learnability').

Among the many challenges to degree-zero learnability, one of the most interesting involves structures such as (43).

(43)

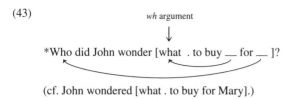

*Who did John wonder [what . to buy __ for __]?

(cf. John wondered [what . to buy for Mary].)

As already noted (see section 1 above and chap. 7), such sentences violate the *Wh* Island condition in that the sentence-initial *wh* word is associated with a gap inside an embedded clause that begins with a *wh* argument. Interestingly, sentences such as these are not ungrammatical in all languages, as example (44) from French helps show. (This sentence is from Lightfoot 1989:328.)

(44) Violà un liste de gens [à qui on n'a pas encore trouvé [quoi . envoyer __ __]]
there-is a list of people [to whom one has not yet found [what . to send __ __]]

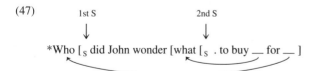

The traditional account for this contrast (e.g., Rizzi 1982) is that UG includes the general principle in (45) (which subsumes the *Wh* Island Condition).

(45) *The Subjacency Condition:*

*Wh [α [β __]]

where α and β are 'bounding nodes'

NP is taken to be a bounding node in all languages, but the status of S varies, in the manner indicated in (46).[7]

(46) *The Bounding Node Parameter:*
Option (a): S is a bounding node.
Option (b): S is not a bounding node.

According to this analysis, English adopts option (a), so that both S and NP count as bounding nodes in its grammar. Assuming that *wh* words are attached outside the S category, sentence (47) is ruled out, since two S nodes intervene between the sentence-initial *wh* word and the corresponding gap in the embedded clause.

(47)   1st S   2nd S
          ↓   ↓
*Who [s did John wonder [what [s . to buy __ for __]

In contrast, French selects option (b) and does not treat S as a bounding node, so there is no violation of the Subjacency Condition in sentence (48).

(48)   ... [à qui [$_S$ on n'a pas encore trouvé [quoi [$_S$. envoyer ___ ___]]]]
        ... [to whom [one has not yet   found [what [. to-send ___ ___]]]]

It is at this point that the challenge to degree-0 learnability arises. Since it is widely assumed that the more restrictive option (a) is the unmarked setting for the bounding node parameter, the acquisition device will have to revise this setting in the case of children acquiring French. But the most obvious piece of data needed to reset the bounding node parameter to the more liberal option (b) involves sentences such as (48), which includes an embedded clause. This is of course inconsistent with the requirement of degree-0 learnability.

Lightfoot acknowledges this problem and proposes an elegant solution: the acquisition device is able to discover that French selects option (b) through exposure to monoclausal sentences such as (49).

(49)
        Combien [$_S$ as   -tu vu [$_{NP}$ ___ de personnes]]?
        how-many [have you seen [___ of people]]
        'How many people did you see?'

If S were a bounding node in French, this sentence would be ungrammatical, since two bounding nodes—one S and one NP—would intervene between the sentence-initial *wh* word and the gap. Exposure to this sort of sentence should therefore alert the acquisition device to the fact that S is not a bounding node in French. Even more significantly, since this type of sentence contains a single clause, the acquisition device is able to make the required adjustment in a manner consistent with degree-0 learnability.[8]

There are many other challenges to degree-0 learnability, including two from among the phenomena considered earlier in this book. The first of these involves Roeper and Weissenborn's (1990) suggestion that the crucial data for determining whether a language permits subject drop comes from embedded clauses (see above and chap. 5). Thus, although speakers of English (a non–subject drop language) occasionally suppress subjects in sentences such as (50), they never do in sentences such as (51).

(50)   Looks good.
        Gotta go.

(51)   *I think [___ looks good].
        *I think [___ gotta go].

In order to avoid the danger of being misled about a language's subject drop status (the problem noted by Valian—see above), the acquisition device should therefore attend to embedded clauses. But this invalidates the thesis of degree-zero learnability, suggesting that at least one level of embedding (degree-1 learnability) may be required for the acquisition device to function properly.

Here again, though, there may be a way to salvage degree-0 learnability. This is because there is a second context in which subjects may not be dropped even in informal English—namely, *wh* questions.

(52)   *What did *pro* see __?

In contrast, true subject drop languages allow null subjects in *wh* questions.

(53)   Qué *pro* vió? (Spanish)
       'What did (s/he) see?'

By attending to monoclausal *wh* questions of this sort, the acquisition device could determine the proper setting for the subject drop parameter in a manner consistent with degree-0 learnability.

A second challenge to degree-0 learnability comes from the domain parameter associated with Principle A. As explained earlier in this chapter, languages such as Japanese differ from English in allowing a reflexive pronoun to have an antecedent NP either in the same minimal clause or in a higher clause. Sentences with the structure of (54) are thus ambiguous in Japanese but not English.

(54)   [Sam believes [that Harry overestimates *self*].]
       ENGLISH: *self* = Harry
       JAPANESE: *self* = Harry *or* Sam

We accounted for this fact by assuming that the domain within which the reflexive pronoun must find an antecedent is the minimal clause containing it in English (option (a)) but the entire sentence in Japanese (option (b)). We further assumed that the initial parameter setting corresponds to option (a) and that the acquisition device resets the domain parameter for Japanese following exposure to sentences in which the reflexive pronoun is unambiguously associated with an antecedent outside its clause. Significantly, however, this scenario appears inconsistent with degree-0 learnability, since the key triggering stimulus for Japanese involves biclausal sentences. There are, however, possible ways out of this problem. For one thing, it has been suggested (e.g., Cole and Sung 1994) that reflexive pronouns that can take an antecedent outside the minimal clause are all monomorphemic (i.e., they consist just of an element equivalent to English 'self'); in contrast, 'compound' reflexives such as English *himself* require a 'local' antecedent. This can be seen clearly in the contrast between *ziji* 'self' and *ta ziji* 'himself' in Mandarin: the former element allows an antecedent in a higher clause but the latter element does not.

(55) [Zhangsan$_i$ zhidao [Wangwu$_j$ hen ziji$_{i,j}$/ ta ziji$_{j,*i}$]].
      Zhangsan knows   Wangwu hate self/ himself
      'Zhangsan knows that Wangwu hates self/himself.'

If this is right, then the domain parameter could conceivably be set based on information about the form of the reflexive itself without the need to consider biclausal sentences.

Problems of other sorts arise, of course. In Navajo, for instance, a certain class of pronouns can attach to verbs, but only in embedded clauses (Wilkins 1989). Indeed, Lightfoot himself acknowledges that the requirement of degree-0 learnability must be relaxed somewhat to allow the acquisition device to 'see' at least some parts of an embedded clause (see, e.g., Lightfoot 1994 for a summary). Nonetheless, research of this sort has pointed to the existence of principled constraints on the type of experience on which the acquisition device can depend, even if these constraints are not yet fully understood.

4. Conclusion

This chapter has focused on the possibility that the acquisition device includes an inborn Universal Grammar whose component categories and principles significantly limit the type of grammatical system that can be acquired. As is widely acknowledged, much of language involves phenomena that have little or nothing to do with the principles and parameters of Universal Grammar: the form and meaning of particular vocabulary items, exceptions to morphological rules (e.g., *union-ize* but not **club-ize*), frozen expressions (e.g., *Be that as it may, So they say*), and 'politeness' conventions—to name a few. For this reason, Chomsky (1981:7–8) suggests that "it is hardly to be expected that [actual languages] will conform precisely or perhaps even very closely to the systems determined by fixing the parameters of UG."

There is nonetheless a very significant body of linguistic phenomena that fall within the domain of UG in the nativist theory. The inventory of categories to which the words of a language are assigned, the mechanisms responsible for the formation of hierarchically structured syntactic representations, and the various principles that apply to those representations (e.g., constraints on pronouns and gaps) are all assumed to be innately given as part of UG.

Since languages differ from each other in systematic ways (in terms of word order, domains for pronoun interpretation, *wh* island effects, and so on), not all innate syntactic mechanisms can be invariant. Rather, it is assumed that some include parameters that make available a small number of alternatives to the acquisition device. Part of the language acquisition process must therefore involve selection of the appropriate parametric option. In the case of English, parameter setting determines that heads precede their complements, that subject drop is not permitted in a finite clause, that the domain for Principle A is the smallest clause containing the reflexive pronoun, and that S counts as a bounding node.

Although very popular among syntacticians, UG-based approaches to language acquisition are far from unanimously accepted. In the next chapter, we will consider some alternatives to the view that the acquisition device includes an inborn Universal Grammar.

14

Alternatives to UG

There is little controversy in contemporary linguistics over the claim that the human mind includes an innately structured acquisition device. There is simply no other plausible explanation for why human beings—but not dogs or rabbits—can acquire and use language. Slobin (1985:1158) observes:

> In one way or another, every modern approach to language acquisition deals with the fact that language is constructed anew by each child, making use of innate capacities of some sort, in interaction with experiences of the physical and social worlds.

As N. Chomsky (1975:13) has remarked along similar lines, "every 'theory of learning' that is even worth considering incorporates an innateness hypothesis."

Despite this consensus, there is disagreement over the precise contribution of the genetic endowment to the language learning capacity. As explained in the previous chapter, the dominant view among syntacticians is that the inborn acquisition device includes highly specific grammatical knowledge in the form of Universal Grammar. However, there has been considerable resistance to this idea, especially among linguists and psychologists whose research focuses on development. Objections to UG seem not to be based on a rejection of nativism per se, but rather on a scepticism (often ill-defined) about the plausibility of the syntactic analyses on which the claims of innate categories and principles are based.

Although UG-based nativism is the best developed and most widely accepted view in the field today, a variety of alternatives have been put forward and are worth considering. I will focus here on work that is compatible with the central theme of this book, namely, that the acquisition process involves the emergence of syntactic representations. I will thus have nothing to say about 'connectionism' (e.g. Rumelhart and McClelland 1987), which denies the existence of syntactic representations altogether, or about approaches to learnability that take syntax to be largely reducible to functional principles (e.g., Van Valin 1991).

1. An Inductivist Approach to Syntactic Categories

The sharpest contrast in the theoretical literature on language acquisition is undoubtedly between the UG-based approach described in the preceding chapter and **inductivist** theories that maintain that language can be learned in its entirety from experience. Such theories minimize the role of inborn mechanisms, recognizing only that certain learning devices and strategies are innate. An extreme form of this view, put forward by Derwing (1973:201), holds that "general learning principles" may be all that is required to account for language acquisition.

One of the best examples of a detailed inductivist analysis comes from the theory of category learning developed by Maratsos and Chalkley (1981), Maratsos (1982), and Braine (1987). The acquisition device posited by these authors consists essentially of a general capacity for distributional learning, i.e., the discernment of recurring patterns and properties in experience. An attempt is made to show that an acquisition device of this sort can discover syntactic categories, which the authors take to be "formed and shaped by . . . sets of grammatical operations" (Maratsos 1982:241), especially positioning and affixation. (Distributional learning also has a prominent place in the semantic bootstrapping hypothesis outlined in the previous chapter, but in the inductivist approach it is the *only* mechanism used to explain category development. There are no innate syntactic categories and no innate linking with a set of corresponding semantic concepts.)

Turning now to a more precise characterization of the inductivist proposal, Maratsos and Chalkley (1981) suggest that syntactic categories are linked to a variety of semantic-structural patterns that involve networks of co-occurring morphological and positional properties. Consistent with this idea, English verbs are defined in terms of their compatibility with past tense marking, progressive aspect, negation by *do + not,* and the like, as exemplified in table 14.1. Nouns, on the other hand, are identified in terms of the distributional characteristics represented in table 14.2.

Initially, Maratsos and Chalkley suggest, the acquisition device simply learns the properties of individual words without realizing that they form part of a larger

Table 14.1 Properties of Verbs

Criterion	Example
Past tense form in *-ed*	*He liked it.*
Present tense form in *-s*	*He likes it.*
Negated by *do + not*	*They don't like it.*
Progressive aspect	*He's liking it more now.*

Table 14.2 Properties of Nouns

Criterion	Example
Plural *-s* [a]	*Boys will be boys.*
Possessive *-'s*	*the boy's achievement*
Determiner *the*	*The boy is outside.*

a. Applicable only to 'count' nouns.

network. Thus, a child might observe that the word *jump* takes the *-ed* suffix to form its past tense, as in (1).

(1)   jump: __ed
                [past]

Eventually, other properties are noted, ultimately giving the information depicted in figure 14.1.

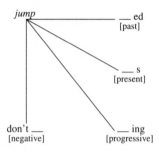

FIGURE 14.1 Properties of *jump*

As other words and their properties are acquired, certain general patterns emerge. For example, it is noted that *spill, kick,* and *realize* resemble *jump* in forming their past tense with *-ed,* their present with *-s,* their progressive with *-ing,* and their negative with *do + not.* These facts contribute to the network of co-occurring semantic and distributional properties illustrated in figure 14.2. A comparable net-work for nouns, based on the properties outlined in table 14.2, is exemplified in figure 14.3. Maratsos and Chalkley suggest that these networks are uncovered bit by bit, with the child first noting the properties of a few words, then observing that many of these properties co-occur throughout the language. Hence, any word that is negated by *do + not* will also form its progressive with the help of the suffix *-ing,* take the *-s* ending in the present, and so on.

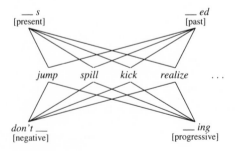

FIGURE 14.2 Some Co-occurring Properties of Verbs

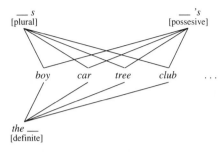

FIGURE 14.3 Some Co-occurring Properties of Nouns

A major advantage of this system from the point of view of language acquisition is that children can learn the 'category' of a new form on the basis of exposure to its use in a single context. Assume, for instance, that the word *motivate* is encountered in the sentence *The teachers don't motivate the students.* Thanks to the network of co-occurring properties illustrated in figure 14.2, the occurrence of *motivate* with *don't* should alert children to the fact that it is a 'verb'—that is, it can be used with *-ed* in the past tense, with *-s* in the present, and so on. Similarly, a child who heard the word *racquet* used in a sentence such as *The racquet is made of metal* would know that it belongs to the 'noun' class and therefore takes the plural suffix *-s,* can appear with the possessive suffix *-'s* (e.g., *the racquet's price*), and so forth.

A further interesting feature of this system is that it predicts errors for forms that are irregular in some way. Hence, if *break* and *see* are classified as 'verbs' on the basis of their use in sentences such as *Don't break that* and *He sees it,* children should erroneously conclude that these elements have the past tense forms *breaked and **seed.* The fact that errors such as these do occur can thus be interpreted as support for the inductivist proposal (Maratsos 1982 : 263).

The distributional approach to category development has a number of shortcomings. As noted by Maratsos himself (1982 : 263 ff.), at least some networks contain troublesome gaps. The noun class in English, for example, must include names such as *Mary* and *Seattle* even though these words typically do not take the plural suffix or occur with a determiner. It is not clear precisely how a child who was trying to classify words in terms of morphological properties would deal with this sort of case. (One possibility, suggested in a different context by P. Bloom (1990b, 1994), is that names in English are NPs rather than Ns. However, it is not clear how this insight could be uncovered using a purely distributional analysis.)

Second, as noted by Pinker (1984 : 49), there is the problem of determining how the acquisition device is able to identify the distributional properties that lead to a fruitful analysis of a language's categories. In the sample cases we have been considering, it was taken for granted that the acquisition device would focus on features such as tense, plurality, occurrence with a definite article, and the like. But, without the guidance of inborn knowledge, what is to prevent the acquisition device from attending to factors such as a word's initial phoneme or its linear position in the sentence? According to this logic, the acquisition device might place *bring* and *boot* in the same category because they both begin with the phoneme /b/. Similarly, it could group together *red, play,* and *boys* on the grounds that they all occur in second position in sentences such as those in (2). (For further criticism along these lines, see Gordon 1985.)

(2)   a. A *red* handkerchief lay on the ground.
      b. They *play* here every Saturday.
      c. Several *boys* were waiting for the bus.

Or, to take another of Pinker's objections, what is to prevent the acquisition device from concluding that *fast* and *trucks* belong to the same category on the basis of their positional similarity in sentences such as (3)? (A parallel case is considered by Maratsos 1982:264 and acknowledged to be problematic.)

(3)   a. Harry drives trucks.
      b. Harry drives fast.

Still another difficulty with the inductivist theory is that it does not provide a universally valid characterization of syntactic categories. As we have just seen, Maratsos and Chalkley's acquisition device characterizes the English noun in terms of properties such as co-occurrence with the determiner *the* and the plural affix *-s*. In Korean, however, there is no direct equivalent of English *the* and the plural suffix (*-tul*) is rarely used, although nouns do occur with a set of case suffixes—for which English has no direct equivalent. Despite these and other distributional differences, the words that we wish to call nouns serve similar semantic and syntactic functions in both languages. All object-denoting words belong to this category, and nouns head phrases that bear grammatical relations such as subject and direct object, carry thematic roles such as agent and theme, participate in operations such as passivization and relativization, and so forth. These facts are not reflected in a purely distributional analysis, which neither predicts that nouns (or any other category) should be found in all languages nor offers a universally valid characterization of their properties.

To date, the inductivist approach to language acquisition has focused on matters pertaining to category development. Virtually nothing has been said about the hierarchical properties of phrase structure or about constraints on gap placement and pronoun interpretation (but see Sampson 1978:199 ff.). Significant break-throughs in these latter areas are necessary before the prospects of this approach to learnability can be evaluated more fully.

2. Semantic Approaches

There have been occasional attempts to circumvent the need for UG by reject-ing the type of formal grammar with which it is associated. In its place, proponents of this view adopt a system of sentence formation that operates on semantically based categories and representations. The most detailed examples of this idea, found in the work of Schlesinger (1982, 1988) and Braine (1992, 1994), seek to reduce syntactic categories to semantic notions such as 'object' for noun, 'action' for verbs, 'attribute' for adjectives, and so on (table 14.3). (This sort of approach is to be distinguished from 'semantic bootstrapping' (e.g., Pinker 1984), which treats syntactic categories as formal primitives despite the existence of links to corresponding semantic concepts.) Schlesinger tries to circumvent the obvious counterexamples (e.g., non-actional verbs and nouns with abstract referents) by proposing that the semantic characterization of syntactic categories is extended (by a process he calls 'semantic assimilation') in response to distributional facts. Thus, he argues (1988:125 ff.), words such as *find, see,* and *remember* get inter-preted as actions (hence verbs) in part because of the formal similarity between the (SVO) patterns in which they occur and the patterns used to express proto-typical agent–action–patient relations.

A similar approach is adopted by Braine, who proposes that the semantic boot-strapping mechanism assumed by UG approaches (see the preceding chapter) can be dispensed with. Categories are defined in terms of notions such as 'object' and 'action' and are allowed to "expand beyond [their] original semantic kernel" (1992:83) in response to exposure to sentences such as *The situation justified the measures,* in which the words occurring in the noun positions seem not to denote literal objects. (Braine refers to this as the 'old-rules-analyze-new-material prin-ciple'; for a similar proposal, see Stemmer 1981:653.) The resulting syntactic representation, Braine argues (p. 88), resembles (4). (P = phrase)

Table 14.3 A Semantic Characterization of Syntactic Categories (Schlesinger 1982:225)

Category	Corresponding Semantic Notion
Verb	Action
Adjective	Attribute
Noun	Agent or patient

(4)

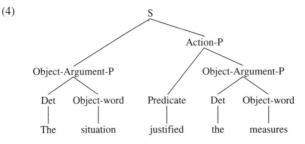

This sort of approach encounters several difficulties. For one thing, the proposal that semantically defined categories can be 'expanded' in the way just illustrated seems to rob the relevant concepts of any content, thereby jeopardizing the claim that syntactic categories can be reduced to a semantic base. By no known definition is the denotation of *situation* an object. Insisting that it is simply robs the notion 'object' of any content, resulting in its treatment as a formal label that fulfills exactly the same function as the more traditional designation 'noun'. The proposal thus becomes purely terminological: what we used to call 'nouns' should now be called 'object-words', with the normal meaning of 'object' suspended.

A further problem with the semantic approach is that it fails to address Maratsos's (1982, 1988) observation that some adjectives (e.g., *helpful* and *quick*) seem more action-like than some verbs (e.g., *belong* and *exist*) and that words with very similar meanings (e.g., *like* and *fond*) can belong to different syntactic categories. In principle, the acquisition device proposed by Schlesinger and Braine (see table 14.3) could analyze *helpful* as a verb (because of its actional meaning) and then compound the error by applying 'semantic assimilation' to formally similar words (e.g., *useful, doubtful,* etc.), incorrectly adding them to the verb class.

Still another shortcoming of the semantic approach is that to date it has said very little about the architecture of syntactic structure (and nothing at all about the principles constraining phenomena such as pronoun interpretation and gap placement). For example, Braine (1992:86) justifies the subject–predicate division in (4) by simply assuming that "agent arguments are specially privileged tree-structurally in having a major branch allotted to them." An obvious problem with this proposal is that it seems to confuse the subject position with agenthood. As the existence of passive sentences show, subjects are not always agents (e.g., *The books were distributed by the teacher*). Moreover, it says nothing about other details of phrase structure, such as the internal hierarchical structure of NPs that contain more than two elements (e.g., *the two old cars*). (Schlesinger 1982:247 seems to assume binary branching, which he attributes without explanation "to the way we conceptualize the world around us," but Braine takes no position on this issue.)

3. The Operating Principles Approach

A somewhat different alternative to Universal Grammar can be found in the work of Dan Slobin and his colleagues, who propose that the acquisition device contains a set of procedures for analyzing linguistic data rather than an actual body of linguistic knowledge. (This is sometimes called 'process nativism' as distinct from the 'content nativism' associated with UG-based theories.) An idea along these lines was first put forward by Slobin (1966:87–88):

> The child is born not with a set of linguistic categories but with some sort of process mechanism—a set of procedures and inference rules, if you will— that he uses to process linguistic data. These mechanisms are such that, applying them to the input data, the child ends up with [a grammar].

Subsequently (e.g., Slobin 1973, 1985), these procedural and inferential mechanisms came to be known as **operating principles.** Slobin (1985) proposes almost forty such principles, which he describes as "procedures for perceiving, storing and analyzing linguistic experience" (p. 1158). A sampling of these principles is given in (5)–(9). (A somewhat different set of operating principles is put forward by MacWhinney 1985.)

(5) *Units:* Determine whether a newly extracted stretch of speech seems to be the same as or different from anything you have already stored. If it is different, store it separately; if it is the same, take note of this sameness by increasing its frequency count by one.

(6) *Functor Classes:* Store together all functors that co-occur with members of an established word class, and try to map each functor onto a distinct notion.

(7) *Word Classes:* Store together as a class all words that co-occur with a given functor or the same groups of functors across utterances.

(8) *Variable Word Order:* If you find that a clause type occurs in more than one word order, attempt to find a distinct function for each order.

(9) *Phrasal Morpheme Order:* Keep the order of morphemes in a phrase constant across the various environments in which that phrase can occur.

Slobin does not take a position on the extent to which the acquisition device (or 'language-making capacity', to use his term) is "specifically tuned to the acquisition of language as opposed to other cognitive systems" (p. 1158). However, unlike the general learning mechanisms of radical inductivist approaches, most operating principles seem to be specifically designed for use with linguistic data— as can be seen from their reference to linguistic notions such as 'word', 'functor', 'morpheme', and 'clause'.

The operating principles approach to language acquisition has been influential and has spurred a great deal of interesting research, but it has met with two serious objections. The first has to do with problems inherent in the operating principles themselves. As noted by Pinker (1989:458), many operating principles provide informal descriptions of *what* children are doing rather than technical explanations of *how* they do it. In the case of (6), for instance, the operating principle instructs the learner to "try to map each functor onto a distinct notion." But how, precisely, is this to be done? Which notions is the acquisition device to consider first? At what point can it decide that a particular functor cannot be mapped onto a distinct notion? A similar problem arises in (8), which instructs the learner to "attempt to find a distinct function" for alternative word orders for the same clause type, but does not indicate how this is to be done or even how to determine whether two patterns are instances of the same clause type.

A further problem with the operating principles approach is that its proponents typically do not take a detailed position on the nature of the grammar that must be acquired, preferring to use data from child language as their sole source of information about the inner workings of the acquisition device (e.g., Slobin 1985: 1158). This is problematic for two reasons.

First, it dramatically limits the amount of data that can be used to understand and explain syntactic development. Because child language is by its very nature the product of an incomplete grammatical system, it can provide information about only part of what the acquisition device must eventually do. A full and undistorted account of the acquisition process seems to require at least a partial theory of the mature grammar that it produces.

Second, it is unclear whether the type of operating principles envisioned by Slobin are even compatible with the sort of grammar that virtually all contemporary syntactic theories attribute to the mature native speaker. (As noted in chap. 12, such grammars include an inventory of syntactic categories, mechanisms for combining these categories to form hierarchically structured syntactic representations with particular architectural properties, and principles that regulate the occurrence of gaps and pronouns in these representations.) Operating principles such as (7) suggest that syntactic categories are to be characterized in terms of their co-occurrence with a set of other elements (whose precise identity is not made clear)—a view not unlike the distributional theory described in section 1 and almost certainly open to the same criticism. There are no clues at all about how operating principles would deal with either the architecture of phrase structure or the principles that regular phenomena such as the placement of gaps and the interpretation of pronouns. This leaves a huge hole in the resulting picture of the language acquisition process, completely ignoring the emergence of two major components of adult syntactic knowledge.

4. General Nativism

Although very different in conception, approaches to language acquisition that rely on UG and on operating principles have in common one important feature: both are committed to the view that the acquisition device includes a set of inborn mechanisms that are specifically linguistic in character (the categories and principles of UG in one case, the operating principles themselves in the other case). Such theories are examples of **special nativism,** the theory that the acquisition device includes innate grammatical mechanisms.

Such approaches contrast with what might be called **general nativism,** the view that the innate knowledge required for language acquisition is more general in nature and does not include actual grammatical categories, principles, or strategies. Technically, the inductivist approaches illustrated in the first section of this chapter are instances of general nativism, since they posit the existence of only the most general inborn mechanisms (e.g., those required for distributional learning). For the purposes of this discussion, however, I will use the term 'general nativism' in a less inclusive sense to refer to theories that posit a more significant innate component than inductivist approaches, but still stop short of adopting an actual inborn grammar.

Work on general nativism is potentially worthwhile for two reasons. First, this line of inquiry is directed by the methodological goal that guides all scientific work—the search for ever deeper, ever more general properties and principles. This goal is pursued within special nativism by proposing principles that account for the widest possible range of linguistic phenomena. In recent years, for example, the leading edge of research has focused on the search for principles that hold both across languages and across structures. Thus, the idea of a 'passivization rule' is rejected in favor of the view that the properties of passive patterns follow from general principles that apply to a wide variety of structure types in all languages (see N. Chomsky 1981 for one proposal). In a sense, the general nativist research program simply takes the quest for generality one step further by considering the possibility that the mechanisms responsible for language acquisition and use are not narrowly linguistic in character.

A second reason for pursuing the general nativist research program is, paradoxically, that the special nativist approach is so widely accepted. In recent years, there has been a virtual consensus among linguists committed to the grammar-oriented study of language acquisition that the inborn acquisition device includes a Universal Grammar with the sort of (faculty-specific) properties and principles considered in the preceding chapter. Under these circumstances, 'contrarian' research that rejects the widely held view and actively seeks out alternatives fulfills a valuable function, allowing the discipline to hedge its bets somewhat and demanding the occasional reassessment of established views.

Of course, proponents of contrarian research must be careful not to underestimate the challenges they confront. As we saw in the preceding two chapters, a strong case can be made for the view that the type of experience to which children have access radically 'underdetermines' the type of grammar required to speak and understand a human language. It seems unlikely that future research will uncover a previously unnoticed type of experience that could somehow erase the underdetermination problem. If the type of grammar assumed by proponents of Universal Grammar is right (i.e., if something like the GB view of syntax is correct), special nativism is inevitable. For the reasons explored in detail in the preceding chapter, the syntactic categories, representations, and principles assumed by that theory are simply too far removed from experience to be learnable. If they do in fact exist, they must be supplied by an innate Universal Grammar, consistent with the central thesis of special nativism.

If special nativism is to be avoided, then, it is clear what path must be taken: advocates of general nativism must propose a system of sentence formation (a grammar) whose emergence in response to experience does not require inborn syntactic categories and principles. Of necessity, this grammar will have to differ substantially from a GB-type grammar, yet still be able to account for the full range of syntactic phenomena found in adult speech. This is obviously a daunting challenge, and very little work addresses it directly. The discussion here extends and refines proposals that have been made in this regard by O'Grady (1987, 1991, in press).

MECHANISMS OF SENTENCE FORMATION

For the purposes of illustration, we can begin with a simple combinatorial system influenced by traditional and recent work in categorial grammar (see, e.g., Bar-Hillel 1953; Dowty 1982; Bach 1988) as well as head-driven phrase structure grammar (e.g., Pollard 1988) and generalized phrase structure grammar (e.g., Gazdar et al. 1985). Because of limitations on space, I will focus on the formation of relatively simple sentence structures consisting of a verb and one or more 'grammatical terms' (subject, direct object), ignoring for now modifiers such as adverbs and adjectives.

The two most important features of the sentence-building system proposed here are both shared by categorial grammars in general. First, the system builds structure from the 'bottom up', combining elements to create phrases and ultimately a sentence. Second, a distinction is made between **functor** categories,[1] which require arguments, and **basic** categories, which do not exhibit such argument dependencies. Categories of the latter type include simple nouns (e.g., *Harry, water*) and Ss. Table 14.4 introduces some verbal functors; the symbol N_a stands for 'nominal bearing an agent role' and N_t for 'nominal bearing a theme role'.

Within this type of system, syntactic representations have the look of the tree

Table 14.4 Some Verbal Functors and Their Properties

Category	Dependencies	Symbol	Examples
Intransitive V	1 agent argument	$V^{<N_a>}$	run, walk, dance
	or 1 theme argument	$V^{<N_t>}$	fall, faint, die
Transitive V	1 agent argument	$V^{<N_aN_t>}$	touch, wash, hit
	and 1 theme argument		

diagram in (10). As in most work in categorial grammar, constituents are marked for category membership, but not for 'bar-level'; thus, N stands for both 'noun' and 'noun phrase' (both of which are nominal); V stands for both 'verb' and 'verb phrase' (both of which are verbal); and so on. S is taken to be a verbal category with no unsatisfied argument dependencies (i.e., $S = V^{(0)}$, as in Keenan and Timberlake 1988:269). (The view that S is a verbal projection is in fact widely accepted outside Government and Binding theory.)

(10)
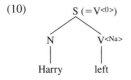

Sentence formation is driven by semantic considerations. In particular, it is assumed that as functor categories combine with arguments of the appropriate number and type, their meanings are amalgamated to form the complex meanings conveyed by sentences. In (10), the verb *leave*—a functor that requires an agent argument—combines with the nominal *Harry,* satisfying or 'canceling' that dependency and creating a phrase whose meaning is the result of combining the meaning of *leave* with that of *Harry.*

Since the combinatorial operation responsible for sentence formation applies to *pairs* of elements (i.e., a functor and one argument), no more than one dependency can be satisfied at a time. This raises two questions: (i) Which of a transitive verb's two arguments should it combine with first? and (ii) What happens to the other argument? The answer to the first question presupposes the existence of an **argument hierarchy** which regulates the order in which a verbal functor should combine with its arguments (e.g., Dowty 1982; O'Grady 1987; Grimshaw and Mester 1988; Larson 1988; Bresnan and Moshi 1990; Li 1990). For our purposes, the hierarchy in (11), which stipulates the relative combinatorial order for agents and themes, will suffice.

(11)   *The Argument Hierarchy:*

Turning now to the second question, any dependencies that remain after a combinatorial operation takes place are passed up to the resulting phrase in accordance with principle (12).

(12)   *The Inheritance Principle:*
        Unsatisfied dependencies are inherited upward.

Example (13) illustrates how this works. (A dotted line represents inheritance.)

(13)

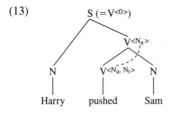

In (13), the transitive verb *push* combines first with the N *Sam.* This satisfies its dependency on a theme argument, leaving the dependency on an agent argument to be inherited by the phrase *pushed Sam.* Combination with the missing argument (*Harry*) then gives an S ($V^{(0)}$), the terminal category that results from having satisfied all the dependencies associated with a verbal functor.

The sentence-building system presented to this point is neutral with respect to word order. It will just as easily form sentences in which both arguments precede the verb as sentences in which the agent argument occurs preverbally and the theme argument postverbally. To remedy this, we can assume that functor categories are 'directional' in the sense that they include information not only about the type of category with which they must combine but also its location. In English, transitive verbs ($V^{(N,N)}$) look rightward for the argument with which they combine, while intransitive verbal categories ($V^{(N)}$) look leftward.

(14)   *Word order conventions* (English):
        An intransitive verb ($V^{(N)}$) combines with an argument to the left.
        A transitive verb ($V^{(N,N)}$) combines with an argument to the right.

This set of conventions ensures that in a simple structure such as (10), the (intransitive) verb will follow rather than precede its subject argument. It also explains why the transitive verb *push* in (13) precedes its theme argument while the resulting phrase *push Sam* (an intransitive verbal category since it exhibits a single unsatisfied argument dependency) follows the argument with which it combines.

Although sketched only in outline, the proposed system of sentence formation satisfies the basic requirements that the grammar for a human language must meet (chap. 12): it includes an inventory of syntactic categories, and it forms syntactic representations with the appropriate type of hierarchical structure. As with the more conventional tree structures considered in the preceding chapter, there is binary branching and there is a 'subject–object asymmetry', with the verb structurally 'closer' to its direct object than to its subject. Taking this very simple system as our starting point, we can now begin to consider the type of acquisition device that is needed to ensure the appropriate syntactic development in response to experience.

THE GENERAL NATIVIST ACQUISITION DEVICE

The goal of a general nativist acquisition theory is to provide an account of syntactic development that does not make reference to inborn syntactic categories or principles. On this view, the acquisition device must consist only of mechanisms that are not inherently syntactic in character; it cannot include UG. These mechanisms may or may not have independent nonlinguistic functions: although some components of the acquisition device (e.g., various 'computational' properties described below) are apparently manifested outside the language faculty, others are arguably peculiar to language (see below for discussion). Crucially, however, the acquisition device does not include conventional syntactic notions such as 'noun' or 'verb' or syntactic constraints such as Principle A or the Subjacency Condition.

The general nativist acquisition device includes several independent modules whose interaction with each other and with experience ultimately gives a grammar. (I use the term 'module' here in the sense of a component with a defined function in a larger system, and not in the more specialized sense of Jerry Fodor 1983.) For the purposes of this illustration, we can take the acquisition device to consist of five modules, each with its own function (table 14.5).

The **perceptual module** is responsible for the analysis of the auditory distinctions underlying the phonemic contrasts of human language and for attention to the cues that make possible segmentation of the speech string into its component words and morphemes. There is reason to believe that the former task is made

Table 14.5 Organization of the General Nativist
Acquisition Device

Module	Function
Perceptual	Provides an analysis of the auditory stimulus
Learning	Provides the means to formulate and test hypotheses
Conceptual	Provides an inventory of notions relevant to grammatical contrasts: singular–plural, definite–indefinite, past–nonpast, etc.
Propositional	Provides a representation of propositional meaning
Computational	Provides the means to carry out combinatorial operations on functors and their arguments

possible by auditory mechanisms that are available by age 1 month or earlier (e.g., Eimas 1974). As noted in chapter 2, the abilities required to segment speech seem to draw heavily on an inborn tendency to focus on salient portions of an auditory stimulus—particularly its beginning and end, as well as stressed syllables (see Peters 1985 and Slobin 1985 for further proposals and discussion).

The **learning module** is responsible for acquiring those aspects of language which do not follow from inborn properties of the acquisition device. Consistent with the widely held view, we take learning to be a process of hypothesis formation and testing. As Pinker (1989:166–67) remarks: "Despite all its complex guises, learning can always be analyzed as a set of 'hypotheses' the organism is capable of entertaining and of a 'confirmation function' by which environmental input tells the organism which one to keep." (See also Fodor 1975:95.) The primary function of the learning module is thus to formulate and test hypotheses derived with the help of the acquisition device's other modules.

The function of the **conceptual module** is to provide the 'vocabulary' of notions in terms of which a language's grammatical contrasts are formulated. Obvious examples of these notions include definite–indefinite (involved in the contrast between English *the* and *a*), past–nonpast (for tense), singular–plural (for the category of number), and masculine–feminine–neuter (underlying the *he–she–it* distinction in the English pronoun system). To date, there is no definitive list of notions that the conceptual system makes available to the acquisition device, although various proposals have been made—ranging from early work in descriptive linguistics by Nida (1946:166ff.) to recent proposals in language acquisition research by Slobin (1985), Bowerman (1985), and Pinker (1989), among others.

The **propositional module** provides a way to represent meaning by analyzing propositions into predicates, modifiers, and arguments bearing a variety of thematic roles. This information contributes to the creation of semantic representations whose properties we will consider shortly.

Finally, the **computational module** determines how the words encoding the elements in the semantic representation can be combined to form sentence structures. As I explain in detail below, properties of the computational module are ultimately responsible for giving syntactic structure its characteristic architecture, including its binary branching.

In order to see how the proposed acquisition device contributes to development, I will summarize and refine proposals made by O'Grady (1991, in press) about the emergence of syntactic categories and hierarchical structure, adding a new suggestion about the origin of a major constraint on reflexive pronoun interpretation.

Syntactic Categories

The purpose of the acquisition device is to discover the grammatical system that a particular language employs, not to explain how it came to be that way in the first place. (Indeed, since actual languages reflect the often idiosyncratic effects of borrowings, historical change, lexical exceptions, and many other factors, an acquisition device that required a rationale for every phenomenon that it encountered would almost certainly fail.) Thus, a theory of category development need not explain the various idiosyncracies that arise in how individual languages draw their categorial boundaries (e.g., the fact that *fond* is an adjective and *like* a verb). Rather, the goal of such a theory, at least initially, is simply to explain how the acquisition device discovers the appropriate category assignments for the words of a language.

Underlying the question of how the acquisition device discovers and assigns syntactic categories is the deeper issue of what a syntactic category is. There are essentially two views in the linguistic literature. The first view, which we can call the 'formalist' theory, treats syntactic categories as formal primitives. (A variant of this view 'defines' syntactic categories in terms of features such as $\pm N$ and $\pm V$, which are themselves treated as formal primitives.) Since primitives cannot be defined in terms of anything more basic, the formalist theory implies that syntactic categories must be directly supplied to the language learner by the acquisition device. This in turn supports the special nativist view that the genetic endowment for language includes knowledge that is purely syntactic in character.

Contrasting with the formalist theory is the 'reductionist' view, which holds that syntactic categories can be reduced to a more basic set of notions—the principal idea underlying the semantic approaches to category development pioneered by Schlesinger and Braine (see sect. 2). The general nativist approach also adopts the reductionist view, characterizing categorial contrasts in terms of a set of inborn semantic notions supplied by the conceptual module. However, unlike the overly restrictive notions employed by Schlesinger and Braine (e.g., 'thing' and 'action'), which must eventually be expanded to the point of vacuity, the key concepts are (by design) broad and potentially overlapping, with boundaries that are determined by distributional criteria to which they are innately linked.

This is probably easiest to illustrate for the V category, whose denotations I take to be instances of an 'event' class broad enough to encompass both actions and states. I take the criterial property of events to be compatibility with the time-based contrasts encoded by tense and aspect. This gives an analysis in which a distributional property (co-occurrence with whatever tense and aspect markers a language employs) indicates category membership, but that distributional property is important for a semantic reason: tense and aspect markers are relevant to the identification of the verb category because they are inherently tied to the inborn 'event' concept to which the verb category is reduced.[2]

This proposal has a number of advantages. First, all languages apparently express tense and/or aspect, albeit in different ways—some by affixes and some by free morphemes (in fact, English uses both). The proposed definition of the verb class is thus a plausible universal, unlike definitions formulated in terms of language-particular distributional properties.

Second, by referring to tense and aspect in our definition, we dramatically limit the set of possible distributional properties that the acquisition device must consider in the course of developing a categorial system. Since compatibility with tense and aspect—inborn notions provided by the conceptual module—is taken to be the criterial feature of 'events' (and hence of verbhood), this is the only distributional property that the acquisition device needs to consider when identifying verbs.

Third, by not equating verbs with 'actions' even as a prototypical correlation (in contrast to Pinker's semantic bootstrapping proposal), we avoid the prediction that children's first verbs should refer to actions. As noted by Maratsos (1988 : 36), non-actional verbs such as *need, want, know, like,* and *sleep* are among the first to be acquired in English. (Yamashita 1990 reports that *inai* 'to not exist' was one of the first verbs acquired by the 2-year-old Japanese child she studied.)

Turning now to the noun class, I propose that its members have denotations that can be 'individuated'—i.e., distinguished in a particular way from other potential referents of the same type. Except for proper names (*Henry, Tokyo*), which are inherently individuating, the most common sign of individuation in the sense intended here is occurrence with morphemes marking specificity/definiteness (e.g., definite articles or their equivalent) and/or deictic determiners (such as English *this* and *that*). Thus, when I say *he read the/that book,* I am distinguishing a particular book from other potential referents of the same type.

Individuation is not restricted just to nouns with countable objects as referents.[3] As the examples in (15) help show, less prototypical instances of the noun category can also occur with determiners and/or deictics.

(15)   a. *Mass nouns:*
             the water, this butter
         b. *Abstract nouns:*
             these truths, a policy, this responsibility
         c. *Nominalizations:*
             the kick, a jump, this running, that departure

What makes these words nouns is not that they always denote individuals—i.e., actual *individuated* things (for some clearly do not); rather, it is that their denotations are *individuatable*. In many (perhaps most) uses, for instance, mass nouns denote non-individuated substances and portions (e.g., *Water is necessary for life; There is water on the floor*). However, as the examples in (15a) show, the denotations of mass nouns *can* be individuated in the sense of being distinguished from other substances of the same type through the use of deictics. On the view put forward here, this is what justifies assignment of the corresponding words to the noun category.

Like verbs, then, nouns are characterized in terms of a semantic notion (individuatability) that is inherently linked to particular distributional phenomenon—
co-occurrence with markers of definiteness/specificity and deicticity. The acquisition device therefore 'knows' precisely which distributional properties to focus
on in order to identify nouns. Moreover, although the precise structural devices
that mark individuation differ from language to language, the fact that all languages have mechanisms to express deicticity contrasts (Anderson and Keenan
1985:308) ensures the universal viability of this approach.[4]

Finally, consider the adjective class. Unlike nouns and verbs, this category is
not found in all languages (e.g., Dixon 1982). However, where it does occur, its
denotations seem to fall into the class of gradable properties (see also Croft 1991:
132). If this is right, then the criterial distributional characteristic of adjectives
will be occurrence with those morphemes that a language uses to indicate gradation (e.g., in English, *very, too,* and so forth).[5] As with verbs and nouns, then,
the distributional criterion that the acquisition device uses to identify adjectives
is determined by the inborn semantic notion to which this category is reduced
(gradability).

In sum, I propose that the conceptual module of the acquisition device includes
an inborn classficatory system that takes each concept that can be encoded by a
'major' lexical item and classifies it as an **individuatable** thing (something that
can be individuated), an **event** (a phenomenon that is situated in time), or a time-
independent, gradable **property.** Just as the human perceptual system forces classification of every speech sound as either voiced or voiceless, so the conceptual
system requires classification of every concept in terms of the contrast among
individuatable things, events, and properties. Moreover, just as the perceptual
module must provide information about the precise acoustic correlates of voicing,
so the conceptual module supplies the specific criteria that are to be used to classify denotations: by definition, individuatable concepts must be compatible with
markers of specificity/definiteness and deicticity; events must permit tense and
aspect contrasts; and properties must be compatible with morphemes encoding
gradation. Figure 14.4 depicts the proposed classificatory operation.

Thanks to the reductionist view of syntactic categories adopted here, the results
of this classificatory operation yield syntactic categories: the category labels N, V,

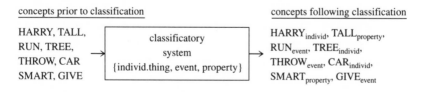

concepts prior to classification   concepts following classification

HARRY, TALL, $HARRY_{individ}$, $TALL_{property}$,
RUN, TREE,   classificatory RUN_{event}, $TREE_{individ}$,
THROW, CAR   system $THROW_{event}$, $CAR_{individ}$,
SMART, GIVE   {individ.thing, event, property} $SMART_{property}$, $GIVE_{event}$

FIGURE 14.4 Operation of the Classificatory System

Table 14.6 Syntactic Categories and Semantic Classes

Category Label	Semantic Class	Corresponding Distributional Properties
N	Individuatable thing	Compatibility with markers of definiteness/ specificity and deicticity
V	Event	Compatibility with contrasts involving tense and aspect
A	Property	Compatibility with markers of gradation, incompatibility with tense and aspect

and A are nothing more than 'shorthand' for the classes consisting of individuatable things, events, and properties, respectively (table 14.6).

Of course, it is easy to imagine criteria for individuatability, eventhood, and propertyhood that would yield different results. (For instance, the term 'event' is often used to include any happening, including the denotations of nominalizations such as *departure* and *restoration*—which would obviously undermine the classificatory system I have proposed.) By the same logic, though, one could easily imagine an acoustic criterion for voicing that would yield the wrong result in the case of phonological development. I assume that whatever the merits of such alternative definitions, they are simply not the ones used by the acquisition device in its categorizational operations.

The theory outlined here differs both from inductivist approaches to category development and from semantic bootstrapping. Unlike inductivist theories, the general nativist approach does not equate syntactic categories with sets of distributional properties. The latter are used as diagnostics for category membership in the general nativist approach, but only because they are inherently linked to the individuatable thing–event–property contrast upon which category distinctions are based.

Unlike semantic bootstrapping, the general nativist approach takes the view that syntactic categories are fully reducible to more basic semantic notions, not just that some instances of particular categories have semantic correlates (e.g., that prototypical Ns refer to 'objects' or prototypical Vs to 'actions'). Thus, in the general nativist theory, all instances of a particular category have the same semantic properties (e.g., all nouns denote individuatable things; see n. 3).

Although the semantic notions underlying the N–V–A distinction are presumably available from the earliest stages of linguistic development, it is unclear at what point the acquisition device is able to actually classify words in terms of this contrast. Even though children do not themselves use determiners and tense markers until age 2 or so (see chap. 15 for further discussion), they may understand enough about the semantic function of these elements to recognize them as markers of individuation and eventhood from an earlier age. (As noted in the preceding chapter, experimental work by Brown 1957; Katz, Baker, and Macnamara 1974;

and Gordon 1985, 1988 has established the sensitivity of children to the presence or absence of determiners before they use these elements in their own speech.) Another possibility, which I will not consider here, is that children initially classify words on some other basis—perhaps their argument structure (e.g., ⟨agent, theme⟩), which play a role in determining a word's gross combinatorial potential and must be learned at any rate. Subsequent identification of the semantic role of determiners, tense, and the like would then lead to further classification in terms of the relevant category constrasts.

Various other issues remain to be worked out. For instance, it is unclear at this time how the acquisition device should deal with words inside idioms (such as *bucket* in *kick the bucket*) or with expletives such as *it* in *It seems that John left* (assuming that pronouns should be assigned to the N class, an issue on which I do not take a position here). Since elements such as these do not denote anything, it is unclear how they can or should be categorized.

A further issue has to do with the possibility that clues other than the distributional properties entailed by a category's semantic characterization are involved in the categorization process. Under some circumstances, semantic considerations alone may suffice to categorize a word. The most obvious example of this involves words denoting discrete objects (*car, book, man,* and so on), which are arguably classifiable as nouns solely on the basis of their meaning (e.g., P. Bloom 1994). It is also possible that 'secondary' distributional properties have a role to play in categorization. For example, once the acquisition device has determined that the possessive morpheme attaches to nominals in English, it could easily make use of this fact to help categorize a novel word bearing the -'s suffix.

Yet another important issue has to do with how the acquisition device distinguishes subclasses within particular categories (e.g., count vs. mass within the noun category, or state vs. activity within the verb category). One possibility is that there are additional inborn concepts with particular distributional consequences. For instance, it has been suggested that within the noun category, the distinction between 'count' nouns such as *rock* and 'mass' nouns such as *dirt* might be reflected in a nominal's compatibility with 'counters' such as *a, one, two, several,* and so on (cf. *a rock* vs. **a dirt*). See Gordon 1985, 1988 and P. Bloom 1994 for discussion. This is similar in spirit to the more general proposal I have made.

Finally, it is necessary to acknowledge that the proposal I have been outlining deals with only the 'core' of the categorization system that is required for human language, and it is obvious that various extensions will be necessary. For example, nothing has been said here about adverbs or the set of 'minor' categories that includes determiners, auxiliary verbs, and prepositions. These and other matters are worthy of careful attention (see O'Grady in press for a proposal), but I will not pursue them further here.

Chapter Fourteen

HIERARCHICAL STRUCTURE

Now let us consider the question of how syntactic representations come to have their characteristic architecture, including hierarchically organized binary branching and a subject–object asymmetry. The components of the general nativist acquisition device most relevant to this problem are the propositional and computational modules.

The propositional module provides a way to represent meaning in an inborn 'language of thought' (e.g., Jerry Fodor 1975; Slobin 1985:1192; Braine 1987); see (16)–(17). Working in tandem with the conceptual module, it is therefore able to provide language learners with a representation of sentence meaning (call it **semantic form**) that includes information about predicate–argument relations as well as the settings for contrasts such as past–nonpast and definite–indefinite. (Consistent with the practice adopted in chap. 12, the formalism used to depict semantic representations is borrowed from Lexical-Functional Grammar.)

(16) Harry studies astronomy.

predicate:	STUDY ⟨agent, theme⟩
tense:	present
agent:	[HARRY]
	[singular]
theme:	[ASTRONOMY]
	[non-count]

(17) Fish swim.

predicate:	SWIM ⟨agent⟩
tense:	present
agent:	[FISH]
	[plural]

Because these representations contain no syntactic labels or phrasal constituents, there is no reason to think that the mechanisms responsible for forming them include inborn *syntactic* knowledge. Rather, it is widely assumed that such representations reflect the inborn architecture of cognition that exists independent of language. This is true not only for the predicate concepts themselves, but also for the thematic (or 'theta') role labels used to classify their arguments. For example, Jackendoff (1976:149) proposes that the characterization of theta roles is nonlinguistic in nature, drawing on "the study of the innate conception of the physical world and the way in which conceptual structure generalizes to ever wider, more abstract domains." Emonds (1991:423) goes even further, suggesting that "theta roles are not part of syntax and are more likely properly associated with the cognitive referents of NPs, and assume significance only in a cognitive psychology for the most part shared by humans and other primates."

The computational module of the general nativist acquisition device regulates the formation of structural representations by stipulating the properties of the underlying combinatorial operations. Three such properties are relevant to our discussion. (All three are manifested in one form or another in many other syntactic frameworks, including GB.)

(18)   *binarity:* Operations apply to pairs of elements.
       inheritability: Operations that cannot apply at one level are carried up to the next.
       iterativity: Operations can reapply without definite limit.

The first of these properties ensures that a functor may combine with only one argument at a time, resulting in the binary branching characteristic of syntactic representations. The inheritability property allows any unsatisfied dependencies to be inherited upward, making it possible for language to have functors that take two (or more) arguments. Finally, the iterativity property permits combinatorial operations to apply as many times as are needed in order to satisfy all dependencies. The syntactic representation in (19), which should be read from the bottom up, helps illustrate the role of these three properties in the system of sentence formation outlined earlier in this section.

(19)

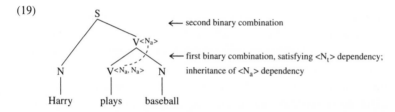

Turning now to the ontogeny of the mechanisms responsible for hierarchical structure, we continue to adopt the view (outlined in chap. 12) that semantic forms such as (16)–(17) above and (20)–(22) below constitute the principal input to the acquisition device.

(20)   John left.

predicate:	LEAVE ⟨agent⟩
tense:	past
agent:	[JOHN]

(21)   John fell.

predicate:	FALL ⟨theme⟩
tense:	past
theme:	[JOHN]

(22)   John builds houses.

predicate:	BUILD ⟨agent, theme⟩
tense:	present
agent:	[JOHN]
theme:	[HOUSE]
	[+plural]

Although these semantic forms—the joint product of the propositional and conceptual modules—contain no syntactic categories or structure per se, they provide information crucial to the development of syntactic representations. For one thing, they include data about the number and type of arguments associated with each functor: *leave* in (20) takes a single agentive argument, while *fall* in (21) takes a single theme argument and *build* in (22) takes both types of argument. This information, together with the results of the classificatory operation discussed in the preceding section, yields a lexicon of the sort illustrated in (23) (see Bach 1979: 517 for a similar proposal). (As before, upper case symbols indicate the word's syntactic category; argument dependencies are recorded inside angled brackets.)

(23)   *A fragment of the English lexicon:*
       John: N
       left: $V^{\langle N_a \rangle}$
       fall: $V^{\langle N_t \rangle}$
       build: $V^{\langle N_a, N_t \rangle}$
       house: N

The impetus to combine these word-level categories to form phrases and sentences has a semantic source: as functor categories combine with their arguments, their meanings are amalgamated to form the types of complex meanings typical of human communication. However, the *manner* in which words combine demands careful attention. In particular, we must ask how the acquisition device determines the actual order and hierarchical organization of the various constituents that make up the syntactic representation.[6]

Matters are relatively straightforward in the case of two-word sentences such as (24) and (25), where the functor (an intransitive verb) combines with a single argument.

(24) $S (= V^{<0>})$
                      /   \
                   N $V^{<N_a>}$
                   | |
                 John   left

(25) $S (= V^{<0>})$
                      /   \
                   N $V^{<N_t>}$
                   | |
                 John   fell

In such patterns, the relative positioning of the functor and its argument can easily be determined from experience (as all approaches to learnability acknowledge), allowing the learning module of the acquisition device to formulate the generalization in (26). ($V^{\langle N \rangle}$ = a verbal category with a single argument dependency; recall that both simple intransitive verbs and verb phrases consisting of a transitive verb and its object argument count as instances of this category type.)

(26)   A $V^{\langle N \rangle}$ combines with an argument to its left.

Matters are more complicated in the case of sentences containing three or more constituents. Sentences such as *John builds houses,* which contains a transitive verb, are a case in point. Because of the (innate) binarity property of the computational module, the verb can combine with only one of its arguments at a time. Fortunately, the inheritability and iterativity properties (also inborn) allow the remaining dependency to be passed up to the resulting phrase and to be satisfied by subsequent combination with an appropriate argument. This leaves the acquisition device with only the problem of determining which argument the verb should combine with first. Put another way, the acquisition device must uncover the content of the argument hierarchy in (11), repeated as (27).

(27)   *The Argument Hierarchy:*
        theme   first
         . . .   ↓
        agent   last

How can the learning module of the acquisition device infer the combinatorial order specified by the argument hierarchy (assuming that the latter is not simply inborn)?[7] One possibility is that it makes use of the word order rule in (26), which was previously inferred from the simple two-word sentences illustrated in (24) and (25). Given that a $V^{\langle N \rangle}$ must combine with an argument to its left, it follows that sentences built around a transitive verb must have the structure in (28) rather than that in (29).

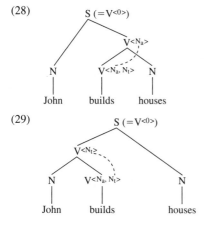

Only in (28) does a $V^{(N)}$ (the phrase *builds houses*) combine with an argument to its left.

Once formed, structures such as (28) allow the learning module to draw two further inferences. The first is simply that a transitive verb (a $V^{(N,N)}$) combines with an argument to its right, a generalization about linear order. The second inference is somewhat more abstract, pertaining to the relative combinatorial order for the verb's arguments, which must be *theme* > *agent* if (28) is the correct structure. This gives the content of the argument hierarchy.[8]

In sum, the proposal that I have been outlining assigns each module of the acquisition device a specific role in syntactic development. A classificatory system grounded in the conceptual module ensures that the words making up a sentence are properly categorized, while the propositional module provides information about the number and type of arguments required by individual functor categories. For its part, the computational module ensures that category combination proceeds iteratively, creating a binary-branching structure. Finally, the learning module is responsible for determining both the relative linear order of a functor and its arguments and the internal organization of the argument hierarchy that underlies the subject–object asymmetry in syntactic structure.

A CONSTRAINT ON REFLEXIVE PRONOUNS

This brings us to the single biggest challenge confronting general nativism—namely, how to account for the abstract principles that regulate phenomena such as gap placement and pronoun interpretation. The fact that a general nativist acquisition device is apparently able to discover the categories and mechanisms responsible for building syntactic structure is an important first step, since it ensures the availability of the syntactic representations to which 'second order' principles apply. But we must still provide an account for the origin of these principles themselves.

At this point, very little can be said about this issue since it is so rarely addressed, even in the literature that is sympathetic to general nativism (but see O'Grady 1987; Van Valin 1991). Nonetheless, for purposes of illustration, I will offer a proposal here about how a general nativist theory might account for the ontogeny of the Prominence Requirement, a component of the system of pronoun interpretation that ensures that a reflexive pronoun must take a 'higher' (i.e., 'c-commanding') NP as its antecedent (see the discussion of 'Principle A' in chap. 11). The sentences in (30)–(32) illustrate the crucial paradigm.

(30)   Harry admires himself.
(31)   Harry's brother admires himself. (*if *himself* = *Harry* rather than *Harry's brother*)
(32)   *Himself admires Harry.

Sentence (30) is acceptable, with the reflexive pronoun taking the NP *Harry* as its antecedent. Sentence (31) is also acceptable, provided that the antecedent is *Harry's brother* rather than the genitive nominal *Harry*. In contrast, (32) is completely ungrammatical.

Although the facts are more or less clear, they are not directly available to the acquisition device. As explained in chapter 12, the acquisition device is not given information about the ungrammaticality of particular sentences, including the fact that (31) has only one interpretation and that (32) is completely unacceptable. Yet children somehow discover that a reflexive pronoun must enter into a certain sort of structural relationship with its antecedent. How can we account for this, short of treating the Prominence Requirement as an inborn syntactic principle?

The proposal described here is built on a two-part suggestion. First, let us assume that the computational module of the acquisition device includes a requirement to the effect that 'dependencies' are satisfied by combination. This requirement has in fact been tacitly assumed throughout our discussion, as can be seen by considering a simple sentence such as (33). (I take the genitive to be a functor that combines with a nominal argument to its right.)

(33)

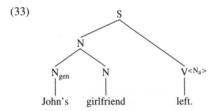

Here it is clear that the agent argument dependency associated with *leave* can only be satisfied by the nominal with which it combines (*John's girlfriend*) and not by the nominal *John*. (This is why the sentence means what it does rather than, say, 'John, who has a girlfriend, left.')

Second, let us assume that the conceptual module of the acquisition device recognizes two types of dependencies. The first corresponds to the previously considered 'category dependencies', in which a functor (e.g., a verb) requires one or more arguments of a particular category type. The second type consists of what we can call 'interpretive dependencies', which occur in cases where one element must look to another for the determination of its reference.

The prototypical instance of an interpretive dependency involves the relationship between a reflexive pronoun and its antecedent. We can represent this relationship by distinguishing between two types of 'referential indices' (the devices that keep track of an NP's referential content)—**functor indices,** which occur on reflexive pronouns and which depend on the referential index of another NP for their interpretation, and **basic indices,** which are found on lexical NPs and which exhibit no such dependencies. (This parallels the distinction between functor and basic categories discussed earlier in this chapter.) For the sake of exposition, we can use 'x' to represent a functor index and numerals for basic indices, as in (34), corresponding to (30).

(34)   Harry₁ admires himselfₓ

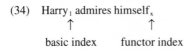

The various modules of the acquisition device now interact to give a very interesting result. Consider first (35), the syntactic representation of the acceptable sentence in (34).

(35)

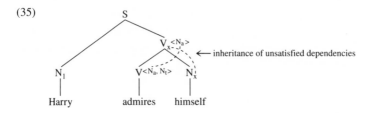

Here the verb *admire* combines first with its theme argument *himself,* in accordance with the argument hierarchy discussed earlier. This combinatorial relation satisfies one of the verb's category dependencies, but it does not satisfy the reflexive pronoun's interpretive dependency. (Recall that dependencies can only be satisfied by combination and that the verb with which *himself* combines does not include a referential index capable of supplying *himself*'s reference.) This suggests that interpretive dependencies must be inheritable, just as category dependencies are. (Precedents for this proposal can be found in the feature-passing analyses of reflexive pronoun interpretation put forward by Gazdar et al. 1985 and especially Kang 1988.)

By the inheritance mechanism in the computational module, then, the interpretive dependency in (35) is passed upward, along with the verb's dependency on an agent argument, to the verbal phrase. Both dependencies are then satisfied by combination with the nominal *Harry,* which is interpreted as the verb's agent argument and which supplies the referential index that determines the referent for the reflexive pronoun.[9]

Now consider (36), which depicts the syntactic representations for the utterances in (31) and (32). (To keep the representations maximally simple, category dependencies are not overtly represented here.)

(36)   a.   b.

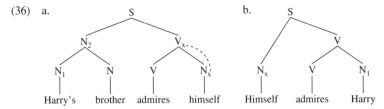

In (36a), the interpretive dependency associated with the reflexive pronoun is once again inherited by the verbal phrase *admires himself.* It can subsequently be satisfied by the referential index associated with the nominal *Harry's brother,* with which the VP combines, but not by the referential index associated with the genitive *Harry,* since the VP does not combine with this element. (Recall once again that the computational module of the acquisition device allows dependencies to be satisfied only by combination.)

Matters are somewhat different in (36b). Here the reflexive pronoun is in subject position and combines only with the verb phrase *admires Harry.* Since this phrase does not bear a referential index (the basic index on *Harry* does not introduce a dependency and therefore is not inherited by the VP), the interpretive dependency associated with the reflexive pronoun is never satisfied and the sentence is anomalous.

The end result of this system is that reflexive pronouns always take higher (i.e., 'c-commanding') NPs as their antecedents. However, this result is not stipulated by a principle of UG (such as Principle A). Rather, it follows from more basic facts—in particular, the fact that reflexive pronouns introduce interpretive dependencies and the fact that even when dependencies are inherited, they must ultimately be satisfied by combination.[10]

The proposal just outlined applies only to the Prominence Requirement on the interpretation of reflexive pronouns (i.e., the requirement that the antecedent be 'higher' in syntactic structure). It says nothing about a second constraint on English reflexive pronouns, the Locality Requirement, which ensures that the antecedent be in the same minimal clause, as illustrated in (37).

(37)   [$_s$ John$_i$ said that [$_s$ Sam$_k$ praised himself$_{k,*i}$].]

This requirement is qualitatively different from the Prominence Requirement: whereas the latter constraint is apparently universal, the former is found in only some languages. As noted in chapter 11, for example, Japanese is not subject to the Locality Requirement, so either of the lexical NPs in structures such as (37) may serve as antecedent for the reflexive pronoun. This suggests that the Locality Requirement does not follow from inherent properties of the acquisition device in the way that the Prominence Requirement does, and that it may in fact have to be learned.

If this is right, then the acquisition device must confront two challenges in acquiring English. First, it must identify the notions in terms of which the 'domain' for reflexive pronoun interpretation is stated. I will not take a position on this matter here, other than to note that the correct notion, whatever it is, must be supplied by the conceptual module of the acquisition device. (For the sake of exposition, I have assumed in this book that the correct notion is 'clause' ($= V^{(0)}$). Wexler and Manzini's 1987 treatment suggests that this is a simplification, but Reuland and Koster (1991) argue that something like the simpler idea may be right after all.)

Second, for the reasons explained in detail in the preceding chapter, the acquisition device must avoid overgeneralization. That is, it must not conclude from a sentence such as (30), repeated as (38), that a reflexive pronoun can have a (higher) antecedent anywhere in the sentence.

(38)   Harry admires himself.

Rather, it must draw the much more restrictive conclusion embodied in the Locality Requirement: the reflexive pronoun is linked to a (higher) antecedent in the same minimal clause. One way to help ensure this result is to assume that the learning module of the acquisition device includes the constraint in (39). (A similar constraint is embodied in the 'Limited Functions' operating principle of Slobin 1985:1199 and, of course, the Subset Principle of Berwick 1985:37 and Wexler and Manzini 1987—see chap. 13.)

(39)   *The Conservatism Law:*
       Construct the most conservative hypothesis consistent with experience.

Thanks to the Conservatism Law, the acquisition device cannot conclude from sentences such as (38) that a reflexive pronoun can take an antecedent anywhere in the sentence. Rather, it must use whatever notions are relevant to the characterization of pronoun–antecedent relations to formulate the most conservative hypothesis consistent with experience (namely, that reflexives take an antecedent in the same minimal clause).

Summary

Table 14.7 provides a summary of the general nativist acquisition device as it has been described to this point.

The proposal that I have made does not claim that the crucial categorial and hierarchical properties of sentence structure are somehow discovered in experience, as might be suggested in an empiricist (i.e., non-nativist) theory. Quite to the

Table 14.7 Summary of the General Nativist
Acquisition Device

Module	Sample Properties
Perceptual	Ends of stimuli are salient.
	Stressed stimuli are salient.
	. . .
Learning	Capacity for forming and testing hypotheses
	Conservatism Law
	. . .
Conceptual	Inventory of 'grammaticizable' notions:
	singular–plural, definite–indefinite, past–
	nonpast, individual, event, property,
	. . .
Propositional	Provides a representation of propositional mean-
	ing in terms of predicates, arguments, and
	modifiers
Computational	Binarity
	Iterativity
	Inheritability

contrary, the categories and geometry of syntactic representations follow from inborn principles and properties. However, in contrast with special nativism, these principles and properties are not specifically syntactic in character, and at least some may be independently manifested in nonlinguistic cognition.

The propositional module, for instance, is arguably present independent of language, since the capacity for propositional thought is retained even in cases of severe language deficits (see, e.g., Zurif 1990: 181; chap. 16 below). Moreover, I have argued elsewhere (O'Grady in press) that the contents of the computational module play a role in arithmetical activity. This is easiest to see in the case of the binarity property, which is manifested in our inability to carry out arithmetical operations on more than two numbers at a time. (Thus, the addition problem 4 + 9 + 6 requires two steps.)

On the other hand, it is unclear whether the grammatically relevant contrasts provided by the conceptual module have nonlinguistic relevance in the sense of being used for the analysis of experience independent of language. Pinker (1989: 359) argues that in general they do not, while at the same time noting that they also are not syntactic in character and that they may overlap with the notions required for other types of cognition.

The status of the Conservatism Law in the hypothesis formation module raises still other questions. As observed in O'Grady 1987: 192–93, it is difficult to establish examples outside language of the type of conservatism in the formation of generalizations that is characteristic of the acquisition device (but see Eckman

1996). It is thus possible that the Conservatism Law, although obviously not a syntactic principle per se, has no role in cognition beyond language acquisition. (Recall that Wexler and Manzini (1987) adopt a comparable position within special nativism.)

The overall picture of the acquisition device that emerges from this discussion is remarkably like a "new machine built out of old parts," to use Bates and McWhinney's (1988:147) metaphor. There is nothing else in the human brain quite like the acquisition device, but when its component parts are examined, none seems to be 'syntactic' or 'grammatical' in the ordinary sense, and some even seem to be relevant for nonlinguistic forms of cognition.

Before concluding this chapter, one final point is worthy of note. Despite the differences between special and general varieties of nativism,[11] there is a striking similarity between the two approaches with regard to 'core' grammatical phenomena: both leave relatively little room for actual learning in the conventional sense. This is obviously so in the case of special nativism, which supplies (via UG) both an inventory of syntactic categories and a template (the X-bar schema) to regulate their hierarchical organization. But it is also so, although perhaps in a subtler way, in the version of general nativism outlined here. According to this proposal, the categorial contrasts found in syntactic structure are determined by the innate classificatory system posited in the conceptual module, while the architecture of this representation is largely derived from inborn properties of the computational module (binarity, iterativity, and inheritability). The role of experience is limited to providing information about the meanings and argument dependencies of individual forms, which is necessary in any case, and to supplying data about two very specific phenomena: the relative ordering of constituents and the combinatorial order imposed by the argument hierarchy, both of which are susceptible to cross-linguistic variation and therefore not eligible for genetic specification in the first place.

4. Conclusion

Special nativism, the theory that the innate endowment for language includes Universal Grammar, is the single most popular approach to the learnability problem. Nonetheless, alternatives of various sorts are being actively pursued. One possibility, put forward in various forms, is that the acquisition device includes a set of 'discovery procedures' rather than actual linguistic categories or principles. Another possibility, which I personally favor, is that the acquisition device consists of several independent modules, none of which contains information that is inherently syntactic in character. There is thus no inborn 'grammar', as proposed in special nativism. At the same time, it is not claimed that the crucial categorial and relational properties of sentence structure are somehow discovered in experience, as suggested in inductivist theories. Instead, the categories and geometry of sentence structure emerge from the interaction of a small number of simple principles and properties, each of which belongs to one of the independent systems making up the acquisition device.

15

Theories of Development

Earlier chapters have provided descriptions of many different developmental phenomena, ranging from the emergence of multiword speech to the mastery of relative clause constructions. Even assuming the accuracy of these descriptions, one important issue remains to be addressed: why does development follow the particular course that it does? That is, why does the acquisition device master certain grammatical phenomena before others, and why does it make errors on certain constructions but not others?

Although descriptions of the *facts* of development are becoming increasingly detailed and far-ranging, progress toward a *theory* of development has been relatively slow. Indeed, Solan (1983:215) suggests that an explanatory theory of development may not be a "fruitful endeavor" or even a realistic goal at this point in acquisition research. Similar pessimism is expressed by R. Clark (1992:128), who insists that a theory of development must be founded on a prior theory of learnability.

One of the reasons for linguists' relative lack of interest in development is that acquisition research in the dominant nativist tradition within linguistics has focused on learnability issues. Such issues are typically studied without regard for developmental data, in accordance with a simplifying idealization that we can call the **Instantaneous Acquisition Assumption** (e.g., N. Chomsky 1975:15, 1986b:53ff.).

(1)   *The Instantaneous Acquisition Assumption:*
       Language acquisition is instantaneous.

The basic hypothesis embodied in this assumption is that certain aspects of language acquisition can be studied independent of mental maturation, intermediate stages of grammatical development, variations in the speech to which the child is exposed, and other 'real time' phenomena. The end product of gradual language acquisition, Chomsky (1986b:54) claims, "is, in fact, identical to the result of applying the [acquisition device] to the available evidence, taken as a set presented at an instant of time."

The importance of the learnability problem notwithstanding, there is an increasing awareness among linguists that the developmental facts must be accounted for—either by explaining them in terms of linguistic theory or by showing precisely how they follow from nonlinguistic factors. A variety of theoretical approaches to development now exist, three of which are worth considering here—the **continuity** theory, the **maturational** theory, and the **incrementalist** theory.
330

1. The Continuity Theory

As noted in chapter 2, many researchers take the view that the language acquisition process is 'continuous' in the sense that the acquisition device analyzes experience in terms of the same notions and relations at all stages of development (the 'Continuity Hypothesis'). In the contemporary literature, the continuity theory is often associated with UG-based theories of acquisition, where it is taken to entail that the entire system of UG is available from the beginning of the acquisition process (Pinker 1984; Clahsen 1992; Poeppel and Wexler 1993).

There are two versions of the continuity theory. According to the **strong** continuity theory (e.g., Poeppel and Wexler 1993; Lust 1995), children are capable of forming full syntactic representations from the earliest stages of syntactic development. Thus, on this view, the structure for a typical biclausal sentence in the speech of a 2-year-old resembles (2)—the very representation posited for biclausal structures produced by mature speakers. (CP = complementizer phrase, the phrasal projection of a complementizer)

(2)

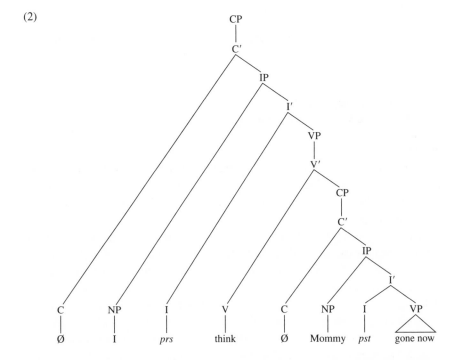

In contrast, the **weak** continuity theory (e.g., Pinker 1984; Clahsen et al. 1984) holds that although children have access to the full set of categories and operations from the beginning of the acquisition process, they may not make use of them in their syntactic representations right away. (For example, children who had not yet

learned complementizers such as *that* and *whether* might not have a C projection
in their representations.) For the purposes of the discussion that follows, I will
assume the strong version of the continuity theory. For further discussion of the
weak version, see Clahsen, Eisenbeiss, and Vainikka (1994) and Vainikka (1993/
94:259–60).

The continuity theory dramatically restricts the domain of syntactic development, essentially limiting it to two phenomena—parameter setting and lexical
acquisition. Let us consider each in turn. As explained in chapter 13, contemporary approaches to acquisition that are based on GB theory assume that Universal
Grammar (by hypothesis, a component of the acquisition device) includes parameters whose precise value must be determined from experience. In the case of
the X-bar schema, for example, the acquisition device must determine whether
heads precede or follow their complements, as in (3).

(3)   *The word order parameter for head–complement order:*
       Option (a): head-initial [e.g., English]
       Option (b): head-final [e.g., Japanese]

Similarly, it must be determined whether finite verbs require an overt subject, as
in (4).

(4)   *Subject drop:*
       Option (a): Subject drop is permitted.
       Option (b): Subject drop is not permitted.

While the continuity theory predicts that both the word order parameter and the
domain parameter are *available* to the language learner from the beginning of the
acquisition process, it does not require that the correct value be immediately determined. Rather, choice of the appropriate option is taken to require interaction
with experience.

The second major type of syntactic development permitted by continuity theories involves lexical acquisition. According to the (strong) continuity theory, for
example, the fact that children under age 3 generally do not use complementizers
such as *whether, that,* and *for* reflects a gap in the lexicon rather than a syntactic
deficit (hence the presence of a C position and a CP projection in (2) above).

In addition to the emergence of specific vocabulary items, lexical acquisition
may also involve the discovery of special properties associated with individual
words. The verb *promise,* for example, is unusual among object-taking verbs in
having its subject serve as 'antecedent' for the understood subject of its complement clause, as in (5a). Most verbs of its type are like *persuade, tell,* and *force* in
having their complement NP serve as controller, as in (5b).

(5)   a. *The verb* promise: *the subject is controller:*

Donald promised Mickey [. to leave]

b. *The verb* persuade: *the object is controller:*

Donald persuaded Mickey [. to leave]

As noted in chapter 6, 5-year-old children tend to misinterpret *promise* sentences by choosing the matrix object as controller for the understood subject. Subsequent lexical development corrects this mistake, uncovering the idiosyncratic character of *promise* with respect to control.

Lexical acquisition may even involve parameter setting: as noted in chapter 13, an influential view within UG-based work on syntactic development is that most (if not all) parameters are lexical in that their values are associated with specific words. If this is right, then the acquisition of pronouns such as *him* and *himself* involves determining the value of the domain parameter in (6) for each element.

(6)   *The domain parameter:*
Option a: domain = the smallest clause containing the pronoun.
Option b: domain = the sentence containing the pronoun.

In English, both *him* and *himself* are associated with option (a); however, in Japanese the pronominal is associated with option (a) and the reflexive pronoun with option (b)—see chapter 13 for further discussion.

In sum, the continuity theory of development takes the view that a full-fledged Universal Grammar is available from the earliest stages of language acquisition. Syntactic development is essentially limited to the selection of parametric options (from a predetermined set) and to the acquisition of lexical items (including any idiosyncratic properties that might have syntactic consequences). Part of the appeal of this view is that it represents the 'null hypothesis' (Macnamara 1982:13; Pinker 1984:7): it posits the least amount of change (i.e., none at all) in the mechanisms essential to language acquisition and, in the absence of evidence to the contrary, it is thus to be preferred to theories that complicate matters by assuming that these mechanisms are subject to change.

However, the continuity theory is not without its problems. Perhaps the single greatest challenge facing this theory involves developmental facts that seem to fall outside existing accounts of parameter setting or lexical acquisition. We have already seen that the continuity theory attributes the late emergence of complementizers to a lexical deficit, but we have not addressed the question of why this deficit should affect complementizers rather than, say, adjectives. In other words, why is it that words such as *that, whether,* and *if* are systematically acquired later than words such as *green, hot,* and *tiny*? Similarly, we have not addressed the question of why parameters are apparently not always set in the earliest stages of syntactic development. Why, for example, does the subject drop stage as described by Hyams (see chap. 5) last well into multiword speech even though the acquisition device has been exposed for months to adult speech in which finite verbs take overt subjects?

Sometimes, the answers to these questions may lie in the nature of experience. For example, Jakubowicz (1994) has noted that Danish children as old as age 9 may not realize that the reflexive pronoun *sig* in their language can have an antecedent outside its minimal clause. (That is, *sig* is wrongly associated with option (a) of the domain parameter.) However, as she observes (p. 216), there is also a straightforward explanation for this apparent delay in syntactic development: sentences contains *sig* are rare in adult speech, which presumably makes it difficult for the acquisition device to get the data that it needs to set the relevant parameter.

PROCESSING AND PERCEPTION

More commonly, though, proponents of the continuity theory find themselves accounting for developmental delays by appealing to extragrammatical factors, particularly those involving children's ability to process and perceive linguistic information. We saw several references to processing considerations in our earlier review of syntactic development. For example, Pinker (1984:160ff.) suggests that children's production of utterances with missing verbs and prepositions (e.g., *Mommy [eat] apple; I sit [on] chair*) during early multiword speech reflects processing limitations rather than the mistaken assumption that these categories are optional (see chap. 3). In a similar vein, P. Bloom (1990a) and Valian (1989, 1990) propose that subject drop in the speech of children learning English is the result of processing factors rather than an incorrectly set parameter (see chap. 5). Pinker, Lebeaux, and Frost (1987) suggest that children's poor performance on passives in many experimental situations is due to the operation of a processing strategy (the ubiquitous Canonical Sentence Strategy) that can actually override grammatical knowledge in many situations (chap. 10).

In some cases, it is even suggested that the design of experiments used to test children's knowledge of particular patterns triggers processing strategies that interfere with the operation of grammatical mechanisms. For instance, Hamburger and Crain (1982) note that act-out tests for relative clause comprehension typically do not provide a set of entities from which a subset is selected with the help of the relative clause. (Thus, the props used to test a sentence such as *The cow pushed the dog that kissed the rabbit* typically include a single dog rather than a set of dogs from which the one that kissed the rabbit can be chosen.) They propose that this flaw—rather than a grammatical deficit—contributes to children's frequent misinterpretation of relative clause patterns as coordinate structures (see chap. 9).

Grimshaw and Rosen (1990:199 ff.) propose that design flaws may also be responsible for the poor performance of preschool children on sentences such as *John saw him*, in which the subject is incorrectly treated as antecedent for the pronoun *him*. They note that since "the pragmatics of pronouns require that they have an antecedent" and since the experimental design provides no alternative, children may deliberately violate Principle B in order to satisfy this pragmatic requirement on the processing of pronouns (see chap. 11).

Although processing effects are a widely acknowledged phenomenon in the acquisition literature, considerable controversy surrounds the suggestion that changes in how children *perceive* linguistic information might have a role in explaining the developmental facts. White (1981:247–48) describes the central thesis of the 'perceptionist' proposal as follows. (Corder 1967 was the first to make the distinction between 'input'—what is available in the environment—and 'intake'—what the child actually pays attention to.)

> Despite apparently similar *input* data at different stages, the child's *intake* actually varies (due to maturational factors, increasing memory, etc.). The child's perception of the data is different from the adult's. The grammar that he comes up with will be optimal for his own perception of the data.

Perceptual considerations have played a prominent role in many accounts of development, with phonetic salience being one of the factors that determines a morpheme's relative order of acquisition (e.g., Peters 1983, 1985; Slobin 1985:1166). Hence, all other things being equal, unstressed morphemes such as tense and number affixes are acquired later than stressed morphemes. See Demuth (1994) for an extension of this idea to a broader range of nonlexical categories.

In some cases, perceptual salience appears to interact with semantic considerations. As noted in chapter 6, for example, Pinker (1984:226) has suggested that children do not "notice" the infinitival marker *to* until after they have acquired the semantically more substantial preposition *to*. Nishigauchi and Roeper (1987) hint at a similar suggestion for the complementizer *for*, which is also acquired after its prepositional counterpart.

Perceptual considerations have even played a role in a well-known proposal about parameter setting. As mentioned in earlier discussion, it has been suggested (e.g., Hyams 1986) that a parameter of UG distinguishes between grammars that require an overt subject and those that do not. Further, it has been proposed that the unmarked or initial setting of the parameter does not require overt subjects— hence children's initial tendency to omit these elements from sentences in their speech, as in (7).

(7)   Made this sit down.
       No fit.
       See window.

One indication that a language requires overt subjects comes from its use of un-stressed pronouns in subject position (e.g., Hyams 1986:95), as in (8).

(8)   He should leave.

As (9) shows, a language that does not require overt subjects (e.g., Spanish) uses a phonetically null pronoun (represented here as *pro*) under such conditions.

(9)   *pro* debe partir.

Since unstressed subject pronouns are presumably used by English-speaking adults in the presence of children throughout the language acquisition process, it is nec-essary for Hyams and others who believe that the subject drop stage lasts for a period of several months to ask why the subject drop parameter is not immediately set in the appropriate way.

> The question thus arises as to how data which are 'ignored' for principled
> reasons suddenly become salient, or, in other words, how can data which are
> in some sense 'filtered out' also act as triggering data? (Hyams 1986:94)

That is, if UG is in fact accessible to language learners in the manner required by the continuity theory, why does it take many months to notice unstressed pro-nouns in English and to realize that the subject drop parameter is wrongly set? Following White, Hyams suggests (p. 94) that this paradox is due to "selective attention" on the part of children, who focus on "certain data for analysis and ignore others." She later (p. 169) describes this phenomenon in terms of the dis-tinction between input and intake, suggesting that changes in children's perceptual and representational abilities enable them to consider data that they had previously ignored.

Unfortunately, it is not clear precisely how the child's perception of the data changes in the case of unstressed pronouns. Perhaps, as Hyams suggests (p. 95), learning the function of contrastive stress allows familiar data to be heard in a new way. Or perhaps the fact that unstressed pronouns are not perceptually salient makes them difficult to discern until other parts of the sentence become more familiar. (Gerken 1991 provides a detailed argument for the relative nonsalience of unstressed pronouns in initial position of a phonological phrase, suggesting that this may be the root of the subject drop phenomenon in early child language; see chap. 5, section 1.)

In other cases, however, it is much harder to identify perceptual factors that might account for the errors found in early stages of development. As noted by

Felix (1987:111), for instance, children's early use of a sentence-initial negative (e.g., *no the sun shining*) can apparently not be explained in perceptual terms:

> [The] theory of perceptual change essentially amounts to claiming that there is some kind of perceptual mechanism that converts an adult utterance into the corresponding child structure. It is only *after* this conversion that the principles of Universal Grammar (as well as any other mechanisms of structural analysis) begin to operate. That is, when an adult says something like *Johnny doesn't like ice cream* the child will perceive this utterance as *no Johnny like ice cream* and it is the latter structure that is the input to the language acquisition device.

While is it conceivable that something like this does happen, Felix notes that such a process of structure conversion is inconsistent with what is known about perceptual mechanisms in general. Moreover, positing modifications of this sort to the input has the effect of creating a mysterious new 'black box' in the mind that affects perception in ways not previously imagined and not currently understood.

2. The Maturational Theory

There is no controversy over the idea that maturation has a role to play in the earliest phases of cognitive and linguistic development. The onset of babbling, for instance, is widely believed to be maturationally influenced (e.g., Oller et al. 1994), and maturation almost certainly has a role to play in explaining why children begin to use language at around age 1 year rather than 1 month. The more difficult question has to do with whether maturational factors are responsible for later features of syntactic development—i.e., from the one-word stage onward.

The key idea underlying the maturational theory of syntactic development is that progression through successive stages of grammatical sophistication is relatively independent of experience (e.g., Gleitman 1981:122). Development, it is claimed, is 'maturationally driven' by a biologically determined timetable not unlike that associated with physical growth. An apparent instance of this sort of phenomenon is reported by Gleitman (1981), who examined the onset of one-word expressions, two- and three-word 'telegraphic' structures, and affixes and minor lexical categories in normal children, blind children, and deaf children of non-signing parents. (The deaf children communicated through a system of invented gestures.) Interestingly, despite the enormous differences in the quality and quantity of the linguistic experience available to these three groups, they all attained the same stages of development at approximately the same ages (table 15.1)—consistent with the existence of a maturationally driven developmental process.

The maturational theory of development also has proponents within the UG-based approach to language acquisition, where it is sometimes suggested that the

Table 15.1 Possible Maturationally Controlled Stages of
Syntactic Development

Stages	Patterns Produced	Approximate Age of Onset
1	One-word	12 months
2	Two- and three-word	24 months
3	Simple fully grammatical patterns	36 months
. . .		

various components of Universal Grammar emerge and become operative in a specific, maturationally given order. (Indeed, Kean (1988:75) suggests that a maturational view of UG is biologically more plausible than the view that it is fully developed from the outset.) For example, Bickerton (1991) suggests that the third step in Gleitman's proposed developmental profile involves the emergence of the X-bar component of UG, which in turn permits children to produce a large variety of different structures. Drawing on longitudinal studies of three children, he notes a sharp increase in the number and type of their structural patterns just after age 3, consistent with the sudden availability of powerful new mechanisms for sentence formation.

According to Felix (1987:114), a leading proponent of the maturational view, the order in which the various components of UG emerge "does not reflect any externally determined factors in the child's linguistic experience, but rather is itself an inherent part of the genetic program." On this view, then, the inborn acquisition device includes not only Universal Grammar but also a maturational schedule for the emergence of its various principles. As Felix puts it (1988:371):

> The mechanism that "pushes" the child through the sequence of developmental stages is therefore the maturational schedule that will successively make more and more UG principles constrain the kinds of hypotheses which the child considers vis-à-vis a given set of data.

In adopting the view that the mechanisms of language acquisition (including UG) become available bit by bit as development unfolds, the maturational theory disputes the central thesis of the continuity theory. What justifies this departure from the null hypothesis? According to Felix (1987, 1988, 1992), only the maturational theory is able to accommodate the known developmental facts. He notes (e.g., 1988:374–75) that during the two-word stage, for example, children produce patterns consisting of a 'relation word' and a complement that have no apparent counterpart in adult speech (e.g., (10)) as well as constructions in which a phrase lacks a head (e.g., (11)).

(10) *Constructions built around a 'relation word':*
      allgone outside
      bye-bye man
      more write
      off bib
      there high
(11) *Constructions in which a PP lacks a P head:*
      Mommy [$_{PP}$ bathroom]
      sit [$_{PP}$ lap]
      Ben swim [$_{PP}$ pool]

      Constructions in which an NP lacks an N head:
      see [$_{NP}$ pretty]
      see [$_{NP}$ hot]
      see [$_{NP}$ broke]

Felix attributes the production of these patterns to the absence of the X-bar schema, which requires all phrases to have heads belonging to a lexical category such as N, V, or P. The disappearance of these patterns and their replacement by more adult-like constructions, he contends, are due to the emergence of the X-bar schema as part of the maturation of UG.

Felix proposes a parallel explanation for a stage that children pass through during the development of pronoun–antecedent relations. As noted in chapter 13, there is some reason to believe that children's first hypothesis about this phenomenon may be that a pronoun must not precede its antecedent. Learners in this developmental stage thus reject (12) along with (13).

(12) After he$_i$ got home, Mickey$_i$ ate lunch.
(13) *He$_i$ ate lunch after Mickey$_i$ got home.

Felix (1988:386) interprets this as evidence that the relevant principle of UG (Principle C, which is sensitive to structural relations rather than just to linear order) has not yet matured.

To take still another example, Borer and Wexler (1987:127–28) suggest a maturational solution to the problem of how the subject drop stage (as conceived by Hyams) ends in English. Rather than assuming that children somehow do not perceive the sentences that establish the need for overt subjects in English (see above), they suggest that the relevant parameter of UG is simply not available for setting until a particular point in the maturational process. (Hyams 1986:169 also raises this possibility.) Prior to that time, it is implied, exposure to the relevant sentences simply has no effect on the child's grammar.

Borer and Wexler also propose a maturational analysis for 'true' (i.e., nonadjectival) passive constructions. Noting that the clearest signs of this structure type (i.e., presence of an overt *by*-phrase and passive forms of nonactional verbs) emerge relatively late, they suggest that the required syntactic mechanisms 'mature' around age 5.[1] Here, however, an empirical problem arises. As reported in chapter 10, Demuth (1989) has found evidence that children learning the Bantu language Sesotho acquire true passives as early as age 2;8. Moreover, Pinker, Lebeaux, and Frost (1987) show that the English passive, including patterns with a *by*-phrase, is acquired much earlier than previously thought (see chap. 10). This suggests either that Borer and Wexler's proposal is incorrect or that the relevant point of maturation is much earlier than they proposed.

MATURATION AND FUNCTIONAL CATEGORIES

The preceding proposals pale in comparison to the comprehensive and detailed maturational theory of syntactic development put forward by Radford (1990). The key claim of Radford's work is that children pass through three maturationally controlled stages of syntactic development (table 15.2). (A similar idea is put forward by Guilfoyle and Noonan 1992; see also Vainikka 1993/94.)

The initial developmental stage proposed by Radford is essentially 'pregrammatical' in character. Utterances in this stage consist of single words that have not yet been categorized syntactically (as nouns, verbs, etc.). There is therefore no possibility of true syntactic structure.

Around age 20 months, however, two striking changes in children's speech mark the onset of a 'lexical' stage. First, there is a sharp increase in the size of their vocabulary, especially in the four 'lexical categories'. The following examples are from the speech of Allison at age 22 months (Radford 1990: 55–56).

> *Nouns:* baby, mommy, doll, horse, cow, pig, hair, knee, back, chair, table, box, can, cup, truck, school, diaper, skirt, dress, blouse, crumb, cookie(s), toy(s), children
>
> *Verbs:* comb, drink, eat, get, open, spill, ride, tumble, help, wait, pull, build, sit, wiping, standing, peeking, eating, walking, squeezing
>
> *Prepositions:* in, on, out, down, up, away, around
>
> *Adjectives:* green, yellow, big, tiny, funny, empty, sharp

Second, at about the same time, a wide range of combinatorial patterns make their appearance (table 15.3). Radford suggests (e.g., pp. 48 ff.) that these patterns re-

Table 15.2 Radford's Three Stages of Syntactic Development

Stage	Characterization
Precategorial	One-word utterances, no categorial structure
Lexical (20 mos., ± 20%)	System of lexical categories and phrases
Functional (24 mos., ± 20%)	System of functional categories

Table 15.3 Combinatorial Patterns in the Lexical Stage

	X + Complement	Modifier + X	Possessor/Subject + X
NP	*cup* tea, *picture* Gia	nice *book*, good *girl*	Mummy *car*, Baby *cup*
VP	*open* box, *go* in	more *write*, no *go* in there	Daddy *gone*, Hayley *draw* boat
PP	*with* ball, *in* bag	right *down*, back *in* (rare)	Doggy *down*, mouse *in* window
AP	*good* to me (very rare)	very *good*, bit *hot*	Lisa *naughty*, hand *cold*

Note: Italics indicate the pattern's head.

flect the emergence of lexical categories (N, V, A, and P) together with the X-bar schema depicted in (14). (Radford takes the specifier position to be filled by possessors in the case of Ns and by 'subjects' in the case of the other three lexical categories.)

(14)

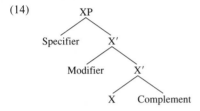

The patterns in (15) illustrate how phrases built around Ns instantiate the various options made available by this template.

(15)

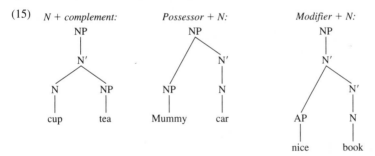

Conspicuously absent from children's speech in the lexical stage are the 'functional categories'—determiners (*the, a, this, some,* etc.), complementizers (*that, whether, if*), and the group of morphemes that proponents of Government and Binding theory group together under the 'inflection' category (e.g., tense suffixes, modal auxiliaries, and the infinitival marker *to*). These categories emerge in the third and final developmental period posited by Radford (the functional stage), resulting in the production of utterances that are much more adult-like in their appearance. The examples in (16) are from the speech of a 26-month-old girl (Radford 1990:277 ff.).

(16)   a. *Utterances containing a determiner:*
          that one, *those* pigeons, *a* teddy, *the* little baby, *some* flowers

b. *Utterances containing 'inflection':*
   It *might* not, *Can* I have it, It tast*es* nice, I tipp*ed* them all, Have *to* lie down

Evidence for the existence of complementizers is somewhat less direct, involving the assumption that this category provides a landing site in question structures for both fronted *wh* words and inverted auxiliaries.[2] Thus, single clause sentences of the sort in (17) are used to support the existence of the complementizer category even though they do not contain a word such as *that, whether,* or *if.*

(17) *What have* you got? *Why has* she gone? *Can* I do that? *Shall* I close it?

What accounts for the relatively late emergence of functional categories in the course of syntactic development? Radford proposes a maturational explanation, suggesting that different components of Universal Grammar "are genetically programmed to come into operation at different biologically determined stages of maturation" (p. 274). In particular, the inventory of lexical categories and the X-bar schema emerge as the result of maturation at around age 20 months, followed by functional categories approximately four months later.

One type of objection to this theory stems from data that appears to contradict the claim that functional categories emerge at a relatively late point in syntactic development. For example, Demuth (1992) notes evidence for the early acquisition of the determiner category in Sesotho, while Whitman, Lee, and Lust (1991) make a similar claim with respect to the complementizer category in Korean relative clauses (however, see Y. Kim 1992a for an alternative analysis of the Korean facts). A very detailed argument along these lines is developed by Poeppel and Wexler (1993) based on data from the acquisition of German.

GERMAN WORD ORDER

The key idea underlying Poeppel and Wexler's work is that German clauses have the verb-final structure depicted in (18), simplifying slightly. (Spec = the specifier position, which for Poeppel and Wexler always contains a phrasal category such as NP or PP.)

(18)

Where the V is nonfinite, it remains in the VP-final position; however, where it is finite, it moves from its underlying position through I to the C position. Movement of the subject or some other phrase to the Spec of C position then gives the characteristic 'verb-second' order of German. This is illustrated for the sentence 'Karl bought this book' in (19), where the finite verb moves to the C position and the direct object NP moves to the Spec of C position.

(19)

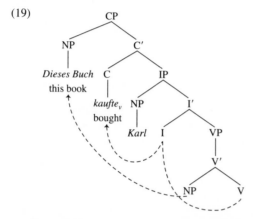

Poeppel and Wexler reason that if German children employ the correct word order in early multiword speech, then their syntactic representations must include functional categories such as C even if complementizer morphemes such as *daß* 'that' are not yet used. Working with a speech sample from a German-speaking child aged 2;1, Poeppel and Wexler identified a total of 251 utterances that are at least 3 words in length (the minimum length for which it is possible to distinguish the second position from the final position). Within this set of utterances, they found that finite verbs occur in the second position and nonfinite verbs in the final position the overwhelming majority of the time (table 15.4).[3] The high incidence of finite verbs in second position (almost 95%) is especially striking, since it suggests the presence of a C position to which the finite V can move.

Further evidence for this conclusion comes from the status of the sentence-initial element in the child's utterances. If the CP projection is in fact present and if the V is in the C position, then the element to its left should often be something other than the subject (since more than just subjects can move to the specifier position under CP). In contrast, if the V is somehow still inside the VP (or perhaps

Table 15.4 Finiteness and Verb Position
(Poeppel and Wexler 1993:7)

	Finite	Nonfinite
In second position	197	6
In final position	11	37

in a pre-VP I position within IP, as in (20)) and there is no CP projection, we would expect the sentence-initial element to always be the subject (this being the only remaining position to the left of the V).

(20)

```
                    IP
                 /      \
             Spec        I'
              ↑        /     \
          subject   I        VP
                    |         |
                    V         V'
                           /      \
                         NP        V
```

Poeppel and Wexler report that of the 180 sentences with overt subjects in their speech sample, 50 (28%) have a nonsubject in the sentence-initial position. These patterns are exemplified in (21) (from Poeppel and Wexler, p. 14).

(21)   a. Eine Fase hab ich.
           a   vase have I
       b. Da   bin ich.
           there am I

As the structure in (22), corresponding to (21a), helps show, the occurrence of these patterns points toward the existence of syntactic representations containing a C position even though children have not yet begun to produce complementizer morphemes per se.

(22)

```
                      CP
                   /      \
               NP          C'
              /__\       /     \
          eine Fase   C          IP
                      |        /     \
                    hab_v    NP        I'
                             |       /     \
                            ich     I        VP
                                             |
                                             V'
                                          /      \
                                        NP        V
```

KOREAN DEMONSTRATIVES

   A quite different critique of Radford's maturational hypothesis accepts the basic correctness of his initial observation (morphemes belonging to the determiner, inflection, and complementizer categories emerge later than nouns, verbs, adjectives, and prepositions) but seeks an alternative explanation for this fact. As Radford himself notes (1990:266 ff.), the morphemes that count as functional categories express meanings that are far more abstract than those associated with the lexical categories found in the speech of two-year-olds. For example, words such as *the, a, would,* and *whether* have meanings that are much harder to identify and define than those of nouns such as *doll* and *hair* or verbs such as *comb* and *eat*. In early work on this topic, Brown and Fraser (1963) proposed that the comparatively concrete meanings of lexical categories (which they called 'contentives') are responsible for their relatively early acquisition with respect to functional categories. Let us call this the 'semantic theory'.

Radford rejects the semantic theory on the grounds that there is no independent way to determine the relative abstractness of meanings or to predict precisely when particular meanings should be acquired (p. 268). Although he is right on this point, the existence of difficulties in measuring semantic abstractness has nothing to do with whether such factors are in fact responsible for the late emergence of functional categories. What is needed is a way to test Radford's UG-based theory against the semantic theory even in the absence of an objective measure of semantic concreteness. This may in fact be possible thanks to an interesting contrast among languages in terms of the words they treat as functional categories.

According to the criteria adopted within GB theory (see, e.g., Fukui 1986), membership in functional categories is determined not on the basis of meaning, but rather on the basis of an element's syntactic behavior. It is therefore possible for morphemes with essentially the same meaning to differ from language to language in terms of whether they belong to a lexical or functional category. For example, whereas demonstratives and other determiner-like words in English are instances of a functional category that heads its own phrasal projection (see (23a)), their counterparts in Korean are lexical categories that serve as 'prenominal modifiers' (see (23b)), as Fukui (1986:206) has suggested for Japanese.[4] (For the sake of concreteness, I will treat Korean demonstratives as a subtype of adjective.)

(23)   a.   b.

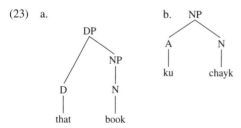

Evidence in support of this contrast comes from differences in the distribution of demonstratives in the two languages. For example, in English, demonstratives must precede any adjectival modifiers.

(24)   a. that big book
        b. *big that book

This is consistent with the claim that demonstratives occur outside the nominal projection and hence cannot be interspersed with adjectival modifiers that occur within that projection.

Just the opposite conclusion seems appropriate for Korean demonstratives. Indeed, their positioning alone is enough to suggest they cannot be heads: they occur prenominally even though the language is uniformly head-final. In addition, as (25) illustrates, Korean demonstratives can be interspersed with adjectival modifiers. (The adjective-first order apparently has the meaning 'that book, which is big' compared to 'that big book' for the demonstrative-first pattern; J.-R. Kim 1992.)

(25)   a. ku   khun chayk
            that big   book
        b. khun ku   chayk
            big   that book

These facts are consistent with the view that Korean demonstratives are a type of adjective and can therefore be intermingled with other modifiers.

The semantic and UG-based theories make different predictions about the emergence of demonstratives and other determiner-like elements in Korean and English. According to the semantic theory, these elements should emerge at a relatively late point in both languages, since they all express comparatively abstract types of meaning. On the other hand, the UG-based theory put forward by Radford predicts relatively late acquisition in English (where determiners constitute a functional category) but makes no such prediction about Korean (in which the corresponding words are a subtype of adjective and can therefore emerge at any time). These differences can be summarized as in table 15.5.

Both theories make the right prediction for English determiners: as Radford (1990:100–1) observes, demonstratives are not employed as determiners (as in *this book, that man*) until after age 2, although they are used as pronominals (e.g., *What['s] this? That [is] Daddy*) from the earliest stages of multiword speech. But what of Korean?

O'Grady (1993) reports (table 15.6) on the productive use of determiner-like words in speech samples from five Korean-speaking children.

Table 15.5 Predictions about the Development of
                Determiner-like Words

Language	The Semantic Theory	Radford's Maturational Theory
English	Relatively late	Relatively late
Korean	Relatively late	No prediction

Table 15.6 Subjects Whose Speech Was Analyzed[a]

Child	Age	Amount of Speech
J	1;9–2;3	10 sessions, approx. 30–50 mins. each
N	1;8–2;1	24 short samples
C	1;9–2;6	short monthly recordings
S	1;1–3;1	short monthly recordings
U	3;10	a single 40 min. recording

a. With the assistance of Sook Whan Cho.

Although Korean allows bare count nouns, demonstratives seem to be quite common in adult speech, where they help encode contrasts between new and old information. H. Kim (1992:223–24) reports that *enu* and *etten* 'a certain' are the markers most commonly used for NPs that introduce new human referents (occurring with 66% of all such NPs in the narrative speech samples that he studied). In the same samples, NPs encoding previously mentioned human referents occurred with demonstrative *i* 'this' or *ku* 'that' over 84% of the time. Thus, even if these elements are not obligatory in the same contexts as they are in English, it seems safe to conclude that children have ample exposure to them.

This notwithstanding, demonstratives and other determiner-like elements are extremely rare in children's early speech. In fact, there was only one example (see (26)) of a determiner-like word in the speech of a child under age 2.

(26) *i*   acwumma, *i*   acwumma po-ki   silh-e. (N at 1;11)
      this lady   this lady   see-NMNLZR hate-INF
      'I hate to see this lady.'

An instance of *ce* 'that there' was found in N's speech at age 2;1, as was one instance of *i* 'this' in the speech of J at age 2;3. (However, the age of these children, as well as the morphological sophistication of N's utterance, suggest that they are already relatively advanced in terms of their overall development.)

(27) *ce* alay   naylye-ka-se, kkem kaci-ko   wa. (N at 2;1)
      that below down-go-and gum   bring-and come
      'Go down there and get chewing gum and come back.'
(28) *i*   cip (J at 2;3)
      this house

As expected, older children produce more determiner-like elements. The following examples were produced by U during a single 40-minute period at age 3;10.

(29) a. *i*   sayngcwi   b. *i*   changko
         this mouse   this   barn
      c. *ce* mentey   sicang-eyse   d. *amwu* yayki-to   an hal-ke-ya
         that far away market-LOC   any   story-even not do-FUT-DECL
         'at that far away market'   'I will not tell (you) any story.'

These results are compatible with those reported by Yamashita (1990, 1995) for a child learning Japanese, a language whose NP structures resemble those of Korean in the relevant respects. (The Japanese data consisted of a series of two-hour tape recordings collected monthly beginning when the child was 12 months old and ending when he was 35 months old.) Yamashita found that demonstratives were acquired at around age 29–30 months, well into Radford's 'functional stage' as shown both by the subject's age and by the structural sophistication of his sentences at this period. Prior to this age, demonstratives were rarely used. (As in Korean, deictics are commonly used in Japanese for NPs with previously mentioned referents—e.g., Gundel, Hedberg, and Zacharski 1993 : 291—so frequency of occurrence in adult speech is apparently not the key factor.)

In sum, it is evident that demonstratives in Korean (and, apparently, Japanese) are acquired squarely in the age range that Radford characterizes as the 'functional stage' (age 24 months or later). Since the relatively late acquisition of these elements cannot be attributed to their categorial status (they are not functional categories in Korean), the crucial factor seems to involve their relatively abstract semantics. (For some discussion of this point with regard to English deictics, see Tfoundi and Klatzky 1983 and the references cited there.) But if this is so, there may no longer be any reason to attribute the late acquisition of English determiners to their status as functional categories: semantic considerations alone might account for their developmental schedule.[5]

The possibility that semantic factors rather than membership in functional categories might explain the relatively late emergence of certain types of morphemes does not refute the maturational approach to development per se. In fact, it may ultimately be necessary to appeal to maturation to account for why certain types of meanings (those deemed 'abstract') emerge at a later point than others. However, if correct, the semantic theory does undermine the claim that the maturation of UG (vs. some other cognitive system) is ultimately responsible for the timing of syntactic development as it pertains to lexical and functional categories.

In concluding this section, it is important to note that while Radford's proposal is by far the most detailed to have been put forward within the maturational framework, it is only one of many contributions to this line of thinking in recent years. Maturational theories of development offer a serious alternative to the continuity theory considered in the preceding section and in the years ahead are likely to elicit further research in both UG- and non–UG-based approaches to language acquisition.

3. The Incrementalist Theory

The key idea underlying the third theory of development to be considered here is that the acquisition process takes place in increments, with each advance adding some element to the inventory of morphemes, categories, and operations acquired to that point. This in turn presupposes the notion of **cumulative complexity** (e.g., Brown 1973:186; see also Brown and Hanlon 1970).

(30) *Cumulative Complexity:*
       X is cumulatively more complex than Y if X involves everything that Y does plus something else.

According to this criterion, for example, the morpheme *were* is cumulatively more complex (table 15.7) than the past tense affix *-ed* in that it not only encodes the notion 'past' associated with the latter morpheme but also the notion 'plural' (since it contrasts with singular *was*).

Cumulative complexity is the principal predictor of developmental order in the incrementalist theory. The key idea is simply that cumulatively more complex concepts and principles are acquired later than their simpler counterparts—all other things (e.g., frequency, perceptual salience, communicative importance) being equal. For expository purposes, let us formulate this idea as the **Developmental Law.** (For variants and further discussion, see Flavell 1972; Atkinson 1982:15 ff.; MacWhinney 1987:267; Lebeaux 1987:38.)

(31) *The Developmental Law:*
       If X is cumulatively more complex than Y, X will emerge after Y (all other things being equal).

So stated, the Developmental Law correctly predicts that plural *-s* will be acquired before the cumulatively more complex *were* (Brown 1973:371).

The incrementalist theory of development differs from the continuity and maturational approaches in minimizing reference to inborn mechanisms of language acquisition such as UG. However, it is not inherently incompatible with UG-based theories in that it has the potential to shed light on those aspects of development that are not directly controlled by inborn mechanisms of UG (e.g., the learning of lexical information, the effect of processing constraints, and the like). A possible example of this comes from Snyder and Stromswold's (1994) work on the development of double object (*I gave John a book*) and *to*-dative patterns (*I gave a book to John*). As explained in chapter 10, section 3, they attribute the comparatively late acquisition of the *to*-dative pattern to cumulative complexity: it requires

Table 15.7 A Simple Case of
Cumulative Complexity

Morpheme	Notions Encoded
-s	plural
were	past
	plural

an understanding of the special role of *to* (which has been 'grammaticized' and no longer denotes movement) that is not necessary for the double object structure. (However, it must be admitted that this is a less than perfect example of cumulative complexity, since the two structures also differ from each other in the mapping of thematic roles onto grammatical relations: the goal is first object in the double object pattern but second object in the *to*-dative construction. Snyder and Stromswold appear to set this matter aside.)

A number of other developmental phenomena considered in earlier parts of this book are also good candidates for an incrementalist analysis. As noted in chapter 5, a morphologically based distinction between tensed and untensed verbs helps determine which VPs take an overt subject and which do not; see (32).

(32) *Tensed VPs:*   *Untensed VPs:*
        With an overt subject:
            John [left yesterday].   *Harry [leaving/to leave today]
            John [will go tomorrow].

        Without an overt subject:
            *Left yesterday   (They tried) [leaving/to leave today].
            *Will go tomorrow

Since a grammar distinguishing between tensed and untensed Vs is cumulatively more complex than a grammar that simply has an undifferentiated V category, the Developmental Law predicts the existence of a stage during which verbs do not exhibit tense contrasts. This in turn allows the incrementalist theory to predict the appearance and relative timing of the subject drop stage.

SOME LIMITATIONS

There are at least two limitations on the use of the Developmental Law as an explanatory tool. First, as Brown and others readily acknowledge, there are many pairs of elements that do not enter into a relationship of cumulative complexity even though one is acquired before the other. An obvious example of this is the past tense affix *-ed* and the plural ending *-s*. While the plural is acquired before the past tense marker, pastness is not cumulatively more complex with plurality (or vice versa). Hence, the Development Law has nothing to say about this particular acquisition fact.

There are many similar examples in the syntactic domain. In chapter 11, for instance, we saw that children apparently do not master the constraint that rules out forward patterns of pronominalization such as *Near John$_i$, he$_i$ saw a snake* until after age 6. On the other hand, the mechanisms required for the production and comprehension of passive patterns seem to be in place around age 3—which is about the time at which children are able to correctly interpret reflexive pronouns. Since the mechanisms involved in producing passive structures are not (as far as we now know) a simple subset or superset of those required either to block patterns of forward pronominalization or to interpret reflexive pronouns, no relationship of cumulative complexity exists among these phenomena. This in turn means that the incrementalist approach has no insight to offer into these particular developmental facts.

At best, then, the incrementalist theory can offer only a partial explanation for syntactic development. While the Developmental Law may shed light on certain acquisition facts, a comprehensive account of development will also have to include other explanatory mechanisms, including perhaps deficits in perception and processing as well as maturational changes in one or more cognitive systems.

A second limitation of the incrementalist approach is that the success of the Developmental Law depends crucially on the calculation of cumulative complexity as determined by a particular grammatical analysis. One of the better known 'dead ends' in language acquisition research was the attempt to predict developmental order in terms of the number of transformations involved in the formation of particular constructions (e.g., Brown and Hanlon 1970). According to this theory, for example, each of the sentences in (33) differs from the others in terms of its degree of cumulative complexity.

(33)   a.   *No movement transformations:*
            Harry is talking to Sue.
       b.   *One movement transformation (Inversion):*
            Is Harry __ talking to Sue?
       c.   *Two movement transformations (Inversion,* Wh *Movement):*
            Who is Harry __ talking to __?

The obvious prediction here is that the developmental order should be: (a) (b) (c). While (a) may emerge before either (b) or (c), the latter two structures apparently appear about the same time (see chap. 8). In fact, in some children, inversion seems to be better controlled in structure (c) than in structure (b), as we have seen. This suggests that, for one reason or another, transformations do not lend themselves to the calculation of cumulative complexity in this case. (For further discussion of this problem, see Maratsos 1978.)

The study of pronoun–antecedent relationships illustrates another aspect of the same problem. As we saw in chapter 11, the grammar of pronoun interpretation may develop in the three steps outlined in (34) in at least some children.

(34)   a.   A pronoun takes an antecedent. (no constraint)
       b.   A pronoun cannot precede its antecedent. (linear constraint)
       c.   A pronoun cannot c-command its antecedent. (Principle C)

The obvious problem here is that the incrementalist approach cannot explain why the second developmental stage should precede the third: since the adult system

(Principle C) is different from the intermediate system, but not cumulatively more complex, the Developmental Law is not applicable.

However, there is perhaps another possibility. It is sometimes suggested that Principle C or its equivalent should also refer to the relative order of the pronoun and its antecedent so as to accommodate contrasts such as (35)–(36) (e.g., Lasnik 1976:15; Kuno 1987:89; O'Grady 1987:131; Jackendoff 1990:436).

(35)   Mary [$_{VP}$ showed John$_i$ himself$_i$ in the mirror].
(36)   *Mary [$_{VP}$ showed himself$_i$ John$_i$ in the mirror].

In both these sentences, the pronoun *himself* c-commands its antecedent because the first XP above it (the bracketed VP) also contains that element. As currently stated, Principle C can therefore not distinguish between the two sentences. Intuitively, the difference lies in the fact that the pronoun follows the antecedent that it c-commands in (35), but precedes it in (36). There are many different ways to incorporate this insight into a grammatical analysis of pronominalization. One possibility is to replace Principle C with the constraint outlined in (37).

(37)   *The Precedence Constraint:*
       A pronoun cannot precede and c-command its antecedent.

This principle rules out (36) while allowing (35), since only the former sentence contains a pronoun that precedes and c-commands its antecedent. The Precedence Constraint also makes the right predictions for (38)–(41), just as Principle C does.

(38)   *[$_S$ He$_i$ visited John's$_i$ mother].
(39)   *Sue [$_{VP}$ told him$_i$ about John's$_i$ exam].
(40)   *[$_{NP}$ his$_i$ report on John$_i$]
(41)   a. On [$_{NP}$ his$_i$ table], John$_i$ put the new book.
       b. After [$_S$ she$_i$ returned home], Sally$_i$ had supper.

In (38)–(40), the pronoun both precedes and c-commands its antecedent, in contrast to the situation in (41) where only the precedence relation holds.

Although Principle C and the Precedence Constraint make similar predictions with respect to grammaticality judgments in many cases, they differ in terms of their compatibility with the incrementalist account of development. In particular, if the Precedence Constraint is the right formulation of the adult system, then the final developmental stage is indeed cumulatively more complex than the intermediate stage, as (42) helps show.

(42)   a. A pronoun takes an antecedent. (no constraint)
       b. A pronoun cannot precede its antecedent. (linear constraint)
       c. A pronoun cannot precede and c-command its antecedent. (Precedence Constraint)

Whereas the final stage makes use of the notions 'precede' and 'c-command', the intermediate stage employs only the notion 'precede'. The Developmental Law thus provides an account for the putative acquisition order.[6]

This illustration underlines an important general point about theories of development: different analyses of the same syntactic phenomenon can lead to very different accounts of its step-by-step emergence. Like theories of learnability, approaches to development are ultimately dependent on an accompanying syntactic analysis. We are thus reminded once again of the inevitable interdependence of grammatical theory and the study of language acquisition.

WEAKENING THE DEVELOPMENTAL LAW

So far, we have used the Developmental Law to provide insight into the 'logic' underlying intermediate steps in the emergence of a particular principle. In the case of the restriction on pronoun interpretation just considered, for example, it can help explain how a linear constraint ('A pronoun cannot precede its antecedent') could be a first approximation of the more mature adult principle ('A pronoun cannot precede and c-command its antecedent').

The success of the Developmental Law in such cases stems from the fact that it forces the acquisition device to proceed step by step in the smallest possible increments. But matters are not always so simple. As observed in chapter 7, for instance, the greater distance between the gap and the displaced element in object *wh* questions such as (43b) makes these patterns cumulatively more complex than subject *wh* questions such as (43a) and accounts for the higher error rate on experimental tasks.

(43)   a. *Subject* wh *question:*
       Who [$_S$ __ will introduce Sue to Max]?
       b. *Object* wh *question:*
       Who [$_S$ will Sue [$_{VP}$ introduce __ to Max]]?

This in turn leads to the prediction that subject *wh* questions should uniformly emerge before object *wh* questions, consistent with the Developmental Law but contrary to fact (see chap. 7 for further discussion).

How can we reconcile this situation with the incrementalist theory? One possibility is that the Developmental Law should be weakened as in (44).

(44)   *The Developmental Law (weak version):*
       If X is cumulatively more complex than Y, X cannot emerge before Y (all other things being equal).

So stated, the Developmental Law is now compatible with two scenarios: one in which X emerges after Y and one in which X and Y emerge at the same time. The

Developmental Law would thus permit subject *wh* questions to emerge before the cumulatively more complex object *wh* questions or at the same time. (Even this weaker prediction may not be correct, however: as noted in chap. 7, Stromswold 1995 has found that some children seem to use object *wh* questions slightly before *wh* subject questions.)

The revised version of the Developmental Law has the further advantage of being compatible with all-at-once acquisition of the constraint on pronoun interpretation. As noted in chapter 11, at least some children seem to acquire the adult version of this constraint at a very early age (perhaps even age 3) without passing through intermediate stages. This is compatible with the weaker version of the Developmental Law, which (unlike the earlier formulation) does not require that the use of precedence to constrain pronoun–antecedent relations predate the joint use of precedence and c-command.

On this view, then, one-step acquisition is possible, in principle at least, in cases where experience provides adequate input to the acquisition device from the earliest stages of development (as it arguably does for *wh* questions and pronominalization patterns). However, individual variation from child to child, perhaps reflecting differences in experience, presumably has a role to play in determining whether the acquisition device functions with such efficiency in actual practice.[7]

4. Conclusion

At the present time, there is no generally accepted theory of development. At least some aspects of development are doubtless due to nongrammatical factors such as attention span, processing difficulty, perceptual salience, frequency effects, and the like. However, it seems reasonable to assume that properties of the acquisition device itself and of the grammatical system that it constructs will also have a significant role to play in an adequate theory of development. Like many of the other issues considered in this book, the resolution of these questions must await further advances in the study of syntactic development.

16

Concluding Remarks

Throughout this book we have been intent on investigating the properties of the acquisition device by studying both the step-by-step development of syntax and the even more puzzling question of how language is 'learnable' in the first place. As we saw in our consideration of the latter issue (chaps. 12–14), there are two quite different views about how the acquisition device bridges the very substantial gulf between the input (essentially, interpretable utterances) and the output (the complex cognitive system that linguists call a grammar).

One view, dominant among syntacticians, holds that the acquisition device must incorporate an inborn Universal Grammar, a full-fledged system of linguistic categories and principles. As noted in chapter 13, the most detailed proposals along these lines have virtually all been made within the framework of 'Government and Binding' theory. Contrasting with this stance is the view that while the acquisition device provides the learner with an inventory of notions and mechanisms relevant to language, these do not include actual *syntactic* categories or principles. As explained in chapter 14, this view of the acquisition device encompasses a diverse set of proposals ranging from distributional learning and semantic assimilation to operating principles and 'general nativism'.

At this point in the evolution of research on the learnability problem, the UG-based approach is deservedly preeminent. Indeed, no other approach offers such detailed proposals about the core components of grammatical knowledge, especially those involving the architecture of syntactic representations and the constraints applying to those representations. (Of course, this does not mean that those opposed to UG should give up their research programs, but it does point toward the need for more explicit and comprehensive counterproposals that can be measured against the currently favored view.)

Turning now to the issue of development, table 16.1 summarizes some of the major findings outlined in earlier chapters of this book. (In assembling this list, I have been deliberately liberal about the scope of the acquisition device, assuming that it includes mechanisms for perceiving and processing data (e.g., properties (a), (j), and (p)) and for formulating hypotheses (properties (h) and (l)) in addition to the inventory of notions needed to construct a functioning grammar (properties (d), (e), and (g)).

In general, the phenomena listed in table 16.1 seem to reflect features of the

Table 16.1 Some Properties of the Acquisition Device Inferred from
Developmental Facts

Property	Chapter
a. Exhibits special sensitivity to items that are stressed and occur in initial or final position	2
b. Differs from child to child in terms of how it segments speech (holistic vs. analytic), and the proportion of social-expressive words it learns in the early stages of development (expressive vs. referential)	2
c. Acquires N before any other major syntactic category (V, A, etc.)	3
d. Formulates generalizations about phrase structure in terms of syntactic notions (N, NP, V, VP, etc.) from very early in the language acquisition process, if not from the very beginning	3
e. Builds hierarchially structured syntactic representations from very early in the acquisition process, if not from the very beginning	3
f. Exhibits special sensitivity to word order conventions, on which it rarely errs	4
g. Can formulate word order conventions in terms of both structural and thematic notions	4
h. Prone to overgeneralization based on generality of occurrence in the formulation of pronoun case rules	4
i. Systematically suppresses the subject NP but not the object NP	5
j. Treats 'gaps' with increasing disfavor the more deeply embedded they are	6, 7, 9
k. Exhibits respect for 'island constraints' from as early as age 3	7
l. Undertakes conservative item-by-item learning of the verbs that can appear in inversion patterns	8
m. Learns auxiliary verbs in VP-internal position first	8
n. Formulates the inversion rule in terms of structural rather than semantic notions	8
o. Can learn 'non-basic' mappings between thematic roles and structural positions (e.g., passive patterns) from age 2 or 3	10
p. Exhibits an initial preference for forward pronominalization	11
q. Identifies the basic mechanisms of pronoun interpretation by age 3 or so	11

acquisition device that have nothing to do with the question of whether there is an inborn grammatical system such as UG. For example, the tendency to be conservative in identifying verbs that undergo inversion (property (l)) and the propensity to overextend case forms on the basis of generality of occurrence (property (h)) provide clues about the nature of the learning mechanism that the acquisition device uses, but they do not help us determine whether there is an innate Universal Grammar. Similarly, the fact that young children exhibit an aversion to gaps in proportion to their distance from the associated 'missing' element (property (j)) or that they prefer forward patterns of pronominalization (property (p)) may tell us something about the processing mechanisms employed by the acquisition device, but it seems not to shed light on the existence of UG.

Among the other development phenomena mentioned in table 16.1, there is little to distinguish between the UG and non-UG views of the acquisition device. True, children seem to master significant grammatical phenomena, including the basic categorial contrasts and the architecture of syntactic representations (properties (d) and (e)), at a very early point in the developmental process, but this does not tell us *how* they do it. A theory that makes the relevant syntactic categories and principles part of the inborn acquisition device obviously offers one type of explanation for these facts, but the general nativist proposal outlined in chapter 14 also posits innate concepts and mechanisms that may be able to account for the rapid emergence of syntactic representations in the earliest stages of development.

There have, of course, been various attempts to use particular developmental phenomena to support the UG-based approach to language acquisition. Among these we can include Lust's suggestion (see (1)) that children learning left-branching languages exhibit no preference for forward patterns of pronominalization (chap. 11, section 1); Hyams's (1986) claim (see (2)) that the end of the subject-drop period coincides with the emergence of modals, verbal inflection, expletives, and contractible *be* (chap. 15, section 1); Déprez's and Pierce's proposal (see (3)) that patterns of sentence-initial negation in children's early speech reflect the subject's 'underlying' VP-internal position (chap. 4, section 1); and Radford's claim (see (4)) that 'functional' syntactic categories emerge a few months after lexical categories such as nouns and verbs (chap. 15, section 2).

(1) *Lust's claim: only children acquiring right-branching languages will find patterns such as (a) easier than (b):*
   a. forward pattern: $NP_i \ldots pronoun_i$
   b. backward pattern: $pronoun_i \ldots NP_i$

(2) *Hyams's claim: a cluster of seemingly unrelated events occur together:*
   obligatory use of overt pronouns instead of null subjects
   appearance of modals (*will, can, should,* etc.)
   use of verbal inflection (tense and agreement)
   emergence of contractible *be* (*He's here*)
   use of expletives (*There's a cat; It's raining*)

(3) *Déprez's and Pierce's analysis of sentence-initial negation: the subject remains inside VP:*
   $[_{IP} \underline{\quad} \text{no(t)} [_{VP} \text{the sun} [_V \text{shining}]]]$

(4) *Radford's claim: lexical categories mature before functional categories:*
   [N, V, A, P] > {Comp, Infl, Det}

While each of these phenomena would be difficult to explain without assuming a GB-style grammar (which in turn entails the existence of UG), there is reason to doubt that any of them actually occurs as described, as noted in earlier commentary. Other phenomena no doubt merit consideration as well, but the trend to this point seems clear: in general, the developmental facts offer no special support for the view of syntax associated with UG-based theories of grammar.

Are there perhaps other phenomena, of a type not considered in previous chapters, that might shed light on the nature of the acquisition device? Two possibilities come to mind, each of which merits at least brief mention here.

THE TRANSITION FROM PIDGIN TO CREOLE

Bickerton (1981, 1984, 1990) has argued that much can be learned about the acquisition device by studying how pidgins evolve into creoles. (A pidgin is the rudimentary 'protolanguage' that develops when speakers of mutually incomprehensible languages come into contact; a creole is the full-fledged language that results when a generation of children adopt a pidgin as their first language.) As Bickerton observes, a child who must learn language based on pidgin data faces an even more severe shortfall in experience than does the child learning an 'established' language such as English. Although the data in the latter situation may not include information about the identity of syntactic categories, the architecture of syntactic representations, or the nature of constraints on gaps and pronouns, it at least consists of sentences from a full-fledged language. In contrast, children exposed to pidgin hear utterances that do not use word order or case to distinguish between subjects and direct objects, that have no gaps of the sort found in *wh* questions and relative clauses, that permit grammatically unconstrained deletion of subjects and objects, that exhibit a paucity of embedding and other types of recursion, and that lack 'grammatical' morphemes such as inflectional affixes, determiners, auxiliaries, and complementizers. Moreover, as noted by Gordon (1990), children in this situation have no opportunity to receive corrective feedback of any sort (including recasts) since there are as yet no speakers of the language being learned. Remarkably, the creole acquired under these circumstances has none of the deficiencies of the pidgin: it is in every respect a full-fledged human language.

As Bickerton rightly observes, the acquisition device must draw on quite extraordinary resources if it is to bridge the huge gap between the experience provided by exposure to a pidgin and the grammar associated with a creole. Indeed, he suggests, by examining the differences between the (first-generation) creole that results from the acquisition process and the pidgin that served as its starting point, we can make very direct inferences about what features of the final grammatical system the acquisition device must supply. At the very least, these include word order, mechanisms for creating and interpreting gaps, constraints on null arguments, recursion (to allow for sentences of unlimited length and complexity), and an inventory of grammatical morphemes.

The crucial question has to do with whether this information allows us to determine anything new about the character of the acquisition device. I believe that it does not, and that the conclusions that can be drawn from Bickerton's work essentially only reinforce the principal conclusions of more conventional work on the acquisition device. In both cases, it is clear that the acquisition process yields as its end result an intricate grammar that is able to form and interpret an unlimited number of sentences with specific structural properties (e.g., categorial contrasts, hierarchical architecture, a subject–object asymmetry, 'island' constraints on the use of gaps, and so on). However, in neither case does describing the 'output grammar' settle the question of how it emerges in the first place (other than to exclude simple induction from experience, which is clear in any case—see chap. 12).

A UG-based theory of the sort that Bickerton favors obviously has a promising proposal to make about the pidgin-to-creole transition—essentially the same proposal, in fact, that is made about language acquisition under more conventional circumstances, which is that most of the grammar is simply inborn. (Bickerton's 1984 proposal allows for less parametric variation than in standard UG accounts, however.) But the general nativist theory sketched in chapter 14 may also have a proposal to make here. The emergence of categories can be attributed to the innate semantically based classificatory system discussed in chapter 14; the architectural features of syntactic structure (including its recursive character) can be explained by reference to the properties that make up the acquisition device's computational module; the development of grammatical morphemes reflects the encoding of the 'grammatically privileged' concepts and contrasts that make up the conceptual module; and so on. General nativist theories encounter no new obstacles in the pidgin-to-creole phenomenon, just as UG-based theories find no special support. The fundamental question of whether the acquisition device includes an inborn *grammar* remains unanswered.

CLINICAL STUDIES

A very different body of evidence relevant to the study of the acquisition device comes from the investigation of linguistic and cognitive deficits of various sorts. Work on this area has converged very strongly on an extremely interesting and important finding: certain aspects of language acquisition and use are dissociated from other types of cognition.

One type of evidence for this conclusion comes from disorders that affect the language faculty but not other types of cognitive activity. A very common example of this involves aphasia, a language disorder caused by damage to the brain. Depending on the location of the lesion, aphasia can occur by itself, with other forms of cognition preserved (e.g., Zurif 1990:181). For example, it is a well-established fact that damage to the left frontal lobe of the brain results in poor articulation, loss of functional categories and affixes, and comprehension difficulties with reversible sentences, especially those containing gaps—the pattern of symptoms often called 'Broca's aphasia'. Other forms of aphasia are even more specific. Pinker (1994b:314) notes that some victims of anomia (an aphasic disorder involving the ability to name) have trouble only with abstract nouns; others can use nouns with animate referents but not those that refer to inanimate things. (There was even a patient who lost the ability to name fruits and vegetables!)

Whereas aphasia is usually the result of a stroke or wound, some language disorders are inherited. A very interesting and unusual disorder of this type has been documented by Gopnik (1990a) and Gopnik and Crago (1991). They report on a highly specific language impairment affecting three generations of a British family—a grandmother, four of her offspring (a fifth is unimpaired), and eleven of their twenty-three children. Although the impaired individuals apparently have normal IQs for nonverbal tasks,[1] they exhibit severe difficulty with those parts of language involving morphological processes—both inflection (e.g., plurals, past tense, subject–verb agreement, and the like) and derivation (e.g., the process that relates words such as *sunny* and *dirty* to *sun* and *dirt* respectively). This deficit results in errors such as those in (5) in spontaneous speech (from Pinker 1994b:49).

(5)   It's *a* flying finches, they are.
       She remembered when she *hurts* herself the other day.
       The neighbors *phone* the ambulance because the man *fall* off the tree.
       The boys *eat* four cookie.
       Carol is *cry* in the church.

In addition, the impaired individuals have trouble with language tests that require them to change tenses (e.g., *Everyday he kisses his nanny. Yesterday he ___*) or to provide the plural of nonsense words (e.g., *This is wug. Here are two ___*). However, they generally know the plural forms of familiar words (e.g., *book–books*) that they have had the opportunity to learn on a case-by-case basis, and they tend to produce irregular past tense forms (*did, ran, saw,* etc.) correctly. All of this points to a disorder focused quite narrowly on the ability to learn and use regular morphological rules in a productive fashion.

The disorders considered to this point all affect language, leaving other forms of cognition more or less undisturbed. Further evidence for the dissociation between language and other mental faculties comes from the reverse situation—the selective sparing of language from a deficit that affects other forms of cognition. A striking example of this, Williams Syndrome (WS), is discussed by Bellugi, Birhle, and Corina (1991). They note that individuals afflicted with this disorder suffer from general mental retardation (the average IQ is about 50), including severe impairment in spatial processing and representation. Remarkably, however,

WS suffers are known for the quality of their speech.[2] The following sample was produced by a 17-year-old girl with an IQ of 50 who is describing what it was like to have a magnetic resonance image made of her brain.

> There is a huge magnetic machine. It took a picture inside the brain. You could talk but not move your head because that would ruin the whole thing and they would have to start all over again. After it's all done they show you your brain on a computer and they see how large it is. And the machine on the other side of the room takes pictures from the computer. They can take pictures instantly. Oh, and it was very exciting! (ibid. 386)

As Bellugi et al. note, this speech sample gives every sign of morphological and syntactic sophistication, with a variety of grammatical morphemes, a passive, and various embedded clauses.

There is a simple and obvious explanation for the series of facts just reviewed: the acquisition device and the grammar it constructs must involve mechanisms that are genetically determined (hence the possibility of hereditary language impairment) and that are located in very specific parts of the brain (hence the possibility of language disturbances due to localized brain damage). This is an important finding, but it is perhaps more limited than one might think. In particular, it says nothing about the design or content of the acquisition device. From the fact that a mechanism is located in a particular area of the brain or is genetically shaped, one cannot conclude that it does not share important features or principles with other mechanisms. Our right and left arms differ from each other in genetically determined ways and are located in different places. But they nonetheless share important features of design and functioning (they include an elbow joint, a forearm, a hand with five fingers, and so forth). Something similar may yet turn out to be true for the relationship between parts of the acquisition device and other cognitive systems in the human brain.

In sum, there is a great deal that we still do not know about the acquisition device. The intense and ever-improving research efforts of the last two decades have produced an impressive body of data about the conditions under which syntactic development takes place and about the nature of the resulting grammatical system, but many fundamental issues pertaining to the design and operation of the acquisition device remain unresolved. Indeed, it would be misleading to end this book without admitting that the ultimate solution to many of the mysteries and puzzles that we have been considering probably lies quite far in the future.

Notes

Chapter One

1. In recent years, some researchers (e.g., Stromswold 1990; Cairns et al. 1994; and McDaniel, Chiu, and Maxfield 1995) have attempted to develop techniques for eliciting grammaticality judgments from children as young as age 3. However, these techniques have not yet become widely accepted or used in the field.

Chapter Two

1. A parallel distinction, proposed by L. Bloom, Lightbown, and Hood (1975), differentiates between **nominal** and **pronominal** children. Children in the former group encode many different semantic relations using nouns but tend to avoid verbs. In contrast, children in the second group employ pronouns (*I* for agents, and *that, this,* and *it* for themes) together with verbs and other relational words. Bretherton et al. (1983) group together referential and nominal children on the one hand and expressive and pronominal children on the other.

2. Even less clear are the reasons underlying the correlations reported by Bates et al. (1994), who coordinated a diary study involving 1,803 children aged 0;8 to 2;6 and their mothers. Bates and her colleagues found a "small but reliable" correlation with birth order (later-born children are less referential) and with maternal education, paternal education, and paternal occupation.

3. In her study of 8 children aged 0;9 to 1;8, Benedict (1979) found a small advantage for 'action words' over nominals in children's early comprehension (especially the first 20 words in their vocabularies). However, she includes in her 'action word class' many words that do not belong to a conventional syntactic category in English, let alone the verb category: *bye-bye, pat-a-cake, nite nite, no, rock rock,* and *ready-set-go.*

4. This figure was even higher for 13 of the children, who underwent what the authors refer to as a 'noun explosion' during a period of rapid lexical growth that began at an average age of 19 months.

5. I use the term 'theme' rather than 'patient' to refer to the entity undergoing an action; for definitions of other thematic roles, see note 1 in chapter 3.

Chapter Three

1. The 'core' set of conventional thematic roles can be defined as follows:

> **agent:** the entity that performs an action
> **theme (patient):** the entity undergoing an action or movement
> **goal:** the end point of a movement
> **source:** the starting point of a movement
> **location:** the place where an action occurs

2. However, some researchers use thematic notions as a 'theory-neutral' way to label the various patterns produced by children without committing themselves to the view that this type of analysis identifies the actual concepts used by the acquisition device in constructing the grammar of the adult language.

3. However, some recent work breaks with this trend (e.g., Wexler 1993, cited by Vainikka 1993/94:261). At any rate, the fact that children have not yet begun to use determiners certainly does not preclude the possibility that the determiner category is *available* to the acquisition device from the outset, consistent with the Continuity Hypothesis. For more on this, see chapter 15.

4. There is also the possibility of crosslinguistic differences. Bates, Bretherton, and Snyder (1988:5) report that the NP–NP pattern is rare in the speech of Italian children, who prefer to omit the subject

rather than the verb. Cho (1981) reports similar findings for Korean. This may reflect that fact that overt subjects in Italian and Korean are optional (see chap. 5) and are therefore more likely than verbs to be omitted. If this is so, it suggests that even young children are sensitive to the grammatical options made available by their language to circumvent processing limitations.

5. Kevin Gregg (pers. comm.) notes that with a strong intonation break before and after the adjective (very unlike the neutral intonation used in Matthei's experiment), *the second green ball* may have the interpretation 'the ball which is both second overall and green'.

6. Matthei (310) reports a parallel error by the same children on phrases such as *the red bird's hat*, where there was a tendency to interpret the phrase to mean 'the bird's hat that is also red'.

Chapter Four

1. Word order can also be used in English to distinguish between statements and questions (*He will leave* vs. *Will he leave?*) and to signal subtle differences in emphasis and focus (*At school, they work hard* vs. *They work hard at school*). The latter type of contrast falls outside the scope of this study, but the former phenomenon is considered in chapter 8.

2. A further problem in this regard is that Déprez and Pierce do not distinguish between 'sentence-initial negation' and 'pre-subject negation'. Thus they count both *Not write this book* and *Not Fraser read it* as instances of the same pattern. This seems methodologically inappropriate, since the first pattern but not the second can be seen as the reduced version of a pattern found in adult speech (e.g., *I did not write this book*).

3. See Oshima-Takane (1992) and the references cited there for discussion of person errors in the acquisition of English pronouns.

4. Chiat (1981:88–89) gives the following examples from the speech of Sally at 2;4.

(i)   I'm gonna put *he* to bed.
        Muppet Show will get a gun and kill *they,* your girls.

Crucially, though, Sally did not use just the nominative form for object pronouns. In other contexts, the accusative form is found.

(ii)   He wants to scratch *him.*
        Get *her* out and then put *her* on your swing.

Chiat also reports that children sometimes alternate between the nominative and accusative form for pronouns that occur alone. For example:

(iii)   EXPERIMENTER: Who's sitting on the chair?
        CHILD (AGE 4;1): *She.*
(iv)   EXPERIMENTER: Who's gonna make the tea?
        CHILD (AGE 4;1): *Me.*

We return to the problem of nominative-for-accusative substitutions below.

5. A less controversial pattern containing an untensed verb with an accusative subject is used to express surprise or disbelief.

(i)   What?! *Me* go to night school!? (in response to 'You should go to night school.')

I know of no data on the acquisition of these patterns.

Chapter Five

1. Hyams's basic idea is that a language that permits subject drop includes a PRO, a special type of null pronominal, under the INFL node in syntactic structure, as in (i). (This type of syntactic structure is employed only in certain versions of government and binding (GB) theory and has no general acceptance outside that framework.)

PRO is governed by the modal

Because PRO includes person and number features that match those of the subject, Hyams proposed that its presence licensed the null subject. Since PRO cannot be governed (roughly, cannot have a head as its sister), and since modals occur under INFL in the version of GB theory assumed by Hyams (see (ii)), it follows that modals should not be possible during the subject drop stage.

2. In addition to being licensed, null subjects must also be identified—either by sufficiently rich inflectional agreement on the verb (the case in Italian) or by a discourse topic (the case in Chinese). Jaeggli and Safir cite German as an example of a language that licenses null subjects (it is morphologically uniform), but cannot identify them (since its system of inflectional agreement makes relatively few contrasts.) For this reason, German is not a full-fledged subject drop language, although it can suppress expletive subjects.

3. Jaeggli and Hyams (1988) attribute the lack of null objects in the speech of the youngest English children to the absence of variables, the type of null category associated with object position in their theory. However, this incorrectly predicts that Chinese children of the same age should also lack null object patterns, which Wang et al. (1992) show is incorrect.

4. Patterns such as those in (i) seem to undermine this generalization.

(i)   Parents want [*their children* to succeed].
        Harry believes [*Mary* to be intelligent].

The italicized NPs are treated as subjects of the embedded infinitival clause in GB theory, but as direct objects of the matrix verb in most other approaches to syntax. Even in GB, it is acknowledged that overt NPs in this position are 'licensed' by an element other than the infinitival verb (see, e.g., N. Chomsky 1981:68), and some recent work (e.g., Authier 1991; Bowers 1993) treats these NPs as 'surface' direct objects.

5. There are at least two possibilities. One is that the lexical properties of verbs such as *gonna* and *try* require a subjectless complement phrase. The other is that a general syntactic mechanism ensures that the lower of two identical subjects must be suppressed.

6. Radford (1990:179) gives examples (i)–(ii) of *wh* questions without an overt subject, both from the speech of Claire at 24 mos. For some other examples, see Vainikka (1993/94:299).

(i)   What doing?
(ii)   Where go?

Other errors produced around this time (e.g., *What dat for?* and *Why tape?*, cited by Vainikka, p. 299) suggest that the acquisition device may not treat all *wh* questions as clausal in the very early stages of development. The prediction would then be that once this fact is established, *wh* questions such as (i) and (ii) would disappear.

7. Weissenborn (1992:291) offers a different explanation, suggesting that if either the head or the specifier position within CP is lexically filled, formation of the topic chain needed to identify the null subject is blocked.

8. Aldridge (1989:64) even cites two examples of missing objects of a preposition.

(i)   Me want stand on __. (20 mos.)
(ii)   Crayon under __. (22 mos.)

Chapter Six

1. Hsu et al. report the subject control responses only for adverbial clauses such as (i) and not for the complement clause patterns studied by Tavakolian and Chomsky.

(i)   The zebra touches the lion [after . drinking the water].

2. This seems to predict that NPs embedded inside PPs, such as *Pluto* in (i), should not be eligible controllers for children, since they are not higher in the tree structure than the missing NP.

(i)   Daisy stood [near Pluto] [before . doing some reading].

This prediction is supported by the experimental results reported in Goodluck 1981 and Hsu, Cairns, and Fiengo 1985, but not those in Phillips 1985, McDaniel, Smith, and Hsu 1990/91, or Goodluck and Behne 1992.

3. The confusion may run in both directions. At age 3;5 and even now at age 4;7, my daughter sometimes uses *tell* in the sense of *ask*.

(i)   In response to 'What was that little girl's name?':
        I don't know. I'll have to *tell* her next time.
(ii)   In response to 'How does Mama say "racoon" [in Japanese]?'
        I don't know, I'll go and *tell* her how she says it.

4. In contrast to the situation in (39), the elements undergoing coordination in these examples form structural units even if no gaps are present.

Chapter Seven

1. De Villiers (1991:158) reports that 3-year-old children often interpret *how* to mean 'why', perhaps because of confusion with *how come*. Thus they respond to questions such as *How did he fix the bike?* by responding *Because it was broken.*

2. Tyack and Ingram's study also included the following two patterns.

(i)   *What subject:* What is touching the boy?
(ii)   *What object:* What is the boy touching?

The results showed superior performance on the *what* object question. However, an examination of the children's errors indicates that pragmatic factors may be responsible for this phenomenon. The dominant error (51.3% of all responses) involved interpreting the *what* subject as if it meant *who*. (Tyack and Ingram's pictures were designed to allow responses consistent with this interpretation.) As Tyack and Ingram note, this suggests that children expect the subject to be animate rather than inanimate (see chap. 3 for further discussion of this point). Interestingly, there is no comparable preference for direct objects: *who* object and *what* object questions yielded a virtually identical number of animacy errors. Since animate *who* is thus natural in both subject and object positions, it seems that the purest test for a structural (vs. pragmatic) difference in the relative difficulty of *wh* questions involves the comparison of *who* subject and *who* object questions, as in table 7.3.

3. The studies by Ervin-Tripp and by Cairns and Hsu each contain unfortunate flaws. The former experiment tested children's responses to questions such as *Who's feeding him?* and *Who's he feeding?* in which pronominal case provides secondary clues about the grammatical role of the *wh* word. Cairns and Hsu's study compares the comprehension of subject questions such as *Who hugged the boy?* with object questions such as *Who did the boy hug?* Since auxiliary *do* shows up only in non-subject *wh* questions in English, its presence provides a second clue to the interpretation of the object *wh* questions (as the authors themselves note)—making a direct comparison of the two patterns difficult. Interestingly, when Cairns and Hsu compared subject *wh* questions with object questions containing the auxiliary *be* (which can occur in either subject or object questions), they found a preference for the former pattern.

4. An unfortunate problem with Hildebrand's design is that although all three types of sentences are roughly equal in overall length, the 'linear distance' (in number of words) between the gap and the sentence-initial *wh* word increases with the depth of embedding (6 words for Type I, 7 words for Type II, and 8 words for Type III). However, an analysis of the children's errors suggests that depth of embedding is the crucial variable, since the predominant deletion error involved suppression of the preposition (rather than, say, an adjective). Only this deletion has the effect of making the gap less embedded.

5. There is a possibility of bias in favor of the LD response in the *wh* argument patterns. If the *wh* word is treated as object of the matrix verb (cf. *Who did Big Bird ask to help someone?*), the most likely interpretation is that Big Bird has requested a particular person to provide help, not that he has inquired whether he himself could help. But de Villiers et al.'s story does not provide the information needed to respond to this first type of question. This may have forced the children to adopt the LD response (cf. *Who did Big Bird wonder if he should help?*), for which the story does provide a plausible answer (Kermit).

6. The most common response for Groups I and II (over 50%) involved interpreting the test question as a 'simple S': 'Who swam in the pond?' (p. 199). In the case of sentence type (i), this calls for the answer 'the dog and the rooster'.

7. A further complication is that even a medial *wh* adjunct can trigger a *wh* island effect if the embedded clause is finite. Thus, (i) is significantly worse than (37).

(i)   ?*What does Harry know [how Mary explained ___ to the students ___]?

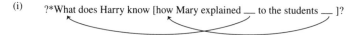

Chapter Eight

1. Even after the various auxiliary verbs have been acquired, the rate at which they are inverted in question patterns can vary for some time. Based on an extensive study of longitudinal speech samples from 14 children, Stromswold (1990:171) notes that the inversion rate is highest for *do* (which is rarely used VP-internally in adult speech), intermediate for auxiliary *be, have,* and the modals, and lowest for copula *be* (the only non-auxiliary to undergo inversion in American English).

2. A qualification may be in order here: based on an elicited production task involving 7 children aged 4;1 to 5;4, Thornton (1995) reports that the type of doubling pattern in (i) is in fact typical of children's negative *wh* questions at a particular point in development.

(i)   What did the spaceman didn't like?

Stromswold (1990:229) suggests that such errors involve the misanalysis of *didn't* as an 'untensed negative'; see Thornton for an alternative proposal.

3. Nakayama does not explain how his hypothesis applies to inversion in *wh* questions. Although copying errors are more commonly reported for *wh* questions than for *yes–no* questions, inversion is obligatory in this structure type in adult speech, as in (i).

(i)   What should we do?
       *What we should do?

This seems to rule out the type of syntactic blending that Nakayama proposes for *yes–no* questions. One possibility is that blending is triggered by the contrast between root *wh* questions, which always involve inversion, and embedded *wh* questions, which never do, see (ii).

(ii)   *Embedded* wh *question without inversion:*
       I wonder [what we should do].
       Embedded wh *question with inversion:*
       *I wonder [what should we do].

Chapter Nine

1. I deliberately exclude from consideration nonrestrictive (appositive) relative clauses. These patterns, which always include a clause-initial *wh* word and 'comma intonation', differ from the restrictive clauses considered here in not picking out a subset of the set denoted by the head. Rather, as in (i), they make a separate assertion about the elements in that set.

   (i)   Those books, which were written by a linguist, received excellent reviews.

2. This may be because the relativized 'object' in Sheldon's SO type (but not Tavakolian's) seems always to be the object of a preposition rather than a true direct object. As we will see later in this section, gaps corresponding to the object of a preposition are more difficult for language learners than gaps in the direct object position.

3. The possible effects of Conjoined Clause Strategy in the OO pattern are harder to discern. Tavakolian (p. 52) reports that children correctly make the duck kiss the sheep in 38% of their responses to patterns such as (i).

   (i)   The horse hits the sheep [that the duck kisses __].

However, as Kevin Gregg (pers. comm.) notes, this same response could be derived from the Coordinate Clause Analysis by assuming that the relative clause had an overt or null pronoun in object position that referred back to the sheep, as in (ii).

   (ii)   The horse hits the sheep [that the duck kisses __]
                                         ⇓
           The horse hits the sheep and the duck kisses him

This might also explain another response pattern reported by Tavakolian: in 22% of their responses, the children had the duck kiss the horse—which could reflect coreference between the putative pronoun and *the horse.*

Tavakolian herself counts neither of these response patterns as instances of the Coordinate Clause Analysis. Instead she considers the effects of this strategy to be manifested only when the children make the horse hit the sheep and then kiss the duck. This response, which accounts for 19% of the children's answers, requires a reanalysis of the grammatical role of *the duck* from subject to direct object.

4. Another possibility, suggested to me by Kevin Gregg, is that the similarity in the type I pattern between the relative clause and the matrix clause (both contain a transitive verb followed by an animate direct object) encourages a coordinate clause interpretation.

5. A type of picture selection task is employed by H. Brown (1971), but his study suffers from other design problems. See de Villiers et al. (1979:503) for discussion.

6. As noted in the discussion of a similar experiment by Hildebrand in chapter 7, the linear distance between the gap and the element that determines its interpretation increases with the depth of embedding. See chapter 7, n. 4 for further discussion of this point.

Chapter Ten

1. This putative preference seems not to be universal: in preliminary work on the passive in Quiché Mayan, Pye and Poz (1988) found no difference in children's ability to understand actional and non-actional constructions.

2. Even higher scores (around 60% for the elicitation of passive action verbs) have been obtained with other children (p. 215), although Pinker et al. admit that these children may have been unusually advanced in their linguistic skills.

3. In assessing the results of early comprehension experiments, the possibility of design flaws must also be taken into account. For instance, the experiment conducted by de Villiers and de Villiers (1973) tested structures such as *Make the dog be bitten by the cat,* which involves the infinitival form of the passive embedded in a larger causative structure. This is far from a pure test of children's

understanding of passive patterns. A different objection can be raised to Baldie's (1976) experiment, which required children to demonstrate their comprehension of passive sentences by selecting from among 5 alternative pictures. The strain that this task must have placed on children's processing mechanisms and working memory may be at least partly responsible for the low scores that Baldie reported.

4. It is interesting to note in this regard that French permits a double object–like pattern when the recipient argument is pronominal but not when it is a lexical NP; compare (i) and (ii).

    (i)   Je lui donne un livre.
            I him give a book.
    (ii)   *Je donne Henri un livre.
            I   give   Henry a book

This suggests that the acquisition device must make a sharp distinction between the two types of pattern.

Chapter Eleven

1. This is Reinhart's (1983) formulation. N. Chomsky's (1981) formulation of Principle C is as in (i).

    (i)   A lexical NP must be free.

An NP is free only if it is not bound—that is, not co-indexed with a c-commanding NP (including, of course, a pronoun).

2. Lust et al. try to dismiss the relevance of these examples on the grounds that Principle C can sometimes be overridden by the pragmatic context. However, it is unclear why the pragmatic context would have this effect in these cases or whether adults (or even older children) would produce such sentences in this sort of context.

3. The more usual formulation of Principle A is as in (i):

    (i)   An anaphor must be found in its governing category.

Anaphors include reflexives and reciprocals (e.g., *each other*); an anaphor is bound if it is coindexed with a c-commanding NP. The definition of governing category, which corresponds to what we are calling a 'minimal domain', varies greatly in the literature, but these complications need not concern us here.

4. There is a simplification here in that more than just the notions 'clausemate' and 'prominence' are needed to account for the interpretation of pronouns across languages. As noted by Wexler and Manzini (1987), for instance, the type of clause in which the pronoun occurs (e.g., root vs. embedded, tensed vs. untensed, subjunctive vs. indicative) may also play a role in determining its interpretation. See also chapter 13.

5. The more usual formulation of Principle B is as in (i).

    (i)   A pronominal must be free in its governing category.

A pronominal is 'free' if it is not bound. See note 3.

6. Bellugi (1971:111) gives the examples in (i) of ungrammatical reflexives in the speech of a child at age 3;6.

    (i)   It's myself.
           Who broke it? Myself or you?

I have observed the apparently ungrammatical uses of pronominals in (ii) in the speech of my daughter.

    (ii) I_i want me_i to help. (2;7) [in response to 'Do you want Chelsea to help?']
           No, I_i see me_i. (3;0) [in response to 'Can you see me?']
           He_i's going to touch him_i. (3;1)
           I_i didn't spill any porridge on me_i. (3;7)

Chapter Twelve

1. Depending on the particular theoretical framework one adopts, the requirement that all branching be binary can yield representations of varying degrees of abstractness and complexity. See Dowty 1982 and Larson 1988 for contrasting proposals (formulated within the frameworks of Categorial Grammar and Government and Binding theory, respectively) about the binary representations appropriate for 'double object' patterns such as *She sent John a message*.

2. Of course, no serious approach to learnability adopts such an assumption. In Pinker's (1984: 31) theory, for example, the acquisition device is assumed to be 'one-memory limited' in that it has no access to previously heard sentences. While this is something of a simplification, since children do commit sequences of sentences to memory on occasion (e.g., nursery rhymes), the point is that the acquisition device is not able to *rely* on such recollections.

3. It is implausible to think that the acquisition device can somehow keep track of the proportion of repetitions given in response to particular structure types and use these to draw inferences about grammaticality. As noted by Marcus (1993), the number of repetitions of a particular utterance that would have to be encountered before a reliable conclusion could be drawn about its status is prohibitively high—at least 85, by his calculation.

4. Of course, there is no reason to think that the acquisition device *requires* such close proximity of the forms *eated* and *ate* in order to note that they do not contrast. It is perfectly plausible to assume that exposure to the form *ate* the next day (or a week later) would lead to the observation that it expresses the past tense of *eat* in adult speech and therefore has the same function as the previously posited *eated* in the child's grammar. The point is simply that parental responses may provide particularly salient triggers for the Principle of Contrast, thereby facilitating the operation of the acquisition device in a modest way.

A similar result can be achieved using MacWhinney's (1987:291) Principle of Competition and Pinker's (1984:177) Unique Entry Principle. A problem with the contrast approach, noted by Bowerman (1987:451), is that children often use several noncontrasting forms interchangeably over a period of time (e.g., *breaked* and *broke* might both be used as the past tense of *break*). If in fact children are guided by the Principle of Contrast, one would not expect them to tolerate forms with identical meanings in this manner.

5. Gleitman's solution to this problem is quite different. She proposes that children must make use of the syntactic context in which words occur to infer their meaning. For instance, words that occur with propositional complements (e.g., . . . *[that it is raining]*) are likely to denote a cognitive activity such as thinking or believing, words that take an NP and a directional PP as complements (e.g., . . . *[a book] [to Mary]*) are likely to denote some type of transfer, and so on. As Gleitman states it, her hypothesis requires that even very young language learners be able to analyze various features of a sentence's syntactic organization in order to understand its meaning. This goes against the more widely accepted view, adopted here and discussed in more detail in the next chapter, that children's understanding of a sentence's meaning helps them to figure out its syntactic structure. Pinker (1994a) provides a detailed critique of Gleitman's proposal.

Chapter Thirteen

1. However, this does not entail that all verbs denote actions (or that all nouns refer to people and things). In Rondal and Cession's data, for example, 22% of the verbs in maternal speech denote states and another 16% refer to mental activities (p. 714). Since 'state' and 'mental activity' do not have inborn correspondences in the bootstrapping system, it is assumed that the acquisition device is not disturbed by encounters with such elements.

2. If this right, the I category would be added to the UG inventory, along with the information that it is prototypically paired with concepts such as tense (e.g., past) and/or modality (e.g., possibility, obligation).

3. In most theories of syntactic structure, the PP in (10a) should be inside the VP. An exception is the version of categorial grammar developed in Steedman 1991, which correlates suprasegmentally

delimited phrases with syntactic units on a one-to-one basis even if that results in unconventional phrase structure configurations.

4. There is a further simplification here. Contrary to what the word order parameter suggests, the relative ordering of heads and their complements is not always uniform in particular languages (Dryer 1992). In Persian, for instance, complements precede a V but follow a P.

5. R. Clark (1992) offers a quite different view of how parameters are set, proposing an evolution metaphor according to which the different parametric values compete for survival, with the 'fittest' hypothesis ultimately winning out.

6. There is a simplification here which can perhaps be overlooked for expository purposes. In fact, non–subject drop languages allow certain structures not found in subject drop languages (e.g., overt expletives such as *it* and *there*). Thus, in addition to allowing sentences with overt referential subjects, each type of language also permits a pattern not allowed by the other (null referential subjects in the case of subject drop languages, overt expletives in the case of non–subject drop languages). This means that the two parametric options license *intersecting* sets of sentences.

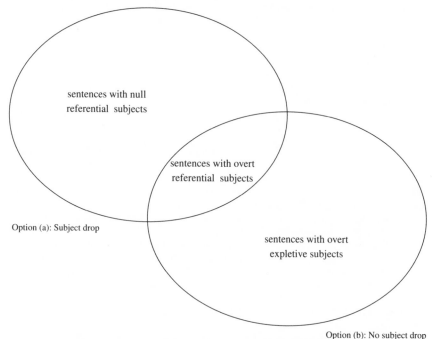

7. We simplify slightly here, since the second option proposed by Rizzi (1982) adds the stipulation that S′ (or CP), the category consisting of the *wh* word and the S to its right, is a bounding node. For some criticism, see Truscott and Wexler (1989).

8. A potential problem for Lightfoot's proposal stems from the fact that children learning English are exposed to sentences such as (i), which seems to resemble the crucial French sentences in the relevant respects.

(i)   Which pictures [$_S$ did Mary take [$_{NP}$ __ of John]?

Yet, we do not want the acquisition device to conclude that S is not a bounding node in English, since this will give the wrong results for the *wh* island cases.

Chapter Fourteen

1. This use of the term 'functor' is unrelated to its use in some of Slobin's operating principles (see section 3).

2. Of course, this assumes that the acquisition device is able to identify the morphemes that express tense and aspect in the language to which it is exposed. This problem arises in all theories of acquisition independently of the issue of category development.

3. The criterion of compatibility with a deictic gives a notion of individuatability broad enough to encompass both count and mass nouns (e.g., *this water, that car,* etc.). This notion should not be confused with that of 'individual', which is used in a somewhat more restrictive sense by Gordon (1985), Bloom (1994), and others to refer to the denotations of count nouns only. On this view, compatibility with the determiner *a* rather than with a deictic such as *this* or *that* is the crucial criterion for class membership. Although I take countability to entail individuatability, the converse is not true.

4. Languages also have deictic expressions such as *here/there* and *now/then* that occur with verbs rather than nouns. However, there seems to be an important difference. When I say *I slept here,* I am not using the deictic to distinguish between two 'sleeping events', one here and another someplace else; rather, I am simply indicating the place where I slept.

5. Various matters remain to be worked out. For example, according to this analysis, words such as *mere* and *utter* cannot be adjectives since they are not subject to gradation. Given their special properties (for example, they cannot occur with a copula verb—**The fact is mere*), this conclusion is perhaps not unacceptable. Also problematic is the fact that adjectives can occur with an apparent deictic in structures such as *The car was this/that blue.* However, the role of the deictic here seems closer to gradation than to individuation.

O'Grady (1996) discusses the status of the tense-bearing modifiers that are common in languages such as Korean and Japanese, arguing that the acquisition device assigns them to a hybrid 'adjectival verb' category.

6. For now, I ignore the question of how phrases are to be categorized. The intuitive idea is that the 'complex concepts' corresponding to phrases are classified in terms of the same three-way contrast used for words. Given that the result of specifying a property of an individual is still an individual, a phrase such as *black sheep* will be assigned to the N category, as desired. Further assuming that specifying the participants and properties of an event leaves an event, phrases such as *eat noodles* and *John eats noodles* should both be treated as categories of the V type just as *eat* is. (See Ninio 1988: 116 and O'Grady in press for independent elaborations of this proposal.)

7. Marantz (1984: 196 ff.) argues that in some languages a transitive verb combines with the agent argument before the theme. This suggests that the argument hierarchy is not innate.

8. In languages that use case marking rather than word order to encode grammatical relations, the last argument can be identified by its case affix rather than its linear position. Special problems arise in 'ergative' languages, in which the subject of an intransitive verb does not bear the same case marker as the subject of a transitive verb. I will not try to resolve this problem here; see Pye (1990) for some discussion.

9. What this means technically is that the 'functor index' associated with the reflexive consists of two parts, a variable and a function. The latter element ultimately applies to a basic index, assigning the value of that index to the variable. (A proposal not unlike this is put forward by Reinhart and Reuland 1992: 286.) Letting 'i' stand for the basic index, 'F' for the function, and 'x' for the variable:

(i) $i + [Fx]$
          $\Downarrow$
          i

In other words, a functor index x takes on the value of a basic index i following combination.

10. I will not take a position here on how to deal with ordinary pronominals such as *he* and *him.* One possibility is that they too introduce interpretive dependencies, but that these dependencies can be satisfied either by the grammar (in which case the antecedent must be higher, just as it is for

reflexives) or by pragmatic mechanisms (in which case the Prominence Requirement would be inapplicable). This gives a system similar to the one proposed within GB by Grodzinsky and Reinhart (1993); see chapter 11.

11. Recently, the conventional view of UG has been called into question by those traditionally committed to special nativism in its strongest form. Within the 'Minimalist Program' (e.g., Chomsky 1993) that has grown out of GB theory, explanatory principles focus on the notion of economy, demanding 'short moves' that are postponed for as long as possible ('Procrastinate') and that take place only to satisfy requirements of the moved element itself ('Greed'). Such principles are broadly computational in character and do not draw on conventional syntactic notions such as 'subject', 'governing category', 'bounding node', and so forth. In this, they are very unlike the inventory of principles making up the sort of Universal Grammar posited in the first thirty-five years of work in the special nativist tradition and seem compatible, in spirit at least, with the version of general nativism adopted here.

Chapter Fifteen

1. Borer and Wexler adopt a 'movement' analysis of true passives in which the theme NP moves from direct object position in deep structure to subject position in surface structure. They assume (1987:149) that maturation must provide a mechanism capable of forming a 'chain' (consisting of the moved NP and its trace) to which a thematic role can be assigned.

2. As (i) shows, inverted auxiliaries 'land' in the empty complementizer position, while fronted *wh* words are placed in the specifier position (C = complementizer).

(i)

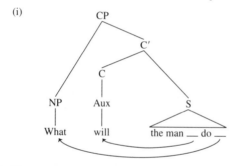

3. These findings seems at least partly at odds with those reported by Clahsen (1986); see chapter 4, section 1. For an alternative analysis of Poeppel and Wexler's data, see Ingram and Thompson (1996).

4. Radford endorses Fukui's account of the difference between English and Japanese (1990:225). However, John Whitman (pers. comm.) notes that he later hedges somewhat on his commitment to Fukui's analysis of Japanese, especially as it pertains to complementizers (p. 273).

The applicability of Fukui's analysis to Korean is not universally accepted. For example, Yoon (1992) argues that Korean has a DP category, although he treats demonstratives as specifiers rather than heads of this projection. (Thus, demonstratives are not themselves taken to be determiners.) Of course, if the Korean morphemes considered here were true syntactic determiners, the data we have presented could no longer be used to choose between the semantic and UG theories.

5. The fact that *here* and *there* as well as pronominal *this* and *that* are acquired relatively early (see above) suggests that deicticity alone cannot account for the late acquisition of the elements we have been considering. At least part of the reason for the difficulty of demonstrative determiners on the meaning-based account must lie in the semantics of the determiner relation.

6. An important issue that arises here, pointed out to me by Kevin Gregg (pers. comm.), has to do with the relationship between the Conservatism Law (chap. 14, section 4) and the Developmental Law. As things now stand, there is a potential conflict between the two principles in that the Conservatism Law seems to require the acquisition device to use the full set of notions relevant to pronoun interpre-

tation (i.e., 'antecedent', 'precedence', and 'minimal XP') in order to ensure the most restrictive generalization possible, while the Developmental Law apparently forces it to use a smaller (cumulatively less complex) set of notions in the initial developmental step(s). One possibility is that this tension is resolved in favor of the Developmental Law. On this view, intermediate developmental stages occur as the acquisition device adds one notion at a time to its formulation of specific principles (consistent with the criterion of cumulative complexity), but each of these formulations would represent the most conservative generalization allowed by those notions and consistent with experience.

7. One possibility is that the two developmental profiles reflect different ways of resolving the tension between the Conservatism Law and the Developmental Law (see n. 6). Where the Conservatism Law is favored, development takes place in a single step; where the Developmental Law is favored, intermediate developmental stages make their appearance.

Chapter Sixteen

1. Bower (1994:347) disputes this, noting that studies by Judith Johnston show that this type of disorder is "linked to deficits on reasoning skills and delays of 1 to 5 years in developing counting skills." Symbolic play is also reported to be less frequent than among unimpaired children. On the other hand, Gopnik (1990b:143) observes that one of her subjects (from a different family) was well "beyond his age level in mathematics and . . . an avid hacker."

2. A curious feature of some WS children is a fondness for unusual words ('hyperlexia'). Asked to name a set of animals, a WS child may give a list that includes *unicorn, yak, ibex, koala,* and *water buffalo* (Pinker 1994b:53).

Glossary

The following brief glossary offers simple definitions for some of the terms and concepts that this book assumes familiarity with. Other technical notions are defined in the text itself upon first presentation.

adjunct: an optional element such as an adverb, an adjective, or a relative clause that denotes properties of the head with which it combines.

agent: the thematic role label reserved for the instigator of an action.

argument: an element denoting an entity or location whose existence is implied by the meaning of a head. For example, the verb *put* has the type of meaning that implies three arguments—an agent, a theme, and a location.

complement: a nonsubject argument.

control: the relation between an NP in a matrix clause and the understood subject of a lower clause whose reference it determines (e.g., in the sentence *John tried to leave, John* is the controller for the unexpressed subject of the infinitival verb).

direct object: the NP complement of a transitive verb.

ergative: the term used for a relation involving only the subject of a transitive verb. Some languages reserve a special case form, agreement morphology, or word order pattern for this relation.

goal: the thematic role label reserved for the end point of a movement or transfer (usually marked by the preposition *to* in English).

head: the word serving as the syntactic nucleus of a phrase (e.g., nouns are the heads of NPs, verbs are the heads of VPs, so on).

intransitive: the category of verbs that take a single NP argument.

MLU (mean length of utterance): the average length of a child's utterances, usually computed in morphemes over a set of at least 100 utterances.

passive: A sentence type built around a verb taking at least two arguments, one of which is an agent that is either suppressed or realized as an oblique and the other of which is realized as subject (e.g., *This house was painted by professionals*).

reversible sentence: A sentence whose component NPs can be reversed without yielding an ungrammatical or nonsensical result (e.g., *The car pushed the truck*).

source: the thematic role label reserved for the starting point for a movement or transfer (often marked by *from* in English).

specifier: in some contemporary theories of syntactic structure, an element occupying the position that is immediately beneath XP and a sister of X′ (the genitive occupies such a position in the phrase *Marvin's recollection of the event*).

subject: The NP that combines with a verbal phrase to yield a sentence.

thematic (theta) **roles:** the labels used to distinguish among the various entities, locations, and times making up the situation described by a sentence (e.g., agent, theme, location, etc.).

theme (patient): the thematic role label reserved for an entity that is affected by an action or to whom a property is attributed (e.g., *Harry* in *The wind knocked Harry down* or *Harry is humble*).

transitive: the category of verbs that take two NP arguments.

References

Akmajian, Adrian, and Frank Heny. 1975. *An introduction to principles of transformational syntax.* Cambridge: MIT Press.

Aldridge, Michelle. 1989. The acquisition of INFL. Bloomington: Indiana University Linguistic Club.

Anderson, Stephen, and Edward Keenan. 1985. Deixis. In *Language typology and syntactic description,* ed. T. Shopen, Vol. 3: *Grammatical categories and the lexicon,* 259–308. New York: Cambridge University Press.

Angiolillo, Carl, and Susan Goldin-Meadow. 1982. Experimental evidence for agent–patient categories in child language. *Journal of Child Language* 9:627–44.

Ardery, Gail. 1980. On coordination in child language. *Journal of Child Language* 7: 305–20.

Atkinson, Martin. 1982. *Explanations in the study of child language development.* Cambridge: Cambridge University Press.

———. 1985. How linguistic is the one-word stage? In *Children's single-word speech,* ed. M. Barrett, 289–312. New York: Wiley.

———. 1992. *Children's syntax: An introduction to principles and parameters theory.* Cambridge, Mass.: Blackwell.

Au, Terry Kit-Fong, Mirella Dapretto, and You-Kyung Song. 1994. Input vs. constraints: Early word acquisition in Korean and English. *Journal of Memory and Language* 33:567–82.

Authier, J.-Marc. 1991. V-governed expletives, Case theory, and the Projection Principle. *Linguistic Inquiry* 22:721–40.

Bach, Emmon. 1979. Control in Montague grammar. *Linguistic Inquiry* 10:515–31.

———. 1981. Discontinuous constituents in generalized categorial grammars. *Proceedings of the North East Linguistic Society* 11:1–12.

———. 1983. Generalized categorial grammars and the English auxiliary. In *Linguistic categories: Auxiliaries and related puzzles,* ed. F. Heny and B. Richards, 2:101–20. Dordrecht: Reidel.

———. 1988. Categorial grammars as theories of language. In *Categorial grammars and natural language structures,* ed. R. Oehrle, E. Bach, and D. Wheeler, 17–34. Dordrecht: Reidel.

Baker, C. L. 1979. Syntactic theory and the projection problem. *Linguistic Inquiry* 10: 533–82.

Baldie, Brian. 1976. The acquisition of the passive voice. *Journal of Child Language* 3:331–48.

Barrett, Martyn. 1982. The holophrastic hypothesis: Conceptual and empirical issues. *Cognition* 11:47–76.

Barret, Martyn, ed. 1985. *Children's single-word speech.* New York: Wiley.

Bar-Hillel, Yehoshua. 1953. A quasi-arithmetical notation for syntactic description. *Language* 29:47–58.

Bates, Elizabeth, Inge Bretherton, and Lynn Snyder. 1988. *From first words to grammar: Individual differences and dissociable mechanisms.* Cambridge: Cambridge University Press.

Bates, Elizabeth, and Brian MacWhinney. 1979. A functionalist approach to the acquisition of grammar. In *Developmental pragmatics,* ed. E. Ochs and B. Schieffelin, 167–211. New York: Academic Press.

———. 1987. Competition, variation, and language learning. In *Mechanisms of language acquisition,* ed. B. MacWhinney, 157–93. Hillsdale, N.J.: Erlbaum.

———. 1988. What is functionalism? *Papers and Reports on Child Language Development* 27:137–52.

Bates, Elizabeth, Virginia Marchman, Donna Thal, Larry Fenson, Philip Dale, Steven Reznick, Judy Reilly, and Jeff Hartung. 1994. Developmental and stylistic variation in the composition of early vocabulary. *Journal of Child Language* 21:85–123.

Bellugi, Ursula. 1967. The acquisition of negation. Ph.D. diss., Harvard University.

———. 1971. Simplification in children's language. In *Language acquisition: Models and methods,* ed. R. Huxley and E. Ingram, 95–119. New York: Academic Press.

Bellugi, Ursula, Amy Birhle, and David Corina. 1991. Linguistic and spatial development: Dissociations between cognitive domains. In *Biological and behavioral determinants of language development,* ed. N. Krasnegor, D. Rumbaugh, R. Schiefelbusch, and M. Studdert-Kennedy, 363–93. Hillsdale, N.J.: Erlbaum.

Benedict, Helen. 1979. Early lexical development: Comprehension and production. *Journal of Child Language* 6:183–200.

Berwick, Robert. 1985. *The acquisition of syntactic knowledge.* Cambridge: MIT Press.

Bever, Thomas. 1970. The cognitive basis for linguistic structures. In *Cognition and the development of language,* ed. J. R. Hayes, 274–353. New York: Wiley.

Bickerton, Derek. 1981. *Roots of language.* Ann Arbor: Karoma.

———. 1984. The language bioprogram hypothesis. *Behavioral and Brain Sciences* 7:173–221.

———. 1990. *Language and species.* Chicago: University of Chicago Press.

———. 1991. The pace of syntactic acquisition. *Proceedings of the Berkeley Linguistics Society* 17:41–52.

Birdsong, David. 1989. *Metalinguistic performance and interlinguistic competence.* New York: Springer-Verlag.

Bloom, Lois. 1970. *Language development: Form and function in emerging grammars.* Cambridge: MIT Press.

———. 1973. *One word at a time* (Janua linguarum, Series minor 154). The Hague: Mouton.

———. 1991. *Language development from two to three.* New York: Cambridge University Press.

Bloom, Lois, and Lorraine Harner. 1989. On the developmental contour of child language: A reply to Smith & Weist. *Journal of Child Language* 16:207–16.

Bloom, Lois, Margaret Lahey, Lois Hood, Karin Lifter, and Kathleen Fiess. 1980. Complex sentences: Acquisition of syntactic connectives and the semantic relations they encode. *Journal of Child Language* 7:235–62.

Bloom, Lois, Karin Lifter, and Jeremie Hafitz. 1980. Semantics of verbs and the development of verb inflection in child language. *Language* 56:386–412.

Bloom, Lois, Patsy Lightbown, and Lois Hood. 1975. *Structure and variation in child language* (Monographs of the Society for Research in Child Development 40).

Bloom, Lois, Susan Merkin, and Janet Wootten. 1982. Wh-questions: Linguistic factors that contribute to the sequence of acquisition. *Child Development* 53: 1084–92.

Bloom, Lois, Peggy Miller, and Lois Hood. 1975. Variation and reduction as aspects of competence in language development. In *The 1974 Minnesota Symposium on Child Psychology,* ed. A. Pick, 3–55. Minneapolis: University of Minnesota Press.

Bloom, Lois, Matthew Rispoli, Barbara Gartner, and Jeremie Hafitz. 1989. Acquisition of complementation. *Journal of Child Language* 16: 101–20.

Bloom, Lois, Jo Tackeff, and Margaret Lahey. 1984. Learning *to* in complement constructions. *Journal of Child Language* 11: 391–406.

Bloom, Paul. 1990a. Subjectless sentences in child language. *Linguistic Inquiry* 21: 491–504.

———. 1990b. Syntactic distinctions in child language. *Journal of Child Language* 17: 343–56.

———. 1993. Grammatical continuity in language development: The case of subjectless sentences. *Linguistic Inquiry* 24: 721–34.

———. 1994. Possible names: The role of syntax–semantics mappings in the acquisition of nominals. *Lingua* 92: 297–329.

———. to appear. Theories of word learning: Rationalist alternatives to associationism. In *Handbook of language acquisition,* ed. W. Ritchie and T. Bhatia. San Diego: Academic Press.

Bloom, Paul, Andrew Barss, Janet Nicol, and Laura Conway. 1994. Children's knowledge of binding and coreference: Evidence from spontaneous speech. *Language* 70: 53–71.

Bloomfield, Leonard. 1926. A set of postulates for the science of language. *Language* 2: 153–64.

———. 1933. *Language.* New York: Holt, Rinehart and Winston.

Bohannon, John, and Laura Stanowicz. 1988. The issue of negative evidence: Adult responses to children's language errors. *Developmental Psychology* 24, 684–89.

Bohannon, John, Brian MacWhinney, and Catherine Snow. 1990. No negative evidence revisited: Beyond learnability or who has to prove what to whom. *Developmental Psychology* 26: 221–26.

Borer, Hagit, and Kenneth Wexler. 1987. The maturation of syntax. In *Parameter setting,* ed. T. Roeper and E. Williams, 123–72. Dordrecht: Reidel.

Bower, Bruce. 1994. Language without rules. *Science News* 145: 346–47.

Bowerman, Melissa. 1973. *Early syntactic development: A cross-linguistic study with special reference to Finnish.* New York: Cambridge University Press.

———. 1979. The acquisition of complex sentences. In *Language Acquisition,* ed. P. Fletcher and M. Garman, 285–306. New York: Cambridge University Press.

———. 1985. What shapes children's grammars? In D. Slobin (ed.), *The crosslinguistic study of language acquisition,* vol. 2: *Theoretical issues.* Hillsdale, NJ: Erlbaum. Pp. 1257–1314.

———. 1987. Why don't children end up with an overly general grammar? In *Mechanisms of language acquisition,* ed. B. MacWhinney, 443–66. Hillsdale, N.J.: Erlbaum.

Bowers, John. 1993. The syntax of predication. *Linguistic Inquiry* 24:591–656.

Braine, Martin. 1963. The ontogeny of English phrase structure: The first phase. *Language* 39:1–13.

———. 1971. The acquisition of language in infant and child. In *The learning of language,* ed. C. E. Reed, 7–95. New York: Appleton-Century-Crofts.

———. 1973. Three suggestions regarding grammatical analyses of children's language. In *Studies of child language development,* ed. C. Ferguson and D. Slobin, 421–29. New York: Holt Rinehart and Winston.

———. 1976. *Children's first word combinations* (Monographs of the Society for Research in Child Development 41 [serial no. 164, no. 1]).

———. 1987. What is learned in acquiring word classes—a step toward an acquisition theory. In *Mechanisms of language acquisition,* ed. B. MacWhinney, 65–87. New York: Erlbaum.

———. 1992. What sort of innate structure in needed to "bootstrap" into syntax? *Cognition* 45:77–100.

———. 1994. Is nativism sufficient? *Journal of Child Language* 21:9–31.

Braine, Martin, and Judith Hardy. 1982. On what case categories there are, why they are, and how they develop: An amalgam of a priori considerations, speculation, and evidence from children. In *Language acquisition: The state of the art,* ed. E. Wanner and L. Gleitman, 219–39. New York: Cambridge University Press.

Branigan, George. 1976. Sequences of single words as structured units. *Stanford Papers and Reports on Child Language Development* 11:60–70.

Bresnan, Joan. 1982. The passive in lexical theory. In *The mental representation of grammatical relations,* ed. J. Bresnan, 3–86. Cambridge: MIT Press.

Bresnan, Joan, and Lioba Moshi. 1990. Object asymmetries in comparative Bantu syntax. *Linguistic Inquiry* 21:147–85.

Bretherton, Inge, Sandra McNew, Lynn Snyder, and Elizabeth Bates. 1983. Individual differences at 20 months: Analytic and holistic strategies in language acquisition. *Journal of Child Language* 10:293–320.

Brown, H. Douglas. 1971. Children's comprehension of relativized English sentences. *Child Development* 42:1923–36.

Brown, Roger. 1957. Linguistic determinism and the part of speech. *Journal of Abnormal and Social Psychology* 55:1–5.

———. 1968. The development of *wh* questions in child speech. *Journal of Verbal Learning and Verbal Behavior* 7:277–90.

———. 1973. *A first language: The early stages.* Cambridge: Harvard University Press.

———. 1977. Introduction. In *Talking to children: Language input and acquisition,* ed. C. Snow and C. Ferguson, 1–27. New York: Cambridge University Press.

Brown, Roger, and Colin Fraser. 1963. The acquisition of syntax. In *Verbal behavior and learning: Problems and processes,* ed. C. Cofer and B. Musgrave, 158–201. New York: McGraw-Hill.

Brown, Roger, and Camille Hanlon. 1970. Derivational complexity and order of acquisition in child speech. In *Cognition and the development of language,* ed. J. R. Hayes, 11–53. New York: Wiley.

Budwig, Nancy. 1989a. Do young children linguistically encode the notion of agent? *Papers and Reports on Child Language Development* 29:133–40.

———. 1989b. The linguistic marking of agentivity and control in child language. *Journal of Child Language* 16:263–84.

———. 1990a. A functional approach to the acquisition of personal pronouns. In *Children's language*, ed. G. Conti-Ramsden and C. Snow, 121–45. Hillsdale, N.J.: Erlbaum.

———. 1990b. Do children linguistically encode the notion of agent? *Papers and Reports on Child Language Development* 29:133–40.

———. 1990c. The linguistic marking of non-prototypical agency: an exploration into children's uses of passives. *Linguistics* 28:1221–52.

Budwig, Nancy, and Angela Wiley. 1991. The contribution of caregivers' input to children's talk about agency and pragmatic control. Paper presented to the Child Language Seminar, University of Manchester.

Cairns, Helen, and Jennifer Ryan Hsu. 1978. *Who, why, when,* and *how:* A developmental study. *Journal of Child Language* 5:477–88.

Cairns, Helen, Dana McDaniel, Jennifer Ryan, and Michelle Rapp. 1994. A longitudinal study of principles of control and pronominal reference in child English. *Language* 70:260–88.

Cambon, Jacqueline, and Hermine Sinclair. 1974. Relations between syntax and semantics: Are they 'easy to see'? *British Journal of Psychology* 65:133–40.

Carden, Guy. 1986. Blocked forwards coreference: Theoretical implications of the acquisition data. In *Studies in the acquisition of anaphora,* vol. 1: *Defining the constraints,* ed. B. Lust, 319–57. Boston: Reidel.

Cazden, Courtney. 1968. The acquisition of noun and verb inflections. *Child Development* 39:433–48.

———. 1972. *Child language and education.* New York: Holt, Rinehart and Winston.

Chiat, Shulamuth. 1981. Context-specificity and generalization in the acquisition of pronominal distinctions. *Journal of Child Language* 8:75–91.

Chien, Yu-Chin, and Kenneth Wexler. 1990. Children's knowledge of locality conditions in binding as evidence for the modularity of syntax and pragmatics. *Language Acquisition* 1:225–95.

———. 1991. Children's knowledge of pronouns as bound variables in a long distance context. *Papers and Reports on Child Language Development* 30:25–38.

Cho, Sook Whan. 1981. The acquisition of word order in Korean. M.A. thesis, University of Calgary.

Choi, Soonja, and Alison Gopnik. 1993. Nouns are not always learned before verbs in Korean: An early verb explosion. Paper presented at the 25th Child Language Forum. Stanford University.

Chomsky, Carol. 1969. *The acquisition of syntax in children from 5 to 10.* Cambridge: MIT Press.

———. 1972. Stages in language development and reading exposure. *Harvard Educational Review* 42:1–33.

———. 1982. 'Ask' and 'tell' revisited: A reply to Warden. *Journal of Child Language* 9:667–78.

Chomsky, Noam. 1965. *Aspects of the theory of syntax.* Cambridge: MIT Press.

———. 1966. *Topics in the theory of generative grammar* (Janua linguarum, Series minor 56). The Hague: Mouton.

————. 1972. *Language and mind*. Enlarged edition. New York: Harcourt Brace Jovanovich.

————. 1975. *Reflections on language*. New York: Pantheon.

————. 1977. *Essays on form and interpretation*. New York: Elsevier North-Holland.

————. 1981. *Lectures on government and binding*. Dordrecht: Foris.

————. 1986a. *Barriers*. Cambridge: MIT Press.

————. 1986b. *Knowledge of language: Its nature, origin, and use*. New York: Praeger.

————. 1993. A minimalist program for linguistic theory. In *The view from Building 20*, ed. K. Hale and S. Keyser, 1–52. Cambridge: MIT Press.

Chomsky, Noam, and Howard Lasnik. 1977. Filters and control. *Linguistic Inquiry* 8:425–504.

Clahsen, Harald. 1986. Verb inflections in German child language: Acquisition of agreement markings and the functions they encode. *Linguistics* 24:79–121.

————. 1992. Learnability theory and the problem of development in language acquisition. In *Theoretical issues in language acquisition*, ed. J. Weissenborn, H. Goodluck, and T. Roeper, 53–76. Hillsdale, N.J.: Erlbaum.

Clahsen, Harald, Sonja Eisenbeiss, and Anne Vainikka. 1994. The seeds of structure: A syntactic analysis of the acquisition of case marking. In *Language acquisition studies in generative grammar*, ed. T. Hoekstra and B. Schwartz, 85–118. Philadelphia: John Benjamins.

Clancy, Patricia. 1985. The acquisition of Japanese. In *The crosslinguistic study of language acquisition*, vol. 1: *The data*, ed. D. Slobin, 373–524. Hillsdale, N.J.: Erlbaum.

————. 1989. Form and function in the acquisition of Korean wh-questions. *Journal of Child Language* 16:323–47.

Clancy, Patricia, Hyeonjin Lee, and Myeong-Han Zoh. 1986. Processing strategies in the acquisition of relative clauses: Universal principles and language-specific realizations. *Cognition* 24:225–62.

Clark, Eve. 1971. On the acquisition of the meaning of *before* and *after*. *Journal of Verbal Learning and Verbal Behavior* 10:266–75.

————. 1983. Meanings and concepts. In *Handbook of child psychology*, ed. P. Mussen, 3:787–840. 4th ed. New York: Wiley.

————. 1987. The Principle of Contrast: A constraint on language acquisition. In *Mechanisms of language acquisition*, ed. B. MacWhinney, 1–34. Hillsdale, N.J.: Erlbaum.

Clark, Eve, and Kathie Carpenter. 1989. The notion of source in language acquisition. *Language* 65:1–30.

Clark, Herbert, and Eve Clark. 1977. *Psychology and language: An introduction to psycholinguistics*. New York: Harcourt Brace Jovanovich.

Clark, Robin. 1992. The selection of syntactic knowledge. *Language acquisition* 2:83–149.

Cocking, Rodney, and Susan McHale. 1981. A comparative study of the use of pictures and objects in assessing children's receptive and productive language. *Journal of Child Language* 8:1–13.

Coker, Pamela. 1978. Syntactic and semantic factors in the acquisition of *before* and *after*. *Journal of Child Language* 5:262–77.

Cole, Peter, and Li-May Sung. 1994. Head movement and long-distance reflexives. *Linguistic Inquiry* 25:355–406.

Collins, Chris. 1994. Economy of derivation and the Generalized Proper Binding Condition. *Linguistic Inquiry* 25:45–61.

Cook, V. J. 1976. A note on indirect objects. *Journal of Child Language* 3:435–38.

Corder, Stephen Pit. 1967. The significance of learners' errors. *International Review of Applied Linguistics* 5:161–70.

Crain, Stephen, and Janet Fodor. 1984. On the innateness of subjacency. *Proceedings of the Eastern States Conference on Linguistics* 1:191–204.

Crain, Stephen, and Cecile McKee. 1986. Acquisition of structural restrictions on anaphora. *Proceedings of the North East Linguistic Society* 16:91–110.

Crain, Stephen, and Mineharu Nakayama. 1987. Structure dependence in grammar formation. *Language* 63:522–43.

Crain, Stephen, and Rosalind Thornton. 1991. Recharting the course of language acquisition: Studies in elicited production. In *Biological and behavioral determinants of language development,* ed. N. Krasnegor, D. Rumbaugh, R. Schiefelbusch, and M. Studdert-Kennedy, 321–37. Hillsdale, N.J.: Erlbaum.

Croft, William. 1991. *Syntactic categories and grammatical relations: The cognitive organization of information.* Chicago: University of Chicago Press.

Cromer, Richard. 1970. Children are nice to understand: Surface structure clues for the recovery of deep structure. *British Journal of Psychology* 61:397–408.

———. 1972. The learning of surface structure clues to deep structure by a puppet show technique. *Quarterly Journal of Experimental Psychology* 24:66.

———. 1974. Child and adult learning of surface structure clues to deep structure using a picture card technique. *Journal of Psycholinguistic Research* 3:1–14.

———. 1987. Language growth with experience without feedback. *Journal of Psycholinguistic Research* 16:223–31.

Cross, Toni. 1977. Mothers' speech adjustments: the contribution of selected child listener variables. In *Talking to children: Language input and acquisition,* ed. C. Snow and C. Ferguson, 151–88. Cambridge: Cambridge University Press.

Dale, Philip. 1972. *Language Development: Structure and function.* Hinsdale, Ill.: Dryden Press.

Davis, Henry. 1986. Syntactic undergeneration in the acquisition of English: WH-questions and the ECP. *Proceedings of the North East Linguistic Society* 16:111–25.

Day, Christopher. 1973. *The Jacaltec language.* Bloomington: Indiana University Press.

de Villiers, Jill. 1980. The process of rule learning in child speech: A new look. In *Children's language,* vol. 2, ed. K. E. Nelson, 1–44. New York: Gardner Press.

———. 1991. Why questions? In *Papers in the acquisition of WH,* ed. T. Maxfield and B. Plunkett, 155–73. Amherst: University of Massachusetts, Department of Linguistics, GLSA Publications.

de Villiers, Jill, and Peter de Villiers. 1973. Development of the use of word order in comprehension. *Journal of Psycholinguistic Research* 2:331–41.

———. 1978. *Language acquisition.* Cambridge: Harvard University Press.

de Villiers, Jill, Helen Tager Flusberg, Kenji Hakuta, and Michael Cohen. 1979. Children's comprehension of relative clauses. *Journal of Psycholinguistic Research* 8:499–528.

de Villiers, Jill, and Thomas Roeper. 1995. Barriers, binding, and acquisition of the DP–NP distinction. *Language Acquisition* 4:73–104.

de Villiers, Jill, Thomas Roeper, and Anne Vainikka. 1990. The acquisition of long-distance rules. In *Language processing and language acquisition,* ed. L. Frazier and J. de Villiers, 257–97. Dordrecht: Kluwer.

Demetras, M. J., Kathryn Post, and Catherine Snow. 1986. Feedback to first language learners: The role of repetitions and clarification questions. *Journal of Child Language* 13:275–92.

Demuth, Katherine. 1989. Maturation and the acquisition of the Sesotho passive. *Language* 65:56–80.

———. 1992. Accessing functional categories in Sesotho: Interactions at the morphosyntax interface. In *The acquisition of verb placement: Functional categories and V2 phenomena in language development,* ed. J. Meisel, 83–107. Dordrecht: Kluwer.

———. 1994. Early underspecification of functional categories. In *Syntactic theory and first language acquisition: Cross-linguistic perspectives,* vol. 1: *Heads, projections, and learnability,* ed. B. Lust, M. Suñer, and J. Whitman, 119–34. Hillsdale, NJ: Erlbaum.

———. 1995. Questions, relatives, and minimal projection. *Language Acquisition* 4:49–71.

Déprez, Viviane, and Amy Pierce. 1993. Negation and functional projections in early grammar. *Linguistic Inquiry* 24:25–67.

Derwing, Bruce. 1973. *Transformational grammar as a theory of language acquisition.* New York: Cambridge University Press.

Dixon, R. M. W. 1982. *Where have all the adjectives gone?* (Janua linguarum, Series maior 107) The Hague: Mouton.

Dore, John, Margery Franklin, Robert Miller, and Andrya Ramer. 1976. Transitional phenomena in early language acquisition. *Journal of Child Language* 3:13–29.

Dowty, D. 1982. Grammatical relations and Montague Grammar. In *The nature of syntactic representation,* ed. P. Jacobs and G. Pullum, 79–130. Dordrecht: Reidel.

Drozd, Kenneth. 1995. Child English pre-sentential negation as metalinguistic exclamatory negation. *Journal of Child Language* 22:583–610.

Dryer, Matthew. 1992. The Greenbergian word order correlations. *Language* 68, 81–138.

Eckman, Fred. 1996. On evaluating arguments for special nativism in second language acquisition theory. *Second Language Research* 17: 398–419.

Eimas, Peter. 1974. Linguistic processing of speech by young infants. In *Language perspectives—Acquisition, retardation, and intervention,* ed. R. Schiefelbusch and L. Lloyd, 55–73. Baltimore: University Park Press.

Eisenberg, Sarita, and Helen Cairns. 1994. The development of infinitives from three to five. *Journal of Child Language* 21:713–31.

Emonds, Joseph. 1991. Subcategorization and syntax-based theta role assignment. *Natural Language and Linguistic Theory* 9:369–429.

Erreich, Anne. 1984. Learning how to ask: patterns of inversion in *yes–no* questions and WH questions. *Journal of Child Language* 11:579–92.

Erreich, Anne, Virginia Valian, and Judith Winzemer. 1980. Aspects of a theory of language acquisition. *Journal of Child Language* 7:157–79.

Ervin-Tripp, Susan. 1970. Discourse agreement: How children answer questions. In *Cognition and the development of language,* ed. B. Hayes, 79–107. New York: Wiley.

Fabian-Kraus, Veronica, and Paul Ammon. 1980. Assessing linguistic competence: When are children hard to understand? *Journal of Child Language* 7:401–12.

Farrar, Michael. 1992. Negative evidence and grammatical morpheme acquisition. *Developmental Psychology* 28:90–98.

Fay, David. 1978. Transformations as mental operations: A reply to Kuczaj. *Journal of Child Language* 5:143–49.

Felix, Sascha. 1987. *Cognition and language growth.* Dordrecht: Foris.

———. 1988. Universal Grammar in language acquisition. *Canadian Journal of Linguistics* 33:367–93.

———. 1992. Language acquisition as a maturational hypothesis. In *Theoretical issues in language acquisition,* ed. J. Weissenborn, H. Goodluck, and T. Roeper, 25–51. Hillsdale, N.J.: Erlbaum.

Ferguson, Charles. 1977. Baby talk as a simplified register. In *Talking to children: Language input and acquisition,* ed. C. Snow and C. Ferguson, 219–35. New York: Cambridge University Press.

Fernald, Ann. 1992. Human maternal vocalizations to infants as biologically relevant signals: An evolutionary perspective. In *Evolutionary psychology and the generation of culture,* ed. J. Barkow, L. Cosmides, and J. Tooby, 391–428. New York: Oxford University Press.

Fernald, Ann, and Hiromi Morikawa. 1993. Common themes and cultural variations in Japanese and American mothers' speech to infants. *Child Development* 64:637–56.

Flavell, J. 1972. An analysis of cognitive-developmental sequences. *Genetic Psychology Monographs* 86:279–350.

Flynn, Suzanne, and Barbara Lust. 1980. Acquisition of relative clauses: Developmental changes in their heads. *Cornell University Working Papers in Linguistics* 1:33–45.

Fodor, Janet Dean. 1992. Islands, learnability and the lexicon. In *Island constraints,* ed. H. Goodluck and M. Rochemont, 109–80. Dordrecht: Kluwer.

———. 1994. How to obey the Subset Principle: Binding and locality. In *Syntactic theory and first language acquisition: Cross-linguistic perspectives,* vol. 2: *Binding, dependencies, and learnability,* ed. B. Lust, G. Hermon and J. Kornfilt, 429–51. Hillsdale, N.J.: Erlbaum.

Fodor, Jerry. 1975. *The language of thought.* New York: Crowell.

———. 1983. *Modularity of mind.* Cambridge: MIT Press.

Foster-Cohen, Susan. 1994. Exploring the boundary between syntax and pragmatics: Relevance and the binding of pronouns. *Journal of Child Language* 21:237–55.

Fox, Barbara. 1987. The Noun Phrase Accessibility Hierarchy revisited. *Language* 63:856–70.

Fraser, Colin, Ursula Bellugi, and Roger Brown. 1963. Control of grammar in imitation, comprehension and production. *Journal of Verbal Learning and Verbal Behavior* 2:121–35.

French, Ann. 1989. The systematic acquisition of word forms by a child during the first-fifty-word stage. *Journal of Child Language* 16:69–90.

Fukui, Naoki. 1986. A theory of category projection and its applications. Ph.D. diss., MIT.

Furrow, David, and Katherine Nelson. 1984. Environmental correlates of individual differences in language acquisition. *Journal of Child Language* 11:523–34.

Furrow, David, Katherine Nelson, and Helen Benedict. 1979. Mothers' speech to children and syntactic development: some simple relationships. *Journal of Child Language* 6:423–42.

Garman, Michael. 1979. Early grammatical development. In *Language acquisition,* ed. P. Fletcher and M. Garman, 177–208. New York: Cambridge University Press.

Gazdar, Gerald. 1981. Unbounded dependencies and coordinate structure. *Linguistic Inquiry* 12:155–84.

Gazdar, Gerald, Ewan Klein, Geoffrey Pullum, and Ivan Sag. 1985. *Generalized phrase structure grammar.* Cambridge: MIT Press.

Gentner, Dedre. 1982. Why nouns are learned before verbs: Linguistic relativity vs. natural partitioning. In *Language development,* vol. 2: *Language, cognition and culture,* ed. S. Kuczaj, 301–34. Hillsdale, N.J.: Erlbaum.

Gerken, LouAnn. 1991. The metrical basis for children's subjectless sentences. *Journal of Memory and Language* 30:431–51.

Givón, Talmy. 1984. *Syntax: A functional–typological introduction.* Vol. 1. Philadelphia: Benjamins.

Gleitman, Lila. 1981. Maturational determinants of language growth. *Cognition* 10:115–26.

———. 1990. The structural sources of verb meanings. *Language Acquisition* 1:3–55.

Gleitman, Lila, Elissa Newport, and Harry Gleitman. 1984. The current status of the motherese hypothesis. *Journal of Child Language* 11:43–79.

Gleitman, Lila, and Eric Wanner. 1982. Language acquisition: The state of the state of the art. In *Language acquisition: The state of the art,* ed. E. Wanner and L. Gleitman, 3–48. New York: Cambridge University Press.

Gold, E. 1967. Language identification in the limit. *Information and Control* 16:447–74.

Goldfield, Beverly. 1993. Noun bias in maternal speech to one-year-olds. *Journal of Child Language* 20:85–99.

Goldfield, Beverly, and Catherine Snow. 1985. Individual differences in language acquisition. In *The development of language,* ed. J. Gleason, 299–324. Columbus: Merrill.

Goldfield, Beverly, and J. Steven Reznick. 1990. Early lexical acquisition: Rate, content, and the vocabulary spurt. *Journal of Child Language* 17:171–83.

Goldin-Meadow, Susan, Martin Seligman, and Rochel Gelman. 1976. Language in the two-year-old. *Cognition* 4:189–202.

Golinkoff, Roberta, Carolyn Mervis, and Kathryn Hirsh-Pasek. 1994. Early object labels: The case for a developmental lexical principles framework. *Journal of Child Language* 21:125–55.

Goodluck, Helen. 1981. Children's grammar of complement–subject interpretation. In *Language acquisition and linguistic theory,* ed. S. Tavakolian, 139–66. Cambridge: MIT Press.

———. 1987. Children's interpretation of pronouns and null NPs. In *Studies in the acquisition of anaphora,* ed. B. Lust, vol. 2: *Applying the constraints,* 247–69. Boston: Reidel.

Goodluck, Helen, and Dawn Behne. 1992. Development in control and extraction. In *Theoretical issues in language acquisition,* ed. J. Wiessenborn, H. Goodluck, and T. Roeper, 151–71. Hillsdale, N.J.: Erlbaum.

Goodluck, Helen, Michele Foley, and Julie Sedivy. 1992. Adjunct islands and acquisition. In *Island constraints,* ed. H. Goodluck and M. Rochemont, 181–94. Dordrecht: Kluwer.

Goodluck, Helen, and Thomas Roeper. 1978. The acquisition of perception verb complements. In *Papers in the structure and development of child language* (University of Massachusetts Occasional Papers in Linguistics 4), ed. H. Goodluck and L. Solan, 85–104.

Goodluck, Helen, Julie Sedivy, and Michele Foley. 1989. WH-questions and extraction from temporal adjuncts: A case for movement. *Papers and Reports on Child Language Development* 28:123–30.

Goodluck, Helen, and Lawrence Solan. 1979. A reevaluation of the basic operations hypothesis. *Cognition* 7:85–91.

Goodluck, Helen, and Susan Tavakolian. 1982. Competence and processing in children's grammar of relative clauses. *Cognition* 11:1–27.

Gopnik, Myrna. 1990a. Dysphasia in an extended family. *Nature* 344:715.

Gopnik, Myrna. 1990b. Feature blindness: A case study. *Language Acquisition* 1:139–64.

Gopnik, Myrna, and Martha Crago. 1991. Familial aggregation of a developmental language disorder. *Cognition* 39:1–50.

Gordon, Peter. 1985. Evaluating the semantic categories hypothesis: The case of the count/mass distinction. *Cognition* 20:209–42.

———. 1988. Count/mass category acquisition: Distributional distinctions in children's speech. *Journal of Child Language* 15:109–28.

———. 1990. Learnability and feedback. *Developmental Psychology* 26:217–20.

Gordon, Peter, and Jill Chafetz. 1990. Verb-based versus class-based accounts of actionality effects in children's comprehension of passives. *Cognition* 36:227–54.

Greenberg, Joseph. 1963. Some universals of grammar with particular reference to the order of meaningful elements. In *Universals of language,* ed. J. Greenberg, 73–113. Cambridge: MIT Press.

Greenfield, Patricia, and Cathy Dent. 1982. Pragmatic factors in children's phrasal coordination. *Journal of Child Language* 9:425–44.

Greenfield, Patricia, Judy Reilly, Campbell Leaper, and Nancy Baker. 1985. The structural and functional status of single-word utterances and their relationship to early multi-word speech. In *Children's single-word speech,* ed. M. Barrett, 233–67. New York: Wiley & Sons.

Greenfield, Patricia, and Joshua Smith. 1976. *The structure of communication in early language development.* New York: Academic Press.

Grimshaw, Jane. 1981. Form, function, and the language acquisition device. In *The logical problem of language acquisition,* ed. C. Baker and J. McCarthy, 165–82. Cambridge: MIT Press.

Grimshaw, Jane, and Armin Mester. 1988. Light verbs and theta-marking. *Linguistic Inquiry* 19:205–32.

Grimshaw, Jane, and Sara Rosen. 1990. Knowledge and obedience: The developmental status of the binding theory. *Linguistic Inquiry* 21:187–222.

Grodzinsky, Yosef, and Tanya Reinhart. 1993. The innateness of binding and coreference. *Linguistic Inquiry* 24:69–101.

Gropen, Jess, Steven Pinker, Michelle Hollander, Richard Goldberg, and Ronald Wilson. 1989. The learnability and acquisition of the dative alternation in English. *Language* 65:203–55.

Gruber, Jeffrey. 1967. Topicalization in child language. *Foundations of Language* 3:37–65.

Guilfoyle, Eithne. 1984. The acquisition of tense and the emergence of lexical subjects in child grammars. *McGill Working Papers in Linguistics* 2.1:20–30.

Guilfoyle, Eithne, and Máire Noonan. 1992. Functional categories and language acquisition. *Canadian Journal of Linguistics* 37:241–73.

Guillaume, Gustave. 1973. *Principes de linguistique théorique.* Quebec: Presses de l'Université Laval.

Gundel, Jeanette, Nancy Hedberg, and Ron Zacharski. 1993. Cognitive status and the form of referring expressions. *Language* 69:274–307.

Gvozdev, Aleksandr. 1961. *Voprosyizucheniya detskoy rechi.* Moscow: Akademiya Pedagogicheskikh Nauk RSFSR.

Hakuta, Kenji. 1982. Grammatical description versus configurational arrangement in language acquisition: the case of relative clauses in Japanese. *Cognition* 9:197–236.

Hamburger, Henry. 1980. A deletion ahead of its time. *Cognition* 8:389–416.

Hamburger, Henry, and Stephen Crain. 1982. Relative acquisition. In *Language development,* vol. 1: *Syntax and semantics,* ed. S. Kuczaj II, 245–74. Hillsdale, N.J.: Erlbaum.

———. 1984. Acquisition of cognitive compiling. *Cognition* 17:85–136.

Hermon, Gabriella. 1992. Binding theory and parameter setting. *The Linguistic Review* 9:145–81.

———. 1994. Long-distance reflexives in UG: Theoretical approaches and predictions for acquisition. In *Syntactic theory and first language acquisition: Cross-linguistic perspectives,* vol. 2: *Binding, dependencies, and learnability,* ed. B. Lust, G. Hermon, and J. Kornfilt, 91–111. Hillsdale, N.J.: Erlbaum.

Hestvik, Arild. 1991. Subjectless binding domains. *Natural Language and Linguistic Theory* 9:455–96.

Hildebrand, Joyce. 1984. Markedness, acquisition, and preposition stranding: What are children born with? M.A. thesis, University of Calgary.

———. 1987. The acquisition of preposition stranding. *Canadian Journal of Linguistics* 32:65–85.

Hirsh-Pasek, Kathryn, and Roberta Golinkoff. 1991. Language comprehension: A new look at old themes. In *Biological and behavioral determinants of language development,* ed. N. Krasnegor, D. Rumbaugh, R. Schiefelbusch, and M. Studdert-Kennedy, 301–20. Hillsdale, N.J.: Erlbaum.

Hirsh-Pasek, Kathryn, Rebecca Treiman, and Maita Schneiderman. 1984. Brown & Hanlon revisited: Mothers' sensitivity to ungrammatical forms. *Journal of Child Language* 11:81–89.

Hochberg, Judith. 1986. Children's judgments of transitivity errors. *Journal of Child Language* 13:317–34.

Hopper, Paul, and Sandra Thompson. 1984. The discourse basis of lexical categories. *Language* 56:251–99.

Horgan, Dianne. 1978. The development of the full passive. *Journal of Child Language* 5:65–80.

———. 1981. Rate of language acquisition and noun emphasis. *Journal of Psycholinguistic Research* 10:629–40.

Hsu, Jennifer, Helen Cairns, Sarita Eisenberg, and Gloria Schlisselberg. 1989. Control and coreference in early child language. *Journal of Child Language* 16:599–622.

———. 1991. When do children avoid backward coreference? *Journal of Child Language* 18:339–53.

Hsu, Jennifer, Helen Cairns, and Robert Fiengo. 1985. The development of grammars underlying children's interpretation of complex sentences. *Cognition* 20:25–48.

Hupet, Michael, and Brigitte Tilmant. 1989. How to make young children produce cleft sentences. *Journal of Child Language* 16:251–61.

Hurford, James. 1975. A child and the English question formation rule. *Journal of Child Language* 2:299–301.

Huxley, Renira. 1970. The development of the correct use of subject personal pronouns in two children. In *Advances in Psycholinguistics*, ed. G. B. Flores d'Arcais and W. J. M. Levelt, 141–65. Amsterdam: North-Holland.

Hyams, Nina. 1986. *Language acquisition and the theory of parameters.* Boston: Reidel.

———. 1987. The theory of parameters and syntactic development. In *Parameter setting*, ed. T. Roeper and E. Williams, 1–22. Dordrecht: Reidel.

———. 1992. A reanalysis of null subjects in child language. In *Continuity and change in development*, ed. J. Weissenborn, H. Goodluck, and T. Roeper, 249–68. Hillsdale, N.J.: Erlbaum.

———. 1994. Commentary: Null subjects in child language and the implications of cross-linguistic variation. In *Syntactic theory and first language acquisition: Cross-linguistic perspectives*, vol. 2: *Binding, dependencies, and learnability*, ed. B. Lust, G. Hermon, and J. Kornfilt, 287–99. Hillsdale, N.J.: Erlbaum.

Hyams, Nina, and Kenneth Wexler. 1993. On the grammatical basis of null subjects in child language. *Linguistic Inquiry* 24:421–59.

Hyman, Larry. 1977. On the nature of linguistic stress. In *Studies in stress and accent*, ed. L. Hyman (South California Occasional Papers in Linguistics 4:37–82), Los Angeles: University of Southern California.

Ihns, Mary, and Laurence Leonard. 1988. Syntactic categories in early child language: Some additional data. *Journal of Child Language* 15:673–78.

Ingham, Richard. 1992. The optional subject phenomenon in young children's English: A case study. *Journal of Child Language* 19:133–51.

Ingram, David. 1976. *Phonological disability in children.* London: Edward Arnold.

———. 1989. *First language acquisition: Method, description, and explanation.* New York: Cambridge University Press.

Ingram, David, and Catherine Shaw. 1988. The comprehension of pronominal reference in children. *Canadian Journal of Linguistics* 33:395–407.

Ingram, David, and William Thompson. 1996. Early syntactic acquisition of German: Evidence for the Modal Hypothesis. *Language* 72:97–120.

Ingram, David, and Dorothy Tyack. 1979. Inversion of subject NP and Aux in children's questions. *Journal of Psycholinguistic Research* 8:333–41.

Jackendoff, Ray. 1972. *Semantic interpretation in generative grammar.* Cambridge: MIT Press.

———. 1976. Toward an explanatory semantic representation. *Linguistic Inquiry* 7: 89–150.

———. 1990. On Larson's treatment of the double object construction. *Linguistic Inquiry* 21:427–56.

Jacobsen, Wesley. 1979. Noun and verb in Nootkan. In *The Victoria Conference on Northwestern Languages* (Heritage Record No. 4), 83–155. Vancouver: British Columbia Provincial Museum.

Jaeggli, Osvaldo, and Nina Hyams. 1988. Morphological uniformity and the setting of the null subject parameter. *Proceedings of the North East Linguistic Society* 18: 238–53.

Jaeggli, Osvaldo, and Kenneth Safir. 1989. The null subject parameter and parametric theory. In *The null subject parameter*, ed. O. Jaeggli and K. Safir, 1–44. Boston: Kluwer.

Jakubowicz, Celia. 1984. On markedness and binding principles. *Proceedings of the North East Linguistic Society* 14:154–82.

———. 1994. On the morphological specification of reflexives: Implications for acquisition. *Proceedings of the North East Linguistic Society* 24:205–19.

Johnson, Carolyn. 1981. Children's questions and the discovery of interrogative syntax. Ph.D. diss., Stanford University.

Jones, Charles. 1992. Comments on Goodluck & Behne. In *Theoretical issues in language acquisition,* ed. J. Wiessenborn, H. Goodluck, and T. Roeper, 173–89. Hillsdale, N.J.: Erlbaum.

Kang, Beom-mo. 1988. Unbounded reflexives. *Linguistics and Philosophy* 11:415–56.

Kaper, Willem. 1976. Pronominal case-errors. *Journal of Child Language* 3:439–41.

Katz, Nancy, Erica Baker, and John Macnamara. 1974. What's in a name? A study of how children learn common and proper names. *Child Development* 45:269–73.

Kaufman, Diana. 1994. Grammatical or pragmatic: Will the real Principle B please stand up? In *Syntactic theory and first language acquisition: Cross-linguistic perspectives,* vol. 2: *Binding, dependencies, and learnability,* ed. B. Lust, G. Hermon, and J. Kornfilt, 177–200. Hillsdale, N.J.: Erlbaum.

Kayne, Richard. 1983. Connectedness. *Linguistic Inquiry* 14:223–50.

Kean, Mary-Louise. 1988. Brain structures and linguistic capacity. In *Linguistics: The Cambridge survey,* ed. F. Newmeyer, vol. 2: *Linguistic theory: Extensions and implications,* 74–95. New York: Cambridge University Press.

Keenan, Edward, and Alan Timberlake. 1988. Natural language motivations for extending categorial grammar. In *Categorial grammars and natural language structures,* ed. R. Oehrle et al., 265–95. Boston: Reidel.

Kessel, F. S. 1970. *The role of syntax in children's comprehension from ages six to twelve* (Monograph of the Society for Research in Child Development 35).

Kim, Daniel H. 1990. The acquisition of subjects by a Korean child: Null subject parameter in child language and its implication for second language acquisition. Unpublished ms. University of Hawaii, Department of Linguistics.

Kim, Haeyon. 1992. Clause combining in discourse and grammar: An analysis of some Korean clausal connectives in discourse. Ph.D. diss., University of Hawaii at Manoa.

Kim, John. 1993. Null subjects: Comments on Valian (1990). *Cognition* 46, 183–93.

Kim, Joung-Ran. 1992. Restriction and apposition. Unpublished paper. University of Maryland at College Park, Department of Linguistics.

Kim, Young-joo. 1987. The acquisition of relative clauses in English and Korean: Development in spontaneous production. Ed.D. diss., Harvard University.

———. 1992a. Korean relative clause acquisition and its implication on the parameter-setting theory of language acquisition. Paper presented to the Seoul International Conference on Linguistics.

———. 1992b. The acquisition of Korean. To appear in *The crosslinguistic study of language acquisition,* vol. 4, ed. D. Slobin. New York: Erlbaum.

Klima, Edward, and Ursula Bellugi. 1966. Syntactic regularities in the speech of children. In *Psycholinguistic papers,* ed. J. Lyons and R. J. Wales, 183–208. Edinburgh: Edinburgh University Press.

Koster, Charlotte. 1994. Problems with pronoun acquisition. In *Syntactic theory and first language acquisition: Cross-linguistic perspectives,* vol. 2: *Binding, dependencies and learnability,* ed. B. Lust, G. Hermon, and J. Kornfilt, 201–26. Hillsdale, N.J.: Erlbaum.

Kramer, Pamela, Elissa Koff, and Zella Luria. 1972. The development of competence in an exceptional structure in older children and young adults. *Child Development* 43: 121–30.

Kuczaj, Stan. 1976. Arguments against Hurford's 'Aux Copying Rule'. *Journal of Child Language* 3:423–27.

Kuczaj, Stan, and Nancy Brannick. 1979. Children's use of the wh question modal auxiliary placement rule. *Journal of Experimental Child Psychology* 28:43–67.

Kuczaj, Stan, and Michael Maratsos. 1975. What children *can* say before they *will. Merrill-Palmer Quarterly* 21:89–111.

———. 1983. Initial verbs of *yes–no* questions: A different kind of general grammatical category. *Developmental Psychology* 19:440–44.

Kuno, Susumu. 1987. *Functional syntax: Anaphora, discourse, and empathy.* Chicago: University of Chicago Press.

Labov, William, and Theresa Labov. 1978. Learning the syntax of questions. In *Recent advances in the psychology of language: Formal approaches,* ed. R. Campbell and P. Smith, 1–44. New York: Plenum.

Ladusaw, William, and David Dowty. 1988. Toward a nongrammatical account of thematic roles. In *Thematic relations* (Syntax and Semantics 21), ed. W. Wilkins, 62–73. New York: Academic Press.

Lakoff, George. 1987. *Women, fire, and other dangerous things.* Chicago: University of Chicago Press.

Lambton, Ann. 1967. *Persian grammar.* Cambridge University Press.

Langacker, Ronald. 1987. Nouns and verbs. *Language* 63:53–95.

Larson, Richard. 1988. On the double object construction. *Linguistic Inquiry* 19:335–92.

Lasnik, Howard. 1976. Remarks on coreference. *Linguistic Inquiry* 2:1–22.

Lasnik, Howard, and Stephen Crain. 1985. On the acquisition of pronominal reference. *Lingua* 65:135–54.

———. 1989. On certain substitutes for negative data. In *Learnability and linguistic theory,* ed. R. Matthews and W. Demopoulos, 89–105. Boston: Kluwer Publishers.

Lebeaux, David. 1987. Comments on Hyams. In *Parameter Setting,* ed. T. Roeper and E. Williams, 23–39. Boston: Reidel.

———. 1988. The feature +affected and the formation of the passive. In *Thematic relations* (Syntax and Semantics 21), ed. W. Wilkins, 243–61. New York: Academic Press.

———. 1990. The grammatical nature of the acquisition sequence: Adjoin-α and the formation of relative clauses. In *Language processing and language acquisition,* ed. L. Frazier and J. de Villiers, 13–82. Dordrecht: Kluwer.

Lee, Kwee-Ock. 1991. On the first language acquisition of relative clauses in Korean: The universal structure of COMP. Ph.D. diss., Cornell University.

Lee, Hyeonjin, and Ken Wexler. 1987. The acquisition of reflexive and pronoun in Korean. Paper presented at the 12th Annual Boston University Conference on Language Development, Boston, Mass.

Lempert, Henrietta, and Marcel Kinsbourne. 1980. Preschool children's sentence comprehension: Strategies with respect to word order. *Journal of Child Language* 7: 371–79.

Levelt, W. J. 1975. *What became of LAD?* Lisse, Netherlands: Peter de Ridder Press.

Li, Yafei. 1990. On V–V compounds in Chinese. *Natural Language and Linguistic Theory* 8:177–207.

Lieven, Elena. 1994. Crosslinguistic and crosscultural aspects of language addressed to children. In *Input and interaction in language acquisition,* ed. C. Gallaway and B. Richards, 56–73. New York: Cambridge University Press.

Lieven, Elena, Julian Pine, and Helen Barnes. 1992. Individual differences in early vocabulary development: Redefining the referential–expressive distinction. *Journal of Child Language* 19:287–310.

Lightfoot, David. 1982. *The language lottery: Toward a biology of grammars.* Cambridge: MIT Press.

———. 1989. The child's trigger experience: Degree-0 learnability. *Behavioral and Brain Sciences* 12:321–34.

———. 1991. *How to set parameters.* Cambridge: MIT Press.

———. 1994. Degree-0 learnability. In *Syntactic theory and first language acquisition: Cross-linguistic perspectives,* vol. 2: *Binding, dependencies, and learnability,* ed. B. Lust, G. Hermon, and J. Kornfilt, 453–71. Hillsdale, N.J.: Erlbaum.

Lillo-Martin, Diane. 1994. Setting the null argument parameters: Evidence from American Sign Language and other languages. In *Syntactic theory and first language acquisition: Cross-linguistic perspectives,* vol. 2: *Binding, dependencies, and learnability,* ed. B. Lust, G. Hermon, and J. Kornfilt, 301–18. Hillsdale, N.J.: Erlbaum.

Limber, John. 1973. The genesis of complex sentences. In *Cognitive development and the acquisition of language,* ed. T. Moore, 169–85. New York: Academic Press.

———. 1976. Unravelling competence, performance, and pragmatics in the speech of young children. *Journal of Child Language* 3:309–18.

Lust, Barbara. 1981. Constraints on anaphora in child language: A prediction for a universal. In *Language acquisition and linguistic theory,* ed. S. Tavakolian, 74–96. Cambridge: MIT Press.

———. 1983. On the notion 'principal branching direction': A parameter in Universal Grammar. In *Studies in generative grammar and language acquisition,* ed. Y. Otsu et al., 137–52. Tokyo: International Christian University.

———. 1986. Introduction. In *Studies in the acquisition of anaphora,* ed. B. Lust, vol. 1: *Defining the constraints,* 3–103. Boston: Reidel.

———. 1994. Functional projection of CP and phrase structure parametrization: An argument for the Strong Continuity Hypothesis. In *Syntactic theory and first language acquisition: Cross-linguistic perspectives,* vol. 1: *Heads, projections, and learnability,* ed. B. Lust, M. Suñer, and J. Whitman, 85–118. Hillsdale, N.J.: Erlbaum.

Lust, Barbara, Yu-Chin Chien, and Suzanne Flynn. 1987. What children know: Methods for the study of first language acquisition. In *Studies in the acquisition of anaphora,* ed. B. Lust, vol. 2: *Applying the constraints,* 271–355. Boston: Reidel.

Lust, Barbara, and Terri Clifford. 1986. Blocked forwards coreference: The 3-D study: Effects of depth, distance, and directionality on children's acquisition of anaphora. In *Studies in the acquisition of anaphora,* ed. B. Lust, vol. 1: *Defining the constraints,* 203–43. Boston: Reidel.

Lust, Barbara, Julie Eisele, and Reiko Mazuka. 1992. The Binding Theory module: Evidence from first language acquisition for Principle C. *Language* 68:333–58.

Lust, Barbara, Kate Loveland, and Renee Kornet. 1980. The development of anaphora in first language: Syntactic and pragmatic constraints. *Linguistic Analysis* 6:359–91.

Lust, Barbara, and L. Mangione. 1983. The Principal Branching Direction parameter in first language acquisition of anaphora. *Proceedings of the North East Linguistic Society* 13:145–60.

Lust, Barbara, and Cynthia Mervis. 1980. Development of coordination in the natural speech of young children. *Journal of Child Language* 7:279–304.

Macnamara, John. 1972. Cognitive basis of language learning in infants. *Psychological Review* 79:1–13.

———. 1982. *Names for things: A study of human learning.* Cambridge: MIT Press.

Macrae, Alison. 1979. Combining meanings in early language. In *Language acquisition,* ed. P. Fletcher and M. Garman, 161–76. New York: Cambridge University Press.

MacWhinney, Brian. 1985. Hungarian language acquisition as an exemplification of a general model of grammatical development. In *The crosslinguistic study of language acquisition,* ed. D. Slobin, vol. 2: *Theoretical issues,* 1069–1155. Hillsdale, N.J.: Erlbaum.

———. 1987. The competition model. In *Mechanisms of language acquisition,* ed. B. MacWhinney, 249–308. Hillsdale, N.J.: Erlbaum.

———. 1991. *The CHILDES Project: Tools for analyzing talk.* Hillsdale, N.J.: Erlbaum.

Marantz, Alec. 1984. *On the nature of grammatical relations.* Cambridge: MIT Press.

Maratsos, Michael. 1974. How pre-school children misunderstand missing complement sentences. *Child Development* 45:700–6.

———. 1978. New models in linguistics and language acquisition. In *Linguistic theory and psychological reality,* ed. M. Halle, J. Bresnan, and G. Miller, 247–63. Cambridge: MIT Press.

———. 1982. The child's construction of grammatical categories. In *Language acquisition: The state of the art,* ed. E. Wanner and M. Maratsos, 240–66. New York: Cambridge University Press.

———. 1983. Some current issues in the study of the acquisition of grammar. In *Handbook of child psychology,* vol. 3: *Cognitive development,* ed. P. Mussen, 707–86. New York: Wiley.

———. 1988. The acquisition of formal word classes. In Y. Levy, I. Schlesinger and M. Braine (Eds.), *Categories and processes in language acquisition.* Hillsdale, N.J.: Erlbaum. Pp. 31–44.

Maratsos, Michael, and Mary Anne Chalkley. 1981. The internal language of children's syntax: the ontogenesis and representation of syntactic categories. In *Children's language,* ed. K. Nelson, 2:127–214. New York: Gardner Press.

Maratsos, Michael, Dana Fox, Judith Becker, and Mary Anne Chalkley. 1985. Semantic restrictions on children's passives. *Cognition* 19:167–91.

Maratsos, Michael, and Stan Kuczaj II. 1978. Against the transformationalist account: A simpler analysis of auxiliary markings. *Journal of Child Language* 5, 337–45.

Maratsos, Michael, Stan Kuczaj, Dana Fox, and Mary Anne Chalkley. 1979. Some empirical studies in the acquisition of transformational relations: Passives, negatives, and the past tense. In *Children's language and communication,* ed. W. A. Collins, 1–45 (Minnesota Symposia on Child Psychology 12), Hillsdale, N.J.: Erlbaum.

Marcus, Gary. 1993. Negative evidence in language acquisition. *Cognition* 46:53–85.

Masterson, Deborah. 1993. A comparison of grammaticality evaluation measurements:

Testing native speakers of English and Korean. Ph.D. diss., University of Hawaii at Manoa.

Matthei, Edward. 1982. The acquisition of prenominal modifier sequences. *Cognition* 11: 301–32.

———. 1987. Subject and agent in emerging grammars: Evidence for a change in children's biases. *Journal of Child Language* 14:295–308.

Mayer, Judith, Anne Erreich, and Virginia Valian. 1978. Transformations, basic operations, and language acquisition. *Cognition* 6:1–13.

McCawley, James. 1976. *Grammar and meaning*. New York: Academic Press.

———. 1988. *The syntactic phenomena of English*. Chicago: University of Chicago Press.

McDaniel, Dana, Helen Cairns, and Jennifer Hsu. 1990. Binding principles in the grammars of young children. *Language Acquisition* 1:121–38.

McDaniel, Dana, Bonnie Chiu, and Thomas Maxfield. 1995. Parameters for *wh*-movement types: Evidence from child language. *Natural Language and Linguistic Theory* 13:709–53.

McDaniel, Dana, Helen Smith, and Jennifer Hsu. 1990/91. Control principles in the grammars of young children. *Language Acquisition* 1:297–335.

McKee, Cecile. 1992. A comparison of pronouns and anaphors in Italian and English acquisition. *Language Acquisition* 2:21–54.

McNeill, David. 1966. Developmental psycholinguistics. In *The genesis of language: A psycholinguistic approach,* ed. F. Smith and G. Miller, 15–84. Cambridge: MIT Press.

———. 1970. *The acquisition of language: The study of developmental psycholinguistics*. New York: Harper & Row.

Menyuk, Paula. 1969. *Sentences children use*. Cambridge: MIT Press.

Mervis, Carolyn, and Jacqueline Bertrand. 1995. Early lexical acquisition and the vocabulary spurt: A response to Goldfield & Reznick. *Journal of Child Language* 22: 461–68.

Miller, Wick, and Susan Ervin. 1964. The development of grammar in child language. In *The acquisition of language,* ed. U. Bellugi and R. Brown (Monographs of the Society for Research on Child Development 29), 9–34.

Mithun, Marianne. 1989. The acquisition of polysynthesis. *Journal of Child Language* 16:285–312.

———. 1991. Active/agentive case marking and its motivations. *Language* 67:510–46.

Morgan, James. 1986. *From simple input to complex grammar*. MIT Press.

Morgan, James, Katherine Bonamo, and Lisa Travis. 1995. Negative evidence on negative evidence. *Developmental Psychology* 31:180–97.

Morgan, James, and Lisa Travis. 1989. Limits on negative information in language input. *Journal of Child Language* 16:531–52.

Morsbach, Gisela, and Pamela Steel. 1976. 'John is easy to see' revisited. *Journal of Child Language* 3:443–47.

Mulder, René, and Rint Sybesma. 1992. Chinese is a VO language. *Natural Language and Linguistic Theory* 10:439–76.

Nakayama, Mineharu. 1987. Performance factors in subject–auxiliary inversion. *Journal of Child Language* 14:113–26.

Nelson, Katherine. 1973. *Structure and strategy in learning to talk*. (Monographs of the Society for Research in Child Language Development 149).

————. 1981. Acquisition of words by first language learners. *Annals of the New York Academy of Sciences* 379:148–59.

Nelson, Katherine, June Hampson, and Lea Kessler Shaw. 1993. Nouns in early lexicons: Evidence, explanations, and implications. *Journal of Child Language* 20:61–84.

Newport, Elissa, Henry Gleitman, and Lila Gleitman. 1977. Mother, I'd rather do it myself: Some effects and non-effects of maternal speech style. In *Talking to children: Language input and acquisition*, ed. C. Snow and C. Ferguson, 109–49. Cambridge: Cambridge University Press.

Nida, Eugene. 1946. *Morphology: The descriptive analysis of words*. Ann Arbor: University of Michigan Press.

Ninio, Anat. 1988. On formal grammatical categories in early child language. In *Categories and processes in language acquisition,* ed. Y. Levy, I. Schlesinger, and M. Braine, 99–119. Hillsdale, N.J.: Erlbaum.

————. 1992. The relation of children's single word utterances to single word utterances in the input. *Journal of Child Language* 19:87–110.

Nishigauchi, Taisuke. 1984. Control and the Thematic Domain. *Language* 60:215–50.

Nishigauchi, Taisuke, and Thomas Roeper. 1987. Deductive parameters and the growth of empty categories. In *Parameter setting,* ed. T. Roeper and E. Williams, 91–121. Boston: Reidel.

Núñez del Prado, Zelmira, Claire Foley, Reyna Proman, and Barbara Lust. 1994. Subordinate CP and pro-drop: Evidence for degree-n learnability from an experimental study of Spanish and English. *Proceedings of the North East Linguistic Society* 24:443–60.

O'Grady, William. 1987. *Principles of grammar and learning.* Chicago: University of Chicago Press.

————. 1991. *Categories and case: The sentence structure of Korean.* Philadelphia and Amsterdam: Benjamins.

————. 1993. Functional categories and maturation: Data from Korean. *Proceedings of the Fifth Harvard International Symposium on Korean Linguistics,* 96–112. Seoul: Hanshin.

————. 1996. The categorial system of Korean: A learnability perspective. In *Essays in honor of Ki-Moon Lee,* ed. J. Shim et al., 1023–49. Seoul: Shin-gu, 1996.

————. in press. The acquisition of syntactic representations: A general nativist approach. In *Handbook of language acquisition,* ed. W. Ritchie and T. Bhatia. San Diego: Academic Press.

O'Grady, William, Sook Whan Cho, and Yutaka Sato. 1994. Anaphora and branching direction in Japanese. *Journal of Child Language* 21:473–87.

O'Grady, William, Ann Peters, and Deborah Masterson. 1989. The transition from optional to required subjects. *Journal of Child Language* 16:513–29.

O'Grady, William, Yoshiko Suzuki-Wei, and Sook Whan Cho. 1986. Directionality preferences in the interpretation of anaphora: Data from Korean and Japanese. *Journal of Child Language* 13:409–20.

Oller, D. Kimbrough, Rebecca Eilers, Michele Steffens, Michael Lynch, and Richard Urbano. 1994. Speech-like vocalizations in infancy: an evaluation of potential risk factors. *Journal of Child Language* 21:33–58.

Osgood, Charles, and Annette Zehler. 1981. Acquisition of bi-transitive sentences: Prelinguistic determinants of language acquisition. *Journal of Child Language* 8:367–84.

Oshima-Takane, Yuriko. 1992. Analysis of pronominal errors: a case study. *Journal of Child Language* 19:111–31.

Otsu, Yukio. 1981. Universal Grammar and syntactic development in children: Toward a theory of syntactic development. Ph.D. diss., MIT.

Owens, Robert. 1984. *Language development: An introduction.* Columbus: Merrill.

Paul, Hermann. 1891. *Principles of the history of language.* Translated by H. A. Strong. London: Longmans, Green.

Pérez-Leroux, Ana. 1995. Resumptives in the acquisition of relative clauses. *Language Acquisition* 4:105–38.

Peters, Ann. 1977. Language learning strategies. *Language* 53:560–73.

———. 1983. The units of language acquisition. Cambridge University Press.

———. 1985. Language segmentation: Operating principles for the perception and analysis of language. In *The crosslinguistic study of language acquisition,* ed. D. Slobin, vol. 2: *Theoretical issues,* 1029–68. Hillsdale, N.J.: Erlbaum.

———. 1994. Strategies in the acquisition of syntax. In *The handbook of child language,* ed. P. Fletcher and B. MacWhinney, 462–82. Boston: Blackwell.

Peters, Ann, and Lise Menn. 1993. False starts and filler syllables: Ways to learn grammatical morphemes. *Language* 69:742–77.

Phillips, Pauline. 1985. The acquisition of control. M.A. thesis, University of Calgary, Department of Linguistics.

Phinney, Marianne. 1981. Syntactic constraints and the acquisition of embedded sentential complements. Ph.D. diss., University of Massachusetts at Amherst, Department of Linguistics.

Pierce, Amy. 1994. On the differing status of subject pronouns in French and English child language. In *Syntactic theory and first language acquisition: Cross-linguistic perspectives,* vol. 2: *Binding, dependencies, and learnability,* ed. B. Lust, G. Hermon, and J. Kornfilt, 319–33. Hillsdale, N.J.: Erlbaum.

Pine, Julian. 1992. How referential are 'referential' children? Relationships between maternal-report and observational measures of vocabulary composition and usage. *Journal of Child Language* 19:75–86.

———. 1994. The language of primary caregivers. In *Input and interaction in language acquisition,* ed. C. Gallaway and B. Richards, 15–37. New York: Cambridge University Press.

Pinker, Steven. 1984. *Language learnability and language development.* Cambridge: Harvard University Press.

———. 1985. Language learnability and children's language: A multifaceted approach. In *Children's language,* vol. 5, ed. K. Nelson, 399–42. New York: Erlbaum.

———. 1987. The bootstrapping problem in language acquisition. In *Mechanisms of language acquisition,* ed. B. MacWhinney, 399–441. Hillsdale, N.J.: Erlbaum.

———. 1989. *Learnability and cognition: The acquisition of argument structure.* Cambridge: MIT Press.

———. 1994a. How could a child use verb syntax to learn verb semantics? *Lingua* 92:377–410.

———. 1994b. *The language instinct: How the mind creates language.* New York: Morrow.

Pinker, Steven, David Lebeaux, and Loren Frost. 1987. Productivity and constraints in the acquisition of the passive. *Cognition* 26:195–267.

Plunkett, Bernadette. 1991. Inversion and early WH questions. In *Papers in the acquisition of WH*, ed. T. Maxfield and B. Plunkett, 125–53. Amherst: University of Massachusetts, Department of Linguistics, GLSA Publications.

Poeppel, David, and Kenneth Wexler. 1993. The Full Competence Hypothesis of clause structure in early German. *Language* 69:1–33.

Pollard, Carl. 1988. Categorial grammar and phrase structure grammar: An excursion on the syntax–semantics frontier. In *Categorial grammars and natural language structures*, ed. R. Oehrle, E. Bach, and D. Wheeler, 391–415. Boston: Reidel.

Prideaux, Gary. 1976. A functional analysis of English question acquisition: A response to Hurford. *Journal of Child Language* 3:417–22.

Pye, Clifton. 1983. Mayan telegraphese. *Language* 59:583–604.

———. 1990. The acquisition of ergative languages. *Linguistics* 28:1291–1330.

Pye, Clifton, and Pedro Quixtan Poz. 1988. Precocious passives (and antipassives) in Quiché Mayan. *Papers and Reports on Child Language Development* 27:73–70.

Radford, Andrew. 1988. *Transformational grammar: A first course.* New York: Cambridge University Press.

———. 1990. *Syntactic theory and the acquisition of English syntax.* Oxford: Blackwell.

———. 1992. Comments on Roeper and de Villiers. In *Theoretical issues in language acquisition: Continuity and change in development*, ed. J. Weissenborn, H. Goodluck, and T. Roeper, 237–48. Hillsdale, N.J.: Erlbaum.

———. 1994. Tense and agreement variability in the child grammars of English. In *Syntactic theory and first language acquisition: Cross-linguistic perspectives*, ed. B. Lust, M. Suñer, and J. Whitman, vol. 1: *Heads, projections, and learnability*, 135–57. Hillsdale, N.J.: Erlbaum.

Ramer, Andrya. 1976. Syntactic styles in emerging language. *Journal of Child Language* 3:49–62.

Read, Charles, and Victoria Hare. 1979. Children's interpretation of reflexive pronouns in English. In *Studies in first and second language acquisition*, ed. F. Eckman and A. Hastings, 98–116. Rowley, Mass.: Newbury House.

Reinhart, Tanya. 1983. *Anaphora and semantic interpretation.* London: Croom Helm.

———. 1986. Center and periphery in the grammar of anaphora. In *Studies in the acquisition of anaphora*, ed. B. Lust, vol. I: *Defining the constraints*, 123–50. Boston: Reidel.

Reinhart, Tanya, and Eric Reuland. 1992. Anaphors and logophors: An argument structure perspective. In *Long-distance anaphora*, ed. J. Koster and E. Reuland, 283–321. New York: Cambridge University Press.

Reuland, Eric, and Jan Koster. 1991. Long-distance anaphora: An overview. In *Long-distance anaphora*, ed. J. Koster and E. Reuland, 1–25. New York: Cambridge University Press.

Richards, Brian, 1994. Child-directed speech and influences on language acquisition: methodology and interpretation. In *Input and interaction in language acquisition*, ed. C. Gallaway and B. Richards, 74–106. New York: Cambridge University Press.

Rispoli, Matthew. 1994. Pronoun case overextensions and paradigm building. *Journal of Child Language* 21:157–72.

Rizzi, Luigi. 1982. *Issues in Italian syntax.* Dordrecht: Foris.

———. 1990. *Relativized minimality.* Cambridge: MIT Press.

———. 1994. Early null subjects and root null subjects. In *Syntactic theory and first lan-*

guage acquisition: Cross-linguistic perspectives, vol. 2: *Binding, dependencies, and learnability,* ed. B. Lust, G. Hermon, and J. Kornfilt, 249–72. Hillsdale, N.J.: Erlbaum.

Roeper, Thomas. 1991. How a marked parameter is chosen: Adverbs and *do*-insertion in the IP of child grammar. In *Papers in the acquisition of WH,* ed. T. Maxfield and B. Plunkett, 175–202. Amherst: University of Massachusetts, Department of Linguistics, GLSA Publications.

Roeper, Thomas, and Jill de Villiers. 1992. Ordered decisions in the acquisition of Wh-questions. In *Theoretical issues in language acquisition: Continuity and change in development,* ed. J. Weissenborn, H. Goodluck, and T. Roeper, 191–236. Hillsdale, N.J.: Erlbaum.

Roeper, Thomas, and Jill de Villiers. 1994. Lexical links in the WH-chain. In *Syntactic theory and first language acquisition: Cross-linguistic perspectives,* ed. B. Lust, G. Hermon, and J. Kornfilt, vol. 2: *Binding, dependencies, and learnability,* 357–90. Hillsdale, N.J.: Erlbaum.

Roeper, Thomas, Steven Lapointe, Janet Bing, and Susan Tavakolian. 1981. A lexical approach to language acquisition. In *Language acquisition and linguistic theory,* ed. S. Tavakolian, 35–58. Cambridge: MIT Press.

Roeper, Thomas, and Jürgen Weissenborn. 1990. How to make parameters work. In *Language processing and language acquisition,* ed. L. Frazier and J. de Villiers, 147–62. Dordrecht: Kluwer.

Rondal, Jean, and Anne Cession. 1990. Input evidence regarding the semantic bootstrapping hypothesis. *Journal of Child Language* 17:711–17.

Rood, David. 1976. *Wichita grammar.* New York: Garland.

Ross, John. 1967. Constraints on variables in syntax. Ph.D. diss., MIT.

Rumelhart, David, and James McClelland. 1987. Learning the past tenses of English verbs: Implicit rule or parallel distributed processing. In *Mechanisms of language acquisition,* ed. B. MacWhinney, 195–248. Hillsdale, N.J.: Erlbaum.

Sadock, Jerrold. 1982. The Bennish optative: The spontaneous ergative construction in child speech. *Chicago Linguistic Society Parasession on Nondeclaratives,* 186–93.

Sampson, Geoffrey. 1978. Linguistic universals as evidence for empiricism. *Journal of Linguistics* 14:183–206.

Scarborough, Hollis, and Janet Wyckoff. 1986. Mother, I'd still rather do it myself: Some further non-effects of 'motherese'. *Journal of Child Language* 13:431–37.

Schieffelin, Bambi. 1985. The acquisition of Kaluli. In *The crosslinguistic study of language acquisition,* ed. D. Slobin, vol. 1: *The data,* New York: Erlbaum. 525–93.

Schieffelin, Bambi and Eleanor Ochs. 1986. Language socialization. *Annual Review of Anthropology* 15:163–91.

Schlesinger, I. M. 1974. Relational concepts underlying language. In *Language perspectives: Acquisition, retardation, and intervention,* ed. R. Schiefelbusch and L. Lloyd, 129–51. Baltimore: University Park Press.

———. 1982. *Steps to language.* Hillsdale, N.J.: Erlbaum.

———. 1988. The origin of relational categories. In *Categories and processes in language acquisition,* ed. Y. Levy, I. Schlesinger and M. Braine, 121–78. Hillsdale, N.J.: Erlbaum.

Schmerling, Susan. 1973. Subjectless sentences and the notion of surface structure. *Proceedings of the Chicago Linguistic Society* 9:577–86.

Shatz, Marilyn, Erika Hoff-Ginsberg, and Douglas Maciver. 1989. Induction and the acquisition of English auxiliaries: The effects of differentially enriched input. *Journal of Child Language* 16:121–40.

Sheldon, Amy. 1974. The role of parallel function in the acquisition of relative clauses in English. *Journal of Verbal Learning and Verbal Behavior* 13:272–81.

Sherman, Janet. 1987. Evidence against the Minimal Distance Principle in first language acquisition of anaphora. In *Studies in the Acquisition of Anaphora*, ed. B. Lust, vol. 2: *Applying the constraints*, 89–101. Boston: Reidel.

Sherman, Janet, and Barbara Lust. 1986. Syntactic and lexical constraints on the acquisition of control in complement sentences. In *Studies in the acquisition of anaphora*, ed. B. Lust, vol. 1: *Defining the constraints*, 279–308. Boston: Reidel.

Sherman, Janet, and Barbara Lust. 1993. Children are in control. *Cognition* 46:1–51.

Slobin, Dan. 1966. Comments on 'Developmental psycholinguistics'. In *The genesis of language*, ed. F. Smith and G. Miller, 88–91. Cambridge: MIT Press.

———. 1973. Cognitive prerequisites for the development of grammar. In *Studies of child language development*, ed. C. Ferguson and D. Slobin, 175–208. New York: Holt, Rinehart & Winston.

———. 1985. Crosslinguistic evidence for the language-making capacity. In *The crosslinguistic study of language acquisition*, ed. D. Slobin, vol. 2: *Theoretical issues*, 1157–1256. Hillsdale, N.J.: Erlbaum.

Slobin, Dan I., and Thomas Bever. 1982. Children use canonical sentence schemas: A crosslinguistic study of word order and inflections. *Cognition* 12:229–65.

Slobin, Dan, and Charles Welsh. 1973. Elicited imitation as a research tool in developmental psycholinguistics. In *Studies of child language development*, ed. C. Ferguson and D. Slobin, 485–97. New York: Holt, Rinehart & Winston.

Snow, Catherine. 1972. Mothers' speech to children learning language. *Child Development* 43:546–65.

———. 1977. Mothers' speech research: from input to interaction. In *Talking to children: Language input and acquisition*, ed. C. Snow and C. Ferguson, 31–49. London: Cambridge University Press.

Snyder, William, and Karin Stromswold. 1994. The structure and acquisition of English dative constructions. Unpublished ms. Dept. of Psychology. Rutgers University.

Solan, Lawrence. 1978. The acquisition of *tough* movement. In *Papers in the structure and development of child language*, ed. H. Goodluck and L. Solan (University of Massachusetts Occasional Papers in Linguistics 4), 127–43.

———. 1983. *Pronominal reference: Child language and the theory of grammar*. Boston: Reidel.

———. 1987. Parameter setting and the development of pronouns and reflexives. In *Parameter setting*, ed. T. Roeper and E. Williams, 189–210. Boston: Reidel.

Sperber, Dan, and Deirdre Wilson. 1987. Precis of *Relevance: Communication and cognition*. *Behavioral and Brain Sciences* 10:697–754.

Steedman, Mark. 1991. Structure and intonation. *Language* 67:260–96.

Steele, Susan, Adrian Akmajian, Richard Demers, Eloise Jelinek, Chisato Kitagawa, Richard Oehrle, and Thomas Wasow. 1981. *An encyclopedia of AUX: A study of cross-linguistic equivalence*. Cambridge: MIT Press.

Stemmer, Nathan. 1981. A note on empiricism and structure-dependence. *Journal of Child Language* 8:649–56.

Stewart, Jean. 1976. Children's ability to understand questions. In *Baby talk and infant speech,* ed. W. von Raffler-Engel and Y. Lebrun, 274–76. Amsterdam: Swets & Zeitlinger.

Stewart, Jean, and H. Sinclair. 1975. Comprehension of questions by children between 5 and 9. *International Journal of Psycholinguistics* 3:17–26.

Stromswold, Karin. 1988. Linguistic representations of children's *wh*-questions. *Papers and Reports on Child Language Development* 20:107–14.

———. 1990. Learnability and the acquisition of auxiliaries. Ph.D. diss., MIT.

———. 1995. The acquisition of subject and object *wh*-questions. *Language Acquisition* 4:5–48.

Stromswold, Karin, Steven Pinker, and Ronald Kaplan. 1985. Cues for understanding the passive voice. *Papers and Reports on Child Language Development* 24:123–30.

Sudhalter, Vicki, and Martin Braine. 1985. How does comprehension of passives develop? A comparison of actional and experimental verbs. *Journal of Child Language* 12:455–70.

Tager-Flusberg, Helen, Jill de Villiers, and Kenji Hakuta. 1982. The development of sentence coordination. In *Language development,* ed. S. Kuczaj, vol. 1: *Syntax and semantics,* 201–43. Hillsdale, N.J.: Erlbaum.

Talmy, Leonard. 1985. Lexicalization patterns: Semantic structure in lexical forms. In *Language typology and syntactic description,* ed. T. Shopen, vol. 3: *Grammatical categories and the lexicon,* 57–149. New York: Cambridge University Press.

Tanz, Christina. 1974. Cognitive principles underlying children's errors in pronominal case-marking. *Journal of Child Language* 1:271–76.

Tavakolian, Susan. 1978. The conjoined-clause analysis of relative clauses and other structures. In *Papers in the structure and development of child language,* ed. H. Goodluck and L. Solan, 37–83. Amherst: University of Massachusetts, Linguistics Department, GLSA Publications.

Taylor-Browne, Karen. 1983. Acquiring restrictions on forwards anaphora: A pilot study. *Calgary Working Papers in Linguistics* 9:75–99.

Tfoundi, Leda, and Roberta Klatzky. 1983. A discourse analysis of deixis: Pragmatic, cognitive, and semantic factors in the comprehension of 'this', 'that', 'here', and 'there'. *Journal of Child Language* 10:123–33.

Thornton, Rosalind. 1990. Adventures in long-distance moving: The acquisition of complex wh-questions. Ph.D. diss., The University of Connecticut.

———. 1995. Referentiality and *wh*-movement in child English: Juvenile *d-link*uency. *Language Acquisition* 4:139–75.

Tomasello, Michael. 1987. Learning to use prepositions: A case study. *Journal of Child Language* 14:79–98.

Truscott, John, and Kenneth Wexler. 1989. Some problems in the parametric analysis of learnability. In *Learnability and linguistic theory,* ed. R. Matthews and W. Demopoulos, 155–76. Boston: Kluwer.

Turner, Elizabeth Ann, and Ragnar Rommetveit. 1967. The acquisition of sentence voice and reversability. *Child Development* 38:649–60.

Tyack, Dorothy, and David Ingram. 1977. Children's production and comprehension of questions. *Journal of Child Language* 4:211–24.

Vainikka, Anne. 1993/94. Case in the development of English syntax. *Language Acquisition* 3:257–325.

Valian, Virginia. 1986. Syntactic categories in the speech of young children. *Developmental Psychology* 22:562–79.

———. 1989. Children's production of subjects: Competence, performance, and the null subject parameter. *Papers and Reports on Child Language Development* 28: 156–63.

———. 1990. Null subjects: A problem for parameter setting models of language acquisition. *Cognition* 35:105–22.

———. 1991. Syntactic subjects in the early speech of American and Italian children. *Cognition* 40:21–81.

———. 1993. Parser failure and grammar change. *Cognition* 46:195–202.

Van Valin, Robert. 1990. Functionalism, anaphora, and syntax. *Studies in Language* 14: 169–219.

———. 1991. Functionalist linguistic theory and language acquisition. *First Language* 11:7–40.

Velten, Harry. 1943. The growth of phonemic and lexical patterns in child language. *Language* 19:281–92.

Wang, Qi, Diane Lillo-Martin, Catherine Best, and Andrea Levitt. 1992. Null subject vs. null object: Some evidence from the acquisition of Chinese and English. Unpublished ms. Haskins Laboratories, New Haven, Conn.

Wanner, Eric, and Michael Maratsos. 1978. An ATN approach to comprehension. In *Linguistic theory and psychological reality,* ed. M. Halle, J. Bresnan, and G. Miller, 119–61. Cambridge: MIT Press.

Warden, David. 1981. Childen's understanding of *ask* and *tell*. *Journal of Child Language* 8:139–50.

Waryas, Carol, and Kathleen Stremel. 1974. On the preferred form of the double object construction. *Journal of Psycholinguistic Research* 3:217–79.

Wasow, Thomas. 1978. Transformations and the lexicon. In *Formal syntax,* ed. P. Culicover, T. Waso, and A. Akmajian, 327–60. New York: Academic Press.

Weissenborn, Jürgen. 1992. Null subjects in early grammars: Implications for parameter-setting theories. In *Theoretical issues in language acquisition: Continuity and change in development,* ed. J. Weissenborn, H. Goodluck, and T. Roeper, 269–300. Hillsdale, N.J.: Erlbaum.

Weverink, Meike. 1991. Inversion in the embedded clause. In *Papers in the acquisition of WH,* ed. T. Maxfield and B. Plunkett, 19–42. Amherst: University of Massachusetts, Department of Linguistics, GLSA Publications.

Wexler, Kenneth. 1993. The development of developmental theories of inflection. Paper presented at the conference on Generative Approaches to Language Acquisition. Durham, N.C.

Wexler, Kenneth, and Yu-Chin Chien. 1985. The development of lexical anaphors and pronouns. *Papers and Reports on Child Language Development* 24:138–49.

Wexler, Kenneth, and Peter Culicover. 1980. *Formal principles of language acquisition.* Cambridge: MIT Press.

Wexler, Kenneth, and M. Rita Manzini. 1987. Parameters and learnability in binding theory. In *Parameter setting,* ed. T. Roeper and E. Williams, 41–76. Dordrecht: Reidel.

White, Lydia. 1981. The responsibility of grammatical theory to acquisitional data. In *Explanation in linguistics,* ed. N. Hornstein and D. Lightfoot, 241–71. London: Longman.

Whitman, John, Kwee-Ock Lee, and Barbara Lust. 1991. Continuity of the principles of Universal Grammar in first language acquisition: The issue of functional categories. *Proceedings of the North East Linguistic Society* 21:383–97.

Wierzbicka, Anna. 1986. What's in a noun? (or: how do nouns differ in meaning from adjectives?) *Studies in Language* 10:353–89.

Wilhelm, Andrea, and Ken Hanna. 1992. On the acquisition of wh-questions. *Calgary Working Papers in Linguistics* 15:89–98.

Wilkins, Wendy. 1988. *Thematic relations.* New York: Academic Press.

———. 1989. Why degree-0? *Behavioral and Brain Sciences* 12:362–63.

Wilson, Bob, and Ann Peters. 1988. What are you cookin' on a hot? *Language* 64:249–73.

Wode, Henning. 1977. Four early stages in the development of L1 negation. *Journal of Child Language* 4:87–102.

Yamashita, Yoshie. 1990. Syntactic theory and the acquisition of Japanese syntax: Radford's GB approach. *Hawaii Working Papers in Linguistics* 22:93–126.

———. 1995. The emergence of syntactic categories: Evidence from the acquisition of Japanese. Ph.D. diss., University of Hawaii at Manoa.

Yoder, Paul, and Ann Kaiser. 1989. Alternative explanations for the relationship between maternal verbal interaction style and child language development. *Journal of Child Language* 16:141–60.

Yoon, Jong-Yurl. 1992. Functional categories in Korean clausal and nominal structures. *Studies in Generative Grammar* 2:427–64.

Yoshinaga, Naoko. 1996. WH questions: A comparative study of their form and acquisition in English and Japanese. Ph.D dissertation, University of Hawaii at Manoa.

Zurif, Edgar. 1990. Language and the brain. In *Language: An invitation to the cognitive sciences,* ed. D. Osherson and H. Lasnik, vol. 1, pp. 177–98. Cambridge, MA: MIT Press.

Index

incrementalist theory of development, 348–54
and cumulative complexity, 349–50
and inversion, 351
limitations of, 350–51
and Principle C, 351–53
and subject drop, 350
and *wh* questions, 351, 353–54
indirect negative evidence, 253, 288–90
individuatable things, 314–17, 372n.3
inductivist approaches, 298–303
infinitival clauses. *See* control
Ingham, R., 92
Ingram, D., 162–63
inheritability property, 319
Inheritance Principle, 310, 324
input (vs. intake), 335. *See also* experience
Instantaneous Acquisition Assumption, 330
Interpretability Requirement, 259–63, 264
inversion, 157–73
doubling errors, 164–68
formulation of, 168–73
and the incrementalist theory, 351
overgeneralization of, 158–59, 164
and structure dependence, 169–73
in *wh* questions, 160–64, 367n.3
in *yes-no* questions, 157–60
islands. *See* extraction, constraints on; gaps
Italian, 60, 83–84, 86–87, 93–94, 230, 291, 364n.4
iterativity property, 319

Jaeggli, O., 87–88
Jakubowicz, C., 228–29
Japanese, 314, 345, 348, 372n.5, 373n.4
branching direction, 217–18
case, 77
subject drop, 84
relative clauses, 184
word order, 60
parameter setting: head–complement order, 280, 332; domain for pronoun interpretation, 281–84, 285, 286–87, 288

Kaluli, 47, 74, 250–51, 252
Klima, E., 157–58, 161–62
Korean, 302, 342, 372n.5
branching direction, 217–18
determiners, 344–48, 373n.4
first words, 23, 24
parameter setting, 287
relative clauses, 183–84
subject drop, 84, 364n.4
wh words, 130

Koster, C., 236
Kuczaj, S., 158–59

language impairment, 360, 374n.1
learnability, 4, 245–64
and general nativism, 307–29
and non-UG approaches, 298–329
traditional view, 245–47
and UG, 265–97
learning module, 312, 320–21, 322, 325–26, 327–28
Lempert, H., 188
lexical learning, 332–33
Lexical Parametrization Hypothesis, 285
lexical stage, 340–41
Lightfoot, D., 292–96
Limber, J., 101–2, 175–76
limited scope analysis, 38–40
Locality Requirement, 227–28, 231
and general nativism, 325–26
and processing, 239–40
See also Principle A
logical problem of language acquisition. *See* learnability
Lust, B., 125–27, 183, 215–18, 222, 357–58

MacWhinney, B., 60
Maratsos, M., 109–10, 299–302
Matching Strategy, 15
Matthei, E., 51–53
maturational theory of development, 337–48
and functional categories, 340–48
and German word order, 342–44
and Korean determiners, 344–48
and passives, 340
and Principle C, 339
and subject drop, 339
and UG, 337–38
and the X-bar schema, 339
Mayer, J., 164–65
McDaniel, D., 113–14
methods of data collection, 5–7
comprehension, 6
diary, 6
experimental, 5–7
grammaticality judgments, 153, 363n.1
imitation, 6
limitations, 7
naturalistic, 5–6
preferential looking, 29, 48–49
production, 6
Minimal Distance Principle, 108–10, 114
vs. the Goal Strategy, 109–10

and the maturational theory, 339
vs. object drop, 98–100, 364n.3
processing theories of, 81–84
in Spanish, 95
subject-drop parameter, 291–92, 294–95
tense-based theories of, 89–93
and VPs, 96–98
and *wh* questions, 95–96, 365n.6
subject-object asymmetry, 248, 263, 322
in difficulty of gaps, 121–23, 126, 131–38,
138–41, 178–81, 188–90, 366n.3
in dropping arguments, 98–100
Subset Condition, 284
Subset Principle, 283–85, 326
Sudhalter, V., 198–99
syntactic analysis of multiword speech, 40–48
arguments for, 43–48
Syntactic Blends Hypothesis, 165–66
syntactic categories
assigning phrases to, 372n.6
errors in, 43–44
formalist vs. reductionist theories of, 313
general nativist approach to, 312–17
inductivist approach to, 298–303
lack of evidence for, 263
maturational theory of, 340–42
semantic approach to, 303–4
and semantic bootstrapping, 266–70
syntax. *See* grammar

Tanz, C., 76–77
Tavakolian, S., 110–11, 177–79, 182–83
tense, 313–14. *See also* finite verbs
that-trace effect, 142–46
thematic analysis of multiword speech, 34–36
thematic roles, 34–36, 47–48, 363n.1, 363n.2
nature of, 318
and word order, 60
Thornton, R., 106–7, 145
to
in dative patterns, 208, 210, 349–50
in infinitival clauses, 103
topic
and case, 75–76
and pronoun interpretation, 225
and word order, 60
Turkish, 24, 261
Turner, E., 193–94
two-word utterances, 34, 41, 46
Tyack, D., 132–33

Universal Grammar (UG)
definition of, 265

lack of evidence for in development, 356–58
and the maturational theory, 337–38
preeminence of, 355
theories of learnability based on, 265–97

Valian, V., 46–47, 83–84, 98–99, 291
verbs
early instances of, 20
general nativist approach to, 313–17
inductivist approach to, 299, 301
novel, 205–8
semantic approach to, 303–4
semantic bootstrapping of, 267–68
See also auxiliary verbs; finite verbs; syntactic categories

Wang, Q., 88
want to, 102–3
Weissenborn, J., 88
Wexler, K., 229–31, 284, 285
Wh Island effects, 149–54
argument vs. adjunct, 151
and degree-0 learnability, 293
and finite verbs, 367n.7
and medial *wh* words, 152–54
and processing, 153–54
wh questions, 129–56
analyses of, 129–30
early examples of, 129–30
in embedded clauses, 138–41, 367n.5
first *wh* words, 130
and the incrementalist theory, 351, 353–54
subject vs. object *wh* questions, 131–38, 141
Wh words
first instances, 130
in embedded clauses, 103
Wichita, 87–88
Wilhelm, A., 133–34
Williams Syndrome, 360–61, 374n.2
word order, 46–47, 55
across languages, 55–57
conventions for in general nativism, 310,
321–22
errors in, 57–66
and finite verbs, 343
in German, 56, 342–44
and negation, 62–66
and the optative, 61–62
and topics, 60

X-bar schema, 270–72, 280–81, 339

Yoshinaga, N., 134–35, 141